ARGUMENTS ABOUT ABORTION

Arguments about Abortion

Personhood, Morality, and Law

KATE GREASLEY

Lecturer in Law, University College London

OXFORD
UNIVERSITY PRESS

OXFORD
UNIVERSITY PRESS

Great Clarendon Street, Oxford, OX2 6DP,
United Kingdom

Oxford University Press is a department of the University of Oxford.
It furthers the University's objective of excellence in research, scholarship,
and education by publishing worldwide. Oxford is a registered trade mark of
Oxford University Press in the UK and in certain other countries

First Edition published in 2017

Impression: 1

Published in the United States of America by Oxford University Press
198 Madison Avenue, New York, NY 10016, United States of America

British Library Cataloguing in Publication Data
Data available

Library of Congress Control Number: 2016962725

ISBN 978–0–19–876678–0 (hbk.)
ISBN 978–0–19–880660–8 (pbk.)

Printed and bound by
CPI Group (UK) Ltd, Croydon, CR0 4YY

Acknowledgements

There are a few people whose help and instruction have been instrumental to my producing this piece of work, and to whom I owe a great deal of thanks. The book is based upon the doctoral thesis that I completed in Oxford in 2014, and I first and foremost owe a huge debt of gratitude to my D.Phil supervisor Leslie Green, who provided invaluable criticism and guidance throughout the course of the project. His input is responsible for the end product being far better than it possibly could have been otherwise, and I consider myself extremely fortunate to have benefited from his insights and intellectual rigour.

As assessors of my work at earlier stages, John Gardner and Jonathan Herring asked many incisive questions that influenced the way I thought about the topic and the work that I ultimately produced. I am very thankful to them for their interest and their suggestions.

There are a number of other people who, whether in conversation or through written comments, have helped to develop my thinking around the subject matter of this book and have pressed me on possible challenges to my arguments. I would like to thank, in particular, Imogen Goold, Carol Sanger, Tom Adams, Sylvia Rich, and Liz Sepper. A special thank you is owed to Matthew Lee Anderson, who provided extensive written comments on a number of important chapters. Thanks also to Lisa Gourd and Carin Hunt for help with the proof-reading and indexing.

Completing this project has been a long and demanding process, and I would not have been able to do it without the support of my family and friends. I am especially grateful to my lovely parents, Peter and Jenny Greasley, who have always unreservedly encouraged my (seemingly endless!) academic endeavours, and who made it possible for me to do well in school many years ago, by taking care of everything else.

Finally, with much love and affection, thank you to Dori Kimel for making me laugh when I needed it, for his constant encouragement, and for always believing I could do this.

Contents

III. PRINCIPLE AND PRAGMATISM

Introduction

This book is about abortion, but it is about a good deal more besides. Part of what makes abortion such a rich and rewarding topic of study is its entwinement with a plethora of other absorbing legal and philosophical problems. Among other things, thinking through the abortion problem forces us to confront questions such as: When is an early human being worthy of strong moral protection? When, if ever, is it justifiable to end the life of another human being? And do we possess the fundamental right to life merely in virtue of being members of the human species, or in virtue of something else?

Given its entanglement with problems such as these, it is hardly surprising that moral disagreement about abortion has been so protracted. Abortion is a hard topic, not just, or even primarily, because it is taboo, emotive, and political. Abortion is hard, first and foremost, because it invites questions that are genuinely complex. The philosopher Margaret Little puts it well when she says that the abortion problem is 'plain old hard'.[1] As she writes:

It touches on an enormous number of complex and recondite subjects, requiring us to juggle bundles of distinctions which are themselves points of contention in morality and law.[2]

As Little incisively notes, the problems of abortion are not just hard the same way that a 'complex math or public policy question is hard'.[3] They are hard in part because when reflecting on the nature of pregnancy and the fetus, the general principles and distinctions of moral and legal analysis with which we are most familiar often seem to come up short. There is, Little sees, 'something about abortion that is not captured however carefully we parse counterexamples or track down the implications of traditional classifications'.[4] Thus, she writes, the 'clear-headed' application of the 'usual tools' of morality and law often fails to construct a wholly satisfactory account of what happens in abortion.

This troubling doubt that abortion could ever be properly analysed using our conventional principles and categories (the 'usual tools') is a worry that pervades the topic, rearing its head at a number of sticking points. At its most sceptical,

---

[1] Margaret Olivia Little, 'Abortion, Intimacy and the Duty to Gestate' (1999) 2 Ethical Theory and Moral Practice 295, 295.

[2] ibid.   [3] ibid.   [4] ibid.

Arguments about Abortion: Personhood, Morality, and Law. First Edition. Kate Greasley. © K. Greasley 2017. Published 2017 by Oxford University Press.

the challenge to which Little refers simply denies that we can argue about abortion *at all* the way we argue about other issues in morality and law—although, when it gets this far, the threat can begin to look a little *too* ominous. Pregnancy may be like nothing else, but then again, no subject of philosophical study is exactly like anything else. The distinctness of a practice or of a situation does not preclude it from also being an instance of a more general kind of phenomenon. Indeed, the entire usefulness of arguing from principles is their ability to capture what is salient and universal about a discrete problem, and thereby gain some insight into how it ought to be appraised, given the more general commitments that we have.

Even with relevant principles to hand, though, navigating a way through all of the pertinent considerations in abortion and assigning them logical order is a significant challenge in its own right, and one with which the first part of this book is exclusively concerned. As will become apparent, deciding what is really at the heart of the abortion controversy is one preliminary inquiry that in fact constitutes a significant proportion of all argument about abortion.

There is a lot that abortion is concerned with which this book is not. Abortion is very often about religious affiliations and beliefs. It is about attitudes to sex—who should be having it, with whom, and how. It is tied up with women's interests in sexual liberation, and men's interests in women's sexual availability. Abortion is often about control: control of a medical procedure, of reproduction, of women as a class, and, from some perspectives, population control. In politics, abortion is about winning elections and judicial appointments, and, in the United States, about the autonomy of states to set their own policies on reproductive choice. Whilst being about all these things sociologically and politically, a main thesis of this book is that at its philosophical heart, abortion is about whether the human fetus is rightly considered a person, in the moral, rights-holding sense. It goes without saying that the answer to this question will probably have implications for a number of problems outside of the abortion dispute, most notably, embryo experimentation and assisted reproduction techniques that typically involve embryo wastage, such as *in vitro fertilization*. I will not be making specific claims about these related topics, but will leave it to the reader to infer what bearing my arguments might have on them, if any.

Abortion is hardly in need of a definition, but in the interests of complete clarity, let me define it as the deliberate ending of a pregnancy with the known or desired result that the embryo or fetus will die. This book is predominantly concerned with how claims about the moral and legal permissibility of abortion intersect with claims about fetal, or 'prenatal', personhood—in other words, claims about whether the fetus is a person in the philosophical sense. In different places, I refer to this issue interchangeably as the question about what constitutes 'personhood', or 'moral status' or 'full moral standing' or full 'moral considerability'. Exactly what is meant by that question, and how the designation 'person' differs from that of 'human being', will be clarified in chapter 1.

Preliminaries

Before we get properly into the discussion, a small handful of issues need to be addressed. Terminology is a common cause of friction in the abortion debate, often for good reason. When still in the midst of argument, it is imperative to avoid stating things in ways that are tendentious. Therefore, I will be using the term 'pregnant woman' rather than the more prejudicial 'mother' to refer to bearers of pregnancies, and 'fetus', not 'baby' or 'unborn child', to refer to all forms of unborn human life, including embryos. (There are notable exceptions when dealing with arguments that explicitly assume, as part of their premises, that the fetus is a person.) My terms are meant not to convey any commitments about the nature of unborn human life but to convey only neutrality about that nature before the relevant arguments have been made.

The designations 'pro-life' and 'pro-choice' are widely disliked for the reason that they imply false leanings on behalf of the opposing camp: opponents of abortion do not view their cause as one that abjures choice for women, and defenders of abortion rights do not see themselves as set against life. I will therefore mostly be employing the less provocative (if slightly more cumbersome) propositions of being in opposition to or in defence of abortion rights. I make an exception in chapter 1, where I refer to the 'pro-life' and 'pro-choice' political movements as they are colloquially labelled.

The extent to which discussants in the abortion debate are entitled to rely on their own, or on common, settled judgements in constructing their arguments is another persistent issue in this topic. I will be following the approach of most discussants by according some presumptive epistemic force to moral judgements that are firmly held by most of us—for instance, the judgement that it is seriously wrong to terminate the lives of healthy human infants. It is not my view that an entrenched judgement such as this should never be reconsidered; to some extent, all relevant moral judgements are held in abeyance at the outset of my inquiry. However, reflecting on what does seem inescapably clear to us, including which practices are plainly morally impermissible, can be an essential step towards gaining understanding about what is less clear. In this discussion, the nature of abortion and the human fetus are the contentious matters. If every other commitment surrounding them were treated as equally contentious, we might struggle to make progress with the subject matter at all. Quite apart from holding the moral prohibition on infanticide very loosely, then, one could instead think that the consensus of judgement there is capable of giving some direction to our deliberations about abortion, and of helping us to see what, in particular, *needs* to be explained.

Some thinkers will no doubt be suspicious of this methodological inclination, and will view any degree of closed-mindedness about ancillary questions (such as the moral permissibility of infanticide) as an impediment to truth-finding, not a partial map. But no theorist can entirely avoid relying at points on propositions that seem to her, and to most people, to be obviously correct. The judgements that human sex cells are not morally considerable beings, and that contraception cannot possibly be murder, are also grounding premises in the abortion debate which, rather than being equally open to dispute, are used by proponents on both sides to shape their arguments about the nature of abortion. This is not to say that our starting presumptions about the moral status of sex cells, or infants, ought to remain immovable in our thinking about abortion, no matter what. But holding everything as equally up for debate at the outset of discussion might only steer us away from the most useful questions there are for understanding the special case of the fetus.

Next, it is important to keep in mind throughout that the questions concerning the moral character of abortion and the appropriate legal response to the practice are distinct. There may well be much that separates the reproductive choices people ought to make and those which the law is justified in enforcing. In regulating abortion, lawmakers must attend to considerations that the moralist need not—considerations like administrability, compliance, the aptness of legal coercion, and its collateral harms. All of these things should alert us to a possible, or even probable, gap between our moral conclusions about abortion practice and the best system of regulation. At the same time, one should expect the two matters—abortion morality and abortion law—to intersect in at least some meaningful ways, even if it is only that our conclusions about the moral nature of abortion practice form the starting point for ascertaining the optimal regulatory regime. The overlap between the correct moral and legal responses to abortion will be greater or lesser depending on what is believed about the nature of the human fetus. What follows about the proper legal status of abortion *if it is the unjustified killing of a person* is different from what might follow if abortion is morally unacceptable but does *not* equal the killing of a person. In particular, the law may have the elbow-room to frame its permissions more loosely than those of morality if the moral cost of abortion does not entail murder, but involves some less grave kind of wrong.

Still, in parts of the book the questions about abortion's moral and legal permissibility will track one another quite closely. This is especially true of chapters 2 and 3, where I consider whether much abortion could be understood as justified homicide or the justified refusal to sustain the life of another person. With regard to the conditions for justified homicide in particular, there is no generally recognized gap between what morality requires and what the law can justifiably enforce. Consequently, much of that discussion will consider the moral and legal landscape in tandem.

It is worth saying one or two more words about the kind of discussion I will be conducting. This book is a work in normative legal and moral philosophy. As such, its primary focus is on the argumentative sustainability of broad propositions about the nature of abortion, about morally and legally permissible conduct, and about the logical consistency of certain sets of claims. It is not primarily concerned with sociological or doctrinal legal questions about abortion, such as how women respond to having abortions and why they have them, or how the law of abortion is and can be applied and interpreted. Though questions of these kinds may prove relevant to the main inquiry at points, they are not approached as independent subjects of investigation. This is not because I regard them as unimportant, but only because their answers do not bear on the particular puzzles central to my discussion.

Like other books about abortion ethics and moral status, I employ the argumentative device of thought-experiments at points. I do this with some awareness of the scepticism harboured by some about the usefulness of abstract hypotheticals for enhancing moral understanding of problems like this. The source of that scepticism is well expressed by Stephen Mulhall when he writes:

> . . . thought experiments in ethics presuppose that we can get clearer about what we think concerning a single, specific moral issue by abstracting it from the complex web of interrelated matters of fact and of valuation within which we usually encounter and respond to it. But what if the issue means what it does to us, has the moral significance it has for us, precisely because of its place in that complex web? If so, to abstract it from that context is to ask us to think about something else altogether – something other than the issue that interested us in the first place; it is, in effect, to change the subject.[5]

With respect to abortion, the concern might be that the use of thought-experiments which are far removed from pregnancy will, in all likelihood, fail to account for many of the morally salient aspects of pregnancy and abortion which are bound up with the real-life context in which it is embedded. Perhaps not everything that is important about pregnancy and abortion can be captured by hypotheticals about violinists with kidney ailments or conjoined twins or intelligent Martians. This issue will be explored in greater detail in chapter 4. As a brief opening apologetic, I will say only that it is extremely difficult to bring more general moral and legal principles to bear on the abortion question *without* looking at how those principles operate outside of the abortion context, and that it is not entirely clear to me how argument about abortion is meant to proceed without marshalling and applying any of our more general moral commitments. I will not, therefore, avoid the thought-experiment method in my discussion. However, mindful of Mulhall's caution, I will try to use them judiciously and to remain alert to important aspects of pregnancy and abortion which they might obscure.

The main stakeholders in abortion rights are of course women. Some readers might therefore be dismayed by the relative sparseness of discussion here about women's interests in accessing abortion and the realities of unwanted pregnancy and abortion prohibitions on women's lives. Philosophical accounts of abortion in which the fetus appears to be central and the pregnant woman somewhat marginalized can be antagonizing to some, and for understandable reasons. The only reason why women's interests in abortion access do not occupy more space in my own analysis is because I take it completely as granted that a considerable amount is on the line for women in securing reproductive control, and that denying them that control is inexorably damaging—damaging to their health, life, happiness,

---

[5] Stephen Mulhall, *The Wounded Animal: J M Coetzee & the Difficulty of Reality in Literature and Philosophy* (Princeton University Press 2009) 27.

and equality. This much is, in my view, beyond serious contention, and it is for this reason that I do not devote more space to expounding the profound negative implications of abortion prohibitions for women.

Neither do I apportion any space to examining the contrary claim that safe abortion provision actually *harms* women, for the simple reason that I do not think it can be taken seriously. This is not to say that no woman could be or has ever been harmed by an abortion, emotionally or physically. That is surely untrue. But almost any medical procedure is potentially harmful to anyone—physically or emotionally—in the right conditions. The prevalent claim by philosophical opponents of abortion that "abortion harms women" can therefore only be understood as the more particular claim that abortion has such a propensity to harm those choosing it, and inflicts a degree of harm which, overall, so far outweighs its benefits, that it is best understood as a bad thing for womankind. This is the claim which I regard as so palpably false as to not warrant any engagement.

The Argument to Come

Does the morality of abortion depend on the moral status of the human fetus? Must the law of abortion presume an answer to the question of when personhood begins? Can a law which permits late abortion but not infanticide be morally justified? These are just some of the questions this book sets out to address.

The book is divided into three parts. Part I is solely concerned with the relevance of prenatal personhood for the moral and legal evaluation of abortion. Contrary to some accounts of the abortion problem, it defends the basic proposition that the argument for abortion rights does indeed critically depend upon whether the human fetus is rightly regarded as a 'person' in the philosophical sense. I examine a few long-standing philosophical accounts of abortion that are alike in concluding that we do not need to decide whether or not the fetus has full personhood status in order to draw the correct conclusion about the morality or legality of abortion.

Those accounts include, most notably, Ronald Dworkin's view that abortion argument is, at root, not about whether the fetus is a person in the philosophical sense, but rather about different interpretations of the intrinsic value of human life, and Judith Jarvis Thomson's argument that even if the fetus is a person, abortion can be considered as the mere failure by a pregnant woman to proffer it non-obligatory life-sustaining assistance. Chapter 3 considers the somewhat different claim that even if the fetus is a person, abortion could be subsumed under moral and legal categories of justified homicide, and chapter 4 examines the view that considerations of sex equality relegate the personhood question to irrelevancy in the abortion debate. Against all such propositions, I argue that deciding what the human fetus is, morally speaking, is of pre-eminent importance in legal and ethical reasoning about abortion.

In Part II, I turn to the substantive debate about the nature of personhood. Disappointingly, no doubt, I do not advance any novel theory about the conditions for personhood or about when persons begin. Instead, I trace the key features of the conventional debate about when persons begin to exist and ask what further beliefs and commitments are seemingly implied by certain familiar strains of argument. In particular, I suggest that arguments in favour of the conception threshold of personhood which point to the putative 'arbitrariness' of all *post*-conception thresholds (viability, consciousness, birth, and so on) seem to presuppose a view about how persons begin, which I term 'punctualism'. Punctualism is the belief that personhood status is acquired completely and instantaneously, and that there can be no vague period in which human beings gradually become persons. In chapter 5, I claim that there is good reason to reject the punctualist thesis and to accept the antithetical 'gradualist' view, which holds that, whatever its constitutive features, the advent of personhood is a process which admits of no non-arbitrarily distinguishable points. In chapter 6, I consider and reject some further arguments for embracing the punctualist thesis and for the view that complete persons must have come into being by the completion of conception. These include arguments which seek to move from claims about the conditions of continuing personal identity to the conclusion that all zygotes are persons.

Chapter 7 is something of a fresh start. I restate the compelling arguments for believing that our concept of a person has chiefly to do with a cluster of sophisticated cognitive and emotional capacities, as well as the perennial problem that not all human beings *post*-birth possess all of those capacities. I argue that some rejections of the so-called 'developmental' (capacities-based) view of personhood's conditions use the wrong test for conceptual salience—that is, they wrongly hold that every constitutive feature of personhood must also be an *essential* feature of all persons. Still, the ostensible absence of *any* sophisticated cognitive or emotional capacities in human beings before birth is also a challenge for so-called 'graduated' accounts of pre-birth moral status, which hold that fetuses become more morally considerable as gestation progresses. Drawing on recent work about the moral status of animals, I suggest instead that the basic (and popular) intuition that later abortion is more morally serious than early abortion can be vindicated by thinking about the moral respect we have reason to demonstrate for human embodiment.

Chapter 8 turns to address two of the most prominent issues in the abortion ethics literature: the human equality problem and the moral difference between abortion and infanticide. The problem from human equality asserts that any account which takes personhood status to supervene on developmentally acquired attributes, such as self-consciousness or rationality, is inconsistent with a commitment to basic human equality, since those attributes can be possessed in greater and lesser degrees by human beings post-birth. The implication, it is argued, is that only a conception of personhood as being constituted by human genetic completeness (a test met by zygotes) can account for human equality. I try to adduce reasons of a moral nature for treating personhood status as a 'range property', meaning that it is fully and equally borne out by all human beings past a minimum threshold. I go on to suggest that there are good reasons for the law in particular to set that minimum threshold at live birth, notwithstanding the close resemblances of late fetuses and neonates. I do, however, partly call into question the popular philosophical view that there are no 'intrinsic' differences between human beings immediately prior to and subsequent to birth.

Finally, Part III turns to some specific issues of abortion law and regulation. Chapter 9 considers what implications my conclusions in Parts I and II have when it comes to framing a good law of abortion, as well as the question of what the serious commitment to a 'right' to abortion (even if only up to a certain gestational point) would require. I also examine some problems arising out of gaps between the morality of reproductive decision-making and the justifications for legal interference, including the well-rehearsed 'back-street abortion argument' based on counterproductiveness of regulation. Chapter 10 considers the special case of selective abortion on the ground of fetal sex or disability of the future child, focussing on the ways in which attitudes towards these special kinds of abortion have been harnessed in the wider moral debate. The final chapter offers some comments on the current controversy surrounding the scope of the right to conscientiously object to participation in abortion provision.

PART I

ORDERING THE ARGUMENT

1

What Should Abortion Argument Be About?

When we argue about abortion, what should we argue about? When a topic is so mired in moral complexity, it can be difficult to gain clarity on just where one's starting point ought to be. Nevertheless, precisely where the locus of debate should reside is not just an interesting question in its own right, but an essential first piece of the puzzle when it comes to thinking through the rights and wrongs of abortion. For many discussants, the argumentative priority of establishing what we are dealing with ontologically or morally in a human fetus—that is to say, whether a fetus is what we understand to be a 'person' or not—is self-evident. Conversely, some serious and influential contributions to the abortion debate have sought to establish that the moral status of the fetus is not decisive either for the morality or legality of abortion, or is even rendered redundant by other philosophical considerations.

Speaking plainly, there is more than one way of telling someone that she is asking the wrong question about a contentious subject matter. On the one hand, one could say that her question misfires because the answer to that question will not, in the end, determine anything critical in the discussion, and then go on to illustrate why this is so. Alternatively, one might claim that there is something inherently defective about the question itself—that it asks something that cannot be answered; that it is irrational or unintelligible; that it is not pertinent to the topic under consideration, or that it is not what disputants are truly arguing about. Challenges of both kinds are captured by certain arguments in academic discussion about abortion. Such arguments seek, in one way or another, to bypass the 'personhood' question in moral and legal reasoning about abortion.

As an example of challenges of the first kind, take the following claim, which we will call the 'Good Samaritan Thesis' (GST):

> *The Good Samaritan Thesis*: Abortion is morally permissible in all (or almost all) cases, *whether or not the fetus is a person*, because gestation is a form of Good Samaritanism—that is, it is a form of supererogatory assistance that no one person could be morally obligated to perform in order to preserve the life of another. Consequently, abortion only discontinues non-obligatory, life-preserving assistance.

The GST claims that abortion is always or almost always permissible, whether the human fetus is a person or not. In effect, it sidelines the personhood question by stating that it is never, or hardly ever, morally obligatory for a woman to carry a pregnancy to term, even to save the life of another person. The most well-known iteration of the GST comes in the way of an analogy drawn by Judith Thomson

Arguments about Abortion: Personhood, Morality, and Law. First Edition. Kate Greasley. © K. Greasley 2017. Published 2017 by Oxford University Press.

between pregnancy and a hypothetical situation in which a person is kidnapped and forcibly connected to a famous, ailing violinist, whose unique kidney condition means that he needs to be connected to the other person's body for the next nine months in order to survive.[1] Thomson's argument is that just as the unfortunate person is surely permitted to unplug the violinist and terminate the bodily support, even with the result that the violinist will die, so a woman is permitted to discontinue her bodily support of a fetus by having it removed from her body.

Another personhood-bypassing challenge of the first kind is what we might call the Justified Homicide Thesis (JHT), which claims the following:

> *The Justified Homicide Thesis*: Abortion is morally permissible in all (or almost all) cases, *whether or not the fetus is a person*, because it is a recognizable instance of justifiably killing another person.

The JHT begins by pointing out that our moral and legal principles make exceptions to the general prohibition on killing other persons. This includes, for instance, situations of self-defence, or just war, or in situations of what criminal lawyers have called 'necessity', where by killing one person is the only way of avoiding an even greater loss of life.[2] It then claims that if the fetus *were* a person, abortion would often or always fit those exceptions. JHT differs substantially from GST by analysing abortion as an act of killing, not just the refusal to save. Hence, the two theses construct abortion's permissibility in different ways. On JHT, abortion is an example of justified killing, and on GST, of a justified refusal to save life.

Let me put the merits of the GST and JHT to one side for now. My concern here is instead with personhood-bypassing challenges of the second kind. As I said, challenges of that kind do not proceed by claiming that, in the final analysis, the permissibility of abortion does not depend upon whether the fetus is a person or not. They have an altogether different character, asserting that the personhood question is a misguided starting point for philosophical discussion and/or legal reasoning about abortion. In what follows I want to examine some such challenges and ask whether they are at all convincing. In short, is there reason to throw out the personhood question in the very early stages of our thinking about abortion?

1.1 Persons and Human Beings

But we may be getting ahead of ourselves already. It might be asked what the category 'person' even means in the context of this discussion, especially in relation to the separate category 'human being'. Most moral philosophers distinguish these two classifications.

---

[1] See Judith Jarvis Thomson, 'A Defense of Abortion' (1971) Philosophy and Public Affairs 1, 47–66.
[2] Both exceptions are, naturally, subject to proportionality requirements. Actions taken in self-defence must be not only necessary to resist the harm threatened by another person but also proportionate to that harm (e.g. one may not kill in self-defence to avoid sustaining only a minor injury). Homicides performed out of necessity are also subject to the proportionality requirement that more of value—namely, human life—is preserved by the killing than is lost by it (and even then, philosophers heavily dispute which side-constraints on necessity killing still apply). These issues are the subject matter of chapter 3.

The ascription 'human being' is taken to be a biological category, encompassing any living creature that is genetically a member of the human species. Any human fetus, or, for that matter, newly formed zygote, is at least a human being in the bare sense that it is an individually identifiable human life. It is definitely not a frog, or a cat.

The ascription 'person', on the other hand, denotes a category of beings which possess a certain kind of moral status, typically elaborated in terms of interests or rights, and yielding a cluster of normative implications concerning how it is morally acceptable to treat such beings. Precisely what all of these normative implications are is a matter of some dispute. At the very least, however, personhood status is taken to entail strict rules about the permissibility of killing the bearers of that status. It is never permissible to kill persons, no matter how painlessly, for reasons of convenience or (on most views) even to promote an appreciable level of welfare among other creatures or persons. The same kind of strict prohibitions on killing are not generally believed to apply to non-persons. The normative classification captured by the term 'person' has, in different places, been expressed in terms of 'moral status', 'metaphysical status', or, in Mary Anne Warren's description, humanity 'in the moral sense'.[3] As I see it, all these terms grasp at more or less the same notion. To ask whether a fetus is any of these things is simply to ask whether it is something that, by virtue of its essence or attributes, is akin to fully matured human beings in the thing that endows *them* with their special status, interests, and rights.

The analytical distinctness of human beings and persons is apparent from the fact that we can at least conceive of non-human persons. Intelligent aliens, angels, and perhaps even some non-human animals could all fit our concept of a person without being biologically human. So 'human being' and 'person' do not *mean* the same thing. It may be true, nevertheless, that all human beings are, necessarily, persons. This would be so if all members of the human species also happened to meet the conditions for personhood, making overlap between the categories 100 per cent. The analytical separateness of the two just means that it is an open, and, hence, an intelligible question whether or not this is so.

Having noted this important distinction, let us turn to the prima facie case for placing the question of prenatal personhood at the forefront of our ethical and legal investigations about abortion. For many, that case is clear and simple. Our moral norms prohibit the intentional killing of other persons in all but the most exceptional circumstances. Without adequate justification or excuse, such killing is legally classified as murder. If a fetus *is* a person, then, abortion is, on the face of it, in the same moral category. At best, defensible homicide. At worst, murder. This sets the stakes high when it comes to the moral status of the fetus. Perhaps even the real *possibility* that a fetus is a person, morally on a par with you and me, is enough to alter the whole structure of the abortion debate. That possibility might prompt us to ask whether abortion could perhaps be subsumed into a moral or legal category of justified homicide, or to think about whether abortion is correctly analysed as an instance of intentional killing.

It should be acknowledged at this point that not everyone engaged in discussion about abortion concedes that the embryo or fetus *is* a human being, where

---

[3] Mary Anne Warren, 'On the Moral and Legal Status of Abortion' (1973) 57(1) The Monist 43–61.

'human being' is taken to mean 'full member of the human species' rather than a form of human life, or human biological material. As can also be true of other animal species, one might argue that there is a difference between what counts as human biological material and what counts as an individual *member* of the human species. A cow fetus is certainly a cow in one sense, that is, it is bovine, but perhaps it is not yet an identifiable instance of *a cow*.

Some philosophers have appealed to the consensus among embryologists when asserting that a new, individual human being is present by the end of conception, when a zygote possessing a complete set of human DNA comes to exist.[4] However, the degree of developmental completeness that is required before a life form may count as a new member of the human species is an evaluative question, not a scientific one. No embryological facts can tell us whether a single-celled zygote properly counts as a whole member of the human species (albeit an immature one), rather than as biological material that is the precursor to a new member, since the idea of a full and complete member of a species is not itself strictly scientific. Returning to the cow example above, a group of zoologists might agree about every biological fact concerning cows and yet disagree about whether a cow embryo should be considered a complete species member.

So the fact that human *beings* begin to exist at conception is by no means a given, depending on what precisely is meant by that designation. I will say nothing further about this issue, however. The distinction between human beings, a biological category, and persons, a moral and evaluative one, is a sufficient primer for my arguments throughout this book without any need to challenge the claim that embryos and fetuses are human beings. In everything that follows, therefore, I am willing to concede that human beings begin to exist at conception.

1.2 Dworkin and the Red Herring

Is it possible, though, that the questions whether, when, and to what degree unborn humans are persons fall far from the true, philosophical heart of the abortion problem? In his book *Life's Dominion*, Ronald Dworkin set out a compelling argument

---

[4] See Robert P George and Christopher Tollefsen, *Embryo: A Defense of Human Life* (Doubleday 2008) chapter 5, citing Bruce Carlson, *Human Embryology and Developmental Embryology* (CV Mosby 2004) 58 and Keith L Moore and TVN Persaud, *The Developing Human* (7th edn, WB Saunders 2003) 40; Patrick Lee, *Abortion and Unborn Human Life* (1st edn, The Catholic University of America Press 1996) chapter 3; Christopher Kaczor, *The Ethics of Abortion* (1st edn, Routledge 2011) 127–9. Others have attacked the proposition that all zygotes and embryos count as individual human beings on the ground that an entirely *individualized* human being doesn't emerge until some days or weeks after conception, either because some parts of the early embryo (or 'blastocyst') eventually become the placenta, or because monozygotic twinning is still possible before the 'primitive streak' (the earliest precursor of the spinal cord) is formed at fourteen days (see: Mary Warnock, *An Intelligent Person's Guide to Ethics* (Overlook 2004) 65–6; Ronald Green, *The Human Embryo Research Debates: Bioethics in the Vortex of Controversy* (Oxford University Press 2001) 31; and Joseph Donceel, 'Immediate Animation and Delayed Hominization' (1970) 31 Theological Studies 76, 98–9).

for believing the personhood question to be, in the main, a red herring in the abortion debate.[5] Rather, he argued, that debate is in truth only a proxy for the genuine disagreement at the root of abortion conflict, grounded in the sanctity of human life, or, more precisely, differing *interpretations* of the sanctity of life and what is required to show that value appropriate respect.

Dworkin's account begins with certain observations about the nature of the public abortion debate. Drawing attention to the fiercely adversarial nature of that debate which, he rightly observed, outdoes practically all other public conflicts in the United States in its upper limits of intensity, Dworkin observed that when conducted in the traditional terms of argument about prenatal personhood (meaning, whether or not the fetus is a person), the abortion conflict appears to be intractable. This owes substantially to the fact that, as Dworkin claimed, 'neither side can offer any argument that the other must accept', since different conclusions about the personhood of the fetus are only, ultimately, a matter of 'primitive conviction'.[6] He wrote:

[T]here is no biological fact waiting to be discovered or crushing moral analogy waiting to be invented that can dispose of the matter. It is a question of primitive conviction, and the most we can ask of each side is not understanding of the other, or even respect, but just a pale civility, the kind of civility one might show an incomprehensible but dangerous Martian.[7]

Fundamentally, either we see a fetus as a person or we do not. This, in Dworkin's eyes, makes debate about fetal personhood interminable, for there will be no trump cards, so to speak. Those who view the fetus from conception onward as equivalent to an unborn child and those who view it as no more than a cluster of cells cannot hope to persuade each other otherwise by recourse to reason, for their beliefs are not grounded in reasoned argument to begin with, only in gut intuition.

Next, so long as abortion disagreement is directed at the moral status of the fetus, that debate will not only be interminable, but also, Dworkin argued, resistant to compromise. Such compromise is 'unrealistic', he claimed, for those who view the fetus as morally analogous to a born human being will not be moved by women's rights arguments which, on their view, are blind to the fact that if a fetus is a helpless unborn child 'then permitting abortion is permitting murder, and having an abortion is worse than abandoning an inconvenient infant to die'.[8] Conversely, those who conceive of a fetus as something hardly different from a body part probably cannot help viewing the opponents of legal abortion as 'either acting in deep error' or out of bigotry, unreflective religiosity, or vindictiveness towards those whom they regard as fallen women. Dworkin concludes:

Self-respecting people who give opposite answers to whether the fetus is a person can no more compromise, or agree to live together allowing others to make their own decisions, than people can compromise about slavery or apartheid or rape . . .

---

[5] Ronald Dworkin, *Life's Dominion: An Argument about Abortion and Euthanasia* (Harper Collins 1993).
[6] ibid 10.   [7] ibid.   [8] ibid 9–10.

If the disagreement really is that stark, there can be no principled compromise but at best only a sullen and fragile standoff, defined by brute political power.[9]

But he did not believe we should resign ourselves to this gloomy prognosis. This is because the entire personhood-centred picture of the abortion conflict was, to his mind, based on a serious 'intellectual confusion'.[10] A good indication that the real nub of that disagreement is something other than as first appears comes in the way of what Dworkin called 'signal inconsistencies' in public attitudes to abortion on both sides of the divide. Opponents of abortion rights, for instance, commonly make concessions where abortion is necessary to save the life of the pregnant woman, or where pregnancy is the result of incest or rape. Furthermore, many are willing to agree that, although abortion is immoral, it should nevertheless be legally permitted, that it ought not to invoke the same penalties as murder, or that despite their moral objection, they would support their own wife, daughter, or friend if she decided to obtain one.

Some 'signal inconsistencies' echo on the 'pro-choice' side too. While supporters of abortion rights clearly do not regard abortion as murder, they do frequently characterize it as a kind of 'cosmic shame' and a 'grave moral decision',[11] not to be undertaken lightly or for trivial reasons, for example because the pregnancy will interfere with a booked holiday. Consequently, supporters of abortion rights often support some legal restrictions on abortion choice, notwithstanding their professed belief that the fetus is not a person in the philosophical sense.

Dworkin pointed out that on the personhood-centred picture of abortion argument, these results seem 'baffling'.[12] How could someone who truly believes that abortion kills a person consign the abortion decision to the realm of personal morality or make concessions where pregnancy is brought about through rape? And why would someone who, say, thinks that abortion is not very different from a tonsillectomy, view it as something obviously to be regretted, or the appropriate target of any legal restrictions? The concessions and exceptions commonly made on both sides seem flatly inconsistent with the traditional account of the abortion conflict as hinging on the personhood issue. In particular, Dworkin claimed:

No one can consistently hold that a fetus has a right not to be killed and at the same time hold it wrong for the government to protect that right by the criminal law. The most basic responsibility of government, after all, is to protect the interests of everyone in the community, particularly the interests of those who cannot protect themselves.[13]

However, Dworkin thought that these signal inconsistencies *are* explicable once the conflict is recast in a different light. Central to a better understanding of abortion disagreement, he claimed, is a distinction between two very different grounds of objection to abortion captured by the interest in 'protecting fetal life'. That interest can, in the one place, refer to what he called the *derivative* objection to abortion. The derivative objection says that abortion violates the fetus's right not to be

---

   [9] ibid 10.   [10] ibid.   [11] ibid 32.   [12] ibid 14.   [13] ibid.

killed, a right which all persons possess. But 'protecting fetal life' can implicate a very different ground of abortion opposition. Dworkin labelled this the *detached* objection to abortion. The detached objection does not depend on ascribing the moral status of persons to any individual fetus. Rather, it claims that all human life has a sacred or, in secular terms, 'intrinsic', value, like the value we might ascribe to a brilliant work of art or a place of natural beauty. The objection holds that abortion is wrong not because it violates a fetus's right to life but because it 'disregards or insults' that intrinsic value.[14]

Dworkin argued that someone who does not regard the fetus as a person may still 'object to abortion just as strenuously as someone who insists it is' if his objection is rooted in detached grounds.[15] Just as someone might object to turning off the life-support of a patient with an incurable and intolerable illness not because of the belief that death is against her interests but because the act of killing insults the intrinsic value of human life, so too might a person object to abortion not because she regards the fetus as having an interest in continued life but because she views the deliberate extinguishing of any human life as an insult to life's intrinsic value, analogous to destroying valuable works of art.

Dworkin believed that almost everyone who objects to abortion practice truly objects to it, 'as they might realise after reflection', on the detached rather than the derivative ground.[16] Once we understand this, he thought, we can make far better sense of why some people believe that abortion is wrong but ought to remain legal, while others think it acceptable, but legitimately regulated. It is perfectly 'consistent', he said, for someone who objects to abortion on detached (sanctity of life) grounds to hold that it is 'intrinsically wrong' to end a human life, but that the decision whether or not to end that life *in utero* must be left to the pregnant woman.[17]

Moreover, on the detached picture of abortion disagreement, supporters of abortion rights actually *share* this appreciation of human life's intrinsic value. They too believe that all human life is extremely valuable, and that its destruction is always regrettable—always a 'cosmic shame'. Thus we should not be surprised that defenders of abortion rights are still sobered by the need for abortion and, frequently, support some restrictions.

This all raises a question, however. If disputants on both sides of the debate share a commitment to the intrinsic value of human life, what are they arguing about? Dworkin's answer was that people *interpret* this value in very different ways. Later in the book, he offered an account of how different interpretations of life's intrinsic value might sponsor radically different conclusions on the abortion question. More fully, he distinguished between two different sources of human life's intrinsic value: *natural* creation and *human* creative investment. Those who place more stock in natural or biological creation are more likely to conclude that the intrinsic value of human life is always insulted when abortion is carried out. But not everyone will agree that premature death in the womb is the most serious frustration of human

---

[14] ibid 11–13.   [15] ibid 12.   [16] ibid 13.   [17] ibid 15.

life.[18] Others may believe that performing an abortion is consistent with respecting human life's intrinsic value if it prevents significant human creative investment in the life of the pregnant woman from being squandered. Disagreement about abortion is, in short, disagreement about which 'mode' of life's intrinsic value has the greater moral importance. Conservatives in the abortion debate are likely to think that natural investment in the form of biological human life is pre-eminent. Liberals, on the other hand, more frequently believe that it is a greater frustration of life's miracle when an adult human being's expectations are disappointed and talents wasted than when a fetus dies before any comparable investment in its life is made.[19]

From all of this, Dworkin drew an important conclusion about political resolution of the abortion problem. Crucially, he argued that disagreement about the meaning and nature of life's intrinsic value has a 'quasi-religious' quality. Our personal interpretations of that value are, he said, 'essentially religious beliefs', relating, as they do, to questions about the meaning of life and death. The end picture is therefore of a conflict which is 'at bottom spiritual'.[20] And recognizing the religious nature of abortion argument has implications for the possibility of principled compromise. For, when the conflict is translated into these terms—into a matter of *religious-like* difference—a pathway to principled resolution is laid out by the doctrine of religious toleration. 'We think that it is a terrible form of tyranny', he wrote, 'destructive of moral responsibility, for the community to impose tenets of spiritual faith or conviction on individuals.'[21] In liberal democracies, the protection of free exercise of religion therefore underwrites a permissive answer to the question of abortion's legality. Since everyone must be free to express her religious beliefs for or against abortion the state must not coercively remove the abortion option. This is a resolution which, Dworkin suggested, those who are morally opposed to abortion have reason to accept if they *are* committed to religious toleration.

Dworkin went on to spell out the ramifications of his argument for the constitutional legality of abortion in the United States in particular. If, as he claimed, beliefs about reproductive freedom are 'essentially religious', then the right to make one's own decisions in such matters can be construed out of the First Amendment, which guarantees the free exercise of religion. Consequently, state prohibitions on abortion are an unconstitutional restriction of US citizens' First Amendment rights. The religious nature of the disagreement settles the constitutional question permissively.

1.3 Personhood v the Intrinsic Value of Human Life

1.3.1 'Signal inconsistencies'

As we have seen, a key aspect of Dworkin's account was the descriptive claim that prenatal personhood is not, in actual fact, at the root of public controversy over abortion—*that it is not what people are arguing about*—and that the features of

---

[18] ibid 90.   [19] ibid. See Dworkin chapter 3 generally, especially 91.   [20] ibid 101.
[21] ibid 20.

that controversy can be better explained when adopting the detached account of abortion's contestedness, revolving around the intrinsic value of human life. The 'signal inconsistencies' were presented as valuable evidence that the crux of abortion disagreement must be something other than prenatal personhood. On Dworkin's view, those inconsistencies, found on both sides of the abortion divide, are simply a bad fit with the derivative account.

Dworkin did not reach far, however, for alternative explanations of those putative inconsistencies which are more in keeping with a personhood-centred view of abortion conflict, despite the fact that many are available. We should probably not be at all surprised to find that many people hold ambivalent and even somewhat contradictory views on such a philosophically complex, politicized, and emotively charged subject as abortion. Such inconsistencies, which are not unique to abortion argument, could owe to any number of things. In the first place, the holders of those views may simply have not thought through their position with much analytical rigour, sheer lack of reflectiveness being, presumably, the most common source of argumentative incoherence. Alternatively, disputants may be led to embrace inconsistent concessions because of emotional or psychological biases, fear of social reproach, or even the need to disingenuously advocate compromise positions for politically strategic reasons.

Strategic necessity in particular strikes me as a very plausible reason why some political opponents and supporters of abortion rights might make concessions which *look like* inconsistencies. Ideological opponents of abortion may support exceptions in cases of rape, incest, or grave risk to the pregnant woman's life for a number of pragmatic reasons: to avoid ostracizing moderates, to focus firepower on the more winnable battles, and so on. If this explanation were correct, we might well expect to see those opponents withdrawing the traditional concessions as and when political climates change and platforms can be radicalized without risking too much of the overall objective: to preserve as much fetal life as possible.

Certain 'inconsistencies' embraced by defenders of abortion rights could equally be driven by a political need to make concessions. Abortion rights campaigners often admit that abortion is always sad or a shame, even when justified. Although this admission does not chime well with the extremely low moral status they accord to the fetus, it can placate moderate sensibilities. As well as being tenable, mundane explanations like these are perfectly consistent with the pre-eminence of prenatal personhood in abortion disagreement.

Thus, there may be little about the public abortion conflict that is left inexplicable on the derivative account. But for what it is worth, the personhood-centred account of abortion disagreement also commands its own fair share of explanatory power, and in some respects outperforms the account based on the intrinsic value of human life. Dworkin noted, we saw, that the abortion conflict is uniquely ferocious as compared with practically all other public disagreements. But this feature accords far better with the derivative than with the detached version of the controversy. This is particularly true of the escalation to violence which has punctuated abortion conflict at times. As a response to the belief that abortion murders children, the shooting of abortionists is at least intelligible, if not justified. This is somewhat less the case when the protest is understood as the expression of just one interpretation of the intrinsic value of human life.

Without doubt, the nature of anti-abortion rhetoric has always lent a good deal of support to the personhood-centred view of abortion opposition. Verbal and pictorial protest messages invoke the language and imagery of murder, and assert or imply the moral equivalence of fetuses and babies. Anticipating this evidence in favour of the derivative view, Dworkin countered that opponents of abortion in fact only employ the rhetoric of murder in order to emphasize their objection based on the sanctity of human life.[22] In short, talk of murdering babies simply packs more punch than spiritualistic rhetoric about life's sacred value, although the real basis for opposition was always the latter.

Dworkin's retort has some initial plausibility. But the idea that the anti-abortion movement's assimilation of abortion with murder is empty rhetoric is increasingly difficult to accept, especially in light of the numerous recent attempts by pro-life politicians in the United States to enact state-level 'personhood amendments' which would redefine constitutional personhood as beginning from conception.[23] If successful, such amendments would have the effect of outlawing most, if not all, abortion in the given state, in direct contravention of *Roe v Wade*. Less obviously, they would also have the effect of prohibiting embryo research and fertility treatments such as IVF which involve embryo wastage, an implication that has not deterred their proponents.

The 'personhood movement' is the most unequivocal demonstration yet of many abortion opponents' depth of commitment to the belief that personhood begins at conception, and renders the derivative account of abortion opposition difficult to resist. To be sure, Dworkin may well have responded by insisting that this is yet another red herring, indicating at most that opponents of abortion are *rhetorically* committed to the notion of prenatal personhood, not that they are truly, deeply committed to it. But the wisdom of Occam's Razor should prompt us to reject his alternative explanations in the absence of a clear need for them. Dworkin believed that the rhetoric and ferociousness of the abortion conflict are explained by the fact that disputants are conflicted over an essentially spiritual issue, whilst being mistaken about the true grounds of their disagreement. The far simpler and more obvious explanation is that one side in the conflict really does believe that murder is at stake, while the other side believes the idea so preposterous that bigotry and oppression is all that they can see as left to be marshalled against them.

---

[22] ibid 20–1. On page 21, he said: 'They declare that abortion is murder, or just as bad as murder, and they insist that human life begins at conception, or that a fetus is a person from the beginning, not because they think a fetus has rights and interests but just to emphasise the depth of their feeling that abortion is wrong because it is the deliberate destruction of the life of a human organism . . . We must be careful not to be led by emotionally charged descriptions about human life and persons and murder that reveal strong emotions but are not a clear guide to the beliefs that people are emotional about.'

[23] In 2011 alone, fourteen state legislatures introduced twenty-six 'personhood' measures. There have been failed attempts to pass such legislation by voter ballot in Colorado, Iowa, Mississippi, and North Dakota. See, http://www.prochoiceamerica.org/media/fact-sheets/abortion-personhood.pdf (last accessed 10 September 2015).

1.4 The 'Anti-Personhood' Argument

Up to this point, I have been examining the proposition that prenatal personhood is not what public abortion argument is about. But one might well ask why, as philosophers or lawyers, we ought to be interested at all in the nature of public discourse, coherent, rigorous, or otherwise. After all, the terms of that discourse do not necessarily bear any relation to the philosophically and legally pertinent issues in abortion.

But Dworkin's own claims about the nature of abortion controversy were not meant to be mere descriptions of the public argument. That is, he was also making the stronger claim that prenatal personhood—or, the 'derivative' question—is not what actually *is* philosophically and legally salient in abortion. One important argument for that claim came in the way of his contention that no one could sensibly regard the fetus as a person with rights and interests of its own, 'in particular an interest in not being destroyed', from the moment of its conception.[24] This is because the fetus has never possessed any mental life, something Dworkin took to be an essential pre-requisite of having such interests. Comparing early fetuses to the assemblage of body parts on Dr. Frankenstein's table before the lever is pulled, he insisted:

... it makes no sense to suppose that something has interests of its own—as distinct from its being important what happens to it—unless it has, or has had, some form of consciousness: some mental as well as physical life.[25]

He may, of course, have been right about that. But as Frances Kamm has pointed out, Dworkin's assertion here is not so much evidence for the irrelevancy of prenatal personhood in abortion as it is an '*anti-personhood argument*'.[26] The fact that Dworkin himself found the notion of prenatal personhood quite implausible (a claim which, apart from asserting the necessity of mental states for interests, he did not accompany with a great deal of argument[27]) does not go to show that the personhood-centred view of the abortion problem is false. This is because the primacy of the personhood question in our philosophical inquiries about abortion can still be demonstrated simply by attending to the fact that *were* the fetus a person, abortion would seem to be tantamount to homicide. Dworkin could therefore dismiss the theoretical importance of the derivative question only by arguing that no sensible individual would classify the fetus as a person.

But Dworkin could be understood to be making a different, even stronger, argument here. By saying that the notion of fetal personhood strikes him as scarcely

---

[24] Dworkin (n 5) 15.   [25] ibid 16.
[26] Frances Kamm, 'Abortion and the Value of Life: A Discussion of Life's Dominion' (1995) 95 Columbia Law Review 167. My emphasis.
[27] Don Marquis remarked that Dworkin accompanied this 'crucial assertion'—that interests require some form of consciousness—'with no argument whatsoever', even though 'his analysis of the ethics of abortion collapses if it is untrue' (Don Marquis, 'Life, Death and Dworkin' (Review Essay) (1996) 22 Philosophy and Social Criticism 127–31).

intelligible, we might take him to be claiming that it is not just false, but conceptually incoherent. Perhaps our shared concept of a person can no more admit fetuses than it can admit rocks, trees, or rabbits. To be sure, *someone* might protest that a rock, a tree, or an insect is in fact a person, and that we have always been mistaken in thinking otherwise. To such a protest, there may be little to say except that the person voicing it does not grasp the concept of a person if she is willing to make such claims. If anything is true about persons, it is that a rock cannot be one. A dispute about whether or not rocks in fact *are* persons could not, therefore, be an argument about the constituent features of personhood, but only an instance of discussants failing to examine the same concept at all. And of course, if it is conceptually incoherent to think of fetuses as persons then it is hardly likely that opponents of abortion believe it. It is far more likely that abortion discussants are conflicted over something else.

If Dworkin were right about the conceptual absurdity of fetal personhood, then the derivative issue would indeed seem to lose much of its argumentative relevance for abortion. It would be pre-eminent only in the sense that something nobody believes, and which is hardly believable, would have serious implications for the legal and moral status of abortion if it happened to be true. This is surely irrelevance of an important kind. It invites the question of whether a fetus should even be considered a serious *candidate* for personhood. Is there more reason to investigate the possible personhood of fetuses than that of insects?

I have not wanted to commit myself so far to any substantive view about the conditions for personhood, taking instead as my subject the prior question whether the personhood issue is critical for our moral and legal calculations about abortion. One thing Dworkin's enterprise may have revealed is just how difficult it is to form a judgement about this prior question that is hygienically separate from one's beliefs about the conditions of personhood. If fetal personhood is an unintelligible proposition, the personhood question will seem to have little place in explaining the moral complexity of abortion, if indeed any complexity then remains.

Still, I believe Dworkin overstated the case if relegating the notion of fetal personhood to the realm of the conceptually incoherent. The human fetus is distinctly unlike rocks, trees, and insects in ways that render ascriptions of personhood more intelligible with respect to them. One obvious difference is that the fetus is a creature which, if left to develop and thrive and to be born, we believe will unequivocally come to possess personhood. It is at least a potential person, in a way that insects or inanimate objects are not. Given this potentiality, and given the biological continuity of fetuses with later humans, there is surely reason enough to consider whether the moral status we accord to developed human beings extends back to human beings *pre*-birth. If we believe that all humans, once born, are persons in the philosophical sense, the next natural question will be why that status is withheld from human beings *in utero*.

The mere fact that a creature will mature into a person if it thrives is not a ground for believing that it already *is* one. But such knowledge could ground an interest in the exact (or as the case may be, inexact) point when that moral status is acquired. Might that creature, which is certainly *en route* to personhood, reach that destination earlier than is entirely apparent? In this respect, unborn humans are much unlike rocks and other entities, which are not generally believed to be developing towards *certain* full-fledged personhood.[28]

Another reason for taking the proposition of fetal personhood more seriously than that of, say, insect personhood, has to do with what constitutional lawyers call 'suspect classifications'. In all other contexts, many now historical, in which the categories 'human being' and 'person' have been distinguished, and where legal systems and social orders have engaged themselves in separating out who is human in the simple biological sense, and who in the moral, rights-holding sense, those applying the distinction have fallen into grave moral error. Familiar examples abound. Genocide, slavery, and racial segregation are, all in a way, an expression of the view that some human beings are not persons, or not in the fullest sense. Our own moral failings in applying this distinction and the purposes to which it has historically been put ought to encourage extreme caution whenever invoking it. If we are right to do so with fetuses, this will turn out to be the only case in which a class of human beings has been correctly excluded from the personhood category. The classification 'human sub-person' is, in other words, a deeply suspect one, and this alone gives us considerable reason to pause and reflect before denying the personhood of fetuses.

Let me emphasize that none of these points in any way go towards proving the personhood status of the fetus. My focus here is entirely with what is logically pre-eminent in abortion ethics, to which end all of the foregoing is only meant to establish this: if it really is the case that the moral status of the fetus is not the core inquiry in ethical argument about abortion, then the burden is still on the proponents of this position to show why.

1.5 Intractability and Compromise

As was seen, Dworkin believed that if the personhood-centred view of abortion conflict is correct, then that conflict is inherently intractable and resistant to principled compromise. Misunderstanding the real nature of the disagreement therefore has serious consequences for resolving abortion politically. As he wrote:

the confusion between the two kinds of objection [derivative and detached] has poisoned public controversy about abortion and made it more confrontational and less open to argument and accommodation than it should be.[29]

As we also saw, Dworkin's pessimistic characterization of the derivative disagreement stemmed from his claim that what is believed about the moral status of the

---

[28] I do not wish to presuppose here that no non-human animals could be persons. The point is only that mature human beings, at least, are uncontroversial examples of persons, and given that human fetuses are the earlier forms of those same biological lives, it seems appropriate to question when, in that biological life, personhood begins. I also do not wish to entirely rule out here the possibility that there born human beings that are not persons.

[29] Dworkin (n 5) 13.

fetus can only ever be a matter of 'primitive conviction'. The personhood question is a philosophical dead end in the abortion debate partly because it cannot sponsor any reasoned exchanges. He made the point that it is not even clear in theory what it would take for all participants in that debate to be persuaded one way or the other. As he put it, 'there is no biological fact waiting to be discovered or crushing moral analogy waiting to be invented that can dispose of the matter'.[30] It is not just that there have been no winning shots in the personhood debate; we cannot even be sure of what one would *look* like.

Insofar as philosophical tractability is thought to be a virtue of any account of the abortion problem, we should of course ask whether the detached view fares any better in that regard. If, as Dworkin argued, the basis of abortion disagreement has in truth been the sanctity of human life all along, the very fact that it shows no signs of abating might be offered up as evidence in itself that the detached dispute is no more tractable than the derivative one. This would not be such a surprise. If Dworkin was correct that the nature of abortion dispute is 'essentially religious', intractability is precisely what one would expect. There is no reason to imagine that a conflict rooted in religious-like commitments would foster *more* reasoned exchanges, or be any more philosophically soluble, than argument about the conditions for personhood.[31] At the same time, the very fact that the public abortion debate has proved so intractable should, by Dworkin's lights, count as good evidence for the derivative account, since intractability is, on his view, a defining characteristic of the personhood conflict.

It is not at all clear, then, that of the two kinds of disagreement, the derivative one is uniquely philosophically intractable. One might also think there is some measure of tension between Dworkin's claims that the derivative question is not amenable to reasoned argument and his own argument against fetal personhood, based on fetuses' lack of mental states. Let us put these complaints to one side, however, and consider Dworkin's main argument about the tractability of the abortion dispute. This was that *if* he is correct that abortion disagreement is 'essentially religious' disagreement about the intrinsic value of human life, a settled constitutional basis for compromise is provided by the doctrine of religious freedom. In the legal realm, he argued, this means that a permissive stance on abortion practice is constitutionally mandated. In the United States, the First Amendment right to free exercise of religion protects the equal right of all citizens to follow their convictions on 'profoundly spiritual matters', with the result that states may not dictate an answer to the abortion question.[32] This constitutional basis for the abortion right is, he argued, one which all those committed to the free exercise of religion therefore have a reason to accept, even if they continue to disagree, 'religiously', about the morality of abortion.

---

[30] ibid 10.

[31] It might be suggested that all moral disagreements are in some way intractable past a point—the point at which their answer depends on more deep-seated philosophical commitments, argument about which is bound to be interminable.

[32] Dworkin (n 5) 165.

Some would no doubt quibble with Dworkin's suggestion that abortion beliefs can be assimilated into essentially religious ones, as well as with the claim that abortion practice counts as an *expression* of those religious beliefs.[33] But let us assume that he was right about those things. The next question is whether it follows, as Dworkin believed, that the personhood issue is not pertinent to the constitutionality of abortion. Dworkin was guilty of a fundamental oversight regarding the limits of the doctrine of religious toleration if he thought that it can ground the abortion right *irrespective* of one's answer to that question. His mistake was in supposing that as soon as religious beliefs are at issue, the derivative worry about causing harm to persons ceases to be relevant for the legal resolution of disputes. The plain falsity of this is apparent when bringing to mind any exercise of religious belief that entails bodily harm to individuals we *are* certain are persons. Liberal democracies cannot, for example, extend tolerance to practices of ritual child sacrifice, slavery, or female genital mutilation if and when those who practice them do so as a matter of religious conviction. The doctrine of religious toleration has clear limits: toleration ends where the infringement of people's rights begins. And the infringement of the right to life is the clearest red line there is.

Dworkin was wrong, therefore, if he believed that applying the doctrine of religious toleration to abortion does not rest on derivative grounds, or presuppose them. If the fetus *were* a person, as one side of the abortion debate insists, the right to abortion could not be defended using the religious freedoms of those that take the opposite view, for the doctrine of religious toleration does not extend to homicide. Indeed, if the religious nature of abortion beliefs mandates toleration of their expression even where that entails harm to persons, we would have to ask why Dworkin's compromise principle does not protect the killers of abortion doctors. Consequently, by even appealing to the doctrine of religious toleration as a basis for political resolution, Dworkin presupposed a particular answer to the philosophical question of prenatal personhood. Toleration of abortion choice, even if a mode of religious expression, cannot be justified if the fetus is a person. And this consideration propels the derivative question right back to the forefront of our reasoning about abortion.

At this point, however, another one of Dworkin's arguments becomes relevant. As well as claiming that fetal personhood is not at the heart of moral debate about abortion, Dworkin argued that the extension of constitutional personhood to fetuses in the United States is quite unthinkable, and that for this reason alone, the personhood question is not constitutionally poignant. If Dworkin was right about this,

---

[33] The definition of religious belief to which Dworkin appeals seems, rightly, to look to the content of the belief rather than the fervency with which it is held, although the content requirement itself is a fairly loose one, capturing everything that, he says, 'touches on' the 'ultimate purpose and value of human life itself'. One might think that abortion beliefs are often religious in a different way, which is that they are mandated by the religious institutions to which many people are affiliated (as is surely true of American evangelicals, Catholics, and so on). On the question of what does and does not count as religious 'expression', it must be borne in mind that not every act which is performed on the strength of a religious belief is an instance of religious *expression* which warrants protection under the right to free exercise of religion. Attending religious services is an important expression of a religious belief, but the persecution of non-believers is not, though it may be carried on the strength of those same beliefs.

then his conclusions about the legal resolution could be left intact, even if the denial of fetal personhood is significant for the morality of abortion.

When *Roe v Wade* recognized the constitutional right to termination in 1973, the Supreme Court addressed itself to the question of the fetus's status under the Constitution.[34] At the time *Roe* was decided, the fetus had never been recognized as a constitutional person under US law. Texas, the state whose abortion legislation was under scrutiny, argued before the Court that the fetus was indeed a person within the meaning of the Fourteenth Amendment. Speaking for the majority, Justice Blackmun held that the law had never treated fetuses as constitutional persons and could not expand the category now. This was despite his acknowledgment that *had* the fetus possessed the constitutional status of a person, it would be entitled to equal protection and abortion would be rendered largely unconstitutional.

Dworkin accepted Justice Blackmun's conclusion about what would follow if the fetus were granted constitutional personhood, but emphatically endorsed *Roe*'s ruling that it lacked such protected status, arguing that the Court could not have come to any other decision on this point. As he wrote, 'almost all responsible lawyers' agree that Justice Blackmun's opinion on the personhood question was correct, since there was no precedent in US law for the proposition that the fetus is a person, and the Supreme Court lacked the power to recognize new constitutional persons.[35] In light of this, Dworkin argued that a contrary ruling would have been legally unsupportable. He did, however, acknowledge the fact that the Supreme Court has been known to upend conventional understandings of the Constitution on questions as fundamental as this—citing *Brown v Topeka Board of Education* as a standout example.[36] Why, then, could the Supreme Court not have broken with tradition here and simply declared the fetus a constitutional person because it regarded it as a person in the philosophical sense?

Dworkin responded to this by restating that the idea of fetal personhood 'is scarcely intelligible and few people believe it'.[37] Yet this is only a reiteration of the 'anti-personhood' argument. Dworkin may think the idea that fetuses are persons unintelligible, but certainly more than a few people believe it. For those who do, the *Roe* majority's refusal to extend equal constitutional status to the fetus was surely its greatest error. The upshot is that Dworkin's argument still fails to displace the primary significance of the personhood question for the constitutionality of abortion. Even if, as Dworkin claimed, little of the academic criticism surrounding *Roe* concerned the personhood ruling, the following two propositions still appear to be true:

1. A finding of constitutional personhood on behalf of the fetus would entail that abortion practice is contrary to the Constitution, and

2. A correct belief in the philosophical personhood of the fetus is a basis for granting it constitutional personhood, even if this breaks with constitutional tradition.

---

[34] 410 US 113 (1973).   [35] Dworkin (n 5) 110.   [36] 347 US 483 (1954).
[37] Dworkin (n 5) 112.

It follows from these joint propositions that whether or not the fetus is correctly regarded as a person in the philosophical sense is indeed integral to the constitutionality of abortion. Consequently, Dworkin cannot use the 'anti-personhood' argument to dismiss the constitutional salience of the derivative question, especially to those who do, in fact, defend the personhood status of the fetus.

1.6 Vagueness and Redundancy

The foregoing suggests that there is a very strong case for thinking that argument about abortion must start, first and foremost, with the question of fetal personhood. But what about Dworkin's deep scepticism concerning that question's propensity to produce principled, reasoned argument? Is the personhood question ultimately, as Dworkin suspected, an argumentative black hole?

As was seen, Dworkin believed that the personhood question is altogether unfruitful for abortion argument because neither side can appeal to a fact or an argument which the other *must* accept. Whatever new is learned or argued about the fetus, it is always open to discussants to maintain that it still does or does not fit their concept of a person.

Some have argued that stalemate in argument about personhood is down to the fact that personhood is *conceptually vague*. The philosopher Jane English claimed that vagueness in the concept of a person means that any attempt to solve the abortion problem using that concept is to 'to clarify *obscurum per obscurius*'.[38] It is nowhere near 'sharp or decisive' enough to do that work, she wrote. And if our concept of a person admits of no clear boundaries, we may well be at a loss when it comes to arguing the case of the fetus. English was particularly concerned with vagueness at the margins of the concept—in the penumbral region which, she claimed, the fetus occupies.

Of course, all of our classifications, including even the scientific ones, are vague at the margins. The concept of a person is not, in this respect, any more nebulous or less usable than many of our everyday concepts. English's view of personhood as too vague to be of use in abortion argument was tied to her belief that it admits of no decisive set of necessary and sufficient conditions—it is, in her words, a 'cluster concept'. This absence of sharp conditions is what produces contestable cases about which it is difficult to know what to say.

Of course, English was wrong if she believed everyone agrees that the fetus is a marginal case of a person. For many discussants on both sides, the fetus is far from a borderline case: it falls squarely within the parameters of personhood, or squarely outwith them. To be sure, these completely opposed viewpoints emanate from deeper disagreements about the core conditions of personhood, which English claimed are

---

[38] Jane English, 'Abortion and the Concept of a Person' (1975) 5 Canadian Journal of Philosophy 233, 236.

ambiguous. But it is disagreement about these core conditions (and in particular, about whether personhood supervenes on human species membership or psychological capacities) rather than vagueness at the margins of the concept which is responsible for the fetus being such a contested case.

Importantly, however, none of this entails that argument about personhood, including fetal personhood, is unreasoned or ungoverned by rules. For one, there are still some clear limits on what sensibly can or cannot be deemed a person—rocks are certainly not people, and normal, mature human beings certainly are. Perceiving those limits and extrapolating from them can be the first step in arguing intelligibly about the concept of a person. One would simply be wrong to think that there are *no* convictions about personhood that we share. There are. And addressing one another with arguments that build on those convictions is precisely how discussants manage to have principled exchanges about the conditions of moral status.

Dworkin's own scepticism about the personhood question stemmed from his worry that no fact or argument could ever settle the matter once and for all, to the satisfaction of everyone. The problem, for him, was that disagreement about the conditions of personhood is interminable. One question is of course why this robs the personhood question of its ethical or legal salience. But one might also question the standards of inquiry Dworkin was insisting upon on pain of dismissing a disagreement as unreasoned. There are few, if any, ethical disagreements about which we would insist on the theoretical possibility of universal agreement or else dismiss the entire debate as irrational and unprincipled; certainly, no one dismisses disagreement about whether a practice is 'just' or 'democratic' on that ground. The standards of argumentation that Dworkin seemed to demand of the personhood debate are never met outside the realm of science, and are not always met within it.

At another point in his argument, Dworkin described the personhood question as 'too ambiguous to be helpful', for the reason that 'it has a great many uses and senses that can easily be confused'.[39] For example, he explained, we might suppose that zoologists one day discover that pigs are far more intelligent and emotionally complex than we have until now believed them to be. The question might then be asked whether pigs should now be regarded as persons in the philosophical sense. But Dworkin argued that there is in fact no need to decide whether pigs qualify for personhood in order to answer the more 'practical' questions that are really of interest to us, such as whether, in light of our new knowledge, we should now treat pigs in many ways as we treat human beings, acknowledging their right not to be killed for food or imprisoned in pens. These answers, he said, do not follow directly from any conclusion about the personhood of pigs, since:

We might believe philosophically that pigs are persons but that human beings have no reason to treat them as we treat one another; or, on the contrary, we may decide that pigs are not persons according to our best understanding of that complex concept but that nevertheless their capacities entitle them to the treatment persons give one another.[40]

---

[39] Dworkin (n 5) 21–3.   [40] ibid 23.

As he thought was true of the example, Dworkin suggested that it would therefore 'be wise to set aside the question of whether the fetus is a person' and focus instead on the key moral questions in which we are interested, such as whether the fetus is owed the right to life or whether its life should be regarded as sacred.

Was Dworkin right to think that the personhood question is merely a distraction from the moral questions that should interest us in abortion? Perhaps the distinction between persons and non-persons cannot, as he suggested, withstand the moral weight we load upon it.

It cannot be doubted that creatures lacking personhood status on our reckoning can still possess a moral standing that is highly significant, especially in some contexts. It is morally impermissible to torture cats or to kill them needlessly just so as with human beings, even if humans are persons and cats are not. Moreover, one might think that it is wrong to torture or needlessly kill cats for much the same reasons that it is wrong to do so to persons: that such actions interfere with the creatures' interests in freedom from pain and in continued life. If it is possible to possess high moral standing without qualifying for personhood, it might be indeed wondered what really turns on personhood status. Why, it might be asked, can the answers to specific moral questions about the treatment of creatures not be answered without recourse to the person/non-person distinction?

These are important challenges. But I do not think they go to show that the personhood inquiry is wrongheaded or redundant in argument about abortion. There exists a shared idea about a class of beings that are endowed, by virtue of their essence or attributes, with the highest moral standing we accord, one equal to that of our own, and which goes hand in hand with certain inviolable rights. So far as the concept of a person has a fixed meaning among its users, this is surely it, and this part of its meaning is unaffected by disagreement about the constitutive properties of a person.

Insofar as the concept of a person is just a placeholder for a kind of being possessing the highest moral standing we accord, it is hard to see why talk of personhood need be confusing or distracting in abortion debate. 'Person' is a classification in common use, one that is readily comprehensible, universal, and is uncontroversial in its invocation of a ready-made package of protections and rights, especially the fundamental right to life.

It is consistent with this common understanding that it is morally wrong to treat non-persons in any number of ways, and quite possibly for reasons that mirror the wrongness of treating persons in similar ways (presumably, we must not torture cats for the same reasons that we must not torture persons). However, it is a core normative implication of personhood status that status bearers are automatically owed strong moral protection against being killed, including in circumstances in which non-persons could not claim that protection. This is particularly true of personhood in its legal sense, recognition of which triggers a catalogue of legal rights and protections, including the almost unqualified right to life. While other normative implications of personhood status may be the subject of greater debate (e.g.: does personhood status entail that the bearer cannot be the object of a proprietary transaction? Does it mean that she may not be treated merely as a means to an end?), ramifications concerning the permissibility of killing are present on any plausible account of what it means to be a person.

When elaborating personhood status in terms of these normative implications, we may still keep as an open question the possibility that the personhood category extends to some non-human animals not generally recognized as such. Such questions will, of course, arise out of discussion about what the constitutive features of a person are. But asking whether the human embryo or fetus in particular belongs in the special moral category which 'person' commonly denotes remains a key question for abortion argument whether or not the class of persons stretches to non-humans as well.

1.7 Conclusion

What if the signal inconsistencies Dworkin illuminated do hold independent rational appeal for us? What is someone to make of the personhood account of the abortion issue if she finds merit in the notion that having an abortion is not just like cutting one's hair or having a tonsillectomy, whilst being, nonetheless, a far cry from murder? For Dworkin, as we have seen, these cross-cutting judgements only went to show that arguing about abortion by way of debating prenatal personhood is profitless. But perhaps he was too hasty in ruling out the possibility that our concept of a person *will* somehow account for intuitions such as these. Where Dworkin saw inconsistency, he might instead have seen ambivalence or nuance. He might have seen discussants grasping at an intermediate category of being—a being that lacks the full status of a person but is not entirely without some of its features and value.

Interestingly, by underscoring putative inconsistencies in hostile and favourable attitudes to abortion, Dworkin demonstrated at least one way to reason fruitfully about fetal personhood. Through pointing out signal inconsistencies in each other's positions, contestants in the debate can appeal to one another through more than just 'primitive conviction'. There is clear argumentative merit in noting, for instance, that someone's failure to treat abortion as in all respects like murder, or as equal to infanticide, challenges her commitment to the belief that a fetus is a person in the fullest sense. Equally, asking someone who flatly denies fetal personhood what meaningful differences hold between late term fetuses and neonates can surely form part of a potentially persuasive argument. Whether they are ultimately winning or not, these are reasoned forms of engagement that seek to change minds by drawing on discussants' own judgements and distinctions, and attempting to reveal inconsistencies within them.

On Dworkin's view, the 'quasi-religious' nature of our beliefs in matters of life and death places the abortion issue firmly in the realm of private morality and out of reach of the law's coercive power, if not its non-coercive influence. In no context, however, is the fundamental right to life of *born* human beings subordinated to religious beliefs in this same way. Homicide crimes are never constructed so as to tolerate someone's acting on such a belief. ('Honour killings', for instance, cannot be shielded by a principle of religious toleration, though they are, in one way, the expression of a view about life's intrinsic value and what does and does not insult it.) If the situation is different for human fetuses, this can only be because they are earmarked from the outset as differently morally positioned. If a fetus is morally on a par with born humans, then something very different from tolerance towards diverse interpretations of the sanctity of life will be required to explain the moral permissibility of abortion.

It may be asked whether, in the end, what Dworkin called the 'detached' inquiry about the intrinsic value of human life captures questions that are truly morally distinct from the 'derivative' one. On one rendering, the question at the centre of the detached dispute is simply when, in the lifespan of a biologically human organism, that organism comes to possess the attributes which grant it strong moral protection, most pointedly protection against being killed in the cause of salvaging creative investment in the lives of others. Is this just the personhood question in another guise? The detached view must still hypothesize a point in the development of human life when terminating that life for anything other than saving the lives of a greater number is an impermissible affront to life's sacred value, the obvious question then being just what it is that ushers in this enhanced moral status. In other words, *whose* life is sacred, and why? These questions lie right at the heart of the personhood inquiry as commonly understood.

2

Gestation as Good Samaritanism

In the previous chapter, I introduced and defended the case for thinking that the question about the moral status, or 'personhood', of the fetus is central for moral and legal argument about abortion. As I pointed out, there are markedly different ways of trying to bypass the personhood inquiry in abortion argument. I have not yet said anything about women's rights and, in particular, the interest that many women undoubtedly have in exercising bodily autonomy through abortion. In light of the importance of women's rights and their potential interests in ending unwanted pregnancy, perhaps it can still be shown that the moral status of the fetus is either irrelevant or secondary in the rights and wrongs of abortion. A claim of this kind might run as follows:

Abortion is clearly permissible in almost all cases whether or not the fetus is a person, because a pregnant woman's right to bodily autonomy supersedes or excludes a fetus's right to life.

Let us refer to this as the Liberal Principle. The crux of the Liberal Principle is the triumph of a pregnant woman's right to bodily autonomy, including the right to terminate her pregnancy, over any competing rights of the fetus, including the right to life. More than one form of argument might be brought under the banner of this principle. What unites arguments falling under the Liberal Principle is just their common conclusion that in the case of a maternal–fetal conflict, a woman's right to decide what happens to her own body ought always (or almost always) to prevail.

Most importantly, the Liberal Principle, if correct, would obviate the need to consider the moral status of the fetus when addressing the morality of abortion. According to it, there is no reason to inquire into what a fetus *is*, morally speaking, since its situation of bodily dependence upon a pregnant woman wholly determines the permissibility of abortion without recourse to that question.

2.1 The Liberal Principle

Often translated into the language of 'women's rights', the Liberal Principle is not an argument in itself, but rather the conclusion to an argument about the interplay of a fetus's supposed right to life and a woman's interests in aborting. The conclusion resolves the abortion question permissively. The moral and legal right to an abortion, it is suggested, can just be read off the right to control one's reproductive

Arguments about Abortion: Personhood, Morality, and Law. First Edition. Kate Greasley. © K. Greasley 2017. Published 2017 by Oxford University Press.

destiny, or to control one's body in general, and cannot be defeated by a fetus's interest in life, even if it were identical in strength to that of a fully realized person.

The landmark US Supreme Court judgment in *Roe v Wade*, which recognized a qualified constitutional right to termination of pregnancy, could be viewed by some as the paradigm legal instantiation of the Liberal Principle.[1] *Roe* recognized that the right to reproductive control contained within the Fourteenth Amendment right to privacy was 'broad enough to encompass the right to a termination', albeit this right could be restricted by 'compelling state interests', including, in the second trimester, the interest in protecting women's health, and, in the third trimester, in protecting fetal life.[2] A first look at the decision in *Roe* may give the impression that the Supreme Court's decision (and the later affirmation of its central ruling in *Planned Parenthood v Casey*[3]) was the legal analogue of the ethical principle outlined above: that a woman's right to bodily autonomy and reproductive control wins out over the fetus's right to life, whatever the moral status of the fetus is believed to be.

That reading would not be accurate, however. This is because the *Roe* Court's rejection of Texas's submission that a fetus was a constitutional person within the meaning of the Fourteenth Amendment was in fact a material part of its reasoning through to the abortion right.[4] Delivering the majority opinion, Justice Blackmun made it unmistakably clear that if Texas's contention in favour of fetal personhood were accepted, the fetus's right to life would consequently be guaranteed by the Constitution and incapable of being abrogated by a pregnant woman's competing right to privacy.[5] In an illuminating footnote to this part of the opinion, Justice Blackmun elaborated that if, as Texas contended, the fetus *were* a constitutional person, then that state's own exceptions to abortion prohibition, which permitted abortion to save the life of the pregnant woman, would be rendered incoherent, along with those of its criminal laws that fixed a lesser maximum penalty for abortion than for murder.[6]

By underscoring these apparent discrepancies, Justice Blackmun cast doubt on the authenticity of Texas's conviction that the fetus really is a person in the philosophical sense. More to the point, however, his remarks about constitutional personhood meant that the *Roe* decision itself did not reflect the sorts of abortion rights arguments which seek to displace the relevance of fetal personhood. It was the very opposite of them. Despite their protestations that 'the difficult question of when life begins' on which those trained in medicine, philosophy, and theology

---

[1] *Roe v Wade* 410 US 113 (1973).

[2] ibid. The constitutional understanding of the notion of 'privacy', which US law uses in a slightly unconventional sense, pertains to the right to control aspects of one's personal life free from state interference, particularly in relation to the sorts of choices that have profound implications for one's sense of personal identity, such as whether or not to become a parent. (See *Griswold v Connecticut* 381 US 479 (1965) and *Eisenstadt v Baird* 405 US 438 (1972), both of which the Supreme Court relied upon when invoking the right to privacy in *Roe*.)

[3] *Planned Parenthood of Southeastern Pennsylvania v Casey* 505 US 833 (1992).

[4] Justice Blackmun summarized the legal position with his remark that 'the unborn have never been recognized in the law as persons in the whole sense' (ibid 162).

[5] *Roe v Wade* (n 1) 156–7.   [6] ibid 157, n 54.

could not agree was not a question for the judiciary to answer,[7] the majority Justices were clear that the attribution of constitutional personhood to the fetus would be a death-blow to abortion rights. As Justice Blackmun conceded in an integral part of the judgment, if fetal 'personhood is established, the appellant's case, of course, collapses, for the fetus's right to life would then be guaranteed specifically by the [Fourteenth] Amendment'. As the Court saw it, then, the abortion right could not survive a finding that the fetus really was equal in moral status to born human beings. Was it correct to determine thus?

Returning to the ethical dispute, the most influential argument in favour of the Liberal Principle comes in the form of an analogy put forward by Judith Jarvis Thomson, now famous (or, depending on one's perspective, infamous) in modern moral philosophy.[8] A discussion of that analogy will dominate much of this chapter and the next, since it forms the basis of a number of arguments that might be used to substantiate the Liberal Principle. If the 'women's rights' claims succeed on all of their own terms, recognition of fetal personhood would not dictate any significant moral restrictions on abortion, if any at all. Such claims therefore warrant extensive consideration.

I shall be proposing that the main versions of those arguments fail on their stated terms. That is, they fail to show that, on the assumption that a fetus is a person, abortion is permissible according to general principles of morality that we can and do accept, and, in the legal context, according to principles of the already existing legal framework.

A qualification should be added here. While I doubt the correctness of the Liberal Principle (as I have stated it) as the basis for abortion rights, even the success of that principle might not completely defeat the relevance of the personhood question. For one, we may still need to make a determination about the moral status of the fetus to even know that 'women's rights' justifications were needed to defend abortion morally. If a fetus is nothing like a person in any case, with no strong moral rights, then it is not clear that pregnant women are even called upon to cite an important, superseding right of their own in order to justify terminating a pregnancy. There is an implicit acknowledgement in Thomson's position, and by those who argue likewise, that if a fetus *is* a person, then abortion is something that at least calls for a defence. Furthermore, even if we were convinced by the thrust of the Liberal Principle, it would still be necessary to ask whether the arguments substantiating it justify abortion in all cases, at all stages of pregnancy, and by all available methods if the fetus is a person. In other words, if even some qualifications remain on which abortions are morally and legally permissible, given fetal personhood, then we will need to decide the independent moral standing of the fetus in many instances in order to correctly map the ethical and legal situation.

---

[7] ibid 159. Justice Blackmun surmised that 'we need not resolve the difficult question of when life begins. When those trained in the respective disciplines of medicine, philosophy and theology are unable to arrive at a consensus, the judiciary, at this point in the development of man's knowledge, is not in a position to speculate as to the answer'.

[8] Judith Jarvis Thomson, 'A Defense of Abortion' [1971] 1 Philosophy and Public Affairs 47.

2.2 The Violinist Analogy

Following the argumentative structure just described, Judith Thomson's philosophical defence of abortion begins by granting, for the sake of argument, that the fetus is a person from conception. Her main argument is then introduced using an imaginary scenario:

You wake up in the morning and find yourself back to back in bed with an unconscious violinist. A famous unconscious violinist. He has been found to have a fatal kidney ailment, and the Society of Music Lovers has canvassed all the available medical records and found that you alone have the right blood type to help. They have therefore kidnapped you, and last night the violinist's circulatory system was plugged into yours, so that your kidneys can be used to extract poisons from his blood as well as your own. The Director of the hospital now tells you, 'Look, we're sorry the Society of Music Lovers did this to you—we would never have permitted it if we had known. But still, they did it, and the violinist is now plugged into you. To unplug you would be to kill him. But never mind, it's only for nine months. By then he will have recovered from his ailment, and can safely be unplugged from you.' Is it morally incumbent on you to accede to this situation? No doubt it would be very nice of you if you did, a great kindness. But do you have to accede to it? What if it were not nine months, but nine years, or longer still?[9]

The scenario described is offered up as an analogy to unwanted pregnancy. But it is important to get clear on the precise position it is meant to rebuff. Thomson is refuting a particular way of thinking about the ethics of abortion once it is granted that a fetus is a person, which runs as follows. If every person has a right to life, and if the fetus is a person, then the fetus has a right to life. The pregnant woman also has the right to decide what will happen to her body. But the right to life is stronger than the right to bodily autonomy, and so outweighs it. Hence abortion is impermissible, even where pregnancy is a result of rape, and perhaps even where abortion is necessary to save the pregnant woman's life. This is what Thomson dubs 'the extreme view'.

But the step from assuming that the fetus is a person to the moral impermissibility of abortion is, on Thomson's analysis, 'neither easy nor obvious'.[10] This is what the violinist analogy is meant to illustrate. If you agree, as Thomson believes you will, that you are allowed to unplug the violinist, then, by analogy, the 'extreme view' about abortion is thrown into doubt. The violinist is unquestionably a person, but you do not believe that this forbids you to unplug him from your body, even if that spells his death. Why does the same not hold for a pregnant woman and her fetus? Why can she not 'unplug' the fetus to free herself from the burdens of supporting its life with her own body?

In describing Thomson's position, David Boonin stresses a key nuance.[11] Her claim, he says, is not that the woman's bodily right simply trumps the fetus's right

---

[9] ibid 48–9.   [10] ibid 48.
[11] David Boonin, *A Defense of Abortion* (Cambridge University Press 2003) 137.

to life. This indeed would be contrary to our very strong judgement that the right to life is more important than the right to control one's own body. The argument is rather that the fetus's right to life '*does not include or entail* the right to be provided with the use or the continued use' of the woman's body in order to go on living.[12] Thomson believes that unplugging the violinist does not violate his right to life to begin with, since he possesses only the right not to be killed *unjustly*, and unplugging him, even if it leads to his death, is not unjust. As Boonin explains, 'even though he has a right to life . . . he has no right to the use of your kidneys'.[13] Regarding abortion, then, Thomson is not attempting to persuade us that in any conflict between bodily autonomy and the right to life, bodily autonomy wins out, but that there is no such conflict in abortion, because the fetus's right is not *violated* by termination of pregnancy.

Thomson's analysis of pregnancy and abortion is brought into sharper focus by her driving claim that *not* unplugging the violinist in the situation she describes would be an act of a Good Samaritan. As she remarks, 'it would be very nice of you' if you allowed him the continued use of your kidneys, 'a great kindness', but not something you can possibly be *required* to do.[14] Boonin regards Thomson's analogical argument as just one example of the more general claim that 'the woman's carrying a pregnancy to term can be subsumed into the wider category of good samaritanism', a claim introduced in chapter 1. How accurate this description of unwanted pregnancy is thought to be is therefore key to the success of the argument.

A crucial premise underpinning Thomson's conclusion on the violinist's—and, by implication, the fetus's—entitlement to the use of another's body for sustained life is that 'we do not have any . . . "special responsibility" for a person, unless we have assumed it, explicitly or implicitly'.[15] On her reckoning, the mere fact that you find yourself in a situation whereby another person, the violinist or the fetus, depends on the use of your body for very survival is not enough to ground such responsibility unless you have done *something* to accept it, at least tacitly. Importantly, Thomson does not regard simply being in a relationship of biological parenthood to the fetus as, without more, a foundation for any such responsibility.

It is noteworthy that the entire thrust of the Good Samaritan Thesis (GST) depicts the potential wrongness of abortion in a very particular way. That is, it suggests that if abortion did happen to be morally deviant, this would only be because it violates a *positive duty* to do something—to give aid to another. As with unplugging the violinist, the thesis supposes that abortion could only be, if anything, a wrongful refusal to save life.

In a different vein, Thomson also suggests that self-defence, or something like it, is a justification both for unplugging the violinist and for performing an abortion, particularly where the woman's life is endangered by her pregnancy. Sometimes it is justifiable to kill another person if they present a serious enough threat. As Thomson argues, 'however innocent the child may be, you do not have to wait passively while it crushes you to death.'[16] Somewhat differently from the GST, this kind of reasoning

---

[12] ibid. My emphasis.   [13] ibid.   [14] Thomson (n 8) 52.   [15] ibid 65.
[16] ibid 52.

categorizes abortion's potential wrongness as a violation of a *negative duty* to refrain from harming others—a duty which can be superseded if the action is justified. If I kill an aggressor to defend my own life, self-defence legitimates what would otherwise be an infraction of the duty to avoid killing. This duty extends to *anyone* I might kill, as opposed to the duty to proffer positive assistance, which is often thought to extend only to particular individuals for whom I have special responsibility.

Translated into a legal framework, the violinist analogy reasoning implies that the law might, with coherence, recognize the personhood of the fetus whilst still declining to treat abortion as unlawful killing, either because it does not regard it as killing at all but only the legitimate refusal to be a Good Samaritan, or because if it is homicide, it has a legally recognized justification, like self-defence (another claim I introduced in chapter 1). I wish to concentrate here on the first argument, what I have been calling the Good Samaritan Thesis.

2.3 Criticism of the Good Samaritan Thesis

Thomson's argument has attracted a considerable amount of criticism in the time since it was written, with the violinist analogy coming under attack on multiple grounds. Boonin devotes a large portion of his book *A Defense of Abortion* to defending the kernel of the GST against sixteen major objections that have been levelled at Thomson's particular version.[17] I will not be tracing all sixteen, but will try to make sense of some of the main reasons why many think Thomson did not manage to show that if the fetus is a person, abortion is still almost always morally permissible.

Typically, responses to Thomson's argument challenge either the strength of the analogy between pregnancy and the violinist scenario or the conclusion about the violinist case Thomson is so confident we will reach. That is, they suggest either that aborting a pregnancy is, in some very important respects, not like unplugging the violinist, or that we cannot be so sure that unplugging the violinist in such circumstances really is morally permissible.

Boonin highlights a third common source of objection, rooted in a more general scepticism that an analogy as odd as Thomson's can elucidate anything about the rights and wrongs of abortion. The 'weirdness objection', as he calls it, 'simply reject[s] the authority of such arguments from analogy to begin with', on the ground that the scenarios imagined are weird, whereas pregnancy is not.[18] Pregnancy is a normal occurrence, and currently the only way of reproducing our species. The violinist scenario, on the other hand, is quite extraordinary. Perhaps this means we cannot rely on it as a guide to the morality of abortion.

The weirdness objection could, of course, be directed at any number of exotic examples conjured up in abortion ethics more widely. In its most developed form, that objection is the more thoroughgoing challenge that all analogical reasoning about abortion is an unhelpful diversion because the pregnancy situation is so

---

[17] Boonin (n 11) chapter 4. [18] ibid 139.

unique. I will say a little more about this kind of objection in chapter 4, but for now let it suffice to say that unless all analogical reasoning in this topic is to be dismissed as invalid, the force of the weirdness objection against Thomson's analogy may have to depend on further argument about the moral relevance of some realities of pregnancy for the GST.

Characterizing continued pregnancy as an act of good samaritanism, and of abortion as the mere failure to save, has significant ramifications for the correct legal analysis of abortion when the personhood proviso is adopted. The law treats acts of killing as very different from the failure to render life-saving assistance. When accompanied by the intention to kill or cause grievous bodily harm, a positive act of killing is murder according to English law, unless a defence can be raised. But only very specific failures to lend positive assistance can ever amount to murder or manslaughter in the law, chiefly when the person who refuses life-saving assistance has a pre-existing responsibility for the victim, arising out of a familial or social relationship, or a voluntary undertaking of responsibility towards her.[19] The mere failure to lend easy, life-saving assistance to someone in mortal peril does not attract any criminal sanction in Anglo-American law (although the duty of 'easy rescue' has been recognized in some other jurisdictions, and the failure of Anglo-American law to impose it has been the focus of some pointed academic criticism[20]). Consequently, if abortion really is only the refusal by a pregnant woman to be a Good Samaritan, its criminalization would not appear to fit with the law of omissions liability in the United States and in Britain as it stands, even if the fetus were a person.

When examining Thomson's argument, it helps to keep in mind what it would take for it to fail. Thomson believes she has a way of showing that the fetus is not entitled to the continued use of a woman's body for survival owing to the situation it finds itself in relative to the woman, regardless of its hypothetical equal moral status. The benefit of the violinist analogy is to provide an analogous situation where the equal moral status of the dependent party is not in any doubt, and hence controlled for. If at any point then, the argument appears to smuggle in a judgement of the fetus's lesser moral status for its sustainability, Thomson will have failed in her stated task.

Next, The GST claims that, if anything, the duty not to abort is the duty to render positive assistance to another—the duty to help rather than to refrain from harming—but that no such duty is owed to a human fetus by a pregnant woman. The thesis will therefore appear to be wrong if either one of two things is true:

1. There *is* almost always a positive obligation on a pregnant woman to continue to gestate a fetus-person through to birth, or

2. Aborting the fetus is not an omission, a failure to save the fetus, but an act of killing, in prima facie breach of the negative obligation to refrain from seriously harming others.

---

[19] See, *R v Stone & Dobinson* [1977] 1 QB 354; *R v Gibbons and Proctor* (1918) 13 Cr App Rep 134; *R v Instan* (1893) 1 QB 450.

[20] See, Andrew Ashworth, 'The Scope of Criminal Liability for Omissions' (1989) 105 Law Quarterly Review 424, and Joel Feinberg, 'The Moral and Legal Responsibility of the Bad Samaritan' in Joel Feinberg (ed), *Freedom and Fulfilment: Philosophical Essays* (Princeton University Press 1994).

If either of these propositions were true, continuing an unwanted pregnancy would not be an act of good samaritanism. It is my contention here that the second proposition is true—that is, that abortion is not the mere failure to save a fetus but the positive act of terminating its life. If this is right, it will be enough on its own to refute the GST without needing to establish any positive obligation on the part of a pregnant woman to aid her fetus by gestating it. Indeed, the second proposition holds that continued gestation is *never* the fulfilment of a special, positive obligation to aid, because the alternative abortion scenario is not the mere withholding of aid, but the act of killing, in breach of the negative obligation to refrain from killing other persons. Because I think the second proposition correct, I will not attempt to make a strong case for the first. However, I think it still worth addressing some aspects of the debate surrounding the question whether a pregnant woman might be obligated to continue to gestate a fetus-person, were the morality of abortion a matter of positive duties to aid.

2.4 A Duty to Gestate?

Thomson's claim that a pregnant woman could have no positive duty to gestate a fetus-person has been paid considerable attention both by those who criticize and those who defend the GST.[21] Some critics have challenged her core premise that obligations to assist others must always be explicitly or implicitly assumed, and its implication that positive duties could not arise circumstantially, especially when that assistance is life-saving. They have also challenged the suggestion that such duties could never be owed to strangers.[22] If I happen upon a seriously wounded hiker on a deserted stretch of terrain, do I not come under an unquestionable moral duty to lend assistance, given I am the only one who can?

Others have sought to adduce a special responsibility owed by a pregnant woman to the individual fetus-person that inhabits her, grounded in her prior responsibility in becoming pregnant, where sex is consensual, or in responsibilities stemming from biological ties.[23] In addition to this, critics of the violinist analogy sometimes point out that the burdens incurred by the person plugged into the violinist are far

[21] Boonin's treatment of this hefty sub-issue can be found at pages 148–88, 227–54, and 266–74 (Boonin, n 11).

[22] See, John Finnis, 'The Rights and Wrongs of Abortion: A Reply to Judith Thomson' (1973) [Wiley] 2 Philosophy and Public Affairs 117, 122–3; Christopher Robert Kaczor, *The Ethics of Abortion: Women's Rights, Human Life, and the Question of Justice* (Routledge 2011), 150–1; and Joel Feinberg, 'Abortion', in Joel Feinberg, *Freedom and Fulfillment: Philosophical Essays* (Princeton University Press 1994).

[23] See, Mary Anne Warren, 'On the Moral and Legal Status of Abortion' (1973) 57 The Monist 43 (Warren objects to Thomson's particular argument on the ground that it does not account for an obligation a woman may be under to sustain the fetus on account of her engaging in consensual sex, although, like Thomson, she rejects the 'personhood proviso' in any event); Kaczor (n 22) 162–8; Patrick Lee, *Abortion and Unborn Human Life* (2nd edn, Catholic University of America Press 2010) 108–10 and 117–20; and Francis J. Beckwith, 'Defending Abortion Philosophically: A Review of David Boonin's "A Defense of Abortion"' (2006) 31 Journal of Medicine and Philosophy 177. Boonin labels the first of these arguments the 'Responsibility Objection', and discusses it at pages 167–88 (Boonin, n 11).

worse than the burdens of typical pregnancy. Pregnancies hardly ever render women bed-ridden and incapacitated for an entire nine months. Perhaps, it is argued, the burdens of sustaining the violinist are not such that any person can be morally required to undertake them in order to save another, but the same is not obviously true of typical pregnancies.

In response, defenders of the GST have rebuffed proposals that consensual sex or biological parenthood could, without more, constitute a source of special responsibility to keep a fetus-person alive.[24] Alternatively, they have argued that in any case, the scope of one's responsibility to assist another, whether that person is a stranger, neighbour, or child, could never encompass the extreme burdens of bodily aid entailed by pregnancy and the violinist scenario.[25] Burdens of this magnitude, it is argued—perhaps, even, *any* burden involving the surrender of one's very body— are simply outwith the scope of the moral or legal obligations people can have in respect of one another, regardless of the circumstances. As Bertha Manninen has argued, American law would not condone the forcible extraction of a kidney or of bone marrow from one citizen on behalf of another, even if the donor were responsible for the needy person's situation of imperilment—for instance, if the need arose because of a car crash injury for which the mandated donor was responsible.[26] Manninen cites the well-known American case *McFall v Shimp*, in which a Pennsylvania court ruled that a man could not be required by law to undergo a bone marrow transplant procedure in order to save the life of his cousin, for whom his bone marrow was the only viable match.[27]

The same is true of English law, which will not compel a parent to deliver up so much as a life-saving vial of blood for his own child, or force a woman to undergo a caesarean section even where it is the only way to preserve the life of her late-term fetus.[28] If a pregnant woman were found to be under a legal obligation to offer bodily assistance to a fetus through continued gestation, this would appear to be the only instance of legally imposed duties of bodily aid to others.

In response to this, it might be pointed out that legal and moral obligation are not the same thing, and that we may be morally required to do, or refrain from doing, many things in respect of which we lack legal duties. Under English law, for example, there is no criminal liability for a person who chooses not to assist a child drowning in a shallow pool, although almost anyone would agree that the failure to do so is morally repugnant. Likewise, just because the law does not generally enforce duties of bodily assistance does not mean that weighty moral duties of the kind do not exist. Moreover, some have argued that legal duties of providing adequate parental care do indeed involve the thoroughgoing use of one's body, if not the actual surrender of flesh and blood. Even those whose parental duties are

---

[24] Boonin (n 11) 148–88, 227–34, and 246–54.

[25] See especially, Bertha Alvarez Manninen, 'Rethinking Roe v. Wade: Defending the Abortion Right in the Face of Contemporary Opposition' (2010) 10 American Journal of Bioethics 33.

[26] ibid 40. See also Bertha Alvarez Manninen, *Pro-Life, Pro-Choice: Shared Values in the Abortion Debate* (Vanderbilt University Press 2014) chapter 2.

[27] 10 Pa D & C 3d 90 (26 July 1978).

[28] See *S v St George's NHS Trust* [1998] 2 WLR 936.

limited to alimony payments must employ their bodies in whatever form of labour they rely on to generate the income with which to pay.[29]

This last observation about the blurred boundaries between bodily and non-bodily forms of assistance strikes me as a bad argument for the legal enforcement of any duty of bodily assistance that clearly exists in morality. There are good reasons to refrain from using the law to coerce forms of assistance which involve interference with our bodily integrity, and it is surely not a good objection to those reasons to point out that the performance of any duty requires the use of our bodies at least in the restricted sense that all activity is physical.

Be that as it may, Thomson is willing to concede that there may exist some circumstances in which the refusal to provide life-saving bodily assistance is morally deficient, even if not in breach of a clear moral requirement. She considers how our response to the violinist analogy might change if the host only had to remain plugged into him for one hour to save his life.[30] In that situation, Thomson admits that it may be 'morally indecent' for the host to refuse, but that acceding the request still falls short of a moral *requirement*. Similarly, Thomson imagines a situation in which she is mortally sick and can be saved only by feeling Henry Fonda's 'cool hand' on her brow. Supposing that Fonda is already in the same room, and need only to cross it to provide the life-saving contact, Thomson admits that it would be ghastly of him to refuse, but maintains, all the same, that he is under no moral obligation to comply.

This, however, leads one to wonder what space Thomson believes exists between 'morally indecent' refusals and a moral obligation to do otherwise. From one perspective, failing to assist someone when it is morally indecent to do so is just one and the same thing as shirking a moral obligation. Doing the morally decent thing is not acting as a Good Samaritan, since moral decency is not moral supererogation; it is the bare minimum that morality requires. Surely Henry Fonda *is* morally obligated to provide Thomson with his 'cool hand' at such little cost, if we are sure that his refusing to do so is quite monstrous.

If moral obligations to provide bodily support are not anathema, it will matter for Thomson's Good Samaritan argument just how onerous pregnancy is compared with being plugged into the violinist for nine months, assuming that we are indeed sure that one cannot be required to sustain the violinist. Whilst it is true that typical pregnancies do not render women bed-ridden for the entire nine months, as in Thomson's example, the bodily burdens and risks accompanying even ordinary pregnancies are fairly significant. Perhaps pregnancy entails the kinds of burdens which no one can be morally obligated to provide in order to keep another person alive. Still, if we are minded to say, in Thomson's amended example, that one *could* be morally obligated to sustain the violinist for an hour, where that is all it takes to save him, the possible

---

[29] Michael Levin, for instance, has argued that 'all child-support laws make the parental body an indirect resource for the child. If the father is a construction worker, the state will intervene unless some of his calories he extends lifting equipment go to providing food for his children' (see Michael Levin, 'Review of 'Life in the Balance' by Robert Wennberg' (1986) 3 Constitutional Commentary 500, 511).

[30] Thomson (n 8) 59.

duty to gestate (if abortion morality *is* a matter of positive obligations) might also depend on how much continued pregnancy is required in order to save a fetus. What if a pregnancy became unwanted only an hour before a fetus can be extracted alive? Following our conclusions about the amended violinist case, it would seem that the pregnant woman might well have a duty to gestate for that remaining hour, unless the cost to the woman of extracting the fetus alive, as opposed to aborting it, is itself above and beyond the things we must do to preserve the lives of others.

It warrants saying something confined about claims to the effect that a pregnant woman may fall under a special responsibility to sustain the fetus inhabiting her owing to her responsibility in becoming pregnant, or to relations of biological parenthood. I have so far mostly been treating pregnancy and the violinist case the same in taking both to ask what level of burdens we are morally bound to undertake if and when we find ourselves in circumstances wherein only our bodily assistance can sustain another person's life. But some have argued that the duties a pregnant woman owes to her fetus may well outstrip those which one person owes to just any other, first and foremost because a woman may owe a special duty of care to a person she brings into existence by foreseeably becoming pregnant.

Boonin labels this the Responsibility Objection. The relevant point of disanalogy with the violinist case is that there you have been plucked at random and forcibly plugged into the violinist. However, where pregnancy results from consensual sex, it could be argued that a woman has at least voluntarily assumed the risk of becoming pregnant. This leads some to say that the violinist analogy only resembles pregnancies that are brought about by rape. In every other case, perhaps a woman's prior responsibility in becoming pregnant could be the source of a special duty to gestate the fetus when the risk of pregnancy materializes. Moreover, even if Thomson were right that one cannot have responsibility for another unless it is assumed, explicitly or implicitly, perhaps consensual sex constitutes such an assumption.

Thomson in fact pre-empts this objection at length. There is not enough space here to relay the entire philosophical discussion surrounding the Responsibility Objection. (And if it is true that, in any event, abortion does not equate to a failure to rescue, the issue will be moot.) Most notably, however, David Boonin has forcefully defended GST from the Responsibility Objection, which he usefully divides into two separate forms. One, which he calls the 'tacit consent version', claims that by engaging in consensual sexual intercourse, a pregnant woman tacitly consents to providing a fetus with bodily aid should she fall pregnant.[31] The other, which he calls the 'negligence version' of the objection, claims that voluntarily engaging in sexual intercourse with the foreseeable risk of becoming pregnant is sufficient to ground a special duty to sustain the fetus whether or not it amounts to an actual assumption of responsibility, in much the same way that we might incur special responsibilities to aid particular individuals whom our negligent behaviour puts in harm's way.

The 'tacit consent version' certainly strikes as the easier to dismiss, since it is far from clear that one can infer actual *consent* to pregnancy from mere willingness

---

[31] Boonin (n 11) 118.

to run the risk of pregnancy. When people knowingly run the risk of contracting sexually transmitted diseases, for instance, we do thereby infer that they consent to fall victim to the disease. The 'negligence version' has more allure, for it seems that we might well hold someone responsible to assist another person in peril (especially mortal peril), and responsible in a way that goes above and beyond ordinary duties of assisting strangers, if they had acted in a way which foreseeably brought about that peril. For instance, as Francis Beckwith has pointed out, we hold drink-drivers responsible for the damage their negligence causes to other people, and duty-bound to rectify the damage, even though they were not *trying* to cause harm.[32] Could the same logic be used to impute to many pregnant women the responsibility to assist their fetuses by gestating them to term?

Boonin attempts to refute the 'negligence version' of the Responsibility Objection by drawing what he believes is a fundamental distinction between being responsible for a needy person's existence and being responsible for his neediness *given that he exists*. He does this with the use of a thought-experiment called the Imperfect Drug story.[33] In 'Imperfect Drug', you are the violinist's doctor and have just discovered that he has a rare ailment on the verge of killing him which can only be cured by a drug with an unfortunate side-effect: five to ten years after administration, it causes the kidney condition described by Thomson. Knowing that you alone have the required blood type to save the violinist when his kidneys fail, you prescribe the drug and cure the disease. You are now responsible for the violinist's existence, in that you have extended his life by offering him the cure. But according to Boonin, this does not now make you responsible for his future neediness, given that he exists. Specifically, you are under no duty to offer him the use of your kidneys later down the line simply because he would not, at that time, be alive but for you. Responsibility in sense one, responsibility for existence, does not entail responsibility in sense two: responsibility for neediness, given that a person exists.

Boonin's retort sounds quite convincing. However, we might feel that some morally salient differences hold between foreseeably bringing a fetus-person into existence and Boonin's Imperfect Drug story. Francis Beckwith believes it an important difference that in Imperfect Drug, the physician is only responsible for the violinist's existence in that she *extends* it.[34] She does not bring the violinist *into* existence. In contrast, the fetus's progenitors do not extend the life of an already existing human being; they bring into being a brand new one, who is needy by nature, and in need of the pregnant woman's body to survive. Beckwith thinks this difference important because, by giving him the drug, the physician has still decreased the violinist's *net neediness*, given that he was on the brink of death at the time. But the pregnant woman can make no such claim. Her voluntary acts have not decreased the net neediness of the fetus, but rather brought into existence a needy-by-nature being which would otherwise not have existed. Beckwith thinks this sufficient to establish negligence-type responsibility in the pregnancy case.

---

[32] Beckwith (n 23) 192.   [33] Boonin (n 11) 172.   [34] Beckwith (n 23) 193–5.

Finally, some people do find merit in the notion that biological ties to other individuals can ground obligations to them that we do not ordinarily owe to others. The putative point of disanalogy here is that the violinist in Thomson's case is a stranger, whereas the pregnant woman stands in a relation of biological parenthood to her fetus. Parents are often thought to owe special duties of care to their offspring, whether they have undertaken them or not. Biological fathers, for instance, are under a duty to pay child support whether or not they intended or accepted their biological parenthood. Perhaps Thomson is simply wrong to deny, as she does, that parents have special responsibility for their children unless they have assumed it. The 'natural claim' children have over their parents, Beckwith argues, explains why we hold parents to account for the fulfilment of their duties, prosecuting them, for instance, when they neglect to provide care. Some may take the view that the duties of child support which the law poses upon biological parents regardless of whether they intended pregnancy (alimony payments, for example) demonstrate our belief that biological parenthood does ground special moral duties to one's offspring, regardless of whether those duties are assumed.

The obvious counter to this objection is that it is simply a mistake to think that biological relations per se ground obligations. Like Thomson, Boonin is extremely sceptical about this possibility. He believes it absurd to think that anything about our reactions to the violinist case should change if it were discovered that the 'stranger' violinist is in fact your son, whom you never knew existed, created *in vitro* years ago from gametes you contributed to a medical study. As Boonin argues, biological parents are commonly thought to have strong duties towards their children because they are their *guardians*. In other words, it is *social parenthood* which is the true source of obligation. Hence, when children are adopted, it is the adoptive parents, not the biological ones, who are held responsible for their welfare. Thomson claims that biological parents typically assume the social role of parenthood when they choose not to abort pregnancies and take a neonate home. For Thomson as well, it is the accepted role of social parent rather than biological relation which is the source of obligation.

Boonin is surely right to think that social parenthood trumps biological parenthood as far as duties of care are concerned. When a child is adopted, it is clearly the adoptive parents and not the biological ones who are specially responsible for her care. However, even on this 'social responsibility' explanation for the typical burdens of biological parenthood, it is not clear that the pregnant woman is off the hook. For Boonin's argument here contains a further premise: that duties of social guardianship only obtain where they are accepted and cannot be a product of circumstance. One might argue that the first rule of social guardianship of children is simply that one is responsible for a child in need if singled out as the only one who *can* help, unless and until that responsibility is transferred to someone else. This is certainly, I think, the working moral presumption when it comes to the finding of abandoned or lost children. In post-birth scenarios, being singled out as the only person who can temporarily care for a child only tends to make the responsibility all the more acute. Of course, in most post-birth scenarios that duty is quite quickly transferable. Not so of gestation, though. Pregnancy is special in this regard in that what is required to keep the fetus-person alive is *not* a transferable duty. No one except the biological 'mother' can provide that aid. In this way, the pregnancy scenario resembles the situation where a biological parent is stuck on a desert island with her child, with no option for transferring guardianship. Presumably, Boonin would not agree that post-birth child abandonment is permissible, even in circumstances where the parent (or adult in *loco parentis*) had no option for transferring social responsibility. It will not be an adequate reply here for Boonin to reiterate Thomson's claim that the parent's assumption of responsibility was originally constituted by not aborting the child and taking her home after birth. The claim thrown into question here is simply the one which holds that responsibilities to children must *always* be voluntarily assumed.

Of course, some discussants are reluctant to relinquish the notion that biological parenthood alone is a meaningful moral relation, and not entirely without reason. Boonin's suggestion that in the amended violinist scenario it would be absurd for you to feel differently upon discovery that the violinist is in fact your son seems to me to be misplaced. Surely most people *would* feel differently upon such a discovery, even more so if the violinist were not a grown violinist at all, but a small child. Moreover, this change of feeling is not one that it seems right to view as inappropriate, pathological, or surprising. It might be replied that even though explicable, the feeling of special responsibility towards one's biological progeny is not a genuine reflection of moral obligation, but only a by-product of the huge cultural significance attaching to biological relations. This cultural significance surely owes in large part to the overwhelming correlation between biological parenthood and social guardianship. Far from showing the pull to care especially for one's biological relations to be irrational or misplaced, however, explanations such as this—as well as theories which carve out an important place for genetic relation in our self-understanding and personal identity[35]—might provide a rational underpinning for those attitudes.

Whatever one's conclusions about the importance of biological relations, though, it is still open for critics of GST to argue that either bodily burdens in general or the typical burdens of pregnancy in particular are simply outwith the scope of any moral obligation one could ever owe to any other, regardless of any special duties of care grounded in either biological relation or negligence responsibility. If this is correct, then arguing successfully for a source of special responsibility will not make a difference to the overall conclusion: that there can be no positive duty on a pregnant woman to gestate a fetus. Reiterating Manninen's argument, someone might also point out that parental and negligence-based responsibilities still have very clear limits in law, and do not ever extend to bodily burdens.

Whatever the legal situation, however, it is far less clear (I think) that bodily assistance could never form the content of a *moral* duty to assist another. And if moral duties of bodily assistance could possibly exist, we can again pose the question whether ordinary pregnancy exceeds the moral obligations of physical help one could ever owe to one's offspring or to those whose needy situation (in the case

---

[35] See J David Velleman, 'Family History' (2005) 34 Philosophical Papers 357.

of pregnancy, needy *existence*) one is responsible for creating. Most, I think, would find it morally deficient to refuse one's child, or the victim of one's negligence, a life-saving bone marrow or blood donation. Whilst I think it clear that even the most straightforward pregnancies go beyond this level of burdensomeness, they are not so burdensome as being plugged into Thomson's violinist for nine months. This makes it a live question whether those burdens go beyond the scope of a possible moral obligation to assist a fetus, and not one that can be answered using the analogy of the violinist.

2.5 Is Abortion the Failure to Rescue?

As I have said, the entire line of argument considered above proceeds on Thomson's assumption that if abortion *is* wrong, that is only because it is a violation of a positive duty to aid another. But much of the criticism of Thomson's violinist analogy contests the very treatment of abortion as an issue of positive obligations. In the violinist scenario, your question is whether you can cause the death of the violinist by unplugging him, if that is what it takes to liberate yourself. But in some ways, 'unplugging' the violinist looks markedly different from many abortive procedures. It is plausible to describe the act of unplugging as one that does not *kill* the violinist as such, but only discontinues his life-support by disallowing him the use of your kidneys, making it inevitable that he will die. But what if you were unable to simply 'unplug' yourself from the violinist? What if freeing yourself from him required bringing about his death in some other way? Would you be permitted to kill the violinist by poisoning him, taking an axe to him, suffocating him, or putting him through an incredibly powerful suction machine that would kill him in the process of detaching him from you, if this is what it took? It is a fairly ubiquitous criticism of the violinist analogy that many abortion procedures do not resemble the clean-cut 'unplugging' in Thomson's scenario, but involve something more like a direct attack on the body of the fetus.[36] Abortion methods better fitting this description include the following:

> *Induction using a saline solution*: A concentrated salt solution is injected into the amniotic fluid, causing the fetus to die from acute salt poisoning. (This method is now obsolete in developed countries.)

> *Vacuum aspiration or suction termination*: This is the most common early surgical technique. The cervix of the pregnant woman is stretched open and the surgeon inserts a plastic tube into the womb. The surgeon then uses a suction tube to evacuate the contents of the womb, in the process of which the fetus is dismembered by the vacuum machine.

> *Surgical dilation and evacuation or, 'dilation and curettage'*: The pregnant woman's cervix is dilated and the fetus is scraped out using a sharp instrument, also killing the fetus by dismemberment.

---

[36] See, for example, Kaczor (n 22) 151–4.

Intact dilation and extraction, or 'partial-birth abortion': The pregnant woman's cervix is dilated and the fetus's head is delivered into the vaginal canal. The doctor then uses a sharp instrument to make an incision into the head, and evacuate its contents with a suction machine. The body of the fetus then passes easily out of the woman. The fetus is killed by the incision.

Perhaps the violinist analogy is misleading for failing to capture the direct nature of the attack on the fetus during many kinds of abortion. If this is so, what implications does it have for Thomson's argument? As John Finnis described it:

... the whole movement of [Thomson's] argument in defence of abortion is to assimilate abortion to the range of Samaritan problems on the basis that having an abortion is, or can be, justified as *merely* a way of *not rendering special assistance*.[37]

Finnis maintained that Thomson's Good Samaritan defence of abortion relied on the important distinction between killing and not keeping another person alive. However, Thomson could not deal with the whole of abortion as a Good Samaritan problem were she to acknowledge that in many instances, it is a positive act of killing rather than a mere failure to continue assistance which is under discussion. If abortion is frequently something very different from merely failing to rescue a fetus, this surely changes what is required to render it morally permissible, on the presumption that a fetus is a person. The negative duty to refrain from killing is largely thought to be far stricter and more general than the positive duty to give life-saving aid. Whereas one needs to locate a source of a duty to lend assistance, the duty to avoid killing applies all the time and in respect of everyone, unless it is displaced by a special justification. As Phillipa Foot explained, 'there is worked into our moral system a distinction between what we owe people in the form of aid and what we owe them in the way of non-interference'.[38] If the fetus is a person, and if aborting it really is to *kill* it, then it would take a particularly strong justification to make that killing permissible. Of course, there are recognized justifications for homicide in both law and morality. Such justifications are typically required to be proportionate to the harm inflicted by killing, and even then the mode of bringing about another person's death may be subject to certain constraints, depending on one's moral outlook. If abortion is a clear-cut example of homicide, only a recognized justification for homicide could vindicate it in morality and law.

Still, there are some abortive procedures that seem to fit the 'unplugging' analogy more comfortably. Abortion by hysterotomy, for instance, is performed through a surgical incision into the pregnant woman's abdomen through which the living fetus is removed. Once outside the womb, the non-viable fetus dies. Abortion can also be (though rarely is) carried out by means of a hysterectomy, whereby the woman's entire uterus is removed and the fetus with it. Again, the fetus subsequently dies not as a result of any direct attack on its body, but because of its expulsion from the environment it needs to survive. We might call these kinds of abortions in

---

[37] Finnis (n 22) 125. My emphasis.
[38] Philippa Foot, 'The Problem of Abortion and the Doctrine of Double Effect' (1967) 5 Oxford Review 5, 9.

which the fetus is ejected but not directly attacked 'extraction abortions'. Another example of a possible 'extraction abortion' is medical abortion procured using the 'abortion pill' (RU-486), an increasingly favoured method. The pill works by triggering contractions which cause a miscarriage, again expelling the embryo or fetus from the only environment in which it can survive. In these examples, there seems to be more scope for characterizing abortion as the discontinuation of life-support rather than the act of killing.

Even in the case of extraction abortions, however, it is possible to challenge the unplugging analogy. The analogy suggests that abortion by these methods merely *allows* the fetus to die. Is that correct? The matter is not settled simply by pointing to the fact that extraction abortions do not involve a direct attack on the body of the fetus, for there are clearly cases where disconnecting life-support without such an attack amounts to killing, not failing to rescue. If a hospital attendant decides to switch off all of the life-support machines on an intensive-care ward without relocating the patients depending on them, she will surely be killing the patients and not just omitting to save them.[39] As in this example, the abortion procedures in question are not *pure* omissions; in each case there is an action being performed which results in the death of the fetus. So the absence of a direct interference with the fetus's body does not appear to settle the question about whether abortion is killing or failing to save.

Those who characterize 'extraction abortion' as allowing death rather than killing tend to claim that the fetus dies not because of the abortion, but because of its own underlying pathology, this being its unsuitability to life outside of the womb—in particular, its underdeveloped lungs. But as an argument for why abortion equates to letting die rather than killing, the claim is not persuasive. If one astronaut aboard a space station ejects another astronaut out into space without a space suit, she has surely killed him rather than just allowed him to die. It is immaterial to the killing description that there is also a physiological explanation for the death of the astronaut, having to do with the unsuitability of his body for survival in space without a space suit.

There is a problem here, however. If one maintains that abortion by extraction kills the fetus rather than fails to rescue it, what is one to say of the violinist case? David Boonin thinks we will not consistently be able to hold that while abortion by hysterotomy or hysterectomy (extraction abortion) kills the fetus, unplugging the violinist only allows him to die.[40] In both cases, the victim is disconnected from vital life-support and is not subject to a direct bodily attack. If the violinist's underlying ailment is the significant cause of his death, why is the same not true of the fetus's underdeveloped lungs?

One way a critic of GST might respond to Boonin's challenge here is to accept that unplugging the violinist does indeed kill him, albeit *indirectly*—meaning, without a direct attack on his body—and to hold out the possibility that there is a justification for killing the violinist that might not be available for many extraction abortions, if the fetus is a person. Alternatively, one might concede that if unplugging the

---

[39] See *Airedale NHS Trust v Bland* [1993] AC 789.   [40] Boonin (n 11) 196–9.

violinist is only the discontinuation of aid, so also is abortion by extraction, and that Thomson's analogy is successful in respect of those kinds of abortions. However, one might still maintain that all *non*-extraction abortions are acts of killing.

But there may yet be further reasons for thinking that extraction abortion and unplugging the violinist are on either side of the killing–letting die divide. Boonin apparently sees no significance whatsoever in the fact that the fetus's biological inability to survive outside the womb is true of all early human life, whereas the condition threatening the violinist is an extraordinary ailment. This probably has something to do with his rejection of the 'weirdness' objection in general. As Boonin sees it, both the violinist and the pre-viable fetus have genetic disposi-tions which mean that they cannot survive when the bodily support of another is taken away, and in both cases those genetic dispositions have the same bearing on whether the dependent party is killed or not rescued when that support is with-drawn. The fact that the violinist's condition happens to be out of the ordinary is beside the point.

But Boonin may be too quick here to dismiss the relevance of the fact that unsuit-ability to life outside of the womb is a condition in which all human beings begin their existence. Without wanting to delve into difficult questions of causation, including whether omissions can be causes, it is at least clear that what is ordinarily required for human beings to remain alive does not usually suffice as an explanation for death. Even a paradigmatic direct killing could be given an alternative descrip-tion that is purely physical and causal. Consider: 'He didn't die because I stabbed him; he died because he couldn't continue to oxygenate his body having lost so much blood from a gash in his skin'. Physical descriptions of inevitable biological failings do not give rise to any doubt about whether a killing has taken place in clear cases. In my stabbing example, the victim's pre-existing need for enough blood to oxygenate his body does not preclude the attacker's actions from being actions that kill.

Pre-viable fetuses are innately incapable of surviving outside the uterine environ-ment, and their dependence on that environment is nothing out of the ordinary; it is the only way in which human beings begin their existence. We do not usually redescribe acts of killing as failures to rescue as soon as it is pointed out that the relevant actions only caused the deprivation of normal conditions for sustaining human biological life. Considering this, it seems we would need a special reason for saying that expelling the fetus from the womb in an extraction abortion does not bring about its death, but only fails to rescue it from the natural consequences of its biological immaturity.

The violinist's situation of dependence is, contrastingly, quite unique. Certainly, one could not very well *explain* the death of the violinist subsequent to his being unplugged from you without drawing special attention to his underlying condi-tion. This is, however, every bit as true for the intensive-care patients whose death you cause by switching off their life-support machines. And you would surely be killing *them*. The predicament of the intensive-care patients is not truly extraordi-nary in quite the way that the violinist's predicament is—it is more familiar and prosaic. But here Boonin might push us to state the exact reason why the sheer weirdness of the violinist's case has a bearing on our assessment of what amounts to killing and what letting die.

One thing to come out of the comparison with the intensive-care patients case is that the accuracy of the killing-versus-letting-die description seems to depend upon more than whether the act is in one clear way just the discontinuation of life-sustaining aid. It seems there must be more involved when applying that distinction properly than looking only to the precise structure of the acts resulting in death, and what the prospects of the victim would have been if left unaided by anyone or anything. Unplugging the life-support patients is a clear act of killing, whilst unplugging the violinist's support seems not to be. Both are alike, though, in being acts which bring about death only by cutting off vital life-sustaining aid. What, then, are we to say about extraction abortion, where the fetus is ejected from a life-sustaining environment by means of a positive act which does not attack it directly? This much seems clear: the determination cannot be made solely by pointing to the fetus's pathological dependence on the uterine environment.

2.6 Killing and Letting Die

Perhaps, however, the killing–letting die distinction is not itself of huge consequence for the GST. Indeed, Thomson's own response to the objection based on that difference is to point out that the violinist analogy is just meant to show that the two cases (the violinist case and abortion) can both be assimilated into the Good Samaritan analysis, being in all relevant respects morally alike, *notwithstanding* that one may be an act of killing and the other not. As she has written:

Now it had not actually escaped my notice that the mother who aborts herself kills the child, whereas a man who refuses to be a Good Samaritan – on the traditional understanding of Good Samaritan – merely does not save. My suggestion was that from a moral point of view these cases should be assimilated: The woman who allows the pregnancy to continue, at great cost to herself, is entitled to praise in the same amount, and, more important, of the same kind, as the man who sets forth, at great cost to himself, to give aid. That is why I proposed we attend to the case of you and the violinist.[41]

In other words, Thomson has gone on to claim that even if abortion *does* entail killing rather than allowing death, the violinist analogy should show us that the distinction is not meaningful here, since the two cases nevertheless amount to the same thing: a refusal to be a Good Samaritan.

Building on this further claim, David Boonin seeks to defend the GST by arguing that killing a fetus-person is morally permissible even if one accepts that killing is, all things equal, substantially morally worse than letting someone die. Boonin begins by presuming that extraction abortion at least, like abortion by hysterotomy, does not in fact kill the fetus, but only allows it to die. Next, he argues that if a hysterotomy abortion is morally permissible, because a pregnant woman is under no positive duty to rescue a fetus by continuing to gestate it, then killing the fetus is *also* permissible if abortion by killing is considerably less burdensome or dangerous

---

[41] Judith Jarvis Thomson, 'Rights and Deaths' (1973) [Wiley] 2 Philosophy and Public Affairs 146, 156.

for the pregnant woman than having it extracted.[42] In contending thus, Boonin relies on the principle that if one may permissibly let another person die in order to avoid some burden or harm, then one may instead kill that same person if the cost to you of letting die rather than killing is great enough. In order to show that killing the fetus is permissible, then, we need only establish that a pregnant woman *would* be permitted to allow the fetus to die by having an extraction abortion, and that an abortion which kills the fetus instead will spare her considerable extra burdens. The second condition might be made out if, for instance, partial-birth abortion or dilation and evacuation were a less risky procedure for the woman than a hysterotomy, or require less recovery time.

Boonin's significant conclusion is that even if killing is substantially morally worse than letting die, abortions which kill the fetus either prior to or in the process of removing it are morally permissible in circumstances where extraction abortion would be. Hence, it is of no consequence to Thomson's argument if unplugging the violinist is a mere failure to rescue whereas many abortions are not.

Boonin is proceeding here on the footing that extraction abortions *are* mere failures to rescue, which some will doubt, and that such refusals of aid are morally permissible given the onerous nature of pregnancy (and considering that a pregnant woman has no special responsibility for her fetus). But the crux of Boonin's argument might come to the defence of the GST even if extraction abortions too are regarded as acts of killing rather than as refusals to rescue. So long as the duty to *volunteer* gestation would still have been absent, killing so as to avoid additional burdens is acceptable.

An integral premise in Boonin's reasoning is that a 'victim' is not *harmed* by being killed if it would have been permissible for the killer or her agents to allow him to die. As he explains his argument at one point, 'if killing is worse than letting die because causing harm is worse than allowing harm, then the doctrine will simply fail to apply in cases where death is not a harm'.[43] Since one would have been permitted to allow the victim to die, then killing the victim does not amount to harm on Boonin's view, for it does not change the morally permitted outcome. Boonin thinks it reasonable to hold that one is permitted to spare oneself the relative burdens of letting die if it makes no difference to the outcome for the victim. This, he sees, is no contradiction of the doctrine that killing is more strictly prohibited than allowing death.

The tenor of Boonin's argument here bears similarities with the philosopher Frances Kamm's well-known argument that abortion is morally permissible because it renders the fetus 'no worse off' than it would have been apart from the pregnant woman's bodily assistance.[44] Kamm also argued that killing a fetus is not necessarily to *harm* it, since, in being killed, the fetus loses only what it had gained through the pregnant woman's bodily support—support that she was, moreover, not obligated to volunteer, due to the special burdensomeness of pregnancy. Consequently,

---

[42] Boonin (n 11) 208–11.   [43] ibid 205.

[44] Cf Frances Kamm, 'Abortion and the Value of Life: A Discussion of Life's Dominion' (1995) 95 Columbia Law Review 160–221.

aborting a fetus by any method does not harm it relative to its 'pre-attachment opportunities', which, Kamm argued, is the correct baseline for assessing what does and does not cause it harm. Kamm argued that in this respect the abortion mirrors the act of detaching Thomson's violinist. In being unplugged, the violinist is also losing only what he had gained through his host's support—continued life—a benefit which the host cannot be obligated to bestow on him at the cost of nine months' connection.

The main strand of Kamm's argument is what she dubs the 'Output–Cutoff Principle'. This states that killing is permissible when it eliminates a life sustained by the use of one's body—a use one is not morally required to offer—in order to end that use. The principle therefore comes into play when the person killed is 'no worse off' than he would have been had he never had the benefit of the host's support. In such a situation, the supporter is justified in cutting off the output of support, terminating the dependant's life. Because the fetus has no opportunities for life apart from attachment to the pregnant woman, and because (let us presume) the woman has no positive obligation to assist the fetus, killing the fetus rather than letting it die is permissible. It leaves the fetus 'no worse off' than it would be but for assistance to which it is not, in any case, entitled. Again, this is meant to hold even if the fetus is a person. In sum:

> The fetus cannot obtain the right to remain in the woman's body, and she cannot be obligated not to kill it, simply because ending its support would require that we take away the life it has only because it received support . . . if letting it die is permissible, then sometimes killing it is permissible as well.[45]

Kamm's argument is similar to Boonin's in that it seeks to move from the absence of an independent positive obligation to gestate a fetus-person to the conclusion that killing the fetus is morally permissible when a few extra conditions are met. Like Boonin, Kamm thinks that there is *some* difference between what is required to permissibly kill a person rather than to let him die. For her, it is that continued support must meet a higher threshold of burdensomeness before killing, as opposed to letting die, is permitted. You may be justified in attacking the violinist to preserve your physical integrity, but not to spare yourself financial sacrifice. Analogously, killing the fetus is permissible if it is the only way to end bodily support without serious cost to the woman. Kamm concedes that if it were possible to safely extract a viable fetus without much cost, a pregnant woman would not be justified in choosing to have it killed rather than extracted, a concession Boonin also makes at one point.[46] But if killing spares the woman additional trouble, the Output–Cutoff Principle renders it permissible.

Both Boonin and Kamm hence reach the conclusion that the killing–letting die distinction is no threat to the GST, even if killing is, in Boonin's words, 'substantially morally worse'. As I suggested above, the best version of the argument need not depend on our being convinced that extraction abortions merely fail to rescue the fetus. Even if all abortion is killing, the argument says, it is permissible if the

[45] ibid 193.   [46] Boonin (n 11) 255.

burdens entailed by *not killing* were such that the pregnant woman could not have been obligated to voluntarily assume them, and choosing to kill rather than to extract is better for the woman. 'No duty to gestate' and 'no duty to refrain from killing' in effect amount to the same thing. This is, it might be said, precisely what Thomson is trying to establish by showing how similar the cases of the violinist and pregnancy really are. But can Thomson's assimilation of the cases—including where abortion clearly amounts to killing—be sustained using Boonin and Kamm's reasoning?

2.7 Harming and Not Helping

Underlying Boonin and Kamm's arguments is the suggestion that the difference between what harms a person and what merely fails to help him can be more morally significant than the difference between what is, strictly speaking, killing or letting die. As they both argue in some way, I simply do not harm someone by killing him if I would not have been under a duty to rescue him (say, because the burdens for me of doing so are too great), and if killing him is the only way to resist helping, or to resist helping without incurring unreasonable burdens by the very act of resistance.

The basic proposition that the difference between harming and not helping can sometimes be the more important one in morality has much to recommend it. Phillipa Foot argued that in many instances, the moral meaning that is perceived in the difference between 'doing' and 'allowing' does not track the difference between acts and omissions, but rather that between not helping and harming.[47] In moral assessments, she claimed, it will not always matter whether a positive or negative kind of obligation is breached. As one example, Foot said, an actor who fails to turn up for a performance will spoil it rather than allow it to be spoiled, even though he does so by an omission. Equally, the parent who starves his child to death harms that child every bit as much as one who kills her through assault. On other occasions, the difference between positive and negative duties is of moral import. Foot's example is that although we allow many people to die in India and Africa by not giving more charitable aid, this is not of a piece with sending them poisoned food. Here, the act is clearly harmful, but it seems the omission is not.[48]

But what really makes the difference between the latter two cases? One is moved to say that the parent who neglects to feed his child does not just fail to rescue her, but that he positively kills her, just as the actor spoils the performance by his absence. Our confidence that harm has been done in these examples seems to lie in

---

[47] Foot (n 38).

[48] Peter Singer has challenged the moral lines some might draw between moral duties and supererogation by arguing that we are in fact duty-bound to give far more charitable aid than we do. While Singer does not expressly argue that we *harm* less fortunate people by failing to provide them with more aid, his argument might help make the case that people are harmed as a consequence of our wrongful omission to give more. (See Peter Singer, 'Famine, Affluence, and Morality' (1972) 1 Philosophy and Public Affairs 229.)

the agents' clear pre-existing obligations to do otherwise. Conversely, by not giving money to charity, I might be failing to save the lives of people in poorer countries, but I am not, on most views, harming any individual as the negligent parent is his child, either because I do not have an obligation to provide such aid, or, more plausibly, because I do not have an obligation to provide it to anyone in particular.

From this it seems Boonin and Kamm would be right to think that whether a withdrawal of aid harms or only fails to help can depend on the agent's existing positive obligations. But Boonin and Kamm wish to say something further: that the same can be true of aggressive acts. On this view, even if the only way to detach the violinist required a fatal attack on his body, your act will still only fail to save rather than harm him if you had no duty to begin with to lend him the use of your kidneys. By the same token, the non-existence of a woman's positive duty to sustain the fetus means that the fetus is not really harmed by being killed.

While we might accept that the prior existence of positive duties sometimes determines which side of the harming/not-helping distinction one's act or omission falls down on, there is, however, something odd about the way that distinction is being relied upon here to show that if unplugging the violinist is permissible, so is aborting a fetus by any method. To start with, it is a clear implication of the argument that if you could only detach yourself from the violinist by decapitating him, stabbing him, or scalding him to death, then you are permitted to do so, or to enlist others to do so. More than this, you are permitted to kill by any of these methods if they are appreciably less burdensome for you than unplugging him (we can imagine that unplugging him will cause you some amount of pain or discomfort which the other methods would not). I imagine that this will jar with what many people believe it is permissible to do to the violinist, especially where the option of unplugging remains, and that this is one reason to question the principle from which Thomson, Boonin, and Kamm are working.

In fact, the principle looks suspect even before it is applied to the violinist's case. Could it be possible that the absence of a positive obligation to rescue someone is the main consideration relevant to the question whether you may kill her in order to avoid the burdens that rescuing her would entail? Suppose that I am rock-climbing alongside a stranger up a cliff face, when the stranger loses her footing and slips. She grabs hold of me to keep herself from falling a long way down to inevitable death, making me slightly unsteady. Her attachment now imposes a danger on me, such that I would not have been morally required to reach out and grab hold of her, and I am also permitted to now refuse to be a Good Samaritan and let go. Suppose also, though, that rather than merely shake her loose, it is less dangerous for me to grab some loose rock and club her over the head with it, simultaneously killing her and detaching her. Or suppose instead that I had a marksman positioned at the top of the cliff, poised to shoot her dead should this very eventuality arise, and that again, it is safer for me to command the marksman to shoot than it is to throw her off me (say, because it will cause me less imbalance). Am I permitted to do either of these things because I was not obligated to endanger myself in order to help her in the first place, and because (as per Kamm) apart from my assistance, she would have slipped and fallen in any case?

Perhaps Boonin and Kamm would argue that this is exactly correct. But many would struggle, I think, to subsume those actions under the refusal to be a Good Samaritan, even in the relevant conditions. In fact, one might just think that this is precisely what is entailed by the proposition that killing is substantially morally worse than letting die, a proposition that Boonin is willing to grant for the sake of argument. If killing is ever subject to constraints to which letting die is not, then surely these constraints will bear out most clearly when all other things are equal but where killing is considerably more convenient than permissibly letting die. This seems to be something that Thomson, Boonin, and Kamm all flatly deny—that is, they deny that there could be any special constraints on killing *when it would have been permissible to let die*, which is in truth just to say that there are no special constraints on *killing*.

But this cannot possibly be right. If it is permissible for me to refuse to save the lives of people dying in poverty by not giving more aid (say, because by refusing, we think I am not in fact *harming* them), this cannot mean it is equally permissible for me to shoot them down to prevent them from taking that aid from me by force. Moreover, the application of Boonin and Kamm's principle does not seem to be affected by the weightiness of the burden which one is not positively obligated to assume. To explain, imagine that the violinist only needed to be plugged into you for one hour to survive (one of Thomson's amended scenarios). And suppose we still accept that you would have no duty to offer the use of your kidneys for that sole hour. Still, one hour is not nine months. But on the principle we are examining, you are just as entitled to kill in lieu of discontinuing support so as to avoid it—a much weaker burden though it is. Just how burdensome the positive aid *would* have been makes no difference. Again, all that matters, it seems, is that by unplugging him you are discontinuing support you had no obligation to provide, and that killing him is sufficiently less burdensome than unplugging. But this again does not seem correct. If the duty to avoid killing is indeed notably stricter than the duty to rescue, the weight of the burden one seeks to avoid by doing *either* (that is, the original burden one could not be obligated to assume) must surely affect whether one is permitted only to let die or to kill as well.

The fact that the principle being considered permits far too much should alert us to some problem. As I see it, the problem is that the argument amounts to the outright denial of the different moral character of killing and letting die. Neither Kamm nor Boonin seems to believe that killing could be prohibited where letting die would have been permissible but killing is less burdensome. But if there is any moral distinction between the two, this is precisely the scenario in which it should be expected to make the difference. If we wish to remain committed to the belief that the rules of permissible killing are different to the rules of permissibly letting die, then 'no duty to gestate' and 'no duty to refrain from killing' cannot amount to the same thing, including when the consequences are the same for the 'victim'. On the contrary: one's conclusion about whether, all things considered, including the weight of the burden to be avoided, there exists a negative duty to refrain from killing the fetus will determine whether there is a duty to continue gestating it if there is no way of ending support *other than* by killing.

For those who still find it too much of a strain to distinguish unplugging the violinist from abortion by extraction, there are two options for how to proceed. First, we can just put extraction abortion in the subsequent discussion and assume that it, at least, is straightforwardly permissible if there is no positive duty to gestate, either because it does not amount to killing the fetus or does not entail harming it. Alternatively, we can assume for the sake of argument that by unplugging the violinist you will in fact be killing him, just as extraction abortion kills the fetus, and turn our attention to justifications for homicide. If unplugging the violinist is an example of justified killing, is the same true of abortion if the fetus is a person?

2.8 Conclusion

This chapter has made one main claim. I argued that whether or not a positive duty to gestate a fetus-person could ever obtain, the problem of abortion, if fetal person-hood is presumed, is a problem not about positive duties to rescue others but about the negative duty to refrain from killing them. Given that this is the case, the GST fails. If abortion is the *prima facie* violation of a strict negative duty not to kill other people, its moral and legal permissibility depends on the applicability of a special dispensation to kill in order to end a pregnancy, rather than on the absence of a duty to volunteer gestational services. It is this former possibility I now want to consider.

3

Abortion as Justified Homicide

In the last chapter, I argued that if a fetus is a person, it is difficult to conceive of most, and possibly all, abortions as anything other than homicide. But killing another person is not always impermissible. In exceptional circumstances, both law and morality allow for it. These permissions have recognition in law in the form of defences to homicide. In particular, the law carves out defences to homicide in limited kinds of circumstances where it is deemed that taking life is, in all the circumstances, the right and justifiable thing to do. If abortion can be brought within a recognized category of justified homicide, then it can be shown to be morally and legally permissible even if the fetus is a person, and even if abortion is killing, not just the refusal to save. I introduced this proposition in chapter 1 as the Justified Homicide Thesis (JHT). I now wish to explore the JHT in greater depth. The question calls for an examination of the moral and legal constraints on permissible killing. Moreover, for those who think that unplugging the violinist in Thomson's thought-experiment is as much an act of killing as any abortion, distinguishing the two cases and answering Thomson's analogical argument will, for them, require showing that the rules about justified killing give different answers for both.

3.1 Self-Defence and the Conflict of Rights

The clearest example of justified homicide recognized in law and in morality is that of killing in self-defence.[1] It is surely permissible for me to kill someone if that is what is necessary to defend myself from her potentially fatal attack on me. Self-defence features to some extent in Thomson's reasoning when she remarks that 'if anything in the world is true, it is that you do not commit murder, you do not do what is impermissible, if you reach around your back to unplug yourself from that violinist to save your life'.[2] Likewise, Thomson is sure that a pregnant woman is permitted to kill a fetus-person to save herself from an otherwise fatal pregnancy.

But legitimate self-defence killing is subject to some very important conditions. The English law of self-defence sets down two main tests for justified

---

[1] See, in English law, the Criminal Law Act 1967, s 3, and the Criminal Justice and Immigration Act 2008, s 76.

[2] Judith Jarvis Thomson, 'A Defense of Abortion' (1971) Philosophy and Public Affairs 1, 52.

Arguments about Abortion: Personhood, Morality, and Law. First Edition. Kate Greasley. © K. Greasley 2017. Published 2017 by Oxford University Press.

self-defence: necessity and proportionality. Harming another person in self-defence must be necessary in order to avoid physical harm threatened by him, and the harm inflicted in self-defence must be reasonable, meaning *proportionate* to the harm threatened.[3] I am not justified in stabbing someone to death in self-defence merely to prevent him from slapping me or pulling my hair. Importantly, though, proportionate need not mean *equal*. As Jane English highlights in support of the self-defence analysis of abortion, it is not the case that you may inflict death only to avoid death, or inflict a black eye only to avoid a black eye.[4] Rather, as she puts it, '. . . our laws and customs seem to say that you can create an injury somewhat, but not enormously greater than the injury to be avoided'.[5] To fend off an attack as serious as rape, you may inflict something as serious as the loss of a finger, and to avoid having your clothes torn, as English says, you can blacken an eye. Other than this, the basic rule in English law is that the injury one inflicts must be the minimum necessary to deter or incapacitate the attacker, with a little leeway to account for calculations made in the heat of the moment.[6]

Despite a certain degree of latitude in the proportionality condition, it still seems that a pregnant woman who aborts will struggle to meet it in any scenario where her life is not put at risk by the pregnancy. Some might doubt that killing another person can ever be proportionate self-defence for any reason other than to avoid risk of death. At the very least, the injury to be avoided must be extremely serious. There is a question, then, over whether the risks associated with normal pregnancy are serious enough to qualify.

Furthermore, there might be particular problems meeting the necessity requirement in the case of late-term abortions. Before the fetus is viable, it is true that aborting and thus killing the fetus is the only way of avoiding whatever physical harms the pregnant woman would be risking through continued pregnancy. Post-viability, however, the necessity part of the test is in doubt if the pregnancy can instead be brought to an end by safely extracting the fetus alive. *Killing* the fetus is not strictly necessary in such circumstances, so an important limb of the self-defence test will not be met.

Responding to the proportionality issue, English acknowledges that the threat posed by the fetus-person would need to be sufficiently serious before defensive killing were justified. As she sees it, though, the threats to a woman's wellbeing, life prospects, and physical and mental health that can unexceptionally accompany pregnancy are comparably serious to other harms the avoidance of which, on her view, warrants killing in self-defence, such as losing a finger, or a serious beating.[7] Whether the normal physical burdens of pregnancy are truly comparable to these sorts of harms is certainly debatable. Pregnancy and childbirth can no doubt be

---

[3] *Gladstone Williams* [1987] 3 All ER 411; *Beckford* [1987] 3 All ER 425; *Whyte* [1987] 3 All ER 416; *Clegg* [1995] 2 All ER 334; *Owino* (1996) 2 Cr App R 128.

[4] Jane English, 'Abortion and the Concept of a Person' (1975) 5 Canadian Journal of Philosophy 233, 237.

[5] ibid 237.   [6] *Palmer* [1971] AC 814 (Privy Council) (Lord Morris).

[7] English (n 4) 237–8.

perilous, but in countries where standards of maternal care are good, few pregnancies involve serious threats to the pregnant woman's health or life.

This said, the physical burdens of pregnancy and childbirth that arise in perfectly typical pregnancies are by no means trivial. They include, among other things: nausea and vomiting, bloating and indigestion, fatigue, weight gain, itching, swelling, sleeplessness, difficulty moving (in the later stages), and, finally, the severe pain of labour, which not infrequently results in tissue damage, and the recuperation process. It is difficult to say whether these burdens are truly tantamount to losing a finger or to a 'serious' beating, as English supposes. They are, I think, less serious in the respect that they do not entail the permanent loss of any function or lasting, debilitating damage. This is a far cry from their being negligible. But the question, remember, is whether they are comparable to the sorts of threats which legitimate defensive killing, the most extreme self-defensive measure.

However, it may be thought that it is far more so the threats to wellbeing, future happiness, and life fulfilment presented by the prospect of unwanted motherhood (or that of surrendering one's child for adoption) that are the truly ominous threats posed by unwanted pregnancy. The problem is that these are not at all the kinds of burdens that people are ever thought justified in using force, let alone lethal force, in order to avoid. A competitor applicant to my dream job who is more likely to prevail might pose an extremely serious threat to my future happiness and wellbeing, but I am not entitled to kill her in self-defence. Nor can romantic rivals claim that killing their competitor is reasonable self-defence because of the perceived threat they pose to life fulfilment. The main burdens of unwanted pregnancy, serious though they are, are simply not of the sort that ever justify killing in self-defence. This is brought out even more sharply when considering the fact that born children can pose exactly the same kinds of threats to their parents. But a parent is not taken to act in legitimate self-defence if she kills her children to live a less encumbered and better life, or because the alternative of having her children adopted entails too much emotional distress.

So far, then, only an abortion carried out to prevent death or serious injury to the pregnant woman—what I will call 'therapeutic abortion'—is even a candidate for justified killing in self-defence, if the fetus is a person and if abortion is homicide. But there are further possible conditions on justified self-defence which raise problems even for therapeutic abortion. First, unlike aggressors in typical self-defence scenarios, the fetus is an innocent party that cannot help its physical imposition on the pregnant woman. English claims that this is immaterial, since it is clearly permissible to kill even an innocent attacker in proportionate self-defence. Suppose, she argues, that a mad scientist had hypnotized some innocent people to jump out of bushes and attack passers-by with knives.[8] Surely, if you are attacked, you have the right to kill your attacker to save yourself from death or serious injury, though his actions are not blameworthy. It is largely thought,

---

[8] ibid 238.

moreover, that English criminal law recognizes the right to defend oneself against an innocent attacker, with fatal force if necessary.[9]

But there may be something amiss with English's analogizing the fetus in the therapeutic abortion to the hypnotized knife attackers. For all their innocence, the attackers are still in the role of aggressors. They are assaulting passers by, and their attacks are patently unjust. But to describe unwanted pregnancy as an 'attack' by the fetus upon the pregnant woman, even a faultless or unwitting one, seems somewhat strained. As Joel Feinberg argued, the bezerk assailant may be innocent, but he is still an assailant.[10] The fetus, on the other hand, is not just innocent; it is not clearly an *aggressor*. He writes:

It did not start the trouble in any fashion. Thus, it would seem that while we are justified in killing an innocent assailant if this were the only way to prevent him from killing us, it does not follow that we are similarly justified in killing a fetal person, since, unlike the innocent aggressor, the fetus is not an aggressor at all.[11]

One possible reason for our difficulty with viewing the pregnancy situation as an attacker–victim scenario is that the fetus is not inflicting, or trying to inflict, any force on the pregnant woman, a paradigmatic feature of justified harming in self-defence. To be sure, its presence affects her body quite dramatically, but these effects arise only as a result of its situation, not its exercise of any agency, faultless or otherwise. Although pregnancy has serious physical effects, Feinberg's claim is that the fetus is simply too passive to be in the role of an innocent aggressor. It cannot do anything other than merely exist, so it surely cannot aggress.

Even if the fetus is not in the role of an attacker, some will still be inclined to accept Thomson's assertion that a pregnant woman does not have to wait passively while it unwittingly kills her. However, therapeutic abortions are rarely performed by the pregnant woman herself; they are performed by third party medical practitioners. The fetus's presence is not threatening *them*. How, then, can they avail themselves of the self-defence justification? This is another possible point of disanalogy with the violinist situation, where the question is whether you may unplug *yourself* from him, not whether someone else may do it for you.

English dismisses this problem by arguing that when a doctor performs an abortion she is acting as the agent of the pregnant woman. If the woman has the right to deadly self-defence, she can just as readily transfer this right to her agent if she cannot safely abort herself. In English law, certainly, actions justified by self-defence can extend to those carried out in the defence of others.[12] But this is an unsatisfactory answer to the third party problem if one is presuming that the right to life of the fetus and of the pregnant woman are equally strong, and that the fetus is not an aggressor. If the lives are pitted against each other, why should the third party not

 [9] See George Fletcher, 'Proportionality and the Psychotic Aggressor: A Vignette in the Comparative Criminal Law Theory' (1973) 8 Israel Law Review 376.
 [10] Joel Feinberg, 'Abortion', in Joel Feinberg, *Freedom and Fulfillment: Philosophical Essays* (Princeton University Press 1994) 62–3.
 [11] ibid.   [12] Thomson (n 2) 54.

choose the life of the fetus instead and act on *its* behalf? Brute hiring power cannot be the tiebreak. Moreover, if there is nothing to choose between them at all, and if, all other things being equal, it is better to allow death than to kill, surely the practitioner should sooner allow the woman to die, thus saving the fetus (where that is possible), than kill the fetus to save the woman.

Like English, Thomson thinks that this problem of choice is a false dilemma. For her, the deadlock between the two innocents is resolved quite quickly once we appreciate that the woman has a prior claim to her own body. As she says several times, 'the body that houses the child is *the mother's body*'.[13] Thomson thinks it plain that a 'third party who says [of the fetus and woman] "I cannot choose between you" is fooling himself if he thinks this is impartiality'.[14] She compares the scenario in which Smith and Jones are both fighting over a coat they need to keep themselves from freezing, even though the coat in fact belongs to Smith. It is not impartiality, she claims, to say: 'I cannot choose between you' *if Smith owns the coat*.[15] It makes all the difference for Thomson that the body belongs to the woman, not to the fetus. But how exactly is the woman's ownership of her own body supposed to establish that the fetus can be killed on her behalf?

The Smith and Jones example provides an interesting insight into Thomson's thinking here. Like Jones's possession of Smith's coat, the fetus's unwanted presence in the woman is, in her view, a bare violation of the woman's rights, whether or not it has yet cost her anything, equivalent to trespass on her property. Since the fetus has no *right* to be in her body in any case, it is legitimate for the third party to choose the woman over the fetus and help her evict it. Thomson's reliance on the pregnant woman's 'just, prior claim'[16] to her own body is a foundational premise which is subsequently used to underpin her further claims that not only can the pregnant woman and the third party choose her life over that of the fetus, but that she and her agents are also entitled to kill the fetus for a 'less weighty reason than preserving her own life'.[17] In fact, since *she owns the house* (her body), Thomson believes that the woman needs no special reason at all to eject the fetus, or to have it removed. To do so is straightforwardly within her rights, given that the fetus's presence there is an unjust invasion of her property.

The problem here is that Thomson seems to be relying on a prior ordering of the respective rights of woman and fetus when characterizing the fetus's unwanted presence in the womb as, to begin with, inherently unjust. Why is the fetus behaving unjustly simply by being where it is? Why is it trespassing? The answer to this cannot be 'because the woman in whose body it resides has the right to have it detached, even if this spells its death'—whether this is so is what is being debated. Thomson answers the question whether the fetus has the right not to be killed by pointing to the woman's prior title to her own body. But we might equally direct the inquiry the other way. We might ask whether the fetus, in all the circumstances, has the right not to be killed, and from that deduce whether the woman's title to her body *entails* the right to kill the fetus in order to be free of it. Just as, as Thomson asserts, a person's

---

[13] ibid. My emphasis.   [14] ibid 53.   [15] ibid.   [16] ibid 54.   [17] ibid.

right to life might not include or entail the right to be supported by another's body at all costs, it is not a foregone conclusion that the moral content of the right to one's own body includes the right to kill a fetus-person inhabiting it in any given circumstance. Whether the fetus (if a person) has the right not to be killed must surely take account of what it will cost the woman to let it live and what is proportionate.

John Finnis has argued that, in likening the fetus to a trespasser, Thomson implies something much stronger than that the woman 'is not under a strict duty to allow it to stay under all circumstances' (which would follow from the simple self-defence argument).[18] She relies, he says, on a different proposition: that the *fetus* is under a duty not to enter or stay in the woman's womb. This he takes to be implied by her claim that the fetus's mere presence in the womb is unjust, the same way that it is unjust for Jones to take Smith's coat. Finnis thinks this analysis comfortably fits the violinist scenario, even though the violinist is innocent. As he describes it, 'our whole view of the violinist's situation is coloured by this burglarious and persisting wrongfulness of his presence plugged into his victim.'[19] But he maintains that it cannot be reasonably said of the *fetus* that it was under a strict duty not to be where it is and is in breach of such a duty by remaining. It is indeed difficult to believe that the fetus is in breach of a duty simply by coming into existence and remaining alive in the womb. For how could it help coming into existence and where else could it conceivably be? In one clear sense, Finnis thinks that the fetus *does* have a right to be where it is. This is the sense that it is not under a strict duty *not* to be there. If this is correct, its very existence is not a bare violation of the woman's proprietary right to her body. Indeed, if the source of the woman's proprietary right in her own body is merely that she exists in it, Finnis asks why the fetus might not lay claim to the same proprietary right for exactly the same reason.

One challenge Finnis faces here if he wishes to preserve the possibility that it is justified for you or your agent to kill the violinist (if unplugging him does amount to killing him) is that the violinist is no more at fault in being in his situation of bodily dependency than the fetus is in being in the womb. The violinist was, after all, plugged into you whilst unconscious, and cannot help his rare ailment. Finnis acknowledges the violinist's faultlessness, but maintains in response that his duty not to be in his current situation—hooked up to your kidneys—is not a fault-based duty. Why, then, not so of the fetus? As we saw, Finnis relies at least partly here on our likely judgement that the violinist's dependency is of an essentially 'burglarious' nature, regardless of fault, whereas the fetus's presence in the womb is not. But what underpins that differing judgement?

Duties not to be a certain kind of imposition, even faultlessly, are sometimes intelligible. English's hypnotized knife attackers might be an example. Although the attackers are not in any way at fault, it makes sense to think of them as nevertheless being in breach of the negative duty not to threaten others. It could be argued that it is equally intelligible for the violinist to be under a strict duty not to impose himself

---

[18] John Finnis, 'The Rights and Wrongs of Abortion: A Reply to Judith Thomson' (1973) [Wiley] 2 Philosophy and Public Affairs 141.

[19] ibid.

on your body. It is at least conceivable that he could avoid being plugged into you, even though in reality he was not at fault. But it is far less easy to make sense of the claim that all human beings begin their existence in prima facie violation of a strict duty not to be where they are. Admittedly, part of what makes this analysis seem so strange is the sheer normalcy of pregnancy and its inextricability from human existence. Can it be possible that all human beings risk violating strict duties to be elsewhere at the very outset of their existence? Given that the only alternative entails their non-existence, this is a difficult proposition to accept.

Of course, one can instead take the position that there is no self-defence justification for killing the violinist unless he poses a threat to your very life, and that third parties may not assist with the unplugging even then, since they may not choose between two faultless antagonists. However, if we agree with Finnis that the very nature of the violinist's imposition on you is 'burglarious', albeit innocent, it follows that a third party can favour you over the violinist if your life were endangered, and perhaps also that you or that third party can unplug him to avoid less harm to you than that. If, on the contrary, the fetus's presence in the woman is not clearly in violation of any duty—is not an instance of trespass—then it remains far from obvious that a third party may, in his capacity as the woman's agent, abort the fetus *even* to save her life.

But if abortion is presumed to be homicide, a greater problem remains for the self-defence justification as regards non-therapeutic (and especially non life-saving) abortions. This is that rights violations do not neutralize proportionality constraints on permissible defensive action. Let us assume that the pregnant woman's 'prior claim' to her own body does mean that the title is hers exclusively, and that the fetus is in violation of that right by being where it is against her wishes. This is still not enough on its own to justify her killing the fetus-person regardless of proportionality, as Thomson seems to believes that it is. Mary Anne Warren put this point well:

Mere ownership does not give me the right to kill innocent people whom I find on my property, and indeed I am apt to be held responsible if such people injure themselves while on my property. It is equally unclear that I have any moral right to expel an innocent person from my property when I know that doing so will result in his death.[20]

Owning a property does not give me the moral right to eject a trespasser from it if this means throwing him out to his certain, immediate death, *unless* his presence places a proportionately serious risk upon me. I am not, for instance, morally entitled to throw an intruder out of the safety of my home to a pack of ravenous wolves outside, simply because the title to the home is mine and I am not in the mood for guests. Indeed, when we look closer at the self-defence justification, it is entirely clear that the initial violation of the defender's right cannot possibly preclude all proportionality constraints. If this were the case, proportionality constraints would never apply to self-defence at all, for the initial violation is a standing feature of the self-defence scenario. There always *is* an unjust threat to the justified

---

[20] Mary Anne Warren, 'On the Moral and Legal Status of Abortion' (1973) 57 The Monist 43–61.

defender, and still the law—and morality too—demands moderation. Given the usual proportionality requirements, it is questionable whether normal pregnancy would meet the conditions for self-defence killing, whether or not the third party problem could be surmounted.

3.2 Necessity and Morally Permissible Killing

3.2.1 'The lesser of two evils'

There is another justification for homicide that has been granted some, albeit heavily qualified, recognition in English law. This is the defence of necessity, also known as the 'the lesser of two evils' doctrine. Put roughly, the doctrine of necessity states that intentionally killing another person may be permissible in exceptional circumstances where it is the only way of avoiding even greater harm.

Necessity as a defence to murder has only ever once been granted by an English court, in the case of *Re A: Conjoined Twins*.[21] The case concerned a pair of conjoined baby twins, Jodie and Mary, whose bodies were fused at the lower abdomen. Mary was incapable of breathing independently and was only kept alive because of a shared artery, which enabled her sister Jodie to circulate blood to both of them. But Mary's weakened state meant that she could not survive for very long. Moreover, the strain she placed on Jodie's heart would soon result in the death of Jodie as well, meaning that without intervention both twins would die within what doctors estimated to be three to six months. Medical professionals wished to perform a separation operation that would result in the near-immediate death of Mary but would save Jodie and allow her to lead a relatively normal life. The Court took the view that by separating the twins, the doctors would indeed be killing Mary, not just omitting to save her, and that, moreover, Mary's death would clearly be intended by the doctors (even though not directly desired), a requisite condition for murder.[22] However, the Court also judged that the operation amounted to the 'lesser of two evils'. In the tragic circumstances, saving one twin was the least detrimental choice. Consequently, the Court ruled that the operation was permissible notwithstanding the fact that the doctors would be intentionally killing Mary, a separate individual person. The doctors would have a defence of 'necessity' to what would otherwise be an act of murder.

The reasoning relied upon in *Re A* pertained to such particular facts that it can be questioned whether a doctrine of necessity killing exists at all in English common law.[23] Be that as it may, the decision bears out the proposition that killing

---

[21] *Re A (Conjoined Twins: Surgical Separation)* [2000] 4 All ER 961.

[22] To be guilty of murder in English law, the defendant must have unlawfully killed another person with the intention either of killing him or causing 'grievous bodily harm' (*R v Cunningham* (1982) AC 566).

[23] The judges in the Court of Appeal were particularly concerned to emphasize just how unique were the facts of the case, and how hard it would be to extract a precedent from the ruling that could be applied to different cases. The fact that the reasoning of all three judges was slightly different also makes it difficult to formulate a more generally applicable necessity doctrine using *Re A*.

another person can be permissible in limited circumstances where doing so is the only way to avoid an even greater loss of life. This can also be formulated as a straightforward moral proposition about exceptional permissions for homicide. Still adopting the personhood proviso, then, perhaps abortion, too, could find a defence in the necessity doctrine, most obviously when it is carried out to save the life of the pregnant woman. In fact, when the English common law first recognized a possible defence to the crime of abortion in *R v Bourne*, the presiding judge, Macnaghten J, surmised that aborting a fetus in order to save the life of a pregnant woman might well be an occasion for a defence of necessity.[24] The *Bourne* decision, which, passed down in 1937, came well in advance of the widespread legalization of abortion by statute in 1967, held that doctors who performed an abortion on a woman would have a defence if it were carried out to prevent her from becoming a 'physical or mental wreck'. Speaking *obiter* in the *Re A* decision itself, ones of the judges, Brooke LJ, described both the *Bourne* decision and the Abortion Act 1967 (the legalizing statute) as examples of the necessity doctrine at work in the law of abortion.[25]

The crucial relevance of the necessity doctrine here is its potential to provide a defence to abortion even when it is assumed that the fetus is a person and that abortion is homicide. However, on the assumption that the fetus is a person, there are precious few abortion scenarios that could meet the basic conditions for necessity killing that are established in law, most notably in the *Re A* decision, and which would be acceptable in conventional morality. To see why this is so requires a closer look at the constraints on morally permissible killing and the features of *Re A* that proved integral to the necessity defence in that case. We can think of these constraints in terms of three broad categories: 1. proportionality constraints; 2. 'victim-centred' constraints on the victim's circumstances; and 3. 'agent-centred' constraints on the manner in which a killing can be performed. I will begin with the first two constraints, which are relatively uncontroversial and find clear articulation in the law.

3.2.2 Morally permissible killing and necessity in the law

The suggestion that one might be permitted to kill another person in exceptional circumstances where greater evil is avoided by killing than would otherwise occur is, first and foremost, a proposition about our extra-legal permissions, and one which the judges in *Re A* clearly found compelling. As is reflected in the conjoined twins case, the paradigmatic necessity scenario in moral theory is where the victim's death is unavoidable in all eventualities but where his being killed can secure the salvation of others. Phillipa Foot famously argued that in some such scenarios, choosing to kill the victim can be morally permissible.[26] Foot imagined the situation in

---

[24] *R v Bourne* [1938] 3 All ER 615, 617.   [25] *Re A* (n 21) 1043.
[26] Phillipa Foot, 'The Problem of Abortion and the Doctrine of Double Effect' (1967) 6 Oxford Review 5.

which, due to some complication, nothing can be done to save the life of a fetus, but in which killing the fetus will save the pregnant woman who would otherwise also perish. She compares that scenario to the imaginary situation in which a person of generous proportions is blocking the mouth of a cave that is gradually filling up with water, and in which others are trapped. If nothing is done, the man is bound to drown with the others. But if the others are somehow able to blow him up, and only if they do this, they can move him out of the way and escape. Foot endorses the view that such an action would be permissible *if he is certain to die soon anyway.* Killing the man is the only way to save as much life as possible in the circumstances, and it does not change the outcome for him.

As with self-defence killing, the first condition we find in the moral version of the necessity justification is a proportionality constraint. In fact, we might say that proportionality is the essential component of necessity. Necessity killing is only justified *because* it averts more harm than it causes; it is the 'lesser of two evils'. More specifically, and as is captured in the cave thought-experiment, killing a person out of necessity is only justified where it is the only means of preventing a greater number of deaths. All candidate scenarios for permissible necessity killing in moral philosophy share this feature. All of them present us with killings which, if carried out, will result in the greatest number of lives being saved. May I redirect a runaway trolley so that it kills one person instead of five? May Jim shoot one Indian to save nineteen others? The stipulation that killing the one will save the most amount of life is the most rudimentary condition of the necessity justification. That condition was iterated in *Re A* when Brooke LJ stated the three core requirements for the application of the necessity defence, which he deemed to be met in the case of the conjoined twins:

[T]hat the act was needed to avoid inevitable and irreparable evil; that no more should be done than was reasonably necessary for the purpose to be achieved and that the evil inflicted was not disproportionate to the evil avoided.[27]

Killing Mary was the only way to avoid the 'irreparable evil' that was the death of both twins. It was not disproportionate, since the overall effect would be to save the most amount of life—one twin instead of no twins.

So the maximization of life is essential to the necessity defence. But this does not mean that necessity is only a numbers game. That is to say, the necessity justification is not made out just whenever it is true that killing one person can save more than one. Foot illustrated this point with another example. If a healthy homeless man walks into a hospital, it is not morally permissible for the doctors at that hospital to kill him and harvest his organs for transplants to save the lives of five others. How is this example materially different from the man blocking the mouth of the cave? Well, for one, the man in the cave is doomed to die soon in any event, whether he is blown up or not. In *Re A*, it was critical for the judicial reasoning that Mary was, sadly, 'designated for an early death'. Because they were unable to save Mary in any scenario, the Court judged the doctors to be in need of an 'escape

---

[27] *Re A* (n 21) 1052.

route' to at least save Jodie. But Mary's poor prospects and the ability to save Jodie were not all that was required for the defence. When restating the 'unique circumstances' for which the decision could be an authority, Ward LJ enumerated the conditions that:

1. It must be impossible to preserve the life of X without bringing about the death of Y,

2. Y by his very continued existence, will inevitably bring about the death of X within a short period of time, and

3. X is capable of living an independent life but Y is incapable under any circumstances (including all forms of medical intervention) of viable independent existence.[28]

All three judges regarded it as essential for the permissibility of the operation that Mary could not be saved at all, as well as that killing Mary was the only way to save Jodie. However, Ward LJ's conditions seemed to extend even beyond this. For him, the only killings for which the decision might be an authority would be those where the victim was *by her very continued existence* threatening to bring about the death of the other. In other words, the victim must present or constitute the threat to the lives of others, as well as being beyond help herself. In *Re A* this condition appeared to be met. Mary's imposition on Jodie was the source of the threat to Jodie's life. As Ward LJ opined, if Jodie could speak, she could rightly protest 'Stop it Mary, you're killing me'. Mary was, he said, 'sucking the life-blood out of Jodie'.[29]

This feature of *Re A* resembles Foot's cave scenario, where the large man is the source of the threat to the other lives, albeit an innocent one. His presence *is* the deadly threat to the greater number; it is not just the case that his death is a means of saving them, as it would be if something else was causing the blockage, and he could be fired in a cannon through the wall of the cave to unblock it. In contrast, the homeless man in the hospital does not present the threat to the other lives; their illnesses do. His death might be a means of saving them, but their imperilment does not owe to his presence. As we noted, the homeless man is moreover not himself destined to die very soon, like the man in the cave, and like Mary. However, it seems clear that the doctors would not be permitted to butcher the homeless man to save five others even if he were certain to die of a terminal illness

---

[28] ibid 1018.

[29] ibid 1016–17. Ward LJ contemplated the possibility that Jodie might have a plea of 'quasi self-defence' against Mary, owing to the parasitic nature of Mary's living and the consequences for Jodie, although he thought it inappropriate to label her an 'unjust aggressor'. If this combination of factors were sufficient to justify killing Mary, then the justification might extend analogously to the simple therapeutic abortion case. However, even Ward LJ did not regard Mary's threat to Jodie as being enough, without more, to justify killing Mary. Like the other judges, it remained integral to his decision that Mary could not be saved (as he said, 'fairness and justice between the children' must take account of the fact that 'Mary is beyond help' (at 1010)). If Ward LJ would not have permitted the operation but for Mary's sealed fate, his quasi self-defence argument will not extend to the therapeutic abortion except where the fetus also is beyond help, at which point it might be argued the quasi-self-defence ground becomes indistinguishable from necessity.

in a few days' time.[30] If this is right, the condition that the victim must present the threat to one or more others seems to apply whatever is true about the victim's fate.

Foot acknowledged that one may *allow* a person to die in order to save many more under less strict conditions. Doctors can surely withhold a scarce life-saving drug from one patient when the same dosage will save a greater number of them. Foot argued only that the rules of morally permissible *killing* place further conditions on the situation of the victim than merely that his death will preserve more life. As she explained further, the asymmetry between the conditions in which it is permissible to withhold aid and to kill is often a function of the relative strictness of positive duties to give aid and negative duties not to injure, a distinction introduced in the previous chapter. On Foot's estimation, the driver of the runaway trolley may steer it into the one instead of the five for, being faced with a conflict of negative duties (not to kill either set of victims), the only rational action is to inflict the lesser injury. But conflicts between negative and positive duties play differently, she claimed. One may not murder someone even to bring food to one's starving children—the weightiest of positive duties. The doctors may not murder the healthy homeless man to fulfil their duty to save the five other patients. Where a positive duty is pitted against a negative one not to kill, the negative duty wins out.

In keeping with Foot's analysis of morally permissible killing, there was evidently far more to the Court of Appeal's decision in *Re A* than a simple calculation of how to preserve the most amount of life. These victim-centred considerations were brought into the foreground by the way in which the Court distinguished the historical case *R v Dudley & Stephens*. There, a necessity defence to murder was withheld from a pair of sailors who, set adrift at sea for twenty days without water or food, killed and cannibalized another member of their party, believing it necessary to preserve their own lives.[31] The judge in the case, Lord Coleridge, famously asserted that 'the temptation to act which existed here was not what the law has ever called necessity'. He reasoned that granting the defence in such circumstances would give rise to a principle which 'might be made the legal cloak for unbridled passion and atrocious crime'.[32] A pressing question in *Re A* was how *Dudley & Stephens* differed from the conjoined twins scenario. Brooke LJ regarded the earlier decision as authority for the law's 'disapproval of the idea that in order to save himself a man is entitled to deprive another of the place of safety he has already secured for himself.'[33] Put otherwise, it was the feature of *choosing* a victim—choosing whom to cannibalize for the sustenance of the others—a victim who, moreover, was not necessarily destined

---

[30] Of course, if the numbers are only large enough, some might hesitate to cling to the usual prohibitions. Would killing the healthy homeless man be morally impermissible if his biological material could be used to cure a deadly disease that would save millions? Can a judge execute an innocent man if it were the only way to prevent nuclear war? Such scenarios would cause most people to pause. However, we need not decide about this further question of whether the constraints on the victim's situation (specifically, her own endangerment) can be relaxed if the numbers saved are great enough. The number of lives saved by an abortion never exceed one, and even this will not amount to the avoidance of greater harm unless *more than one* (woman and fetus) would otherwise be lost.

[31] *R v Dudley & Stephens* [1881–5] All ER 61.   [32] ibid 67.   [33] *Re A* (n 21) 1034.

to die soon, which placed an act of intentional killing firmly out of reach of the necessity defence.[34]

In this respect, Mary's terminal condition distinguished *Re A* from *Dudley & Stephens*. Mary was, unfortunately, doomed to die soon in any eventuality.[35] This took the choice of whom to save out of the doctors' hands. Nature had individuated Mary as the only twin whose death could result in the most life, and Jodie was the only twin that could be saved. In stark contrast, the sailors in *Dudley & Stephens* chose from a number of candidates (themselves included) whom to sacrifice to save the rest. The law's conclusion that they were not entitled to do so made it abundantly clear that the 'lesser of two evils' defence will not countenance the destruction of a person who, apart from the choice to kill her, may well have survived. Given his distinguishing of *Dudley & Stephens* on this basis, it can be deduced that an action to avoid 'inevitable and irreparable evil' according to Brooke LJ's test would not have included the killing of one of the twins if there were any choice over whom to kill. This would have been so where killing Mary could save Jodie, but where killing *Jodie* might equally save *Mary*. In this situation, making a choice one way or the other meets the proportionality constraint of the necessity doctrine, since it is the only way to save the most amount of life (one twin rather than no twins). But it will not meet the victim-centred constraints on necessity killing.

From all of this, we can draw the following conclusions. A necessity defence to homicide would not have been afforded to the doctors in *Re A* if either: 1. Mary had not been beyond saving; 2. her attachment to Jodie had not been the source of Jodie's endangerment; and 3. if it were possible to save *either* twin through a procedure which killed the other, thus leaving nothing to choose between them. If any of these things were true, the doctrine of necessity as articulated in *Re A* could not have justified the operation.

Still working on the presumption that the fetus is a person, what do these conditions suggest about the scope for the application of the necessity defence if aborting a fetus is indeed to kill it? First, it is clear that only in the most extreme circumstances will an abortion situation come close to paralleling the genuinely taxing thought-experiments concerning the justification of killing in moral philosophy. The man in the cave scenario is not the parallel of the straightforward therapeutic abortion to save the life of the pregnant woman. For this, the fetus would have to be destined to die soon no matter what course of action was taken. In fact, only one abortion situation is even a candidate for justified killing through necessity: where the lives of both pregnant woman and fetus are endangered, and where killing the woman to save the fetus is futile, but aborting the fetus *can* save the woman. Here, as in *Re A*, there is no forbidden choice between lives, the 'victim' cannot be saved in any eventuality, the victim's presence constitutes the threat, and killing the victim

---

[34] Lord Coleridge in *Dudley & Stephens* also pointed to the criminal law's denial of duress as a defence for murder, set down in *R v Howe* [1987] 2 WLR 568, as exemplifying the general legal principle that one may not take the life of another to save oneself, or even others, where the killing amounts to a choice between lives (*Dudley & Stephens* (n 31) 66).

[35] *Re A* (n 21) 1051.

preserves the most amount of life. The same permission to kill the fetus would not extend to what Foot regarded as the 'worse dilemma' where the fetus is *not* destined to die in every alternative, but where the woman can still only be saved by killing it. That is not like the man in the cave or like Mary and Jodie. As Foot explained, 'on a strict parallel with cases not involving the unborn' it appears that intentionally killing the fetus-person would not be permissible here. She explained further:

Suppose, for instance, that in later life the presence of a child was certain to bring death to the mother. We would surely not think ourselves justified in ridding her of it by a process that involved its death.[36]

If fetus and woman are presumed to be of equal moral worth, it seems that only the scenario in which the fetus cannot be saved but aborting the fetus will save the pregnant woman meets both the proportionality and the victim-centred conditions on morally permissible killing. This conclusion might sound fairly radical. It means that therapeutic abortion to save the life of a pregnant woman is not even a hard case on the assumption that abortion is homicide; it is a case where abortion is clearly impermissible unless the fetus is incapable of sustained life in any event. Thus Foot suggested that those people who accept the justifiability of therapeutic abortion 'probably equate the life of the mother against the unborn fetus as the many against the one'.[37] They may be correct to do so, but this would mean surrendering the personhood proviso and the putative strength of Thomson's position.

I have already adumbrated the 'victim-centred' constraint on necessity killing that one cannot *choose* one's victim. Thus in *Dudley & Stephens* the sailors were not permitted to choose someone to cannibalize, even to save the greatest amount of life, whereas the doctors in *Re A were* permitted to kill Mary because nature had already marked her out for death. I argued that as regards therapeutic abortion, given the personhood proviso, the upshot is that abortion is not permissible where killing the fetus could save the woman, but where killing the woman or allowing her death could equally save the fetus. However, it is worth noting that Foot took the contrary view here. That is, Foot believed it permissible to choose between the life of the fetus and the pregnant woman where either one can be saved by killing the other, but where otherwise both will be lost. She argued that in choosing to kill either, one can be acting reasonably, so long as uncertainty does not obscure the absolute necessity of acting in such a way.

Consequently, Foot concluded that in principle, it may have been reasonable for the sailors in *Dudley & Stephens* to kill and eat the cabin boy, since it is better to save some than none, *even if this requires choosing a victim* (although she acknowledged that we might respect someone who would prefer to perish than commit such an 'appalling action'). She equally thought that if the certainty were absolute, as it can be in the abortion case, it is better to choose to kill one than save none. Given the choice, she predicted that most people would kill the fetus and thereby save the pregnant woman. However, this can only be because they struggle to accept the personhood proviso. Taking the personhood proviso seriously, the most

---

[36] Foot (n 26) 15.   [37] ibid.

that comes out of Foot's argument at this point is that it is equally permissible to kill the fetus to save the woman *or* to kill the woman so as to save the fetus. This does not make for a robust defence of therapeutic abortion.

The conjoined twins case also helps to clarify the implications of the pure bodily imposition of a fetus upon a woman, assuming that both are persons. Had Jodie's life not been in danger, it would be unthinkable for the Court to have ordered the separation, knowing that Mary would die, on the ground that Jodie simply had the right to have her detached so as to end the bodily imposition. Mary's physical dependency on Jodie could not have been justification enough were both capable of living a normal life span in their conjoined state. This is so despite the fact that the nature of their physical union was far more thoroughgoing, and, if they had survived a normal life span, far more burdensome for Jodie, the supportive twin, than nine months of normal pregnancy. Extrapolating from this to the abortion scenario, it appears that the fetus's physical dependency on the pregnant woman could not suffice for a necessity defence to abortion.

This may raise new questions about Thomson's violinist. Although his imposition does not threaten to kill you, here the common intuition is that you are permitted to have him detached merely to end the bodily imposition. Why (assuming still that unplugging the violinist is killing him and not just refusing to give life-sustaining aid) is the amended Mary and Jodie case, where the burdens for Jodie are far greater and indefinite, any different? Defending this difference would, I presume, require one to argue that unlike the unconscious violinist, the conjoined twins predicament does not clearly entail the unjust imposition of one person upon another. Although Mary's parasitic living is a burden on Jodie, it may be difficult to describe her as being under a duty not to be where she was. One question this raises is whether the imposition of the fetus upon the pregnant woman better resembles the conjoined twins scenario or the violinist scenario in terms of the inherent unjustness of the weaker party's imposition on the stronger one. However, our certainty that Jodie does not have the bare right to have Mary detached, at the cost of Mary's life, puts immense pressure on Thomson's claim that a pregnant woman has such a right in respect of a fetus-person.

All in all, the proportionality and victim-centred constraints on necessity killing bring us to the inescapable conclusion that, on the presumption that a fetus is a person and that abortion is killing, a simple therapeutic abortion to save the life of the pregnant woman fails to meet the conditions for the defence, let alone abortion for any less urgent reason, such as temporary physical discomfort, derailment of life plans, or emotional turmoil. The only abortion scenario that meets the *Re A* conditions is where killing the fetus is the only way of avoiding the deaths of both parties, and where there is no choice about whom to save. It is an implication of this that were the fetus to be granted personhood under English law, both the *Bourne* decision and the Abortion Act 1967, which widely legalized abortion, would be flatly inconsistent with the common law doctrine of necessity and murder.[38]

[38] One of the *Re A* judges, Walker LJ, came close to acknowledging as much when he opined that exploring the defensibility of abortion was of limited use as an analogy for how to respond to conflicting medical duties between actual persons, since fetuses are not regarded as such until delivery (*Re A* (n 21) 1066).

3.2.3 Intention and the doctrine of double-effect

So far, we have found that the proportionality and victim-centred conditions on so-called necessity killing already drastically limit the scenarios in which abortion is permissible if it amounts to homicide. In fact, as I have said, the relevant conditions are only ever met where killing the fetus can save the life of the pregnant woman but where the fetus itself cannot be saved by any action.

According to some, however, there are yet further constraints on morally justified killing. One of these putative constraints stems from a distinction, often made in moral philosophy, between killings that are directly intended and those which are indirectly intended. To kill a person with direct intention is to kill her either as a means to an end or as an end in itself. To kill with indirect intention is to bring about someone's death as a known side-effect of some other desired result which could be logically, although maybe not practically, achieved without causing the death. For example, a burglar who shoots and kills an apprehender in order to silence him and eliminate any witnesses kills with direct intention, since the death of the victim is something he is aiming to achieve by shooting. We can contrast this with Glanville Williams's famous insurance bomber, who places an expensive package on a plane along with a bomb, intending to blow up the plane and collect the insurance on the package. The bomber knows that all of the plane passengers will be killed when the bomb explodes, but he does not aim directly at their deaths, since those deaths are not integral to his fulfilling his purpose. The same distinction is sometimes described as the difference between killing with the intention to kill or with the mere knowledge or foresight that one's actions will cause death (or what some, differently again, distinguish as 'direct' versus 'oblique' intent).

Some would argue that there is an absolute prohibition on the directly intentional killing of an innocent person. If this were true, then, on the personhood proviso, most forms of abortion would appear to be prohibited *even* where the first two conditions on necessity killing—the proportionality constraints and the victim-centred constraints—are met. Moreover, those who read an important moral difference into the difference between direct and indirect intentional killing may attempt to distinguish the violinist case from abortion on this ground, if it were assumed that the other conditions for necessity killing are equally met in both. Is it possible to claim that when unplugging the violinist one only indirectly intends his death, but that all or some abortion directly intends the death of the fetus? If this were true, it may be another route to claiming that abortion is impermissible whereas unplugging the violinist is not.

In the previous chapter, we already encountered some important distinctions between kinds of conduct: that between killing and letting die, and between doing and allowing harm. The distinction between killing directly and indirectly is different from both of these. Indirect intentional killing is not the same as failing to save. As Thomson acknowledges, 'an indirect killing is perforce a killing', whereas a man who has never killed may still have failed to save many lives.[39] Thus, the proportionality

---

[39] Judith Jarvis Thomson, 'Rights and Deaths' (1973) [Wiley] 2 Philosophy and Public Affairs 146, 157.

and victim-centred conditions for the necessity defence to killing apply regardless of whether the killing in question is directly or indirectly intended. One clearly does not have carte blanche to kill whomever so long as one does it with indirect intention.

The difference between directly and indirectly intended killing will only ever be relevant, then, where the other conditions for morally permissible killing are already made out. Where this is so, the key claim is that there are residual side-constraints on the manner in which one or more persons may kill another: whereas killing with indirect intent is sometimes permissible where the gain in terms of life preserved is great enough, directly intended killing is absolutely prohibited and does not ever admit a results-based justification. As we shall see, the implication of this claim for those propounding it is that the causal structure of an abortion might determine whether or not it falls under the absolute prohibition. On John Finnis's view, an abortion by hysterectomy (the removal of an entire womb and the fetus with it) could conceivably be permissible even if the fetus is a person, but an abortion that crushes the fetus's skull in order to extract it never could be. Underlying the suggested importance of this distinction is the more general proposition that there are some sorts of acts it is never permissible to perform even despite a great pay-off in terms of life saved, net welfare, or some other calculable good. These are what philosophers call 'deontological constraints'.

As Finnis points out, Thomson seems to acknowledge in principle the existence of such constraints when she recognizes that there are 'drastic limits' to the right to self-defence, such as that one probably may not torture another person even to protect oneself from deadly harm.[40] However, she is not convinced that any side-constraints render abortion impermissible merely because fetal death is more directly intended than the death of the violinist in her scenario.

To reiterate, it is not the case that one has permission to kill whomever so long as death is not specifically aimed at but is rather the known side-effect of some ulterior purpose. For the most part, English law does not distinguish the two, and for good reason. The insurance bomber example is a good illustration of why intention to kill in criminal law encompasses both the direct and indirect kinds. Even though the deaths of all of the passengers are, strictly speaking, side-effects without which the bomber's purpose would still have been accomplished, it would be absurd if this could make a difference to his liability for murder, which requires an intention to kill or cause grievous bodily harm. The general rule in English law, set down by the House of Lords in *R v Woollin*, is that what is foreseen as a *virtually certain* consequence of one's act will almost always be regarded as intended.[41]

There is an exception to the assimilation of direct and indirect intent in the English law of murder, however. This is the 'doctrine of double-effect' (DDE). The typical example of DDE at work in the law concerns the administration of high doses of pain-relieving medication by physicians to patients near the end of life, with the purpose of providing comfort, but in the certain knowledge that they will hasten death. In this circumstance, the law does not impute the intention to kill to the physician. Even

---

[40] Thomson (n 2) 53.   [41] *R v Woollin* [1999] AC 82.

though death was foreseen as inevitable, harm to the patient is taken to be so at odds with the overarching aim or purpose of the act—bringing the patient relief—that it is altogether struck out as the meaningful intention. Here, at least, the law accepts that the difference between what is foreseen as virtually certain and what is aimed at can matter for the morality of homicide.

With all of this in mind, we can pose two questions about intention-based side-constraints. First, is there an important moral difference between directly and indirectly intended killings, such as would render abortions which *aim* at the fetus's death absolutely prohibited? Second, if a moral difference of the kind exists, could the DDE be used to show that most abortion is in fact a species of indirectly rather than directly intended killing, even if it involves a fatal attack on the body of the fetus?

3.2.4 The manner of killing

Whether the specific manner of a killing can make a moral difference when all other things are equal is where Finnis and Foot part ways. As Finnis has argued, directly intended killing is prohibited in every scenario, even if it is the only means of preserving the most amount of life. The most obvious example of directly intending fetal death in abortion is, of course, where fetal death is desired in itself as the purpose (or one of the purposes) of the abortion. But what if this were not so? It may be argued that in many abortions, it is not fetal death but an end to the pregnancy which is being aimed at; the death of the fetus is merely the inevitable side-effect of terminating the pregnancy, like the insurance bomber example.

Importantly, Finnis argued that the distinctive feature of directly intended killing has much to do with the causal structure of the act. By his lights, killing the fetus is directly intended if it is used as a means of securing the end of the pregnancy and if *that* wider purpose cannot be achieved without it. The example he uses is where a craniotomy is performed on a fetus during a partial-birth abortion as a means of extracting it from the woman, killing the fetus by crushing its skull. The same analysis would appear to apply to most methods of abortion, including abortion by vacuum aspiration or dilation and curettage, where the fetus is killed in the process of being extracted. In such abortions, the death of the fetus is inextricably linked to the extraction procedure—killing the fetus is an unavoidable *part* of the extraction. As Finnis sees it, such abortions are 'inescapably' characterized as 'anti-life', and thus subject to the absolute prohibition on killing.[42] Whether or not one wills it as an independent aim, he argues, to *choose* fetal death as a means to an end is a 'choice against life' of the kind that cannot have a results-based justification. Given the personhood proviso, Finnis concludes that:

The traditional condemnation of therapeutic abortion is the straightforward application of the intention/foresight distinction to the case where mother and child are equally persons, and neither is to be directly attacked.[43]

[42] John Finnis, 'The Rights and Wrongs of Abortion: A Reply to Judith Thomson' (1973) [Wiley] 2 Philosophy and Public Affairs 129.

[43] ibid 132.

For Finnis, the absolute prohibition on direct killing simply applies both ways. One cannot fatally attack the woman to save the fetus, and one cannot fatally attack the fetus to save the woman, whether or not the other conditions for the necessity defence are made out. But not all abortions are directly intended killings on Finnis's definition. This includes the abortion by hysterectomy, where, for instance, a pregnant woman's cancerous womb is removed in order to save her life, in the knowledge that the non-viable fetus within it will die. The traditional condemnation does not apply here, he explains, since the DDE exception extends theoretically to an abortion where there is logical room to characterize the overriding intention as that of preserving life rather than destroying it. This is true of removing the malignant womb because it involves no attack on the fetus's body, does not depend for its success on the death of the fetus, and would have been carried out all the same if the fetus were not present. In Finnis's view, these features mean that removing the womb better resembles unplugging the violinist, where death is foreseen as inevitable but not aimed at directly.

Finnis thus posits a crucial difference between the therapeutic removal of a cancerous womb containing the fetus, and the therapeutic abortion by craniotomy. In contrast to the removal of a malignant womb, the craniotomy abortion cannot but be construed as directly intending fetal death as a means to an end, even if it is not an end in itself (say, because fetal death per se is not wished for, but only an unavoidable consequence of saving the woman). This, it seems, is because the fatal attack on the fetus's body cannot logically share space with the hope that it will live.

A killing that DDE precludes from being directly intended is still subject to proportionality requirements, and Finnis expressly reminds us of this. Thus, even abortion by hysterectomy is justifiable for nothing less than saving the life of the pregnant woman. But Finnis is convinced that the craniotomy is absolutely prohibited regardless of proportionality. Just as you cannot kill the violinist by having someone chop him into pieces, even to save your own life, so a pregnant woman cannot have her fetus aborted in a manner that aims at its death as a means or an end.

Foot disputed Finnis's claim that the causal structure of a directly intended killing will absolutely bar its permissibility. 'If you are permitted to bring about the death of the child', she asked, 'what does it matter how it is done'?[44] As far as Foot was concerned, the people in the cave will act permissibly if they kill the large man by blowing him up (a direct attack), since he will perish in either case, and only by doing so can they be saved. The difference between direct and indirect intention is not morally relevant, she argued, when killing directly does not cause any more harm to the victim than he will in any event sustain, and is in the interests of saving more life. As she said of the cave scenario:

It is a great objection to those who argue that the direct intention of the death of an innocent person is never justifiable that the edict will apply even in this case.[45]

---

[44] Foot (n 26) 6.   [45] ibid 14.

Foot applied the same reasoning to the death of the fetus in therapeutic abortion where the fetus cannot be saved. If nothing can be done to save the life of the fetus, the doctrine Finnis espouses will fly in the face of what she said most reasonable people would think. Foot was aligned with Finnis in thinking that extracting the fetus by craniotomy to save the woman is impermissible if the fetus is a person and is *not* beyond saving anyway; one cannot kill one innocent person to save just one other if the victim would not otherwise die, since the balance of life is equal on both sides, but killing one person is worse than letting another person die. Where Finnis and Foot differ is in Foot's denial that where an abortion by hysterectomy is permissible (on her view, when neither woman nor fetus would otherwise live), an abortion by craniotomy is not. This denial has an important place in Thomson's defence of abortion, made more explicit in her own reply to Finnis's criticism. Thomson argues that for Finnis to be correct, it needs to be shown that the difference between the two kinds of killing is pertinent when everything else is equal. But along with Foot, she cannot bring herself to believe that this is true. The idea that 'abortifacients taken by a teaspoon' could sometimes be 'morally safe' but that a craniotomy for the same reasons is just 'far too messy' to be permissible strikes her as absurd.[46]

It is clear that on Finnis's view, even the circumstances in which 'abortifacients taken by a teaspoon' could be morally safe would be extremely circumscribed. The medicine would have to be, first and foremost, necessary for curing the woman of a life-threatening ailment, and only destructive to the fetus as a side-effect. It would also have to be the case that she would have taken the medicine even if not for the fetus's presence in the womb. Thomson's criticism here should therefore be read as one which rejects the importance of these kinds of features. When abortion meets the conditions for proportionate killing, and the respective prospects of woman and fetus also meet the general conditions for morally permissible killing, the fact that a killing directly aims at a fetus's death, and that the act which kills wouldn't be chosen but for its presence, is not prohibitive in effect.

Finnis's response to this scepticism about the moral difference the manner of a killing can make when all other things are equal directs the inquiry back to the existence of deontological constraints per se. As he reasons, to deny that the directness of a killing has moral import is in a way to eschew deontological constraints on killing altogether, and this is something he believes Foot and Thomson would be loath to do. Clearly, Foot did not believe that the maximization of life is justification enough for any kind of a killing. She did not believe the doctors may cut up the healthy patient to use his organs to save five others, or that a judge may execute an innocent man in order to avoid a bloody riot. But she did think it permissible to blow up the large man to save others trapped in the cave so long as he is certain to die soon anyway. Finnis asks whether this is not 'an unwarranted though plausible concession to consequentialism'.[47] The only reason Foot thought it acceptable to kill the man in the cave through direct attack is because it would maximize life

---

[46] Thomson (n 2) 151.   [47] Finnis (n 42) 134.

saved, without changing the outcome for him. But if this is sufficient justification for directly killing the large man, it would also seem to justify cutting up the patient if he is fated to die imminently of a terminal illness. Finnis has pointed out that Foot's principle might also justify an agent (D) killing an innocent person (V) when ordered to do so under threat from P, in circumstances when P would otherwise kill V along with D. The fact that neither Foot nor Thomson would countenance 'moral horrors' like these, including 'saving life by killing innocent hostages, etc', is, for Finnis, testament to their belief that it *does* matter whether one's choice aims at death as a means or an end, or just accepts it as an unavoidable side-effect of saving the greatest amount of life.

It is not my ambition here to make the case for the existence of deontological constraints on killing or injuring. No doubt there are many who would object to the notion that there are any actions the nature of which renders them absolutely prohibited regardless of what gains can be made by performing them. But Finnis's wider point is that moral philosophers who deny the moral difference between direct and indirect intentional killing in the therapeutic abortion of a fetus-person do, nevertheless, accept the operation of side-constraints in other scenarios where the consequentialist position is in fact far more seducing. (We might take, for example, the permissibility of using torture to extract information from a terrorist when we are certain he knows where a bomb is planted.) Finnis's starting point— that some actions are too set against the value of human life to be performed—is one that Foot and Thomson do seem to share. However, while they regard factors such as the victim's own imperilment (for Foot) or her imposition on others (for Thomson) as relevant to that characterization, they do not accept the same thing about the causal structure of killing. As Thomson has it, when all else is equal, the distinction between directly and indirectly intended killing is simply too technical to be of consequence. Is she right to believe this?

3.2.5 Double-effect and comparing intentions

There are two main ways one might seek to argue that Finnis's further constraint on killing does not lead to the impermissibility of practically all abortion if the fetus is a person. One is to show that many or most abortions involve only the indirect intention of fetal death. The other is to try to collapse the moral distinction Finnis draws between directly and indirectly intended killing in abortion.

With regard to the first strategy, the violinist scenario can be brought into play again. Finnis sees it as a relevant point of disanalogy between unplugging the violinist and almost all abortion that whereas the violinist's death is only indirectly intended, abortion aims directly at fetal death. When you unplug yourself from the violinist, you foresee that his death is inevitable, but you do not will it or aim at it as part of your enterprise. If he happened to survive, your purpose would not have been frustrated. In contrast, abortion often does seem to aim at fetal death either as an end in itself or as a necessary means of detaching the fetus from the woman, not merely a by-product of doing so.

It is important to note at this point that the violinist scenario will mirror most abortions in failing to meet the strict proportionality requirements for necessity killing. Only if both violinist and host are doomed to die imminently in any event, and only if unplugging the violinist can save the host but nothing can be done to save the violinist, will Thomson's scenario be a candidate for a 'lesser of two evils' justification for homicide. So let us amend the violinist case to assume that these conditions are met. The scenario therefore reflects the therapeutic abortion where nothing can be done to save the fetus. We can reframe Finnis's argument as stating that when the proportionality condition is equally met in both cases, the difference between directly and indirectly intentional killing would still show us that unplugging the violinist is permissible whereas therapeutic abortion is not.

One apparent objection to this is that in therapeutic *extraction* abortions at least, the fetus's death is no more directly chosen than is the violinist's death in Thomson's analogy. In neither case is the victim attacked directly, we may say, but rather just separated from a source of life-support. In both cases, therefore, the death of the victim might be understood as a foreseen consequence but not an aim of that separation. Should either the fetus or the violinist live, the aim, which is to discontinue bodily support, would still be achieved. Finally, in neither case is the death of the victim even an interim aim of the separation process: neither fetus nor violinist needs to be killed *in order to be* detached. Thomson consequently argues that that death is no more intended in an extraction abortion than when unplugging the violinist.

With regard to most abortions, however, whichever method is used, the death of the fetus *is* specifically intended by the pregnant woman and her doctors. Indeed, I think it fairly transparent that the main intention most women have in procuring abortions is not to end their pregnancy by extracting the fetus, but to avoid motherhood or the emotional turmoil of adoption by ending the life of the fetus through the abortion. This is a serious problem for the claim that the death of the fetus is no more directly intended in extraction abortion than in the violinist's unplugging.

David Boonin responds to this objection by claiming that if an abortion is otherwise justified, say, to spare the woman the physical burdens of pregnancy, that justification will not be invalidated merely because those performing it also happen to desire the fetus's death.[48] Suppose, he imagines, that you wanted to unplug the violinist and win back your freedom, thus killing him intentionally, and are permitted to do so. However, suppose that the violinist also happened to be your chief rival in a symphony, and that you independently wished him dead. Boonin argues that so long as one acts on a 'permissible' intention (to unplug oneself), an additional, 'impermissible' intention (to kill the violinist) will not render the conduct impermissible. Just so with abortion and fetal death.

If Boonin's answer is sound, it will still, at this point, only act as a defence of abortion by extraction where the other necessity conditions obtain: where the abortion is carried out to save the woman and fetal death is proportionate (it will save

---

[48] David Boonin, *A Defense of Abortion* (Cambridge University Press 2003) 216–20.

more life than if nothing is done). Consequently, it can be argued that equating the violinist's unplugging with extraction abortion in terms of the directness of the intention to kill does not provide a defence for *killing* the fetus where it could be safely extracted alive in the alternative. Were the fetus capable of being extracted without being killed, there would be no way to claim, by analogy with the violinist, that it is equally permissible to abort in a way that ensures its death. This suggests that the necessity doctrine can therefore only offer a defence to the therapeutic *extraction* of the fetus.

Thomson is in fact willing to grant that a pregnant woman has no right to demand fetal death in abortion as an end in itself where a viable fetus can be safely extracted alive.[49] However, she nevertheless disputes Finnis's central claim that abortions which directly aim at fetal death as a means or an end are prohibited in every eventuality. In effect, she denies that a hysterectomy or a craniotomy for the same reason really can be distinguished solely in terms of the directness of the intention to kill. Along similar lines, Boonin contends that directly intended killing is plainly permissible in the same circumstances where it is permissible to kill as a side-effect *if* choosing the direct form of killing involves less risk of harm to the agent or the beneficiary. If the craniotomy is safer for the woman than the abortifacient medicine, and the outcome is the same for the fetus, surely it is unreasonable to prohibit *that procedure* specifically. Boonin's argument is, in short, that killing directly rather than indirectly (through extraction) does not manifest greater disrespect for the value of the fetus's life if it avoids a more 'dangerous and invasive' procedure for the woman. He explains:

[I]t is extremely difficult to see how causing a person to die by one means, rather than causing him to die by another, in cases where it is permissible to cause death by the first means and the cause of death makes no difference to him, is using him as a means, or failing to respect him as an end.[50]

Boonin's denial of the moral difference between killing directly and indirectly where it makes no difference to the victim might cut against our moral reactions to amended violinist scenarios. If unplugging the violinist could only safely be performed by first ensuring that he is dead, could we be so confident that a third party is justified in killing the violinist in order to detach him from you? Would the Court of Appeal in *Re A* have consented to separating Mary from Jodie if this could only be achieved by first poisoning, stabbing, or suffocating her? I think it doubtful that the Court would have consented to such a thing even if it were the *only* means of detaching Mary, let alone only a safer means for Jodie.

But the deeper problem with Boonin's argument here bears some similarity to the pitfalls of his argument (considered in the previous chapter) that the difference between killing and letting die is of no moral consequence where there is justification enough for letting die, but where killing is safer for the agent. Boonin expressly grants that there *is* a substantial moral distinction between indirectly and

---

[49] Thomson (n 2) 66.   [50] Boonin (n 48) 223.

directly intended killings.[51] He only seeks to show that the distinction does not affect the permissibility of killing directly where indirect killing would be permissible, but directly intended killing has some distinct advantage for the agent or beneficiary. Yet again, however, one might answer Boonin by pointing out that if there is such a moral distinction, as he grants, it will only ever make a difference when everything else is equal but when killing directly has some added advantage. If the moral distinction does not affect one's permissions in *these* cases—when all else is equal but killing directly is better for the agent—then it surely does not exist at all. It simply follows from there being a moral distinction between directly and indirectly intended killing that the difference must matter when it is the only difference there is.

Rather than denying that the indirect–direct distinction matters for morally permissible killing when all other things are equal, a defender of Thomson might instead draw on the DDE to question whether therapeutic abortion by direct attack on the fetus really intends fetal death any more or less directly than extraction abortion by hysterectomy. Finnis claims that when a malignant womb is removed to save the life of a pregnant woman, DDE can be deployed to show that the overriding intention of the operation is that of saving life, not killing, notwithstanding the fact that the fetus's death is inevitable. But for his conclusions to be correct, we must be confident that the same cannot be said of therapeutic abortion by craniotomy. Can a doctor who performs an abortion by craniotomy not say, in the end, that the fetus's death was, here too, neither a means nor an end for her—not an end because it was not directly desired, and not a means because the fetus's death is not logically necessary for ending the pregnancy, the true aim, but only practically inevitable? If the fetus *happened* to survive its skull being crushed, the purpose of the abortion, to end the pregnancy, could still be achieved. We can also ask whether the fetus's death in this scenario is really any more *aimed at* than the violinist's death in Thomson's case.

An important part of Finnis's direct intention test looks to whether there is logical room to hope that a victim of killing will live by asking if 'the same action would have been chosen if the victim had not been present'.[52] This is true of removing the cancerous womb, but not of the therapeutic craniotomy, or of any extraction abortion other than the hysterectomy. Where a hysterotomy (removal of a pre-viable fetus by caesarean section) or a medical abortion (inducement of miscarriage using drugs) is concerned, it cannot be said that the same action would have been chosen completely apart from the fetus's presence, even if the reason for the abortion is that the pregnancy poses a risk to the pregnant woman's life. But as Thomson points out, this condition does not hold for the violinist either: his presence is a *sine qua non* of your decision to unplug. Thus the following question is raised. If the death of the 'victim' is logically severable from the agents' intentions in the violinist scenario, why is the same not true of *all* life-saving therapeutic abortions by extraction, which do not directly attack the body of the fetus, and

---

[51] ibid 213.   [52] Finnis (n 42) 137.

whose purpose is not to kill the fetus but only to end the bodily imposition of the fetus upon the woman?

Interestingly, Finnis's condition that the fatal action would be performed even without the presence of the victim does not hold true for the conjoined twins' separation either. That operation would not have been performed if it were not for Mary's existence and situation. In *Re A*, the Court of Appeal in fact considered whether the DDE could be invoked to reach the conclusion that the doctors who performed the operation would not truly intend Mary's death (and would not be guilty of murder for that reason). Two out of the three judges, Ward LJ and Brooke LJ, thought that it could not be.[53] Although the operation would save Jodie, it would not benefit Mary in any way, and it was their view that DDE could not apply where the 'overriding' benevolent intention concerned one person and the foresight of death another. The judges were surely right in making this determination about DDE. *Re A* could be contrasted with the typical DDE case of the death-hastening pain relief, where both effects, good and bad, are experienced by the same person. Surely, the doctrine could not similarly be relied upon to displace the intention to kill if, for instance, the patient could be relieved of his pain only by an action which also speeds up the death of *another* patient in the bed next to him.

Working from the Court of Appeal's analysis of DDE, it might seem that Finnis is in error to think that the doctrine even applies to the removal of the malignant womb. Just like the conjoined twins' separation, the hysterectomy in this case does not aim at the victim's death as a means or an end. But similarly also, the 'good' intention (saving life) is not directed at the victim, the fetus, which, I suggested, it must be. If this second condition on DDE is correct, then it will not be possible to distinguish the intention in a life-saving therapeutic hysterectomy from that of every other kind of extraction abortion by using DDE.

In spite of the Court of Appeal's refusal in *Re A* to apply DDE to the twins case, however, the causal structure of Mary's death still seemed to matter a great deal. The majority of judges believed that the doctors performing the separation would indeed intend Mary's death. But there was greater ambivalence about whether the separation procedure would constitute a direct *attack* on Mary. They agreed that, by separating the two, the doctors would be committing an assault on the weaker twin. However, both Brooke LJ and Walker LJ proposed that the separation would also confer on Mary a certain kind of bodily integrity that she had been denied through being joined to her sister, restoring her, in a way, to some natural state that she ought to have been in—a state of individual embodiment.[54] Furthermore, while the operation certainly interfered with Mary's body, it might be argued that it did not attack her in any way certain to bring about death if not for her unusual situation of dependence. Notwithstanding their rejection of DDE, the judges seemed influenced by this idea not only that Mary's death was not the aim of the operation, nor an intermediate aim of the procedure, but more than this, that it would not

---

[53] *Re A* (n 21) 1012; 1030–1.   [54] ibid 1052; 1066–7.

be the result of a kind of attack on her bodily integrity that would have killed her completely apart from her strange state of dependence.

Like the violinist's death and the therapeutic hysterectomy, it can be argued that the causal structure of Mary's death was consistent with it being only indirectly intended, even though the separation procedure would not have taken place but for her existence (a part of Finnis's indirect intention test). Doubtless, the Court would not have authorized the procedure if it had required a truly direct attack on Mary's body either prior to or as part of the separation—the sort of interference that no normal baby could survive.

But the therapeutic craniotomy abortion is different from unplugging the violinist, from the therapeutic hysterectomy, and from the conjoined twins' separation in some meaningful respects. Like the latter three scenarios, it might be argued that its true purpose is to preserve the life of another, the fetus's death being only a regrettable yet unavoidable consequence. But where the fetus is directly attacked, its death is not merely a consequence of a procedure with a different aim; it is logically inseparable from the nature of the act performed. A big part of why it seems that to aim to crush another person's skull is to aim directly at his death, no matter what ulterior purposes lie behind the act, is that there is no counter-factual in which that act might not amount to a choice to end his life. More like Dudley and Stephen's act of cannibalism, and less like *Re A*, one could argue there is no logical room to wish that the fetus could survive, but only to wish something incoherent: that crushing skulls did not cause death, or that people did not have to be killed to be eaten.

I think Finnis was correct to say, in his response to Thomson, that these counterfactual thoughts 'remove morally relevant intention too far from common sense intention'.[55] By the same analysis, even the sadist who kills for pure satisfaction could argue that she does not directly intend her victims' deaths since she would be just as satisfied if they came back to life without her knowledge. We cannot say that a killing is not truly 'aimed at' only because one can imagine different laws of biology according to which death is not an inevitable consequence of, say, a point blank shooting, a stab to the heart, or holding someone underwater for ten minutes.

It is true that, at points, the distinction can seem extremely fine-grained. Is the death of a fetus in a therapeutic, life-saving vacuum aspiration abortion truly more aimed at than in the life-saving hysterectomy? Again though, Finnis might retort that this is simply the upshot of it *ever* mattering how a killing is performed, and with what kind of intention, and that if Thomson and Foot wish to dispute his conclusion on the ground that the difference is negligible in terms of outcome, this may call into question their broader acceptance that there are some acts which cannot be given results-based justification.

Still, Foot's 'man in the cave' scenario may give us reason to hesitate before concluding that directly intentional killing is never permissible. Can the trapped people really not blow up the large man to save many lives? One might think that what one is permitted to do when there are many more lives at stake is a different question

---

[55] Finnis (n 42) 136.

from what one may do to save only one. Foot's own condemnation of the simple therapeutic abortion (where the fetus *can* live if the woman were left to die), given the personhood proviso, was simply that one may not choose to *inflict* death on one rather than *allowing* another to die, since the amount of life preserved is equal in both scenarios, and killing is worse than not saving. But Foot still believed that one may inflict death directly in order to maximize life saved in the cave scenario, and in the therapeutic craniotomy where the fetus cannot possibly be saved. This is the only point on which she and Finnis differ. Even, then, if one were to side with Foot and reject the absolute constraint on directly intended killing, the circumstances for permissible abortion if the fetus is a person are still reduced to one: where the fetus cannot be saved at all, but aborting the fetus *can* save the woman.

There is one remaining problem for Finnis, however, if one believes both that unplugging the violinist kills him only indirectly, and that in the scenario where he is hooked up to your kidneys, you are permitted to unplug. This is that abortion by extraction to spare a woman the burdens of pregnancy seems to be no more direct a killing than unplugging the violinist. In a hysterotomy or a medical abortion using drugs, the fetus is not directly attacked. Unlike the removal of the malignant womb, these abortions do not meet Finnis's condition that the action would be chosen even without the victim's presence, but neither does unplugging the violinist. This is a serious problem for Finnis if he wishes to maintain that my amended violinist case (where both parties will die if nothing is done) and the therapeutic extraction abortion, say, by inducing miscarriage, can be distinguished in terms of the directness of the intention to kill. As Thomson argues, if unplugging the violinist is only an indirect killing, then a woman's taking medication to bring on miscarriage is surely as indirect. Consequently, it could be argued that all extraction abortion should amount to indirectly intended killing if this holds for unplugging the violinist.

This difficulty may well indicate that analysing the act of unplugging the violinist as the failure to save rather than as an indirect killing is more integral to Finnis's position than might first appear. Ultimately, Finnis still maintains that unplugging the violinist is only, in any event, the denial of life-sustaining aid, whereas almost all abortion, including by extraction methods, positively kills the fetus.[56] This ground of distinction was the subject of the last chapter and the core issue for the Good Samaritan Thesis (GST). If Finnis is right that, in the final analysis, unplugging the violinist is still only a failure to save, whereas ejecting the pre-viable fetus is killing it, he may be able to maintain that unplugging the violinist is permissible to avoid the sorts of burdens that would not justify extracting the fetus. However, when the comparison is between extraction abortion and unplugging, he cannot rely on the causal structure of death to argue that the former is killing and the latter failing to save. The causal structure is the same in both, and neither entails a more directly intended death than the other. Finnis would have to find some other reason, therefore, for claiming that only the abortion is an act of killing, if he wishes to defend

---

[56] ibid 139–40.

the general impermissibility of extraction abortion while granting that you or others may unplug the violinist.

3.3 Conclusion

The last two chapters have covered a lot of ground, and it may be useful to take stock. In the previous chapter, I argued that all abortion, including by extraction methods, is better understood as an act which kills the fetus rather than fails to save it. In the course of this chapter, I considered a couple of routes to the proposition that if the fetus is a person and if abortion is killing, then most abortions are instances of justified homicide. I argued that with very limited exceptions, the attempt to subsume abortion under one or more categories of justified homicide cannot be reconciled with the moral and legal constraints on killing that are otherwise generally accepted. If normal abortion is an instance of justified homicide, then it is an entirely anomalous one that explodes the conventional boundaries of permissible killing. Consequently, accounts of the abortion problem that treat it as an example of justified homicide fail to dislodge the centrality of prenatal personhood for the moral and legal status of abortion. If all of this is correct, then neither the GST nor the JHT can be relied upon to show that the moral status of the fetus—that is, whether or not the fetus ought to be regarded as a person—is extraneous to the moral and legal permissibility of abortion.

4

Analogical Arguments and Sex Equality

4.1 The Use of Analogies in Abortion Argument

The last two chapters gravitated around Judith Thomson's well-known violinist analogy argument about abortion. In the course of considering the Good Samaritan Thesis and the Justified Homicide Thesis, we considered various points of disanalogy between pregnancy and the violinist scenario, and asked whether those disanalogies were morally relevant to our appraisal of the two cases. But some people might feel deeply unsatisfied with the extensive use of the violinist analogy in moral reasoning about abortion. For that matter, they may feel that *all* such analogies— conjoined twins, hypnotized knife attackers, cannibals at sea—fail to serve as any kind of useful guide to the moral and legal constraints on abortion that apply if we assume the fetus is a person. On the contrary, perhaps reasoning using cases such as these, which are so different from pregnancy in so many ways, is only likely to impede clear moral thinking on abortion.

The philosopher Margaret Little has argued that being pregnant involves a very unique kind of physical intertwinement that is not easily reflected by analogies of any kind.[1] This is the fact that, for the pregnant woman, being pregnant is to be literally *occupied* by another life form:

To be pregnant is to be *inhabited*. It is to be *occupied*. It is to be in a state of physical intimacy of a particularly thoroughgoing nature.[2]

In this respect, even the conjoined twins example clearly differs. Although their intertwinement is certainly of a 'thoroughgoing' nature, it does not (and did not in the *Re A* case) involve the complete occupation of one person by another. If the fetus is a person, this kind of intertwinement is unique to pregnancy. Little argues more broadly that the nature of the union between woman and fetus cannot be properly analogized at all. For her, the unique physical intimacy that pregnancy entails 'means that the fetus, the gestating woman, and their relationship do not fit ready-made categories'.[3] In attempting to fit them into such categories, she warns that we will often appeal to analogies which are 'at best awkward, at worst dangerous, but always distorting'.[4] Attempting to understand pregnancy by considering

---

[1] Margaret Olivia Little, 'Abortion, Intimacy and the Duty to Gestate' (1999) 2 Ethical Theory and Moral Practice 295.
[2] ibid 301.   [3] ibid 296.   [4] ibid.

Arguments about Abortion: Personhood, Morality, and Law. First Edition. Kate Greasley. © K. Greasley 2017. Published 2017 by Oxford University Press.

situations which lack the same degree of physical enmeshment will always miss something important. Little draws on the feminist theorist Catharine MacKinnon's well-known remarks that 'nowhere in law is a fetus a fetus', with a concept of its own. Rather, it must always be defined by some existing classification, whether a person or a body part.[5] But why, MacKinnon asks, should we do things this way round? Why not treat the fetus and the pregnancy relationship as paradigmatic categories and analogize other things to *them*?

Little thinks we should expect that a tradition which has always imagined persons as physically separate will not fare well in analysing situations where 'persons *aren't* as it imagines them'. Hence it is not surprising if we find ourselves scratching our heads about what follows if a great number of persons actually exist inside of others.[6] But her main problem with traditional analyses of abortion is that they do not 'take as pivotal the fact that gestation occurs inside of someone's body'. Once one focuses on pregnancy's unique form of physical intimacy, Little thinks it will become apparent that the moral permissibility of abortion does not depend on prenatal personhood. This owes to the fact that the kind of occupation entailed by gestation requires a special form of consent. Consequently, for Little, mandating continued gestation when that consent is missing is to inflict unjustified harm on a pregnant woman, much like an assault.

In effect, Little doubts that anything at all can be learned about the nature of pregnancy and abortion through analogies about violinists, conjoined twins, or, indeed, anything else. Her argument might be understood as the 'weirdness objection', introduced in chapter 2, in a more developed form. The weirdness objection, we saw, claims that exotic thought-experiments cannot tell us much about abortion because they are weird, whereas pregnancy is not. Little's argument is that we should resist the temptation to analogize pregnancy to *anything* else, weird or not, since doing so is likely to direct us away from the unique and morally pertinent features of pregnancy—specifically, the bodily occupation of the pregnant woman by the fetus.

This scepticism about the usefulness of analogies might, in turn, speak to an even more general scepticism about the value of thought-experiments in ethics. Such hypotheticals typically require us to filter out any number of complicating realities in an effort to, in Stephen Mulhall's words, 'clear the scene of any other potentially polluting concerns'.[7] To demonstrate this sort of disagreement about thought-experiments in ethics, Mulhall describes a widely cited study conducted by the psychologist Carol Gilligan:

[The conductor of the study] presented groups of students with a problem case: would it be morally permissible for an impoverished person to steal medicine from a chemist in order to save the life of her sick child? The men argued with one another about the immorality of

---

[5] Catharine A MacKinnon, 'Reflections on Sex Equality under Law' (1991) 100 Yale Law Journal 1281, 1314.

[6] Little (n 1) 297.

[7] Stephen Mulhall, 'Fearful Thoughts' (2002) London Review of Books http://jeffersonmcmahan. com/wp-content/uploads/2012/11/London-Review-of-Books.pdf (last accessed 28 March 2014).

theft and the sanctity of human life; the women inquired: 'Why doesn't she ask the chemist to give her the medicine she needs?' Some will take it that the women had simply misunderstood the point of the problem case, and of problem cases in general; for to include such a dialogue between chemist and parent is to change the case, and thus to avoid responding to the particular issue of principle it was intended to abstract from the complexity of reality. Others will take it that the men had been distracted by matters of principle from attending properly to the concrete reality of moral experience and the possibilities of human fellowship.[8]

When confronted with Thomson's violinist analogy, the women in Gilligan's experiment might well have pointed out that people never do, as a matter of course, find themselves in the situation of having their bodies connected up with that of an unconscious violinist, or anyone else. Can it possibly not matter that Thomson's scenario is not a regular part of human life, or that if this really were to happen to you, you would be the first and only known person to be subjected to that bizarre imposition? Perhaps the relative normalcy of pregnancy cannot be dismissed as a morally irrelevant feature of the pregnancy situation. Rather, perhaps the fact that pregnancy is so embedded in everyday human life colours the entire meaning of pregnancy, and abortion, for those who experience it. There are, for instance, no websites and stores exclusively dedicated to selling merchandise to people currently supporting violinists, no 'violinist leave' standardly worked into employment contracts to cater for the very realistic eventuality that the Music Society might kidnap you for nine months at any time, and no general understanding of and allowance for the implications of hosting the violinist and the setbacks it entails. The reality of pregnancy is, of course, drastically different. It is everywhere, affects everyone, is not generally regarded as an unfortunate occurrence, and is often celebrated even when unintended. (By way of contrast, were anyone at all to celebrate the fact of their having been kidnapped and plugged into the violinist, we could only conclude that she was of unsound mind). It is, moreover, *the* way that human beings reproduce. All of these features, along with the intimacy of fetal occupation, affect the real life implications of pregnancy in ways that cannot be replicated in the violinist scenario.

In the course of her discussion, Thomson offers up some further analogies which better capture the normalcy of pregnancy, including the scenario in which 'people-seeds' routinely drift around in the air and might drift through windows and take root in homeowners' carpets. The people-seeds might then begin to grow into 'person-plants' for whom the proprietors become responsible for keeping alive.[9] In this scenario, Thomson thinks it obvious that you are not responsible for maintaining the life of the person-plant if that means continuing to suffer its imposition within your house, merely because you knew that people-seeds are generally drifting around and failed to batten down the hatches or stop any air from getting in.

---

[8] ibid 2–3.
[9] Judith Jarvis Thomson, 'A Defense of Abortion' (1971) 1 Philosophy and Public Affairs 59.

The person-seed analogy appears to replicate the normalcy of pregnancy in the respect that the burdensome imposition is not extraordinary or wacky as the violinist situation is—not in the world we are imagining, anyway. However, Thomson's alternative analogy fails to import any *further* likely consequences of our living in a world in which new humans standardly come to exist in this way, and the effect that these additional features might have on our appraisal of the moral problem with which we are presented. The normalcy of pregnancy in the world in which we live embeds it in a whole number of social realities which inform its wider meaning and burdensomeness, as well as the burdensomeness of avoiding it. These realities include the fact that pregnancy is the consequence of sexual intercourse, not the drifting of seeds to which we are totally unconnected; the fact that it is often celebrated, that it is the cause of our own coming into being, and so on. Thomson does not try to account, in her analogy, for the different ways our living might be structured if people-seeds were drifting around everywhere, or if they were the main source of human reproduction. How, for instance, might the social significance of leaving one's windows open change if this were the case? Would someone not have developed a high-tech security system for keeping one's windows shut, except when people-seeds are desirable, or innovative strategies for filtering them out, or alternatives for ventilating the home? These are the kinds of background circumstances that the women in Gilligan's experiment might well want to know about, not because they miss the point of the inquiry, but because they understand the relevance of this surrounding context to the questions Thomson and her challengers are asking, which include considerations about the burdensomeness of avoiding pregnancy.

In his rebuttal of the weirdness objection, Boonin maintains that the mere strangeness of the violinist scenario cannot matter unless it constitutes a morally relevant difference. He writes:

If the differences do not themselves prove to be morally relevant, then the mere strangeness of the example in and of itself will provide no further reason for rejecting the argument's soundness.[10]

I agree with Boonin that strangeness per se is not a reason to reject a thought-experiment in the course of abortion argument. But as the people-seeds analogy may demonstrate, it can be difficult to isolate the strangeness of an analogy from a host of features that *are* morally salient. As Mulhall argues, the moral significance that an issue has for us often owes to 'the complex web of interrelated matters' within which we actually encounter it. Rather than helping us to gain clarity about the rights and wrongs of the problem, extracting it from its actual context may just, in effect, 'change the subject'.[11]

In the violinist's case then, the concern may stand that putting its weirdness entirely out of our minds might only cause us to miss truly important differences

---

[10] David Boonin, *A Defense of Abortion* (Cambridge University Press 2003) 141.
[11] Mulhall (n 7) 3.

between Thomson's analogy and pregnancy that emerge from their different surrounding contexts. Indeed, we may miss the fact that the violinist scenario is really *nothing like* pregnancy except in the single sense that it too involves bodily intertwinement with another human being for nine months.

Does this mean Little is right to claim that philosophers are in error whenever they argue about abortion by reference to broader categories or analogies? This will present great difficulty if we are asking ourselves what follows about abortion if the fetus is a person, for, other than by appealing to the rules about refusing aid or permissible killing which we accept outside of the abortion context, how can we reason about that matter at all? Pregnancy is of course unique. But so are many problems the moral implications of which we may want to assess, including Mary and Jodie's predicament and that of Dudley and Stephens's. Pregnancy is not unique in being unique. And like any other kind of life and death problem, discussants will find themselves in an argumentative vacuum if they cannot search outside of the pregnancy situation for more general principles that can help shed light on it. Those principles must be extrapolated from other contexts if they are to provide moral insight based on more general commitments, rather than generating an ad hoc conclusion about abortion.

This does not mean that the specific features of the pregnancy situation are irrelevant to moral and legal reasoning about abortion. There is always scope to differentiate pregnancy from a comparator case, and thus to refine the principle one is considering or show that it does not apply to abortion. But pregnancy's uniqueness per se cannot be offered up as a point of distinction unless one explains in what respect it is unique and why this matters for our moral evaluations.

Still, perhaps the most outlandish thought-experiments lack usefulness for a very particular reason: that they cannot produce reliable intuitions from which to make further deductions. Take the following thought-experiment presented by Nicole Hassoun and Uriah Kriegel as part of an argument about the relevance of *potential* personhood for moral rights:

Suppose that many years from now, a space elevator is installed between Earth and Mars, and that an oyster finds its way to the elevator. At this point, the normal course of events should lead to that oyster's becoming conscious *in the absence of intervention*. The oyster on the elevator is thus potentially conscious in the sense in which fetuses and neonates are—it is, so to speak, *en route* to consciousness. Yet it still seems intuitively permissible to kill the oyster.[12]

The point these authors are trying to make is that if we think it permissible to kill the oyster, it seems we do not believe that being on an uninterrupted path towards full consciousness endows a creature with the fundamental right to life. If this is correct, then embryos and fetuses will not possess the right to life merely in virtue of being on that same path. But it may be objected that the oyster scenario is *so* other-worldly that it is difficult to draw any firm conclusions about it. How would

---

[12] Nicole Hassoun and Uriah Kriegel, 'Consciousness and the Moral Permissibility of Infanticide' (2008) 25 Journal of Applied Philosophy 45, 51 (emphasis in original).

we feel about killing oysters if there were space elevators to Mars onto which oysters tended to climb, at the end of which they were transformed into conscious beings? Perhaps such a scenario is so far removed from the possibilities around which our moral sensibilities are constructed that there is really no second guessing how we might assess it as a reality. If this is indeed the case, we may not be able to deduce anything useful about the grounds for attributing moral status to fetuses from our unreliable intuitions about the oyster scenario. Moreover, to help us know whether a creature's being on a path to consciousness is sufficient for a fundamental right to life in circumstances analogous to pregnancy, we would have to construct the example so that, somehow, the implications of *not* permitting 'oystercide' were roughly comparable to the burdens of unwanted pregnancy and childbirth, including their particular effect on one already disadvantaged class of persons. Whatever imaginative twist to the thought-experiment could account for this calls for more creativity than I can muster. It might also be objected that, for true comparability, we should imagine a different reality whereby all clear cases of persons of which we are aware, including ourselves, start out as oysters, even though countless oysters never attain consciousness. How might this affect our judgements about oystercide? It is admittedly difficult to say. Like Thomson's people-seeds analogy, it seems that much more of the surrounding context of pregnancy would have to be imported into the thought-experiment to reflect all of the morally relevant aspects. Once the relevant modificaions are made, however, we may well find ourselves hesitating to draw any firm conclusions at all.

The violinist and conjoined twins analogies are, in these respects, somewhat different. In the violinist scenario, the supposition is, I take it, that what takes place *is* extremely out of the ordinary. There is thus no need to perform the imaginative feat of deciding how everything else might be if this sort of occurrence happened all the time, and how that might affect our reactions, once every other morally relevant feature of pregnancy is built in. This difference might itself be considered an important point of disanalogy, as has been noted. The 'weirdness objection' may be apt insofar as our conclusions about abortion do not flow directly from our conclusions about unplugging the violinist when the latter case is so alien whereas the former is not. Quite apart from suggesting that the analogy is too weird to yield reliable reactions, the problem here is that the conclusion we *do* form about the violinist might not clearly carry over to abortion when all the morally relevant implications of the extraordinariness of the violinist case, as compared with the familiarity of pregnancy, are factored in. But this does not mean the analogy is unhelpful. On the contrary: distilling the meaningful differences between the violinist situation and pregnancy is precisely what may help us to isolate some morally relevant features of pregnancy and abortion.

The conjoined twins analogy is not quite the same in terms of sheer outlandishness. It is certainly extraordinary in one sense, that is, in its rarity. This is not the same extraordinariness that we encounter in the oyster case, because the conjoined twins case is real and, hence, perfectly possible. It is therefore a moral problem that can arise without anything else about the world around us having to dramatically change. Consequently, we need not hold our moral reactions to the problem quite as loosely as in the truly extraordinary oyster scenario. And if this is so, our moral evaluation of the conjoined twins problem can tell us something about the broader principles we accept regarding the killing of one person who is bodily dependent upon another. Again, some people will point out disanalogies arising between the conjoined twins case and pregnancy, even on the assumption that a fetus is a person. But attending to these disanalogies and whether they make a moral difference will again be an integral part of our reasoning about abortion.

Returning to Little's argument, it may be suggested that she *is* in fact really pointing to a morally relevant difference between pregnancy and everything we might be tempted to analogize it to when she underscores the outright occupation of the pregnant woman by the fetus. As Little says, it is *inside* her, not just attached to her. This is one aspect of pregnancy's uniqueness that clearly differentiates it from the violinist case and from the conjoined twins. Is it a difference that matters for the analysis of abortion as a category of justified homicide? Little claims that the special level of intimacy entailed by unwanted bodily occupation makes mandated gestation intolerable, whatever moral status one assigns the fetus.[13] But it is interesting that she also regards the personhood category as particularly unsuited for conceptualizing the fetus because of the difficulty we will have imagining persons that are not 'physically separate'. Little does not deny that such persons *could* exist. She only suggests that our conventional ideas about what persons are like will make it extremely hard to imagine them thus.

This observation could have more than one implication. Little, it seems, intends it to speak to the treacherousness of all analogies, extraordinary or not, which try to discern what would follow about abortion if the fetus were a person. It would be difficult, on her view, to see clearly on this question when the 'person' we are thinking of is so different from persons as we ordinarily think of them. Little takes it to endorse her wider point that when arguing about abortion, people should steer clear of subsuming the fetus under any of the traditional categories, such as 'person' or 'non-person'. But the fact that discussants struggle to keep to the brief when trying to imagine what moral consideration is owed to persons entirely enclosed within others can equally reveal something about how they think of persons. Why do these thought-experiments stretch the imagination to breaking point? Why is it that discussants can only begin to formulate thoughts about what is owed to persons *like that* by analogizing them to partially separate persons, physically attached to others but still visible in the world and in direct contact with it, like the violinist or the conjoined twin? Rather than suggesting that all analogical argument in this topic is unhelpful or distorting, the struggle to account for the fetus's complete enclosure whilst maintaining the personhood proviso could reveal something significant about our concept of a person.

---

[13] Little (n 1). Little goes on to define exactly what kind of attitude towards the fetus ought to, on her view, accompany pregnancy, this being a simple openness to developing a relationship with the fetus which, if entered into, would ground some responsibility to sustain it.

The question also remains as to how moral and legal reasoning about abortion is to proceed *other than* by looking outside of the abortion context, since there is no other ostensible way to draw conclusions that are grounded on, and consistent with, the more general commitments that we have. Someone may press the objection that the violinist or conjoined twins scenario reflects some of the features of pregnancy but not *all* of its features. But this just misses the point of the examples. The analogous cases are not *meant* to resemble pregnancy in all respects, but to isolate certain features whose ethical significance we are testing. With the violinist, this is the bodily dependence of one person upon another at a considerable cost to the host. With the conjoined twins, it is the effect of bodily dependence by one person upon another when the weaker party's dependence threatens to kill the other party, and where they themselves are beyond saving. If a discussant thinks that other features of pregnancy not captured in either case are also ethically salient to abortion, even on the assumption of fetal personhood (including the fact that the fetus is entirely enclosed within the woman), then she will have to explain what they are and why they are morally meaningful. But engaging in this kind of reasoning *is* the process of discerning and refining the more general principles we are prepared to defend, and what bearing this has on abortion morality.

Interestingly, it seems that even Little's own analysis of abortion cannot do without reliance on more general categories and principles. Her argument is that pregnancy entails a particularly thoroughgoing degree of intimacy, one which cannot be legitimately forced upon someone. As she says, 'To mandate that the woman remain pregnant is to mandate that she remain in a state of physical intertwinement against her consent.'[14] Being in a state of physical intertwinement with another being must be consensual. Little derives this conclusion from some of the concepts and categories that we employ outside of the abortion context. She writes:

Just as sexual intercourse can be a joy under consent and a violation without it, gestation can be a beautiful experience with it and a harmful one without it. To think that the above concern insults the meaningfulness of pregnancy is simply to misunderstand the point. We don't impugn how meaningful it is to have willing sex when we protest against a rape; the fact that sexual intercourse can be wonderful doesn't mean we would think it appropriate for the state to conscript people into serving as prostitutes.[15]

Little takes these thoughts about rape to indicate that 'consent determines valence on matters of physical integrity . . . a trip to a beautiful country turns into a kidnapping, a surgery into an assault, when they are done against one's consent'.[16] In other words, we accept the general principle that non-consensual bodily invasions are not acceptable, and that principle is meant to tell us that gestation without consent is no different, and that mandated pregnancy through abortion prohibition is consequently unacceptable. This is in truth not methodologically all that different from Thomson's use of the violinist scenario to tell us that gestating a fetus cannot be morally obligatory, or from my use of the conjoined twins case to tell us whether

---

[14] Little (n 1) 301.   [15] ibid 302.   [16] ibid.

abortion might amount to justified homicide in morality or law. Someone deploying Little's original complaint might direct it back at her here and claim that we cannot learn anything about pregnancy abortion by thinking about rape, the two being such distinct things. But she would be right, as I see it, to respond that there is no way to make her argument against mandated gestation without appealing to extra-pregnancy contexts, and that the point of the examples is simply to prove the independent significance of consent in scenarios of bodily interference. One potentially significant point of disanalogy between the bodily invasion involved in rape and mandated pregnancy, however, is that the perpetrator of a rape is *inflicting* a non-consensual bodily invasion upon a person, whereas those who refuse to perform abortion are only failing to help end her non-consensual occupation by the fetus. Because of this difference, there may well be difficulty likening mandated pregnancy (through the prohibition of abortion) to bodily *interference* akin to assault.

If Little's argument is wrong, it will be because morally pertinent differences like this hold between pregnancy and abortion and non-consensual sex or surgery, either meaning that the consent principle does not apply in the same way (perhaps because pregnancy is not the 'invasion' that rape and assault are), or because other considerations override it. I do not want to pronounce on Little's argument here. My point is only that Little can no more manage to draw out the morally important features of pregnancy by discussing pregnancy alone than those who compare it to somewhat wilder scenarios.

4.2 The Sex Equality Argument

I have suggested that we cannot reject all arguments by analogy and hope to make progress in our reasoning about abortion. Moreover, uncovering important points of disanalogy between abortion and other moral problems does not show analogical reasoning to be distorting. Instead, those disanalogies can prove useful for distinguishing the features of pregnancy which correctly affect our moral accounting. So far, though, I have paid scant attention to one very striking distinction between pregnancy and anything to which we might want to analogize it, when thinking about abortion. That is, I have made very little of the fact that unwanted pregnancy only happens to women.

This is an obvious point of disanalogy with the other scenarios discussed. In Thomson's violinist analogy, for example, it is not specified that the person whose kidneys are used to keep the violinist alive is a woman. The analogy is in this way sex-neutral. Some feminist theorists have taken issue with the fact that the supporter in the example is not sexed. MacKinnon has argued that by leaving out the fact that the supporter in pregnancy is always female, Thomson's parable fails to underscore the astronomical damage to sex equality for which mandated pregnancy is responsible.[17] According to this perspective, reproductive control is

---

[17] Catharine A MacKinnon, 'Privacy v Equality: Beyond *Roe v Wade*', in Catharine A MacKinnon, *Feminism Unmodified: Discourses on Life and Law* (Harvard University Press 1987) 98.

vital for combating the social inequality of women and their oppression by men. Denying women abortion, it is argued, exacerbates existing sex inequality in a number of ways, including by entrenching women's dependence on and vulnerability to men. Why this is so is not all too difficult to see. Pregnancy and childrearing can aggravate a woman's condition of poverty, reduce her chances of a good education, diminish her career prospects, and keep her dependent on men, perhaps in a situation of abuse. For feminists, abortion cannot be considered separately from this context, which includes the background conditions of inequality between the sexes that already persist with or without abortion rights. Susan Sherwin summarizes the point this way:

Since we live in a patriarchal society, it is especially important to ensure that women have the authority to control their own reproduction . . . virtually all feminists seem to agree that women must gain full control of their own reproductive lives if they are to free themselves from male dominance.[18]

Both Sherwin and MacKinnon have also argued that reproductive control is central to women's liberation because it is linked to the control of sexuality itself.[19] Their accounts lay emphasis on the way in which structures of male dominance can often make pregnancy difficult to avoid in the first place. Sherwin explains:

Few women have not found themselves in circumstances where they do not feel free to refuse a man's demands for intercourse, either because he is holding a gun to her head or because he threatens to be emotionally hurt if she refuses (or both) . . . Under such circumstances, it is difficult to argue that women could simply 'choose' to avoid heterosexual activity if they wish to avoid pregnancy.[20]

Openness to sex can be the price of domestic peace, continuing emotional support, or economic survival. As Sherwin explains, sexual coercion is not always recognized as such. Moreover, both Sherwin and MacKinnon make the point that contraceptives cannot always be relied upon to afford women reproductive control. The most effective and reliable contraceptives can be hazardous to health and future fertility if used for prolonged periods, and often come with undesirable side effects. Barrier methods do not have the same health drawbacks but are far less reliable, and there are often social impediments to using them. As Sherwin underscores, women are discouraged from 'preparing' for sexual activity, and many find their male partners unwilling to use barrier methods.

On the feminist picture then, the subjugation of women by men can make sex— and hence, pregnancy—difficult to avoid in the first place. Furthermore, however, unwanted pregnancy and childrearing can itself contribute further to the erosion of sexual autonomy. The more dependent women are, the less free they are to refuse

---

[18] Susan Sherwin, 'Abortion Through a Feminist Ethics Lens' (1991) 30 Dialogue: Canadian Philosophical Review/Revue canadienne de philosophie 327, 330.
[19] See Sherwin (n 18) and MacKinnon (n 5).
[20] Sherwin (n 18) 330.

sexual access. Given that the abortion option is often the only means of exercising reproductive control, the feminist argument concludes that the option must be protected if we are to take sex equality seriously. Abortion is, first and foremost, an issue of equal rights for women, since only by controlling their reproduction can they place themselves on a more equal footing with men.

As MacKinnon has explained, the feminist critique of abortion restrictions differs substantially from the mainstream 'liberal' defence of abortion, exemplified by the Supreme Court's reasoning in *Roe v Wade*.[21] The latter proceeds by locating reproductive control in a zone of personal privacy out of reach of governmental interference. The reasoning of the US Supreme Court reflected this public–private distinction, grounding abortion rights on the liberal notion of personal autonomy, and the specific right to control one's reproductive destiny, rather than in the need to secure sex equality. MacKinnon criticizes the 'privacy doctrine' of *Roe* for its failure to vindicate abortion rights using what she believes is the correct constitutional basis.[22] By consigning legitimate abortions to the realm of 'private choice', MacKinnon argues that the Supreme Court neglected the public interest in securing sex equality, which is heavily implicated in the issue of abortion freedoms. Liberal theories of reproductive rights that rely on the public–private distinction are erroneous, she argues, in assuming that the private sphere *is* free and equal, rather than constituting a zone where male dominance is permitted to reign unchecked by state power. *Roe v Wade* was therefore right, but for the wrong reasons.

What does all this mean for abortion morality? The relation between procreative control and sex equality cannot seriously be doubted. Indeed, few philosophers writing about abortion do, I think, question the claim that mandated pregnancy and childrearing compound women's inequality in a number of ways (although some opponents of abortion rights surely underestimate the effects of mandated pregnancy on the status of women).[23]

Since few 'non-feminist' philosophers (whether of a 'pro-life' or 'pro-choice' persuasion) would deny these claims, we must look further to discern the real point of conflict between traditional philosophic and feminist approaches to abortion. Sherwin claims that a feminist analysis, unlike non-feminist accounts, 'regards the effects of unwanted pregnancies on the lives of women individually and collectively

---

[21] See MacKinnon (n 17) and *Roe v Wade* US 410 113 (1973).   [22] ibid 93.

[23] It should be acknowledged that certain contributions to the abortion debate also criticize *permissive* abortion laws on the ground that they are damaging to sex equality. So-called 'pro-life feminists' draw attention to the way in which the availability of abortion as 'back-up' contraception can in fact weaken women's sexual autonomy, or that abortion choice fails to exemplify 'feminine' caring values (see Sidney Callahan, 'Abortion and the Sexual Agenda: A Case for Prolife Feminism' (1986) 123 Commonweal 232; Celia Wolf-Devine, 'Abortion and the "Feminine Voice" ' in Joel Feinberg and Susan Dwyer (eds), *The Problem of Abortion* (3rd edn, Wadsworth Publishing Company 1997) 160.)

MacKinnon also draws attention at several points to the way in which the abortion option can and has been used to strengthen male sexual dominance over women in a matrix where 'private' interactions are deemed to be outside of the law's concern (MacKinnon (n 17)). In a background context in which women do not control access to their own sexuality, she argues, 'the availability of abortion removed the one remaining legitimized reason that women have had for refusing sex besides the headache' (above, n 17, at 99).

as a central element in the moral evaluation of abortion'.[24] Feminist ethics, she says, 'demands that the effects on the oppression of women be a principal consideration when evaluating abortion policies'.[25] Perhaps, then, the distinguishing feature of *non*-feminist abortion ethics is not resistance to the idea that abortion rights are intimately bound up with sex equality, but where and how this consideration is positioned in the overall argument. For feminist ethicists, it is *the* principal consideration. For non-feminists, it is perhaps just one piece of a larger puzzle.

Let me state, then, what we can call the sex equality argument in favour of abortion rights. The argument holds that the necessity of abortion rights for securing sex equality is sufficient to show that abortion is morally permissible and that abortion rights are necessary as a matter of justice. I think that most non-feminist philosophers would reject this argument, even though they would not deny that prohibiting abortion impedes sex equality. Their disagreement, I believe, is with the suggestion that the sex equality interest in reproductive autonomy is sufficient to justify abortion rights without needing to make any claim about the moral status of the fetus. Understanding this can go a long way towards understanding why it is that non-feminist accounts seem to pay so little attention to the women's interests issue.

MacKinnon, Sherwin, and other feminist theorists undoubtedly identify a pertinent consideration for abortion policy when drawing attention to the various ways in which abortion restrictions entrench sex inequality. However, a full moral appraisal of abortion will not be complete until we consider how the sex equality interest weighs against countervailing considerations. It may well be that 'traditional' philosophers are not, on the whole, explicit enough about weighing the sex equality interest in their moral calculations. In some cases, though, this may only be because the factual claim that abortion rights are necessary for sex equality is seen as axiomatic. It is not given more air time only because it is not in dispute.

Whilst agreeing entirely with the claim that women's equality with men depends, to a very significant degree, on the procreative and bodily control which abortion affords, I nevertheless think it is possible to show that the sex equality interest is neither sufficient nor necessary for a philosophical defence of abortion. If I am right about this, it may help to explain why the sex equality interest is often at the margins of philosophical abortion argument, without casting any doubt whatsoever on the undeniable claim that prohibiting abortion damages women as a class and exacerbates their social disadvantage.

4.3 Sex Equality and Fetal Personhood

The sex equality argument as I have defined it appears to be neutral on the question of fetal personhood. That is, it seems to claim that sex equality is a sound basis for abortion rights whether or not the fetus is a person with the same moral status as born human beings.

---

[24] Sherwin (n 18) 330.   [25] ibid.

MacKinnon asserts straightforwardly that because 'fetal rights as such are in direct tension with sex equality rights', they cannot be tolerated.[26] This assertion is not accompanied by any consideration of how things would stand if the fetus *were* a person in the philosophical sense. The question can be asked, then, whether MacKinnon believes the sex equality interest is sufficient to justify abortion rights with or without an accompanying denial of fetal personhood.[27] This 'sufficiency thesis' is implied by MacKinnon's comment that once one recognizes sex equality as part of the abortion problem, it will no longer matter that the fetus is a 'form of life'. For why, she asks, should women *not* make life and death decisions?[28] MacKinnon's comments here are suggestive of the view that even if the fetus is a person, abortion might be considered a form of justified homicide, owing to the interest in sex equality that it protects. In short, the sex equality interest resolves the abortion question permissively *whatever status one accords to the fetus*.

But if this is indeed a claim that MacKinnon and others are making, it is one that is extremely difficult to accept. This can be shown by the following consideration. MacKinnon and Sherwin correctly point out that it is not chiefly pregnancy but more so unavoidable *childrearing* which threatens to socially disadvantage women and curtail their independence from men. Thus, laws which prohibit infanticide of born children up to any age at which they are still significantly dependent *also* impede sex equality, if women would otherwise choose to liberate themselves that way. Women could probably secure better equality with men if they could have their born children exterminated at any time. But it is unthinkable that the sex equality interest could ever be strong enough to justify that. This thought-experiment tells us that we do not think furthering sex equality is a justification for homicide. And we do not even need the infanticide example to tell us this. There is a good case to be made that the plight of women will be greatly improved by dropping a bomb on Playboy magazine's headquarters, but this is not a justification for doing so. Consequently, if the fetus is presumed to be a person, the sex equality interest is not sufficient to show that abortion is morally justified. Such a claim would rely on the argument that conduct otherwise amounting to murder is transformed into justified homicide if it is needed to combat sex inequality. But any further thinking shows this is not a principle we can reasonably accept.

Against the infanticide counter-example, it may be objected that, post-childbirth, women can always extricate themselves from social motherhood at any time by having their children adopted, and that infanticide would therefore never be practically necessary for the furtherance of women's equality. Hence the comparison is not apt. This objection fails for two reasons. First, it is equally true of many pregnant women that they can arrange adoptions to relieve themselves of childcare responsibilities following childbirth, which presents the main threat of social disadvantage. But if the avoidance of either motherhood *or* adoption can justify killing a fetus-person in the furtherance of sex equality, it should also, in theory, justify killing a five-year-old for the same reason. Second, if it is still considered a serious point of

---

[26] MacKinnon (n 17).   [27] MacKinnon (n 19) 1315.   [28] MacKinnon (n 17) 94.

disanalogy, the thought-experiment could simply be amended to exclude adoption as an escape route. In a country where adoption agencies did not exist, or were outlawed, and where the only means by which women could relieve themselves of onerous and socially disadvantaging duties of childcare were infanticide, could the value of sex equality justify the practice? I think not. If the sex equality argument is intended to succeed in spite of any presumption of fetal personhood, it surely relies on a principle of permissible killing that would not be accepted in any other context. The fact that this is so serves as a good indication that the denial of fetal personhood is integral to the feminist case for abortion rights.

This all serves to show that the sex equality interest in reproductive control is not sufficient to justify abortion philosophically. Other things must also be true—namely, that the fetus is not a person, morally equal to born human beings. If the interest in sex equality justifies abortion rights, this can only be because the fetus is something less than a person, since the furtherance of sex equality is not a justification for homicide.

It could be objected here that feminist perspectives on abortion do indeed engage with the question of fetal moral status. Sherwin argues that 'because of a fetus's unique physical status—*within* and dependent on a particular woman—the responsibility and privilege of determining its specific social status must rest with the woman carrying it'.[29] She also points out that, unlike born human beings, fetuses are by nature limited regarding the relationships in which they can participate. Being enclosed in the womb, it is simply impossible for them to fulfil the kinds of relational roles that it is possible to fulfil after birth. Hence, although fetuses are, on her view, morally significant, their status is 'relational not absolute'. By this, I take it Sherwin means that their moral status can only be dictated by the pregnant women in whose bodies they reside.

These are indeed arguments about fetal moral status, and they are also arguments about moral status as such. The claims are, at bottom, that situations of complete bodily dependence or lack of access to certain social goods, like relationships, preclude a human organism like the fetus from possessing full moral status. These arguments may be correct, or they may be wrong. Moral philosophers spend a good deal of time debating their veracity. As we should know by now, Thomson's famous violinist analogy *is* an argument that complete bodily dependence on another human being alters the moral status of the dependent being (for her, it alters it in such a way that the dependent being has no right not to be killed by the host being or her agents).

Thomson, in effect, reaches the same conclusion as does Sherwin—that bodily dependence on another determines moral status, especially one's right not to be killed—albeit in her case, it is the conclusion to a lengthy argument by analogy. Sherwin's 'relational' view of the fetus is a different argument about the conditions for moral status, or 'personhood'. By offering it to us, Sherwin demonstrates some agreement that individual or class interests in ending unwanted pregnancy

---

[29] Sherwin (n 18) 10.

would struggle to justify homicide unless the fetus's right to life is, to begin with, weaker than that of born human beings. But of course, many will want to look more closely at the idea that the fetus is differently positioned at the outset, including at the claim that the inability to partake in relationships strips a being of full moral status. This too is a general claim about the conditions for moral status, and one about which some discussants may raise doubts. They may ask whether it can really be correct that moral status depends on the relationships one forms, or is able to form, with others—what about the misanthropic, the perpetually isolated, the man stranded alone on a desert island? These doubts may lead in turn to larger questions about what sort of access to human fellowship is needed for full moral status (actual, or only hypothetical?), if indeed such access is. Whatever our answers to these questions, it seems that the wider complexities bound up with the issue of moral status cannot be avoided in abortion argument by underscoring the sex equality interest in reproductive control, or by pointing out plain facts about the fetus's particular situation of dependence, without explaining how and why these facts pertain to the general conditions for moral status. Because of this, the sex equality argument for abortion rights cannot bypass the central question about the moral status of the fetus.

PART II

THE THRESHOLD OF PERSONHOOD

5

Personhood Thresholds, Arbitrariness, and 'Punctualism'

5.1 Thresholds of Personhood

The discussion in Part I was meant to establish one main thing: that a sound moral or legal basis for abortion rights cannot bypass the question of the moral status of the human fetus. The permissibility of most abortions does indeed depend upon that status and upon whether the fetus qualifies as a fellow person. After surveying some of the main attempts by defenders of abortion rights to strip the personhood question of most of its relevance, I concluded that those attempts ultimately fail. In sum, those seriously engaged in ethical and legal reasoning about abortion must confront the fetal personhood issue and make up their minds about it.

Still, it is little wonder that some discussants have made such concerted efforts to sidestep that question. How does one even begin to make persuasive arguments about whether or not the human fetus is a person? Whether it belongs to that class of beings or not is a fact which, for many, is simply self-evident, resisting systematic argument. Roger Wertheimer believed that the sheer self-evidence of the fetus's lack of personhood in the eyes of supporters of abortion rights is a key reason why they 'so consistently fail to make contact' with the terms of the anti-abortion challenge.[1] He wrote:

He [the supporter of abortion rights] doesn't know how to respond to the argument [that the fetus is a person], because he cannot *make sense* of that premise. To him, it is not simply false, but wildly, madly false, it is nonsense, totally unintelligible, literally unbelievable. Just look at an embryo. It is an amorphous speck of coagulated protoplasm. It has no eyes or ears, no head at all. It can't walk or talk; you can't dress it or wash it. Why, it doesn't even qualify as a Barbie doll, and yet millions of people call it a human being, just like one of us. It's as if someone were to look at an acorn and call it an oak tree, or, better, it's as though someone squirted a paint tube at a canvas and called the outcome a painting—a work of art—and people believed him. The whole thing is precisely that mad—and just that sane. The liberal is befuddled by the conservative's argument, just as Giotto would be were he to assess a Pollock production as a painting.[2]

---

[1] Roger Wertheimer, 'Understanding the Abortion Argument' (1971) 1 Philosophy and Public Affairs 67.
[2] ibid 73–4.

Arguments about Abortion: Personhood, Morality, and Law. First Edition. Kate Greasley. © K. Greasley 2017. Published 2017 by Oxford University Press.

Of course, opponents of abortion who attribute philosophical personhood to the human fetus often think their position equally self-evident to any reasonable person assessing the facts. In their defence of embryo rights, Robert P George and Christopher Tollefsen present a real-life tale from the 2007 Hurricane Katrina disaster, in which a team of rescue officers entered a flooded hospital and salvaged fourteen hundred frozen embryos in canisters of liquid nitrogen.[3] George and Tollefsen take it that had the officers never made it to the hospital, 'there can be little doubt that the toll of Katrina would have been fourteen hundred human beings higher than it already was . . . ' In this passage, the authors' use of the term 'human being' is clearly meant in the moral, rights-holding, sense—the 'person' sense. But this proposition, which they believe can *hardly be doubted*, is the very same one which supporters of abortion rights think not only incorrect, but, in Wertheimer's words, 'literally unbelievable' and 'wildly, madly false'.

As one might expect, appeal to sheer self-evidence is symptomatic of great difficulty in marshalling arguments about prenatal personhood. But why is that task so immensely difficult? A large part of the answer is that arguing about fetal personhood requires one to define personhood universally. What is it that makes *us* persons with the moral rights that we possess? Is personhood status a matter of capabilities, or some sort of essence? Is it human species membership which is the defining characteristic of a person, and if so, why? The problems inherent in these questions clearly extend far beyond the abortion debate. They go to the very heart of our beliefs about what kind of beings we are, what makes us uniquely valuable (if anything does), and why we possess the interests and rights we do, including the fundamental right to life. Given the deep-rooted nature of disagreement about our own metaphysics, it is hardly surprising that disagreement about personhood at the beginning of life is so intractable.

Those with some exposure to academic argument about abortion will be familiar with the conventional discourse surrounding fetal personhood. Contestants on both sides begin by singling out a particular biological, psychological, or, in some cases, sociological benchmark in the career of the emerging human, which they regard as transformative: conception, implantation, quickening, viability, consciousness, birth, rationality, and so on. The relevant benchmark is then offered up as the threshold of philosophical personhood. The favoured threshold will be taken to *mark* the beginning of personhood, but an argument will need to be made that it corresponds to a criterion (or criteria) that *constitutes* personhood.

The relation between the threshold of personhood and the criterion of personhood might be different depending on the argument. The threshold could be treated as evidence for the emergence of the criterion, for example where the development of certain brain structures is taken to be evidence for the capacity to form conscious desires—one proposed criterion of personhood. Alternatively, the threshold and the criterion might be one and the same thing, for instance where birth is put

---

[3] Robert P George and Christopher Tollefsen, *Embryo: A Defense of Human Life* (Doubleday 2008) 1–3.

forward as the threshold of personhood on the ground that *having being born* is constitutive of personhood. Or the two may be thought to generally coincide, for example where the threshold for personhood is placed at twenty-eight weeks with the rationale that this is when fetuses tend to become viable, and that separate independent living ability is what turns human beings into persons.

No proposal will last long unless it is accompanied by an account of what confers or constitutes philosophical personhood in universal terms. But this universalizing requirement poses significant challenges for the proponent in excluding from the definition the class of beings it seems reasonable to exclude whilst including those it seems reasonable to include. Opponents of any given threshold largely proceed by summoning forth *reductio ad absurdum* arguments, intended to show that the threshold or criterion commits its defenders to untenable implications concerning who is in or out of the person category. In the alternative, it will be argued that in stepping between all the cracks (the *reductios*), those defenders forfeit a coherent, universal theory for their proposed threshold. In particular, subscribers to the view that full-fledged personhood begins at conception typically allege that *post-conception*—or, what they call, 'developmental'—criteria for personhood, such as consciousness, rationality, or independent living ability, exclude too many born human beings from the community of persons.[4] Neonates and young infants are not rational. Comatose human beings are not conscious. Intensive care patients on life support may not be capable of independent breathing. But surely all of these human beings are persons. Counter-examples such as these can be mustered for almost any developmental criterion one might pick, and, it is argued, go to show that each of the developmental thresholds is unsupportable.

The conception threshold has its own *reductio* problems to contend with, however, although they come in a different form. For instance, if a human organism is a person in the philosophical sense from the moment of conception, then spontaneous miscarriage must be the greatest natural threat to the human race—the single biggest killer, outrunning cancer, malnutrition, and natural disasters by a huge margin.[5] If zygotes and embryos are persons, therefore, it would seem to follow that more resources should be devoted to preventing natural miscarriage than to anything else. This will strike many as an absurd implication.[6]

Further again, and somewhat strangely, the conception threshold entails that the majority of people who have ever existed perished as blastocysts before they

---

[4] For good illustrations of arguments of this sort, see Christopher Robert Kaczor, *The Ethics of Abortion: Women's Rights, Human Life, and the Question of Justice* (Routledge 2011), chapter 4 generally.

[5] For a developed explanation of this point, see: Toby Ord, 'The Sourge: Moral Implications of Natural Embryo Loss' (2008) 8 American Journal of Bioethics 12.

[6] It should be noted that defenders of the conception threshold have posited answers to this *reductio*, an important one of which simply embraces the putatively 'absurd' conclusion that embryos are equally morally valuable with born human beings, but points to the inadequacies or impossibilities of embryo-saving interventions (especially at such an early stage of pregnancy) as an explanation for why we would not want to devote more resources to preventing natural miscarriage. This, to my mind though, does not address the palpable absurdity that *should* such interventions be effective and easy to deploy, they ought to take primacy over the prevention of disease, famine, road accidents, and the like.

ever implanted in the womb. It also seems to imply that embryo loss ought to be mourned every bit as much as the deaths of small children. In the commonly rehearsed 'Embryo Rescue Case' scenario, someone who faced the choice between saving one newborn baby or five human embryos from a burning down hospital would act more reasonably in choosing the embryos, given that this would amount to saving the greatest number of people.[7] These all appear to be absurd but unavoidable implications of the belief that personhood begins at conception.[8] Needless to say, some opponents of abortion will not find these implications absurd at all. Hence some emerging pro-life advocacy of 'embryo adoption', which is considered to be a form of child rescue. However, prima facie, and for the as yet uncommitted thinker, they are at least as hard to accept as the 'developmental' criteria *reductios*.

At a glance, then, it seems that counter-examples and *reductio* arguments can be deployed against thresholds of all kinds. The challenge for each proponent is to address the *reductios* without modifying her personhood criterion beyond the limits of its rationale or embracing conclusions that most will struggle to accept, such as that infants or radically cognitively disabled humans lack philosophical personhood, or that the death of a single-celled zygote or, even, a pair of sex cells, is as lamentable as the death of an adult human being. As Don Marquis explains, discussants who arbitrarily tweak their criterion of personhood so as to avoid putatively absurd conclusions lay themselves open to the allegation that their arguments are 'atheoretical', not proceeding in terms of principles which are universally true.[9] But just like the rules of a game, certain generally accepted rules and constraints direct the structure of the exchanges between contestants, refereeing the philosophical moves that can legitimately be made and dictating the standards of correctness to which proposed thresholds are held. The nature of those rules and the deeper commitments they might presuppose are a central concern of mine in this chapter.

5.2 Arbitrariness of Different Kinds

As we have seen, one guiding rule in the conventional debate about the conditions of personhood is the avoidance of *reductios*. There are, on the whole, two different ways of dealing with *reductio*-type counter-arguments. The first is to amend or refine the conditions of personhood that one endorses in order to avoid the *reductio*. So, for instance, if a theory which grounds personhood status in conscious desires seems wrongly to exclude sleeping persons or those in reversible comas, incapable of such desires, the theory might be adjusted to locate moral standing in a more specific trait, such as the latent capacity for conscious desires or, perhaps, the past experience of conscious desires. It is important to understand that the success of

    [7] See: S Matthew Liao, 'The Embryo Rescue Case' (2006) 27 Theoretical Medicine and Bioethics 141.
    [8] There have been attempts to rebut the conclusion that these are necessary implications of the belief that personhood begins at conception. One or two of them will be considered in chapter 7.
    [9] Don Marquis, 'Why Abortion Is Immoral' (1989) 86 Journal of Philosophy 183, 188–9.

this strategy of avoidance depends on the theory's ability to explain and justify the amendment. It will not adequately answer a *reductio* if a discussant changes her criterion by fiat, just so as to dodge the counter-example, without being able to explain why the kernel of her argument about personhood makes the right discriminations when taken to its natural conclusions. In the example I gave, one must explain the justificatory basis of a 'past conscious desires' criterion of personhood.

The second strategy is to try to deny that the *reductio* is really a *reductio* by challenging the notion that the ostensibly absurd implication is really absurd. This strategy is favoured by some philosophers who, in response to the challenge that their criterion of personhood excludes young infants, respond by contesting the conventional moral standards according to which infanticide is strictly morally prohibited. Some historical cultures, they might mention, did not hold the same view about the moral status of young infants as do we. Perhaps we are simply in error in attributing full moral status to neonates. Perhaps, as Michael Tooley suggests, our absolute prohibition on infanticide is really just another kind of unsupportable social taboo.[10]

A related, but somewhat different, kind of objection is also ubiquitous in conventional debate about personhood. Contributors to that debate routinely demand of one another that their respective thresholds of personhood avoid *arbitrariness*, although the same word can, in this context, denote distinct kinds of objections.

In the first place, a personhood threshold might be decried as 'arbitrary' in the sense that it lacks a defensible, corresponding criterion for personhood. Take the conception threshold. Those who defend the conception threshold presumably do so because they endorse a criterion of personhood based on genetic humanity. Something is a person, on this view, if it belongs to the species Homo sapiens, which it does if it is an individual organism possessing a full set of human DNA. I am granting for the sake of argument in my discussion that all forms of human life post-conception are at least human beings in the strictly biological sense, albeit radically underdeveloped ones. But the defender of the conception threshold cannot just presuppose that all human beings are necessarily persons—that is what his argument needs to establish. If he is unable to explain the independent moral salience of human species membership, he will lay himself open to the challenge that his criterion is morally 'arbitrary', meaning simply that it lacks adequate justification.

Michael Tooley has argued that attributing special value to biological humanity *per se* is morally arbitrary in a very particular way—that is, it is *speciesist*.[11] The speciesism challenge can be explained this way. Many would not consider it seriously morally wrong to abort a cat fetus. Although a human embryo is genetically human, it does not possess psychological capacities that are any more developed than that of the cat fetus; it is not more sentient or intelligent. Proponents of the speciesism challenge take psychological capacities such as these to be the morally relevant ones for personhood. It seems therefore that there is no reason to treat the human fetus as more morally considerable than the cat fetus. If one just asserts that

---

[10] Michael Tooley, 'Abortion and Infanticide' (1972) 2 Philosophy and Public Affairs 37.
[11] ibid.

the human fetus is owed more protection in virtue of being human, Tooley contends that this will entail 'arbitrarily' preferring one species over another, meaning, without reference to morally differentiating characteristics.

Tooley believes that the speciesism problem frustrates all proposed benchmarks of personhood during gestation, as well as the birth threshold. If one chose, for example, to propose viability as the threshold of personhood, the question will become why viable cat fetuses are not equally morally important, if speciesism is not silently in play. Tooley proposes instead that a human being is not a person until she is self-aware in the sense of possessing 'a concept of oneself as a continuing subject of experiences'—a morally distinguishing feature that is not merely a matter of human species membership.[12] This, he argues, is what is required before an individual is capable of having desires that could be satisfied by continued life, and hence, a strong interest in living. Since infants only begin to think and to become self aware at a few months of age, it is only around then that, on Tooley's analysis, they acquire the fundamental right to life.

Defenders of the conception threshold in particular will push back against the 'speciesism' allegation by attempting to show that their preference for human species membership is not without justification. Homo sapiens *are* special, they often argue, in possessing the unique capacity for rationality and higher thinking, complex desires, unique forms of sociability, and so on. The fact that these capacities are typically borne out by adult human species members is, they say, a morally distinguishing characteristic of the human race. Against the speciesism challenge, they might retort that if an alien culture were discovered whose mature members *also* typically exemplified traits like rationality and higher thinking (like the Vulcans from *Star Trek*), all members of that species would *also* be persons from the beginning of their biological existence. It is not 'sheer' humanity, but the distinctive forms of human flourishing, which are the morally relevant characteristics.

But refining the criterion of personhood even further to 'being a member of a species the adult members of which are typified by higher forms of consciousness' (rationality, higher-level desires, etc) does not quite address the justification problem. One can just pose a further question. Why is it that merely belonging to a biological species the *typical adult members of which* are capable of higher forms of thinking itself suffices for personhood status?

Related to this first kind of arbitrariness problem—the problem of justifying a personhood threshold—is what Mary Anne Warren termed the 'intrinsic properties assumption'.[13] As she described it, this is the assumption that only facts about the 'intrinsic' properties of individuals can justify ascriptions of moral standing. Conversely, properties that are only circumstantial or relational, like the property of being in a certain location, or of being wanted and loved, are irrelevant to moral standing. It is plain to see how the intrinsic properties assumption underlies many of the key moves in the traditional debate about prenatal personhood.

---

[12] ibid 9.
[13] Mary Anne Warren, 'The Moral Significance of Birth' (1989) 4 Hypatia 46, 47–8.

Characteristics like human appearance, size, and movement in the womb are often quickly dismissed as lacking intrinsic enough a quality to be meaningful for personhood. Surely human beings do not derive their moral status from how they look, their size, or how much they can move (what about the permanently paralyzed?). It is only morally meaningful, or 'intrinsic', properties which matter.

The intrinsic properties assumption is an important pillar of the discussion about the birth threshold of personhood and the moral difference between late abortion and infanticide. One very familiar claim is that the mere fact of having been born cannot alter a human being's moral status, since it is not an 'intrinsic' property, but only a matter of location. A thirty-week-old fetus *in utero* is not intrinsically different from a baby born prematurely at twenty-four weeks, or so it is claimed. How can the fact of being one side or the other of the vaginal canal make such a difference to their respective rights to life? It is in this precise way that birth is said to be an entirely 'arbitrary' threshold of personhood. From here it is argued that the defender of the birth threshold must, for consistency, either concede that late abortion is morally impermissible, or relax her moral opposition to infanticide.

The intrinsic properties assumption also drives objections against other thresholds of personhood that appear to depend on allegedly *extrinsic* factors, including the viability threshold. Whether a twenty-four-week fetus can survive outside of the womb or not, it is argued, largely depends on the standard of neonatal care in the place which it is born.[14] A twenty-four-week fetus inside a pregnant woman on a plane is not viable for the few hours it is in the air, but could become so again when the plane lands and neonatal care units are in close proximity. Could personhood status be as periodic as this? Similarly, 'relational' theories which seek to tie the acquisition of personhood to a certain kind of relation to born human beings— being wanted by them, or able to interact with them—are criticized for grounding personhood in purely 'extrinsic' properties.[15] It seems altogether wrongheaded to argue that an unloved and unwanted newborn is, by virtue of those facts, less of a person than a cherished one, and this seems to be implied by the relational view. Equally implausible is the idea that a human being who finds himself isolated from other humans from birth, like Tarzan in the jungle, consequently lacks personhood status.

It is not always noted that we should expect the distinction between 'intrinsic' and 'extrinsic' properties to blur at some point. The capacity for rational functioning is widely regarded as an intrinsic feature of human beings, but it too may often *depend* on 'extrinsic' factors. For example, someone who suffers severe brain injury in an accident might be unable to regain rational functioning without the existence of advanced medical care, the availability of which is a matter of circumstance.

Which side of the intrinsic–extrinsic divide a property falls down on will also depend on just how one expands the definition of those terms. Viability is often

---

[14] Kaczor (n 4) 68–71.
[15] For an example, see Jonathan Herring, 'The Loneliness of Status: The Moral and Legal Significance of Birth' in Fatemah Ebtehaj and others (eds), *Birth Rites and Rights* (Hart Publishing 2011).

considered an extrinsic property because it can depend on so much outside of the fetus itself. However, reaching a gestational age from which it can survive outside of the womb without extraordinary efforts of modern medicine might plausibly be described as an intrinsic developmental threshold, mostly having to do with lung development. As H Tristram Engelhardt noted in his discussion of the viability threshold, viability in this sense is more of a biological than a situational fact, and is far less of a moving goalpost. In fact, the lower limit of 'biological' viability has not been significantly affected by advances in neonatal care.[16] It might also be wondered whether its location inside the womb could not be an 'intrinsic' property of a fetus, where intrinsic is taken to mean innate or non-circumstantial. The fetus could not have existed in any other situation, and its dependence on the pregnant woman's body for survival is certainly no less a biological fact than facts about its brain development. Is enclosure within the womb a strictly extrinsic property of some human beings?

The kinds of judgements driven by the intrinsic properties assumption also point to a second form of potential arbitrariness in the personhood debate: that of not treating like cases alike. This is not exactly the same as arbitrariness in the sense of lacking good reason or justification for one's proposed criterion (or criteria) of personhood, although it certainly springs from it. Part of the infanticide problem, for instance, is that the birth threshold seems to treat late fetuses differently from newborns without clear justification. The threshold thus seems to make 'arbitrary' differentiations between morally similar cases. It is generally seen as a failing of any account of personhood if it appears to treat creatures possessing the same *intrinsic* features differently. The speciesism challenge could be partly understood as an objection based on arbitrariness of this kind, since it entails the claim that various accounts of personhood fail to treat intrinsically similar creatures—cat fetuses and human fetuses; or human infants and adult chimpanzees (whose cognitive capacities may be more or less on a par)—alike.

There is a third kind of arbitrariness complaint frequently directed at attempts to locate the beginning of personhood during gestation or beyond. This is arbitrariness of the *sorites* kind, captured by the classic paradox of the heap. Suppose I begin to pull grains of sand together, one single grain at a time. Eventually, if I keep going, a heap of sand will materialize. I ask you to tell me at exactly which point the heap comes into existence. Which individual grain makes the difference? There you will have a bit of a problem. This is because there is no single grain about which it can plausibly be argued that *its* addition turned a non-heap into a heap. For whichever grain one might choose, there is nothing to distinguish *it* from the immediately

---

[16] H Tristram Engelhardt, Jr, 'The Ontology of Abortion' (1974) [University of Chicago Press] 84 Ethics 217, 228–30. In 2007, after reviewing all the evidence on fetal viability, the House of Commons Science and Technology Committee concluded that while survival rates of twenty-four weeks' gestation and beyond had improved in recent years, there was no evidence to suggest that fetal viability had been significantly lowered since the upper time limit for abortion had last been set (House of Commons Science and Technology Committee, 'Scientific Developments Relating to the Abortion Act 1967' http://www.publications.parliament.uk/pa/cm200607/cmselect/cmsctech/1045/1045i.pdf, 13–15 (last accessed 11 October 2016)).

succeeding or preceding ones. Why the one hundred-thousandth grain, and not the grain immediately before or after that? Surely the collection of sand does not become something altogether different between those individual grains.

In the debate about prenatal personhood, it seems that defenders of the conception threshold sometimes impugn post-conception benchmarks of personhood for being arbitrary in the sorites sense. That is, they take it to be a failing of developmental thresholds that they cannot be non-arbitrarily distinguished from the closest neighbouring points in the biological life of a human being.

Take the birth threshold. The challenge based on sorites arbitrariness will ask how the moment of birth can be distinguished from the moments immediately preceding it, when the fetus passes down the vaginal canal. As Christopher Kaczor asks: 'is there really any important difference in the personhood of a human being one minute before birth and one minute after?'[17] But it is equally as impossible to non-arbitrarily distinguish the few moments before birth from the moments immediately preceding *them*. So things get even worse for developmental thresholds, or so the argument goes. Whichever development is settled upon as the critical benchmark—be it birth, viability, sentience, or consciousness—will ultimately equate personhood's beginning with a threshold that is not morally distinguishable from the developments occurring just moments before, and the same will continue to be true however far back one moves the threshold. This is owed to the incremental nature of all human development before birth, and indeed, after it. Kaczor sums up the apparent problem this way:

The conception of personhood used by defenders of infanticide also leads them to posit arbitrary deadlines to separate who may live from who may be killed. Indeed, setting the age for voting or driving is indeed arbitrary . . . However, in matters of life and death we must do better than picking a random cut-off point. Life itself is at stake, the existence of innocent human beings, and so a vision of personhood that rests on the arbitrary decisions of the powerful against the weak cannot be in conformity with the demands of justice or equality.[18]

The claim that developmental criteria for personhood cannot be reconciled with basic human equality is an independent problem that I will consider in chapter 8. The claim I am interested in here holds that the correct threshold of personhood must not be arbitrary in the sorites sense (we can say: must not be *sorites-susceptible*). It is a problem of *cut-off* points.

For Kaczor and other critics of developmental thresholds, the fact that those thresholds do not pick out a precise, non-arbitrary cut-off point is a fundamental flaw, and attests to their falsity. In particular, it is often argued that where a posited threshold of personhood is sorites-susceptible, no reason exists to refrain from pushing it further and further forward. If twenty-four weeks' gestation, why not twenty-five? If birth, why not a few hours after? If two weeks of infancy, why not a month? The result, it is argued, is a disconcerting slippery slope, which threatens to rationalize a later and later threshold of personhood.

---

[17] Kaczor (n 4) 49.   [18] ibid 36.

As Kaczor acknowledges, sorites arbitrariness rears its head in all kinds of other contexts too. When we set the voting age at sixteen, or the driving age at seventeen, we cannot explain why a teenager a day before her sixteenth or seventeenth birthday is less capable of voting or driving competently than she is the day after. But this does not render the threshold unreasonable. In many contexts, then, sorites arbitrariness simply does not worry us, and does not logically entail any kind of slippery slope. Those who, like Kaczor, believe that it is uniquely problematic in a proposed threshold of personhood will therefore need to explain why.

Along these lines, it seems that the question about the threshold of personhood will need to be distinguished from the paradox of the heap itself. In the sorites paradox, *we know* that the grains of sand become a heap at some point, even though we cannot pinpoint any non-arbitrary moment when this occurs. The reasonable conclusion, in the heap case, is not to say that the heap exists with the first grain of sand, just as the reasonable response to sorites arbitrariness surrounding our driving age limit is not to allow babies to drive. These are clearly absurd reactions to sorites arbitrariness. Again, then, a defender of the conception threshold who believes that the continuous nature of human development helps her case will have to explain why the sorites-susceptibility of any developmental threshold of personhood has such a radically different implication, compelling us to identify personhood at the very beginning of biological human life.

As I said, the three kinds of arbitrariness I have outlined are not entirely distinct from one another, but are in significant ways related and mutually reinforcing. If a threshold is revealed to be arbitrary in one sense, it could quite possibly, and for the same reasons, be described as arbitrary in one of the other two senses as well. But all three capture standards of correctness that are accepted by many discussants in the personhood debate and used as grounds for criticism of competitor thresholds. Here, I wish to focus special attention on arbitrariness in the third, sorites sense. In particular, I wish to consider what deeper commitments about the nature of personhood one might need to embrace before imperviousness to sorites arbitrariness can be set up as a standard of correctness that a threshold of personhood needs to surmount. What kind of property must one take personhood to be for such a standard to apply? And which personhood threshold could possibly meet it? Subjecting these underlying commitments to scrutiny will, I think, reveal something about how it is reasonable to think that persons begin.

5.3 Conception and the Sorites Paradox

To recap, the problem of sorites arbitrariness is usually advanced by defenders of the conception threshold against so-called 'developmental', or post-conception, thresholds of personhood. As they see it, milestones like birth, viability, sentience, or brain development are all unacceptably arbitrary, since they equate personhood's beginning with minor developments not at all morally distinguishable from those occurring moments before or after. Kaczor points out that the birth threshold in particular is not nearly as definitive as might be supposed. Is the crucial moment when the human being exits the uterus, or the vaginal canal? Need it be all the way out of the woman before it is born, and hence a person, or just some of the way out? Those who criticize developmental thresholds on this basis presumably believe that the conception threshold is immune from sorites arbitrariness. They must believe, that is, that conception *is* an entirely discrete event in the life of a new human, and one that is non-arbitrarily distinguishable from all of the developments leading up to and after it.

But proponents of the conception threshold would be mistaken in thinking that only post-conception thresholds are sorites-susceptible. Indeed, even the very description of conception as a discrete, identifiable 'moment' is considerably misleading. Here are some of the numerous, individual events comprising the conception 'moment':[19]

1. The sperm approaches the unfertilized egg cell.
2. The sperm passes the egg's layer of follicle cells, and will make contact with the zona pellucida (the outer matrix of the egg) in one millionth of a second.
3. The sperm makes contact with the zona pellucida (the outer matrix of the egg).
4. One of the proteins in the egg's outer layer binds to a molecule on the head of the sperm.
5. The molecular interaction causes part of the sperm to release its contents, including enzymes that will enable it to penetrate the zona pellucida.
6. Finger-like extensions of the egg cell take the whole sperm cell into the egg.
7. The cell membranes of the egg and sperm fuse and break down.
8. The nuclei of the egg and sperm form 'pronuclei'.
9. Membranes of the pronuclei break down and become arranged for 'mitotic cell division'.
10. The first division is the zygote, a single cell with 46 chromosomes, 23 from each pronucleus.

Of all these stages, which is the exact moment when personhood begins? Does the new person come into being the millisecond when the sperm first makes contact with the egg, or the next millisecond when it just begins to release enzymes and penetrate it, or during one of the milliseconds when the pronuclei are fusing? If penetration of the egg is *the* moment, how far must the sperm penetrate before a person exists, and why is any one of those microscopically distinct advances more significant than the adjacent ones? Even penetration by the sperm is not

---

[19] The descriptions are taken from Michael Tooley's contribution in Philip Devine and others, *Abortion: Three Perspectives* (Oxford University Press 2009) 44–5 and Keith L Moore and TVN Persaud, *Before We Were Born: Essentials of Embryology and Birth Defects* (5th edn, WB Saunders 1998) 36–7. Tooley credits many of his descriptions to Neil A Campbell, *Biology* (4th edn, The Benjamin/Cummings Publishing Company 1996).

truly a 'point', but, at the quantum-mechanical level at least, is distributed over innumerable events. In truth, there are no 'points' of the non-sorites-susceptible sort *anywhere* in the biological world, if everything is only considered through microscopic enough a lens.

A proponent of the conception threshold of personhood who attacks later thresholds for being sorites-susceptible will need to show that his preferred benchmark *is* non-arbitrarily distinguishable from the adjacent developments on either side. But it does not look as though he can show this about conception. Whichever 'moment' is settled upon as the salient one *will* be arbitrary in the sense that no reason can be adduced for distinguishing it from the next closest, especially since the moments can always be individuated evermore finely. Moreover, it would be unfair to reply that the moments constituting the process of conception are too closely gathered to give rise to a problem of arbitrariness, but that those constituting birth are not. The problem of being unable to non-arbitrarily distinguish one moment from the closest neighbouring ones, if it is a problem, is exactly the same regardless of how long or short the time slices are. On the conception theorist's reasoning, the logical 'slippery slope' moving the threshold of personhood later and later in human development would still exist even if the increments of development are minute.

Further to this, it will seem that whatever considerations supporters of the conception threshold can bring to defend it against the sorites problem will also be available to those who support post-conception thresholds such as birth. It might be argued, for instance, that sorites-susceptibility at the borderline of personhood does not obviate the existence of clear cases, and that humans are clearly persons once conception has certainly been completed. But those defending the birth threshold can respond thus to the sorites problem as well. They can contend that the progressive nature of birth does not preclude there being clear cases on one side and the other: humans that are clearly born, and those that are clearly not. If the suggestion is that sorites-susceptibility rules out any proposed threshold of personhood, some explanation must be given as to why it does not rule out all of them, conception included.

5.4 Punctualism v Gradualism

At this point, it looks as though a certain amount of vagueness around the threshold of personhood is inescapable on any account. I think it apparent, though, that those defending the conception threshold typically take a very particular view of such vagueness. The entire thrust of the sorites critique of post-conception thresholds takes it as given that the inability to eliminate vagueness at the margins of personhood is a huge obstacle for any claim about when personhood begins. But we might wonder why anyone would believe such a thing to begin with. The premises underlying the sorites objection are, I think, multi-layered and fairly contentious. But the most fundamental of them is the premise that there is *a* single moment when human material (be it sperm and ovum together, zygote, fetus, or human infant) is instantaneously and wholly transformed into a morally considerable person. Although it may be impossible to say exactly when, on the microphysical level, that moment occurs, the presumption is that this impossibility is only due to the limits of our knowledge and perception. In other words, the precise moment is certainly there, whether it can be pinpointed or not.

This is the nub of what I will call the 'punctualist' thesis about the emergence of personhood. Punctualism is the belief that, to borrow an expression of Warren Quinn's, the beginning of personhood is something like an 'existential pop'.[20] On one side of the 'pop' there exists only human material, and on the other, a being which is essentially and completely a person. Persons do not emerge vaguely and incrementally, like human anatomy does; the beginning of their existence is instead sudden and absolute. Punctualism contrasts starkly with a very different view about how persons begin to exist: what we might call 'gradualism'. Gradualism eschews the idea that persons come into existence instantaneously and completely—in the manner of an 'existential pop'—and claims instead that personhood emerges gradually and incrementally. Consequently, there may well be a period of time during which the personhood of a human being is something of a grey area, being partial or indeterminate. The possibility of vagueness around the margins of personhood follows from the 'gradualist' thesis about personhood's emergence.[21] But any vagueness of this kind is excluded on the punctualist view, which regards personhood as an 'all or nothing' property.

Let us assume for the moment that the punctualist thesis is correct and that new people do begin to exist instantly and completely. The first question to arise is why, given this belief, the conception threshold fares any better than its rivals. The punctualist thesis as I have formulated it simply states that *somewhere* the life-span of a new human being is punctuated by the beginning of personhood—the 'existential pop'. But why could the pop not take place during the later stages of fetal development, or the process of birth? Presumably, one *could* be committed to the punctualist thesis about personhood's emergence whilst endorsing birth or some other post-conception milestone as the threshold of personhood. One would simply need a reason to believe that the 'existential pop' occurs somewhere between, say, the beginning of birth and its completion, even if one cannot say at exactly which point, down to the millisecond. The defender of the conception threshold presumably just finds no reason to believe that the moment of existential import happens during the change of location from womb to world (or, equally, during the acquisition of independent breathing ability) and good reason to believe that it occurs some time during conception. But what is the basis

---

[20] See W Quinn, 'Abortion: Identity and Loss' (1984) 13 Philosophy and Public Affairs 24.

[21] The terms 'gradualist' and 'gradualism' are not new; they have been employed by a few philosophers to date in discussion about the acquisition of personhood or 'moral status' at the beginning of life (see: Margaret Little, 'Abortion and the Margins of Personhood' (2008) 39 Rutgers Law Journal 331). Exactly what theory of moral status 'gradualism' is taken to denote is not always abundantly clear, and can vary between uses. I use the term here to label the basic proposition that personhood emerges at the beginning of life incrementally or vaguely.

for this assumption? Why is it any more likely that the conception process is the window within which personhood begins? The tempting answer is just to say that conception *is* an instant, whereas the later developments are not. But we already know that isn't true.

A different argument might run along the lines of claiming that all human developments subsequent to conception are simply not cataclysmic enough to suggest that somewhere buried within them is such a substantial and meaningful change as the advent of moral personhood. It is often suggested that post-conception developments only ever amount to the acquisition of a little more of one property or another—for example, gaining conscious awareness is only a matter of gaining a few degrees more sentience than shortly before, when a human being is sensitive to its environment in many ways, but not quite fully conscious. On the other hand, it is argued that conception marks the beginning of an essentially new kind of being, rather than the augmenting of certain existing features, like sentience. George and Tollefsen make an argument to this effect in the following passage:

> [T]he difference between a being that deserves full moral respect and a being that does not (. . .) cannot consist only in the fact that, while both have some feature, one has more of it than the other.
>
> In other words, a mere quantitative difference (having more or less of the same feature, such as the development of a basic natural capacity) cannot by itself be a justificatory basis for treating different entities in radically different ways. Between the ovum and the approaching thousands of sperm, on the one hand, and the embryonic human being on the other, there is a clear difference in kind ... But between the embryonic human being and that same human being at any later stage of its maturation, there is only a difference of degree.[22]

It jumps the gun somewhat in the present discussion to accept, without argument, that conception is a qualitative change and every development following it merely quantitative, *or* that quantitative differences cannot add up to qualitative or 'intrinsic' differences. The most meaningful differences between typical adult humans and chimpanzees consist in only a few more degrees of intelligence, sociability, and emotional breadth. Presumably, George and Tollefsen would not dismiss *those* differences as meaningless—as being *merely* quantitative.[23] Conception is certainly not quantitative in the sense that it does not continue to augment during the life of a human being, but neither does the acquisition of consciousness, or birth, once those benchmarks are passed. One does not become any *more* conscious after acquiring the capacity for conscious thought, and the characteristic of 'having been born' does not come in greater and lesser degrees. These developments do come about incrementally, in many successive moments, but as we saw, so does

---

[22] George and Tollefsen (n 3) 120.

[23] Incidentally, George and Tollefsen think that, by this point, they have already established the claim that conception marks a difference in kind in an earlier chapter (ibid, chapter 2). It is not entirely clear why, however, given that the relevant chapter is in fact only a detailed exposition of the fertilization process which features no argument *from* the biological facts considered *to* the moral conclusion that conception is morally significant in a way that later human developments could not possibly be.

conception. Thus, if the incremental nature of their coming to be is what makes these milestones 'quantitative', so is conception.

George and Tollefsen are in fact independently committed to the view that a life form with a complete set of human DNA is fully a person. Believing this, they might have reason to think, if accepting punctualism, that the 'existential pop' must have happened by the end of conception, even if they can find no ground for placing it at the millisecond during which the sperm first penetrated the ovum, the millisecond during which the gametes' nuclei first begin to fuse, or any of the milliseconds in between or after. But just as George and Tollefsen are convinced that conception is a more fundamental event in the life of an early human being than any other, so the proponent of the consciousness, viability, or birth thresholds could argue that the change taking place by the completion of these processes marks the beginning of a morally different kind of being. At issue here is whether there is better reason to believe that conception, rather than some other process of human development, is punctuated by the beginning of personhood on the ground that conception is a definitive moment, whereas the others are not. But if sorites-susceptibility is the thing which disqualifies post-conception processes in this inquiry, conception is in the same boat.

Be that as it may, punctualism, if true, may have extremely important implications for discussion about the advent of personhood. For one, whether it recommends the conception threshold or not, the punctualist thesis can make certain worries intelligible, including concerns which arise out of sorites arbitrariness. A belief in punctualism may, for instance, provide an explanation as to why sorites arbitrariness surrounding a proposed personhood threshold is found so troubling.

Vagueness is everywhere in the world (consider: at what precise moment does day turn into night?), but in few other places is it ever thought to be as worrisome as at the margins of personhood. Only philosophers are vexed by the question of how many grains of sand constitute a heap. But when the same puzzle is apprehended at the threshold of personhood, it is regarded by many as far more than a theoretical curiosity. If punctualism were correct, the seriousness of the sorites problem at the borderline of personhood might be explicable, since it posits that there *is* a determinate answer to the question whether the fetus is already a person at twenty-three weeks and six days, or becomes one at some time during the following day. This view effectively loads up the stakes of the sorites problem, by suggesting that it is possible to mistake the threshold of personhood by the most marginal fraction, and that the consequences of such a mistake are gravely serious: the killing of a *complete, fully realized* person, instead of a cluster of human biological material. It is as if the punctualist thesis pictures a policy-maker engaged in the enterprise of line-drawing as being like the protagonist in an action movie who is forced to decide whether to snip the red or blue wire of a ticking bomb, with nothing to choose between them and everything on the line. It is possible to see how this picture of what is entailed by settling on a threshold of personhood can make the sorites problem significant in a way that it is not in the context of other vague thresholds, like the difference between night time and dusk.

5.5 Personhood Continuums

I have just sketched two competing conceptions of the emergence of personhood at the beginning of human life and some rough implications of what I am calling the 'punctualist' thesis. It is possible to see why someone committed to the punctualist thesis would worry about arbitrariness of the sorites kind at the threshold of personhood and might, for that reason, want to reject any putative threshold which cannot be non-arbitrarily pinpointed, even though, as I have said, this would present problems for all possible thresholds. I believe, however, that there are good reasons to reject the punctualist thesis and to accept its antithesis, gradualism.

The main challenge to punctualism can be put in the form of an adapted version of a thought-experiment proposed by the philosopher Derek Parfit, originally used in the service of defending a particular view of personal identity, or, what it means to remain the same person over a period of time.[24] Let me call the adapted experiment the 'Brain Cell Spectrum'. It runs as follows:

The 'Brain Cell Spectrum'
Consider a range of cases along a continuum. On the near end there is an uncontroversial example of a non-person, let us say, a human being that is irrevocably and completely brain-dead, kept alive only by an artificial ventilation machine. On the far end is a clear case of a person, let us say a mature, normally functioning human being. Suppose that scientists have developed the capability to replace every cell of a brain-dead human's brain, one by one, with exact replicas of the brain cells as they were when they were alive. In the case on the nearest end of the continuum, they replace only 1 per cent of the dead cells with functioning, living ones. In each subsequent case the doctors continue to replace more cells at a time—40 per cent, 60 per cent, 70 per cent—until in the case at the far end there are none of the original dead cells left and the human being has the normal brain functioning of a living, adult human being.

Suppose we are convinced that what started out at the near end of the spectrum as a non-person is, at the far end of the spectrum, clearly a person. What are we to say in all the intermediate variations, where the scientists replace 10 per cent, 40 per cent, or 90 per cent of brain cells cloned from the human? If we accept the punctualist thesis, we must believe that one particular variation marks the point when a human body has become a person. And we would have to say that, for any given variation along the continuum, the individual has either completely acquired the property of personhood, or he has not. Yet it is hard to believe that there exists any sharp point—any critical percentage of brain cell substitution—which is responsible for such a dramatic change. If one simply cannot entertain the idea that personhood is gained instantaneously and entirely with a single percentage variation, there will be ground for serious scepticism about punctualism.

It is irrelevant to the point being made here that the brain experiment is technically impossible. The mere fact that we could not justify identifying the beginning of personhood with a single variation in the abstract hypothetical still reveals something

---

[24] Derek Parfit, *Reasons and Persons* (Oxford University Press 1984).

about the plausibility of the punctualist thesis. If we *were* committed to that thesis, we should be able to say quite confidently that one of the variations marks the attainment of personhood, however impossible such an experiment might be. But one could also posit a less fantastical version of a 'Brain Cell Spectrum' by inverting the example. In the inverted version, the near end is the case of a human being with a fully functioning brain, whose brain cells die off rapidly one at a time until, at the far end, we are left with an irrevocably brain-dead human being. Again it does not seem plausible to identify the end of the person with the death of any particular cell, although it is evident that the organism at the far end is not a person and that the organism at the near end *is* one. Our reactions to these cases show that we struggle to accept the 'existential pop' idea, particularly because it does not seem reasonable to identify that existential pop with any one of the minute brain variations.

A defender of the conception threshold might object here that brain functioning is not, on her view, the criterion of personhood; genetic humanity is. Being a creature with a set of human DNA, she might argue, is not a question of degree. Thus, the person-making feature, the human genome, *does* have a sharp borderline. Firstly, however, it must be understood that endorsing a species membership criterion of personhood cannot evade the problems of vagueness showing up on the 'Brain Cell Spectrum'. The human being in question has a full set of human genes both at the near and far ends of the continuum. Unless the proponent of punctualism is going to say that that the subject *is* a person at the near end, even when irreversibly brain-dead, he will have to say that somewhere along the continuum the human being transforms suddenly into a person (or vice versa, in the case of someone dying one brain cell at a time). And this is the very thing which it seems unreasonable to say.

Secondly, even if we grant that species membership itself is not a question of degree, *the coming into existence* of a new individual human life form is still clearly gradual. As we have seen, conception is a process like everything else. New, genetically complete human beings come into existence through a succession of infinitesimal events that are non-arbitrarily distinguishable from immediately adjacent events. The advocate of punctualism would still be forced to make the improbable claim that one of these tiny microphysical developments is the sharp borderline between persons and non-persons. Yet the choice between fractional developments here seems just as unintelligible, if not more so, than the choice between brain cell percentages.

However, vagueness can surround the very criterion of species membership as well, at least in theory. To illustrate this, let me introduce another spectrum thought-experiment, formulated by Jeff McMahan:

The 'Transgenic Spectrum'
The Spectrum begins with a chimpanzee zygote that has an unaltered genome. In the next case, a single human gene is inserted into a chimpanzee zygote and a chimp one swapped out. In the third case, two human genes are inserted. In each case further along in the spectrum, one more human gene is inserted while the corresponding chimpanzee gene is deleted. Thus, at the far end of the spectrum is a case in which *all* of the chimpanzee genes are replaced by corresponding genes from a human source, and the creature is fully human.

In all cases the genetically altered zygote is implanted in a natural or artificial uterus and thereafter allowed to grow to adulthood.[25]

McMahan surmises that 'individuals at one end of the spectrum with only a tiny proportion of human genes are unambiguously chimpanzees' and that 'those at the other end with only a tiny proportion of chimpanzee genes are unambiguously human beings'. And this certainly seems to be true.[26] He offers the 'Transgenic Spectrum' as a straightforward argument against treating human species membership as a 'source of moral status'. He asks whether it can be plausible that the moral status of any individual creature on the spectrum can depend solely on having a 'sufficiently high proportion of human genes to count as a member of the human species'. He answers that it is not. In particular, he thinks it difficult to believe that an individual on the spectrum whose genes have given it the brain of a dull chimpanzee should come within strong moral protection simply because a sufficient proportion of its *other* genes are human, or that such an individual should be treated any differently from a neighbour on the spectrum whose proportion of human genes *just* fell short of making it overall human, even though its brain functions more like that of a human than that of a chimpanzee. This is intended to demonstrate that moral status is not a matter of human genetics per se.

McMahan worries it may be mistakenly inferred that he is claiming there must be some sharp borderline between the human and the non-human in the spectrum experiment. That he is not. Rather, he is claiming only that, whether the property of 'being genetically human' is a matter of degree or not, it seems that membership in the human species itself is not the morally salient feature of creatures who have claims against being harmed for certain reasons. The humanity of the transgenic creatures will clearly vary if it attaches to their brute proportion of human genes, yet this does not appear to be the real basis on which we should morally distinguish between them. The creatures that are more valuable than others along the spectrum will be so in virtue of their enhanced cognitive capacities, not their pure number of human genes relative to chimp ones.

My own use of the 'Transgenic Spectrum' is meant to demonstrate something different. I want to assume for the moment that we have good reason to believe moral status supervenes on human species membership rather than on something else, like cognitive capacities. Granting this, I believe our reactions to the 'Transgenic Spectrum' suggest that the punctualist thesis is still difficult to believe. We must ask what the punctualist would have to say about the spectrum. It seems he will have to assert that one of the minute variations along the spectrum marks the difference between being a person and not being a person. But this is precisely what it is hard to accept. With which additional human gene does the transformation take place? There is no reason to believe of any single gene that *it* rather than another makes such a huge difference. Is it the substitution of the *last* chimp gene for a human one that brings a person into existence? It is hard to find reasons for this as well. Before the substitution of that final gene, the creature is only *barely* less human than it was

---

[25] Jeff McMahan, 'Infanticide' (2007) 19 Utilitas 131, 146.   [26] ibid 146–7.

before. It is far more human than it is chimp. So it will be tough to argue that the sharp borderline between persons and non-persons is the addition of that last gene. Needless to say, the same challenge will arise whichever additional gene is proposed as the borderline.[27]

Defenders of the species membership criterion of personhood may retort that the 'Transgenic Spectrum' has little bearing on their appraisal of abortion, since, if they are right, all embryos and fetuses will nevertheless warrant strong protection, being genetically complete human beings. But this would be to miss the lesson from the spectrum experiment. The point is not that hypothetical vague cases of human beings preclude clear cases. Obviously they do not. What the spectrum shows is that, whether the species membership criterion is correct or not, punctualism is nonetheless difficult to defend, since it seems clearly to be the case both that there are examples of persons and non-persons along the spectrum, and that no individual variation marks that difference. And if punctualism is not believable, as its implications for the spectrum suggests, then it cannot be relied upon by defenders of the conception threshold to disqualify later thresholds of personhood on the ground of sorites-susceptibility.

Does punctualism seem more credible if the criterion for personhood is switched to some particularly high level of sentience, characteristic only of developed humans? Let us amend the spectrum accordingly:

The 'Sentience Spectrum'
A serum has been invented which, when injected into kittens, can heighten their sentience and eventually transform them into beings that are as rational and self-aware as typical humans. If a full dose of the serum is injected, the kitten will acquire the ability for self-awareness and higher thinking equal to that of a mature human being. If only one drop of serum is injected, the kitten will become just *slightly* more self-conscious and rational than it was before. If all but the last drop of serum is injected, the kitten will be almost as fully sentient as a typical human being—only *slightly* less self-aware and rationally capacitous. A scientist injects a kitten with one drop of the standard dose at a time. With every additional drop, the kitten increases in sentience until, with the addition of the final drop, it is brought up to the same sentience level as the typical adult human. There are 100 drops in the standard dose.[28]

If punctualism is correct, what follows about the kitten's acquisition of personhood on the 'Sentience Spectrum'? At the near end of the spectrum, the kitten is certainly not a person, and at the far end it certainly is one. Again, if punctualism is true, one would have to hold that at all intermediate points on the spectrum, the kitten either is or is not yet fully and completely a person. One must believe that at all points, the question 'is this kitten a person *now*?' has a determinate, all-or-nothing kind of an answer, and moreover, that there is some additional drop of serum—a

---

[27] Although the thought-experiment is merely theoretical, the existence of grey areas between species which the 'Transgenic Spectrum' demonstrates are not at all fantastical, see John Dupré, 'Natural Kinds and Biological Taxa' (1981) 90 Philosophical Review 66.

[28] The example is an adaptation of a thought-experiment constructed by Michael Tooley (Tooley (n 10) 60–1).

critical quantity—which corresponds with the beginning of personhood. Yet again, it is hard to believe when surveying the spectrum that any of these things are true, because there is no ground for believing that it could be true of any particular drop of serum.

It is worth emphasizing that the purely theoretical nature of these thought-experiments does not diminish their usefulness in drawing out clashes between what follows from punctualism and what it is reasonable to believe about person-hood's emergence. If we really believed that there is a sharp borderline between human material and persons, we could comfortably claim that *if* any of these hypo-thetical continuums were possible, there would be a precise variation with which personhood begins, even if we cannot say for sure which it is. But it is exactly this claim that the spectrum thought-experiments show to be implausible, for there is simply no reason to believe that a sharp borderline exists between any two neigh-bouring variations on any of the spectrums.

Interestingly, the existence of sorites arbitrariness between the variations in the spectrums is the very thing which makes punctualism seem so unreasonable. The sorites-susceptibility of each individual point on the personhood continuums cuts against the belief that personhood begins at a non-arbitrarily distinguishable 'moment'. None of this shows punctualism to be utterly incoherent. It *might* still be true that in each of the spectrums there is a sharp borderline when personhood obtains or vanishes. It is simply difficult to square that notion with the fact that there is no single increment on the spectrum of brain-functioning, genetic human-ity, or sentience, which it seems reasonable to think marks the sudden emergence or disappearance of a person.

Finally, the very same judgements which place the punctualist thesis in doubt also seem to lend some measure of support to the gradualist thesis. To reiterate, the central tenet of gradualism is that personhood at the beginning of life emerges pro-gressively, and that personhood status can, therefore, be indeterminate at points. Gradualism does not posit a single point of complete metaphysical change. It sup-poses, to the contrary, that no such moment exists. The spectrum experiments show that whichever properties upon which personhood is thought to supervene, *physical or psychological*, it does not seem to admit of sharp boundaries.

6

Dualism, Substantial Identity, and the Precautionary Principle

6.1 What Would Make Punctualism True?

In the last chapter, I suggested that there is good reason to favour the gradualist view of personhood's emergence at the beginning of life over the punctualist one. I did not claim, however, that punctualism is incoherent or impossible. It *could* conceivably be true that the beginning of personhood in an early human being is like an 'existential pop'. It is only that what this commits us to holding in the personhood continuums makes it difficult to believe.

But perhaps there is nevertheless a basis for accepting the punctualist thesis. It is worth asking what, if anything, would make punctualism true. More specifically, I want to consider whether any particular view about the nature of personhood and the sort of quality it is might lead to the punctualist thesis, and whether there is any good reason to accept those further commitments.

As part of their rejection of all 'developmental' (or, post-conception) theories about the beginning of personhood, Robert P George and Christopher Tollefsen argue that such accounts rely on an incoherent and erroneous conception of the kind of fact personhood is.[1] They first reiterate their claim that all post-conception thresholds make arbitrary determinations (ones which they do not believe the conception threshold has to make) between degrees of maturation which cannot be morally distinguished. Consequently, they think it an implicit claim of developmental views that what makes a human being a person is ultimately a *decision* or *stipulation* by an individual or society as a whole that personhood obtains at a particular point—a point deemed pragmatically desirable or appropriate.

The authors call this the 'Attribution View'.[2] They attack the Attribution View for being hopelessly relativistic on the question of when and if personhood ever obtains, making it possible that two people holding contradictory views on the question could both be right. They say:

But any view that holds, in regard to some type of claim or other, that there are no facts, no 'right answers,' but that answers, knowledge or truth are merely a matter of decision,

---

[1] Robert P George and Christopher Tollefsen, *Embryo: A Defense of Human Life* (Doubleday 2008).
[2] ibid 124.

Arguments about Abortion: Personhood, Morality, and Law. First Edition. Kate Greasley. © K. Greasley 2017. Published 2017 by Oxford University Press.

radically removes the possibility of error by making virtually every answer the right one. And this, in turn, radically eliminates, it seems to us, any possible motivation for studying biology or any other area of science.[3]

The suggestion that the Attribution View relativizes *science* is both odd and telling, for up to that point in their discussion the authors are considering conflicting accounts of the beginning of philosophical personhood, or of 'human being' in the morally meaningful sense, not of biological facts. It is therefore difficult to know what they have in mind when they refer to personhood as a biological or scientific category here. Of course, even some scientific categorizations must ultimately be decided by stipulation, such as the determination of whether Pluto is a planet or a large asteroid. No one thinks that the need for stipulation at the outer limits of astrological classifications means that the classification 'planet' is not a scientific one, that it is ungoverned by rules, or relativistic. Yet George and Tollefsen appear to believe that any need to stipulate a precise beginning of personhood within a certain margin has precisely these implications.

What would make their suggestion that the need for stipulation 'radically removes the possibility of error' about the beginning of personhood intelligible? Again, the claim here seems to assume the punctualist thesis is true, so far as it presupposes that there *is* a non-arbitrarily distinguishable 'moment' when persons begin. But it also seems to imply a very particular view about what kind of property personhood is—a view which, in turn, could help make the punctualist thesis explicable.

Consider the question: 'Is *this* fetus a person?' What is the answer to that question like? One view might conceive of the answer as being like one contained in a sealed envelope. When discussants attempt to give an answer, they are really guessing, albeit making reasoned guesses, at what is contained in the envelope. Moreover, each guess will be determinately right or wrong even if the answer inside the envelope can never be revealed—even if it remains permanently sealed with indissoluble super glue. On this view, the personhood status of a fetus is a completely independently existing fact. It is not a moral quality which simply supervenes on one or more physical or psychological properties, like human species membership, or consciousness, or rationality. It is a quality that has, in a sense, an autonomous kind of existence, completely set apart from all other facts about creatures which possess personhood status.

What I have described is a kind of non-reductionist view of personhood. The view suggests that the property of personhood is not reducible to other facts about human beings, but is instead separate from and further to them. The easiest route to this kind of belief about personhood is the claim that personhood consists in something supernatural (in the sense of being beyond and outside of the physical world, not in the sense of being spooky), like my body being possessed by a soul or some other 'immaterial substance', such as a Cartesian pure ego. Philosophers know this belief as *dualism*, famously described by Gilbert Ryle as the 'ghost in

[3] ibid 130.

the machine' idea. On the dualist picture, persons are immaterial substances that inhabit human bodies but are not reducible to or identical with those bodies. They may be operating the bodies—pulling the levers, so to speak—but they are, in the most basic way, something set apart from them.

The dualist view of persons and the kind of non-reductionism about person-hood that it entails seem to fit well with the punctualist thesis. Firstly, if person-hood consists in *this* kind of a fact, the fact about whether an immaterial substance is yet inhabiting a human body, it would suggest that the question 'is X a person yet?' is in every case like the answer in the sealed envelope: separate and independently existing. If personhood consists in the possession of a soul or some other immaterial substance, irreducible to and non-identical with our human bodies, it also seems to follow that persons begin absolutely and completely, even if there is insurmountable uncertainty about exactly *when* they begin. It is easy to see why someone committed to dualism might embrace the punctualist thesis about how persons begin. Immaterial person substances like souls or Cartesian egos are not thought to obtain in degrees. On the dualist view, personhood seems to be all or nothing and immediately occurring. Consequently, for any given moment in the development of a new human, it is always either determinately true or false that a person has come into being: has the existential pop happened yet or not? It is possible to see why someone committed to dualism would be minded to look for a sharp threshold with which to identify the beginning of personhood, and to eschew any threshold that fails to pick out a non-arbitrarily distinguishable 'point' of moral import. If persons are separately existing immaterial substances, we will presumably want to know, and know with some degree of certainty, when those substances come to exist in human organisms. The absence of a good explanation for why a person substance has not begun to exist shortly before a putative thresh-old of personhood will be deeply disconcerting, especially where that threshold is used as a cut-off point for abortion. In summation then, this non-reductionist view of personhood suggests that there is no vagueness surrounding the beginning of persons, except of the epistemic kind.

6.2 Dualism

It is worth noting at this stage that George and Tollefsen do not support a dual-ist conception of persons. In fact, the refutation of dualism is a key move in their defence of the conception threshold of personhood. We will see more on this pres-ently. Still, we can see why those who subscribe to some form of dualism could be committed to the punctualist thesis about the emergence of personhood. 'Immaterial substances', like souls or Cartesian egos, are not usually thought to obtain in degrees or admit of vagueness at the margins. They are either there, or they are not. The immaterial substance view is, needless to say, difficult to prove or disprove. Many people have great difficulty believing that once they come to exist as a subject of consciousness, they, or their essence, could ever cease to exist, even once their body and brain are dead and gone. But the mere fact that our imaginations falter when contemplating our own disappearance from existence is not good evidence for the belief that persons are immaterial substances.[4] Even so, it is difficult to imagine what a hard disproof of that proposition would look like. How could one show that intangible person essences do *not* exist?

Convincing arguments have nonetheless been proposed that challenge the dualist conception of persons. One possible problem, pointed out both by philosophers and scientists, is that the 'immaterial substance' belief is not required to explain the manifestation of typical 'person-like' traits, such as self-awareness and rationality, in human beings. Neuroscience has an explanation for the manifestation of these capacities, based in the physical properties of the human brain. This is why those capacities are destroyed or damaged when, for instance, brains are injured in accidents, or fail to develop properly because of congenital defects. One puzzle for the dualist view asks why it is, if the mental states possessed by persons (like self-awareness and intelligent thinking) are produced by an immaterial substance transcending human anatomy, that those states are affected by purely physical changes, like brain injury or drug use. Presumably, the immaterial substance thought to be responsible for mental states is not affected itself by physical changes.[5] We might wonder, therefore, if dualism is true, why physical events that happen to the brain would alter those capacities.

A possible dualist answer to this problem might be that, on the dualist conception, the psychological capacities of the animal being in which person substances reside are in fact separate from the immaterial person substance. They are possessed by the animal, the physical being, not by the person. Thus, we should expect them to be affected by physical events. This does not imply that dualism is false.

But this answer introduces a different problem for dualism highlighted by philosophers of mind. This concerns what dualism must hold about the conscious life of the human animal that the ghostly substance inhabits. Is the suggestion that the 'host' human body, complete with a sophisticated brain, is not itself a thinking being? If this is true, and if only humans are persons, then humans are the only sophisticated mammals whose large cerebral cortexes do not generate conscious life. On the other hand, if both the immaterial 'person' substance and the 'host' human animal are thinking beings, it follows that every mature human being possesses not one but *two* subjects of consciousness, a notion which is quite extraordinary. How would each of us even know if we were the thinking person or the thinking animal? There would be no way of telling. This is known as the 'too many thinkers' problem.[6]

---

[4] For an inconceivably long stretch of time, none of us *did* exist as subjects of consciousness, from which fact alone it must be accepted that it is possible for persons to exist at one time and not at another.

[5] For a detailed exposition of this problem, see Paul Churchland, *Matter and Consciousness* (Revised edn, MIT Press) 30–33.

[6] For a fuller explanation, see Eric T Olson, *The Human Animal: Personal Identity Without Psychology* (Oxford University Press 1999) and Eric T Olson, ' "Personal Identity", entry in the Stanford Encyclopaedia of Philosophy' http://plato.stanford.edu/entries/identity-personal/ (last accessed 10 October 2016).

These may be good reasons for doubting the dualist account of personhood in the absence of compelling evidence for believing it. However, it is not my intention here to make a firm case against dualism. This is because it may not even be necessary to establish the falsity of the 'immaterial substance' belief in order to refute the punctualist thesis, or challenge its use in defence of the conception threshold of personhood.

First, even if the dualist picture of persons is correct, it is still not entirely clear that it entails the punctualist thesis about the beginning of personhood. Let us assume for the sake of argument that persons *are* immaterial conscious substances that inhabit and animate human bodies. Must such substances come into existence immediately and wholly? Could they too not emerge incrementally, like the biological or psychological properties that human beings possess? If immaterial person substances of the kind did exist, perhaps the very fact that the sorts of psychological capacities for which those substances are thought to be responsible themselves emerge gradually is good reason for believing that the same is true of the immaterial substances responsible for them.

Secondly, even if the punctualist thesis necessarily follows from dualism, does it follow from dualism that the 'existential pop' must occur at some time during the process of conception, and not at any later stage of human development? There is no reason that I can think of for believing that dualism implies this, and therefore that dualism supports the conception threshold of personhood. We must look further, then, for a persuasive argument that the beginning of personhood in humans is contemporaneous with conception.

6.3 Personhood Essentialism and the Argument from Substantial Identity

One such argument begins with a proposition which, along with others, George and Tollefsen advance in support of the conception threshold. This is *personhood essentialism*, or the belief that personhood is an essential property of all creatures that are persons. Personhood essentialism has been relied on extensively in antiabortion philosophy in defence of the view that all human. beings are persons from conception.

Philosophers who rely on this claim draw a distinction between 'accidental' and 'essential' characteristics of individuals. An accidental characteristic is a trait which an individual could either possess or lack whilst still being the same thing. I would still be me if I did not play the guitar but enjoyed ballroom dancing instead. Essential characteristics, on the other hand, are qualities without which an individual or object would not be the same basic thing that it is. It is an essential property of mine that I have the biological parents I actually have; I could not have had different biological parents and still be me. George and Tollefsen use a different example to illustrate the distinction.[7] They claim it is an essential property of a dog,

---

[7] George and Tollefsen (n 1) 58–9.

Rufus, that he belongs to the kind 'dog'. Rufus will not cease to exist if he ceases to possess the ability to run, or loses his teeth, but he could never exist as something that is not a dog; that is an essential property of his.

'Personhood essentialism' states that the property of 'being a person' is essential, not accidental. For George and Tollefsen, this means that the same human being could not be a person at one time and not at another. This is because to lose or gain the property of personhood means becoming a different thing altogether. Nothing could lose or gain that property without simply going out of existence, just like a dog cannot cease to be a dog and persist as the same thing. Consequently, it is argued, if I am a person now, I must always *have been* a person from the very beginning of my existence. And since I began to exist as an individual entity at conception, I must have been a person from conception.

The argument rehearsed here by George and Tollefsen is recurrently used by defenders of the conception threshold of personhood. Sometimes termed the 'substantial identity' argument, it is in large part an argument about the possibility of *substantial change*: the possibility that an object or an individual can change in respect of a substantial—meaning, an *essential*—characteristic, and still remain the same basic thing. Those who, like George and Tollefsen, defend the conception threshold by appeal to the substantial identity argument hold that an individual or object cannot change substantially and continue to exist. When this premise is joined with personhood essentialism, and with the belief that 'we' are identical with biological organisms which began at conception, it supposedly yields the conclusion that the beginning of personhood is contemporaneous with conception. Conception is when all human beings begin to exist biologically, so if essential or 'substantial' change is impossible, and personhood is an essential characteristic, all adult human beings must have been persons from the very beginning of their existence.

From here, the task of conception threshold advocates seems, to them, to be fairly straightforward. All they need show is that human beings do in fact begin to exist as individually identifiable organisms at conception and their work is done. Once this is established, the argument from substantial identity demonstrates that, in George and Tollefsen's words, all Homo sapiens 'have always been persons, and will cease to be persons only when [they] cease to be, by dying'.[8]

What it means to 'remain the same thing over time' in the context of the substantial identity argument is not always perspicuous. In George and Tollefsen's iteration, it seems they mean to say that a human being cannot change essentially and be *numerically identical* with her earlier self. An object at an earlier time is said to be numerically identical with an object at a later time if it is one and the same thing with the later object. Numerical identity can be contrasted with *qualitative* identity, where two objects are exactly alike in all of their properties but remain separate individual things, like two separate but exactly similar apples. The substantial identity argument starts out by presupposing that zygotes, embryos, and

---

[8] ibid 81.

fetuses (but not the sex cells which created them) are numerically identical with the mature human beings they will or might later become; they are the same individual *things*. I, for instance, am numerically identical with my fetus-self; it was me and I am it. It then runs from the claim that personhood is an essential property to the conclusion that zygotes, embryos, and fetuses must be persons. This is because of their numerical identity with mature human beings and because of the impossibility of substantial change.[9] If I am identical with my fetus-self, and I am a person now, then I must have been a person as a fetus, since personhood essentialism holds that my fetus-self and I cannot be numerically identical without possessing all of the same essential properties.

The argument can be broken down as follows then:

1. A being cannot change substantially (or essentially) and remain the same individual thing.
2. Mature human beings are numerically identical with the zygotes and embryos which begat them. I was once a fetus and that fetus was me.
3. Personhood is an essential property of all creatures which are persons, thus,
4. C1: If I am a person, so was the zygote, embryo, and fetus which were identical with me, and
5. C2: I *am* a person, therefore so was the zygote, embryo, and fetus from whence I came.

We should note that nothing about the substantial identity argument and personhood essentialism implies punctualism. That is, it does not entail that the beginning of personhood is a sharp threshold, or that conception is such a threshold. Rather, it argues that the kinds of creatures that can be persons at *some point* must be persons from the beginning of their existence, which, in the case of human beings, is conception. It is compatible with this argument to think that persons also fade into existence non-instantaneously, as newly conceived zygotes come into being. The significant conclusion is only that, once clearly in existence, those newly conceived zygotes must be persons since they are numerically identical with later persons and given that personhood is an essential property.

We can see from all of this that the argument will fail if any one of the following propositions is true:

1. Substantial change is possible.
2. Mature human beings are not numerically identical with the zygotes that begat them; I was *never* a zygote.
3. Personhood is not an essential property of mature human beings.

---

[9] It is probably immaterial to the argument that the fetus's identity with the later human-person would be only theoretical if the fetus were fated to die before it becomes that human. For the argument might be read as seeking to establish that fetuses as a kind must possess the same essential properties as mature human beings they are able to develop into, given that all mature human beings were once fetuses.

The first alternative—the possibility of substantial change—is reflected by Warren Quinn's 'process theory' of the way morally considerable persons begin.[10] This theory states that basic kinds of things such as persons could fade in and out of existence gradually. Just as we might perceive that something which is basically and essentially a house might come into existence *as a house* slowly during the process of construction, so Quinn suggests that the coming-to-be of things that are substantially persons may be a process during which human beings are at different times more or less complete versions of the same basic kind of thing. If, whilst going through this construction process, the thing retains its numerical identity, then substantial change will be possible. The same individual which is only a person-in-process at one stage will be a person at another. As Quinn argues, there are certain basic kinds which it only seems accurate to describe as partial instantiations of something else, like a *house-under-construction*. If the same human being is a person-in-process at one stage and a person at another, then it will have changed substantially whilst remaining the same thing numerically.

Alternatively, it might not be true that personhood is an essential property of all beings which are persons. This is alternative 3. Many will maintain that personhood is only an accidental property of mature human beings, similar to the ability to play a musical instrument. If this were true, it would be coherent to hold that the same human being goes through phases of being a person and not being a person throughout its existence, whilst remaining the same numerical thing. Again, the fact that quintessentially 'person-like' traits such as self-awareness and consciousness do come and go in human beings might only bolster the claim that personhood is an accidental property. Quinn calls this the 'stage theory' of personhood. The stage theory holds that a human organism can remain the same (numerically identical) thing whilst going through distinct stages of lacking personhood and possessing it.

One question that might be asked of George and Tollefsen is whether they believe there are any qualities *other* than personhood that typical, mature human beings possess essentially. Could it not be an essential characteristic of someone that she is a mother, or that she is deaf? If these too are essential characteristics, they at least are clearly able to appear and disappear in the same human being. If the claim is rather that personhood is the *only* essential characteristic of human beings, we will require some further explanation as to why human beings can change in innumerable ways and remain the same numerical thing, yet cannot change in this one respect. What is so special about personhood that it, but absolutely nothing else about human beings, is like that?

What about the second alternative? The critic of the substantial identity argument might instead respond by just denying that mature human beings are in fact numerically identical with the embryos and fetuses that produced them, if numerical identity is taken to imply substantial identity. The later human beings, she might say, are basically *different* beings from the earlier life forms. Consequently,

---

[10] Warren Quinn, 'Abortion: Identity and Loss' (1984) 13 Philosophy and Public Affairs 24.

personhood could be an essential property of the mature human being without being a property of the earlier human organism. For proponents of the substantial identity argument, this response is taken as a challenge to defend the claim that fetuses are indeed identical with the mature human beings they become, although it is interesting to observe where this takes their argument.

Along with others who defend the conception threshold this way,[11] George and Tollefsen believe that their task here is to *refute* the dualist conception of persons—the view that 'we' are ghostly substances inhabiting human machines—and they devote an entire chapter of their book to doing so. This is because of what they take dualism to imply about the conditions for persisting identity. If 'we' are basically immaterial substances, it seems that we could come and go from our human bodies and, consequently, that we are not identical with those bodies. If this were true, it would *not* follow from personhood essentialism that all human beings, including zygotes, are persons (or in other words, that humans are persons from the very beginning of their existence), since human beings would never be identical with person substances. Persons and the human bodies they inhabit would be two separate numerical things, not one and the same. Consequently, the 'ghost in the machine' might exist in the machine at one time and not another, and there is no reason to think that human organisms are persons at every stage of their existence, even if personhood essentialism is true.

Following this thinking, George and Tollefsen bring a whole selection of arguments to attack the credibility of dualism and endorse the antithetical view that we—the subjects of consciousness with which we identify ourselves—are identical with our human bodies, a view known as 'animalism'. If we are one and the same thing as our human bodies and *not* immaterial substances, then we begin to exist when those bodies do, which, they argue, owing to biological continuity, is conception. And if we are essentially persons, then so were the zygotes with which we are identical.

It is in some ways strange, though, that the authors believe their argument for the conception threshold turns on the triumph of animalism over dualism. Firstly, the animalist criterion for persisting identity over time does not establish the truth of personhood essentialism, the main premise that George and Tollefsen need to be true. To claim that we are our bodies, and that the conditions for our continued existence as the same thing over time are merely biological, is to claim only that we are the same numerical things as the zygotes and embryos which begat us, not that being a person is an essential property of any personhood-possessing thing. The authors conclude their discussion of animalism by stating that it (unlike dualism) is not 'in tension' with the view that we are essentially persons.[12] But it does not entail that view either. Animalism is also compatible with the suggestion that human

---

[11] See also Christopher Robert Kaczor, *The Ethics of Abortion: Women's Rights, Human Life, and the Question of Justice* (Routledge 2011) 102–21; Patrick Lee, *Abortion and Unborn Human Life* (2nd edn, Catholic University of America Press 2010) 33–45 and Baruch A Brody, *Abortion and the Sanctity of Human Life: A Philosophical View* (MIT Press 1975) 134–44.
[12] George and Tollefsen (n 1) 81.

beings *acquire* the property of personhood at some stage in their development. Animalism claims that the criterion for persisting identity is bodily continuity, not that personhood is an essential property. Thus, on animalism, the later human beings might still be persons even if the earlier ones are not.

In making the case for animalism, George and Tollefsen rely on an argument put forward by one of its chief proponents, Eric Olson. Olson calls it 'the fetus problem'.[13] Put succinctly, the problem is that if we are *not* identical with our bodies (if animalism is not true), but instead with a substance or with mental states which animate that body, it follows that the fetuses we came from must go out of existence in order for *us* to materialize. Before the immaterial substance or mental states exist, the fetus is certainly an identifiable thing. But if the thing that it is—human material—cannot be identified with the later person, it seems that it must somehow just disappear when 'we' arrive on the scene. This seems to be clearly wrong. It is apparent to most people that fetuses are one and the same thing with the persons they turn into, not that the early human being simply ceases to exist when the person arrives (And where would it have gone? It certainly did not die).

But George and Tollefsen omit to mention that on Olson's account, the 'fetus problem' is not taken to show that all biological human beings are persons from conception—that *we* were always persons. Quite the opposite. Olson thinks it plain that if the criterion of numerical identity is biological, the fetus may just come to be a person 'the same way it may later come to be a musician or a philosopher'.[14] For Olson, the animalist view of identity *solves* the fetus problem by explaining that fetuses and the mature human beings they turn into are identical with one another solely in virtue of their physical continuity, even though the later organisms may be persons and the earlier organisms not. In other words, animalism is as compatible with the 'stage theory' of personhood as dualism.

Dualism need not, in fact, be in any tension with the view that 'we' are essentially persons, depending only on how the 'we' is defined. If the 'we' that is being identified here is the immaterial person substance, then it is certainly clear that *this* substance does not at any time lack the property of being a person. Given that it is this substance with which dualism takes me—my subject of consciousness—to be identified, and that this is a separate numerical thing from the human animal it inhabits, it follows from dualism that personhood essentialism could still be true, and that 'we' have always been persons. But it will not follow that all human organisms—separate numerical things—are persons from conception.

Next, the truth of animalism does not prove the impossibility of substantial change, another thing George and Tollefsen need to be true. If substantial change is possible, then the fetus *can* gradually become an essentially different kind of thing—a person, not just a human being—without going out of existence altogether and being replaced by something else, the same way that a caterpillar metamorphoses into a butterfly, a different sort of creature, whilst persisting as the

[13] Eric T Olson, 'Was I Ever a Fetus?' (1997) 57 Philosophy and Phenomenological Research 95.
[14] ibid 106.

same numerical thing. As H Tristram Engelhardt argued, we cannot just *presuppose* substantial continuity from conception to death.[15] Maybe substantial change is just part of the life cycle of human beings. The problem of how things can change whilst also remaining the same thing is a philosophical issue that naturally extends far beyond the abortion debate. George and Tollefsen clearly do not mean to deny the possibility of all change, but only of substantial change. Things, they say, cannot change in respect of their *essential* properties and remain the same thing, which is just the same as saying that things cannot change essentially, full stop.

But we will still require an explanation for why things can change in all sorts of respects whilst retaining their numerical identity but cannot change in other 'essential' respects, as well as some account of what makes a property 'essential' as opposed to 'accidental'. It seems to be true both that a caterpillar does change substantially when it metamorphoses into a butterfly *and* that the caterpillar and butterfly are the same numerical thing, just as someone might think it seems obviously true both that the fetus and the developed human being it transforms into are one and the same thing, *and* that this individual undergoes a substantial change when it turns into a thinking, self-conscious being. It may be replied that it is just part and parcel of something's being an essential property that the same being cannot possess it at one time and not at another, and that if anything is an essential property, personhood surely is. But if a belief in essential properties commits us to accepting something that seems dubious—such as that the same individual cannot be a person at one time and not at another—we should not rule out the possibility that the belief rests on a mistake. Perhaps no essential properties of this kind really exist.

In a different vein, one might argue instead that the criterion of continuing numerical identity over time, whatever it is, is the *only* essential property which we possess, since that criterion is the only thing in virtue of which we remain the same individual thing over time. This, to me, just seems to follow from the nature of the inquiry into the persistence conditions for numerical identity. Another way to pose that question would be just to ask what is that one property which, so long as it persists in an individual, means that the individual remains one and the same thing over time. If George and Tollefsen are correct in supporting biological continuity as the criterion of persisting numerical identity (as I suspect they are), this would imply that our animal bodies are our *only* essential properties, and that our moral status as persons is, hence, a non-essential one. Only if we are numerically identical not with our human bodies but with a separate person substance, the crux of the dualist view, would it seem to follow that there can be no time in our existence that we were not persons. But even if this were true, it does not entail that all *human beings* are persons throughout their existence. For, once we swap the criterion of numerical identity for the one we get on the dualist picture, it is perfectly coherent to hold that we, the immaterial substance, always remain the same thing, but that not every living human body is at all times animated by an immaterial substance.

---

[15] H Tristram Engelhardt, Jr, 'The Ontology of Abortion' (1974) [University of Chicago Press] 84 Ethics 223.

6.4 Quantitative Properties

Attacking the credibility of dualism is a somewhat surpising move by defenders of the conception threshold given the fact that, as I recounted, dualism is the only view about the nature of personhood that even appears to lend credence to the punctualist thesis, and hence, to the kind of arbitrariness critique of other personhood thresholds defenders of the conception threshold often put forward. If personhood is not an immaterial substance like a soul or an ego, but instead just supervenes on other physical or mental base properties, it ceases to be clear what reason anyone might have for suspecting that the beginning of personhood is an 'existential pop', rather than the gradual fading in of a quality. Whatever those base properties are believed to be, *they* certainly come into existence gradually, and this is as true of species membership as of anything else because of the progressive nature of conception. Unless some one is committed to the belief that persons begin when immaterial substances animate human material, what reason would he have to believe that they begin wholly and instantaneously? And if there is no good reason to accept punctualism, sorites-susceptibility will not be a legitimate critique of any theory of emerging personhood.

But George and Tollefsen may object that this misses the emphasis of their own argument. In fact, they state explicitly that to read their argument against all post-conception thresholds of personhood as a form of sorites paradox is a misunderstanding.[16] They attribute this misunderstanding to Michael Sandel's criticism of their position.[17] Sandel suggests that their arbitrariness objection to post-conception thresholds of personhood mirrors the problem of the heap in which, we saw, someone is asked to specify which individual grain of sand makes the difference between a non-heap and a heap.[18] Sandel rightly points out that the mere fact that the addition of one more grain cannot ever seem to make that difference does not mean that there *is* no difference between a grain and a heap, or that it is reasonable to say that the heap begins with the first grain of sand. By analogy, then, the continuity of human physiological and psychological development, and our inability to specify an *exact* threshold of personhood which is non-sorites-susceptible, are not a reason to hold that personhood begins at conception.

George and Tollefsen believe this misrepresents their argument. They write:

What the sorites analysis overlooks, however, is that we *have* specified a non-arbitrary difference in human development. For while it is true that there is no non-arbitrary difference between a blastocyst and a later embryo or infant, there is a non-arbitrary difference—a difference in kind—between male and female gametes and the single-celled human embryo. The embryo is *a new human being*—the same complete human organism, as Sandel himself seems to acknowledge, as the later child and adult. While subsequent changes exist on a

---

[16] George and Tollefsen (n 1) 122.   [17] ibid.
[18] Michael Sandel, *The Case Against Perfection: Ethics in the Age of Genetic Engineering* (Harvard University Press 2007) 118.

continuum, the change from gametes to a new human individual does not. The union of gametes effects a substantial change that brings into being a new and distinct entity—in this case a human individual, *a human being*—in question.[19]

By claiming that they *have* specified a non-arbitrary point in human development, the authors seem themselves to miss part of the objection Sandel is raising. Sandel uses the sorites paradox to explain that, like in the problem of the heap, there is no *reason* to search for a beginning of personhood which is non-arbitrary in this particular sense—the sense of being non-arbitrarily distinguishable from its closest neighbouring points. There simply *is* no beginning of personhood which is distinguishable in this precise way, just as there is no sharp beginning of a heap of sand, unless, in the case of personhood, the punctualist thesis is true. Hence, the inability to specify such a point anywhere along the continuum of human development should not point in favour of the conception threshold.

Moreover, as we saw in the previous chapter, the claim that 'the change from gametes to a new human individual' does not exist on a continuum is false. The coming to be of a new human organism is a process, comprised of infinitely divisible successive points, none of which can be non-arbitrarily distinguished from their immediately adjacent points.

But George and Tollefsen might well interject here to charge me also with failing to understand the nature of their arbitrariness argument against all post-conception thresholds of personhood. Perhaps their continuum problem is not at all as I describe it, and their sense of 'arbitrary' not the sorites sense that I am using.

The authors point out that qualities like consciousness and sentience exist on a spectrum in a way that the quality of 'being a conceived human being' does not. Late fetuses might well be conscious and sentient *to a degree*, but not enough to warrant personhood status, given a cognitive capacities-based view of personhood's conditions. For that, conscious desires or rationality or self-awareness would be required on many accounts. Yet, as George and Tollefsen see it, the differences between these levels of mental functioning 'is merely a difference between stages along a continuum', stages which, moreover, may develop in the same creature gradually over time.[20] Hence they describe such differences as merely 'quantitative', or differences in degree, which, they claim, cannot be the basis for treating creatures in different ways. Rather, moral rights, including the right to life, can only be possessed by a creature in virtue of *the kind of being it is*. 'Human beings', they say, 'are intrinsically valuable and deserving of full moral respect in virtue of *what* they are'.[21]

If George and Tollefsen are right in supporting the 'animalist' view that we are our human bodies, then it follows, for them, that all developmental changes subsequent to conception 'exist on a continuum' in a way that 'the change from gametes to a new human individual does not', even though it, too, comes about, like everything else, in non-arbitrarily distinguishable increments.[22] The sorites problem here would be beside the point. It will not matter, on this argument, that the very coming-to-be of a new human organism is a continuous microphysical process

---

[19] George and Tollefsen (n 1) 123.   [20] ibid 119.   [21] ibid 123.   [22] ibid.

admitting of no non-sorites susceptible points. The argument is rather that we only possess moral rights in virtue of what we unchangeably are, that (according to animalism) what we are is human bodies, and that those bodies begin to exist, as individual organisms, at conception. Hence, the transition from gametes to zygote *is* non-arbitrary in a way that all subsequent changes are not, in that only *it* amounts to a 'substantial change'—as they say, the kind of change 'that brings into being a new and distinct entity, in this case, a human individual'.[23] And it is only in virtue of being human individuals that we possess moral rights, since individuals can only possess such rights by dint of being the kind of things that they basically are.

I believe and hope that this is a fair rendering of George and Tollefsen's argument at this point in the book. According to this argument, the issue with 'quantitative properties' is not that they represent some degree of a broader property, the way that consciousness might be expressed as a degree of sentience. The problem is rather that no post-conception developments, whether 'quantitative' or not, are developments that go to the substantial nature of personhood-possessing creatures. If the animalist criterion of numerical identity is true, only the quality of 'being human', established at conception, is part of our substantial nature.

George and Tollefsen define the view they are attacking at this juncture as 'moral dualism'.[24] Moral dualism is the belief that there is a difference between human beings and persons, and hence that not all human beings are necessarily rights-holding persons. Perhaps all human beings begin their lives as non-persons. Understood as the idea that human beings and persons are analytically distinct, even if they overlap, moral dualism is a claim I have accepted from the beginning of this book. I take it that George and Tollefsen do not intend to challenge the analytical distinctness of humanity and moral personhood, because I think they would want to accept that the members of an intelligent alien species could be persons. It is clear, however, that they wish to challenge the view that there could be any instances of living human beings that are *not* persons. In other words, they may be distinct classifications, but their correspondence is complete.

For clarity, we ought to distinguish moral dualism from the kind of metaphysical dualism we were considering earlier. The dualist thesis I considered before holds that we are numerically identical only with an immaterial mind or essence which can inhabit a human body at one time but not another. The 'moral dualist' only claims that humanity and moral personhood are distinct properties, and that one may be a human without being a person. George and Tollefsen's argument above is effectively meant to establish that moral dualism is incompatible with the animalist conception of numerical identity. The argument and its conclusion can therefore be broken down as follows:

P1. We are owed the moral rights associated with personhood only in virtue of what we are unchangeably, meaning our substantial properties.
P2. We are our human bodies (animalism).

<hr />

[23] ibid.   [24] ibid 112.

Hence:

C1. Our moral rights supervene on our human biology.

P3. We begin to exist as individual human beings at conception.

Hence:

C2. All human beings from conception are persons (moral dualism is false).

From one angle, this seems to be just another iteration of the substantial identity argument considered above. As was the case there, I believe this argument pushes the conclusions of animalism too far. Even assuming that the animalist view of numerical identity is correct, it seems that personhood essentialism remains a core premise of the argument, and this is a claim the authors have not given us compelling reason to accept. A moral dualist who does not accept personhood essentialism might well agree with the animalist criterion of persisting identity— the view that we are identical with our bodies—but simply hold that 'we', human beings, do not possess the quality of personhood at all times in our existence. It is also still open to the moral dualist to deny the impossibility of substantial change and claim that even though personhood is an essential property, it is possible for individuals to change in respect of such properties and still remain the same numerical thing.

It is of course precisely the compatibility of moral dualism and animalism which the authors are contesting. On their view, moral dualism does not fit with the animalist view of numerical identity, since if both were true we would have to abandon the clearly correct proposition that creatures which are persons are worthy of moral respect only in virtue of the kind of things they are. Animalism says that all human beings are numerically and substantially identical with their human bodies, hence come into existence, *as the thing that they are*, at conception.

Yet the moral dualist might respond that it is not human beings that are persons in virtue of what they unchangeably are, but, rather, personhood-possessing creatures. If *those* creatures ceased to be persons, they would still be human beings, and still be numerically identical with the thing they have always been. It would remain true, then, that they are in possession of personhood by dint of the *kind* of thing that they are, even if that nature does not necessarily go hand in hand with the conditions for their persisting numerical identity. To be a person is, surely, to be a very particular (and special) kind of a thing, even if one could cease to be a person and still survive as the same identifiable individual.

Another questionable implication of George and Tollefsen's argument can be brought out by considering the hypothetical case of zombies. The authors wish to claim both that we are numerically identical to our bodies and that we are persons at all times that we exist as the same living human organism. This seems to give a strange result in the zombie hypothetical. A zombie, we may suppose, is biologically continuous with the human being as she existed before she was zombified. Endorsing the animalist criterion of identity, we would have to say that the human and the zombie it turns into are one and the same thing. And this seems to make sense. When characters in zombie apocalypse dramas suffer the misfortune of being bitten, it strikes us as rational for the other characters to feel pity for the victim who has become something so loathsome, a reaction which would lack intelligibility if the zombie were not identical with the victim. But it seems clearly wrong to say that if the human being pre-zombification was a person, and identical with her human body, then the zombie is also a person. And this is what George and Tollefsen's argument would apparently commit us to saying in this fantasy scenario.

Lastly, let me return once more to the issue of 'merely quantitative' characteristics. For those who believe that certain cognitive abilities or levels of biological development are the conditions for personhood, it will just be true that differences between creatures which are on one metric quantitative can add up to morally significant differences. George and Tollefsen compare a conception of personhood which rests on capacities such as these with the racist attribution of moral worth on the basis of skin colour. 'The racist', they say, 'picks out a shade of skin as a more important characteristic than common humanity in deciding the worth of human beings'.[25] However, they continue, 'between any two human beings, the difference in colour will always be only a difference of degree, a difference that makes no difference to the sorts of beings that each is'. The authors propose that identifying personhood with the onset of developmental capacities which also exist on a spectrum is discriminatory in much the same way. Defenders of developmental thresholds are just like racists who wrongly regard someone as inferior by 'picking out a characteristic that should be irrelevant to moral respect'.[26]

This, however, conflates the differences of degree issue—the continuum problem—with their argument about the sorts of morally intrinsic differences that can be relevant for moral status. It is not the fact that shades of skin colourings lack sharp borderlines which leads us to believe skin colour is irrelevant to moral status. It is the fact that we cannot see how skin colour is related to the strong moral considerability that personhood entails. George and Tollefsen seem to make use of the skin colour analogy in the service of arguing that any criterion of personhood which can be located on a wider spectrum (e.g. self-consciousness or rationality on a 'Sentience Spectrum') disqualifies that criterion as constitutive of personhood. So the right analogy with skin colour and racism would be to imagine that we *did* otherwise have sound reason to think that moral status supervenes on a particular skin colour, and *then* to argue that the fact that colour is a spectrum, or that shadings are never precise, precludes us from identifying personhood with white, black, brown, or yellow skin.

But the fact that all shades of colour exist on a spectrum and blend into one another is not the reason that grounding personhood in skin colour is so obviously erroneous. The reason is that skin colour has no bearing on any of the attributes or capacities which we believe generate moral rights. If, however, we *did* have sound reason for regarding skin colour as relevant to personhood, the fact that colours sit on a spectrum with no sharp boundaries would be no objection unless

---

[25] ibid 120.   [26] ibid 121.

we were convinced that any property which is on *some* metric quantitative cannot be constitutive of personhood. As we have seen, George and Tollefsen's main argument for this is that personhood can only supervene on substantial properties, of which, it seems, there is only one: the property of being an individual human organism. This argument I have found unpersuasive. None of this poses any problem with answering the racist of course, because we already know why skin colour has nothing to do with moral status.

6.5 The Precautionary Principle

Finally, I want to address one more argument in favour of the conception threshold. Let us assume again for the moment that the punctualist thesis is true. One question I have asked is whether it follows necessarily from that thesis, or from metaphysical dualism, that the critical moment when personhood begins must occur during the process of conception and not in a later phase of human development. For a long time, the doctrine of the Catholic Church was that ensoulment took place at forty days of gestation in the case of a male fetus and ninety days in the case of a female, and that only abortion of an ensouled fetus was tantamount to murder.[27] This doctrine is not obviously incompatible with a punctualist view of personhood's beginning. Indeed, it seems, on the face of it, to assume that punctualism is true, and that there is a distinct moment when a complete person arrives on the scene, through ensoulment. But earlier Catholic doctrine does not equate personhood with the very beginning of a human organism.

Perhaps, however, one might defend a precautionary principle in favour of *presuming* that humans become persons at conception. If punctualism is true, vagueness about when the 'existential pop' occurs will only be of the epistemic kind. There *is* a sharp borderline when personhood begins; we just cannot be sure where it is. When this epistemic problem is viewed alongside the moral risk of getting the threshold wrong, it could be argued that the only reasonable answer is to treat human organisms *as if* they were persons from conception, just in case. As Kaczor suggests, choosing a threshold of personhood is not like just choosing a minimum driving age. Specifically, what is at stake in choosing a personhood threshold seems far greater in the way of consequences of getting it wrong. Considering the gravity of the line-drawing exercise, perhaps a precautionary principle of assuming personhood from the earliest conceivable point is the soundest policy.

It is worth underscoring, first of all, just how integral the punctualist thesis is to the reasoning behind this precautionary principle. Those making the case for a risk-averse principle of this kind have presented analogous scenarios in which protagonists are unsure whether there is a tramp roaming around in a building about to be demolished, or are considering whether to risk shooting children accidentally

---

[27] Cf Engelhardt (n 15).

by placing a firing range next to a playground.[28] Should we blow up the building, or construct the firing range, if we cannot be sure whether or not they will result in the death of a person? Would we not do better to err on the side of caution and abstain? The very nature of these analogies reflects a clear prior commitment to the belief that for any week, day, or hour of gestation one might pick, the developing human being either is or is not determinately a person. That is, they assume the all-or-nothing, punctuated picture of how personhood begins. Asking whether a twenty-four-week gestated fetus is yet a person is like asking whether there is a tramp in the building; it is determinately true or false, and if we are unsure, we had better not take the risk.

The gradualist picture of personhood's emergence does not suggest the same thing about the threshold of personhood. On that picture, it is not the case that between twenty-four weeks and twenty-three weeks and six days there is a determinate, independently existing answer to the question whether the fetus is yet a person or not, such that if we cannot find a reason for believing a transformation took place within that critical day, we run the clear risk that abortion at the earlier point kills a morally considerable person. Gradualism allows that the beginning of personhood is not a sharp threshold. Hence, while there may be good reason to limit abortion at, say, twenty-four weeks, no supportive argument need be made that the fetus is a radically different being one day or one hour earlier.

Perhaps, though, the defender of a precautionary principle can disavow punctualism and argue something different. That is, she might argue that whether or not the beginning of personhood is a gradual emergence of a property or a sharp borderline, it remains the case that we cannot know *for certain* when a morally considerable person has arrived on the scene. Even if personhood has no sharp beginning, we cannot be sure that a complete person has not materialized *by* twenty-four weeks' gestation, twelve weeks, or even by the end of conception. Moreover, the stakes involved in making a mistake in either direction seem to go very strongly in favour of refusing abortion. If we wrongly assume that human beings have already achieved complete moral status from conception and on this basis deny abortion, a huge injustice will be done to countless women that are unjustly made to endure the burdens of unwanted pregnancy. However, if we mistakenly fail to attribute personhood to fetuses and for this reason permit abortion, the consequences will be countless unjustified deaths, a far worse prospect. Thus, the argument goes, any uncertainty should tilt us in favour of prohibiting abortion.

It is clear, however, that those who invoke precautionary reasoning must understand the uncertainty surrounding the beginning of personhood in a very particular way. Specifically, they must think that we have, in truth, *absolutely no idea* whether a fetus is a person at any given stage of gestation; hence we must presume that it is from the earliest conceivable point. We cannot so much as assume that the

---

[28] See Margaret Brazier, 'Embryos' "Rights": Abortion and Research' in M Freeman (ed), *Medicine, Ethics and the Law* (Stevens 1988) and Francis Beckwith, *Defending Life: The Legal and Moral Case Against Abortion Choice* (Cambridge University Press 2007) 60–1.

early human organism must acquire *some* physical properties in addition to human genes, or some psychological ones, before it is possible that it might be a person, since, for all we know, personhood does not require such things at all. This is surely the thought that is needed to ground a precautionary assumption that zygotes are persons. However, this construction of the epistemic problem involves a view of personhood as something that does not just transcend physical or psychological facts about human beings—that is greater than the sum of its base properties in the way that a painting is more than the sum of the brush strokes and droplets of paint which constitute it. Rather, it treats the property of 'being a person' as utterly separate from all other properties of creatures that are persons, such as that we could know everything it is possible to know about the physical and psychological nature of a creature and *still* be unable to say with enough confidence whether or not it is a person.

What could underwrite this sort of view about the nature of personhood? One might wonder whether it follows from metaphysical dualism. Returning briefly to the argument in chapter 5, someone committed to the dualist view of persons might question the whole relevance of transgenic, sentience, or brain-based continuums for the truth of the punctualist thesis. She might argue that personhood does not supervene *at all* on facts about human genes, sentience, or psychological states, but instead consists in a completely independent and separate property, irreducible to such things. It matters not then, she might say, that the coming-to-be of genetically complete, conscious, or sentient human beings involves a spectrum of innumerable variations, and that any variation one might propose as the absolute beginning of personhood cannot be non-arbitrarily distinguished from the previous one, because personhood has nothing *whatsoever* to do with any physical or psychological developments in human beings.

However, on a picture like this, which entirely disassociates personhood status from all other facts about human beings, puzzles will begin to arise regarding the limitations of the precautionary principle. For one, if personhood's emergence does not supervene on any other facts about human biological or psychological properties, then there is no special reason for suspecting that human beings *in particular* are persons (let alone persons *already* as embryos) any more than there is reason for suspecting that rocks, trees, or non-human animals of all kinds are persons. Indeed, once the conditions for personhood are set loose from absolutely all other properties of personhood-possessing creatures, even basis for ascribing personhood to typical, mature human beings starts to give way. Mature humans are rational, self-conscious, communicative, capable of intelligent learning, and so on. But the view we are considering here treats the fact of personhood as separate from all such things. For all we know, then, mature human beings could be exactly as they are—thinking, feeling, and intelligent—and *still* lack personhood. Consequently, it will not look as though the precautionary principle has any particular reason to pick out genetically complete human beings as objects of our caution, or that there is any more reason to suspect that they are persons than to suspect the same about rocks, trees, or rabbits.

The defender of the precautionary principle will want to reply that only human beings could ever be *candidate* persons, since an individual human organism is the very least required for personhood. Thus, conception really is where the precautionary principle bottoms out. We should take caution with all human beings, but not with anything else. But I do not think she could make such a move fairly. If the precautionary principle could be limited by appealing to obvious basic conditions of personhood, this would go equally for the whole of gestation and beyond. Discussants would then be at liberty to argue that a being clearly lacking mental states is surely not a person, so we should take the precautionary approach of assuming personhood only once mental states of some sort (or whatever other features one thinks obviously required for personhood) are apparent. But if uncertainty about the beginning of personhood really is as thoroughgoing as precautionary reasoning needs to assume it is—if personhood does not depend on anything else about human beings that can be perceived—then even human genetic makeup cannot provide limits for the precautionary presumption. On the picture that such reasoning provides, the property of being a person might just as plausibly be possessed by a pair of gametes as by an embryo or fetus. True, gametes do not possess a complete set of human chromosomes, but on the view we are considering, this is not what personhood reduces to in any case; it is a property wholly independent from and separate to human physical properties.

Following this, it is difficult to see how the precautionary principle can limit the duty to take precautions at conception. Surely we should exercise caution with gametes too and treat all contraception as homicide. Nor, it seems, can the presumption be limited to living human beings. Are we entirely sure that dead human bodies are not persons? If personhood does not supervene on any mental or physical states whatsoever, it is not clear why they could not be. Given what one risks in making a mistake, and following precautionary reasoning, we had better take care and treat them as if they were persons, even if decomposing. These are clearly untenable implications of a precautionary principle.

Ultimately, an argument which relies on the complete disassociation of personhood status from any other facts about the physical or mental constitution of human beings runs the risk of casting off all conceptual constraints when it comes to what can be a person. If one's metaphysical commitments about personhood entail that, for all we know, insects might be persons, this is, I think, an indication that one has taken a wrong turn. This is not to suggest that the question of who or what can be plausibly described as a person is merely a question about how we use language. I do not think this is so. But as Engelhardt helpfully points out, 'syntactically deviant' uses of language *can* provide insight into the outer limits of concepts.[29] 'That is', he says, 'when one recognises that it is nonsensical to speak of stones as having pains, one realizes something about the kind of objects stones are – what falls within and what exceeds the sense of their type.'[30]

---

[29] Engelhardt (n 15) 219.   [30] ibid.

When personhood is not thought to depend on any base properties, even the hypothetical discovery that fetuses could do quadratic equations and contemplate the meaning of their life in the womb would not resolve the question of fetal personhood. For all we know, they may *still not* be persons. If this is the nature of the epistemic problem that sponsors the precautionary principle, then it seems to collapse the meaning of personhood altogether en route to advocating caution at the margins of life.

7

Gradualism and Human Embodiment

7.1 Gradualisms

In chapters 5 and 6, I contrasted two very different views about the emergence of personhood, or 'moral status', in human beings: the punctualist thesis and the gradualist thesis. I suggested that there is no compelling reason to accept punctualism, but good reason to accept the gradualist thesis, which holds that no sharp borderline exists between the absence of moral personhood and its attainment. I noted that, on one reading, the crux of the conception threshold argument is that personhood is not a property which is *attained* at all, but that it is just always present in personhood-possessing creatures, throughout their existence. Thus, human beings must always be persons from conception. I raised doubts about this argument, and about the notion that any particular view of the conditions for persisting numerical identity lends support to the conception threshold of personhood.

Still, the gradualist thesis as I have sketched it does not refute the proposition that all human embryos are persons. It says only that there is no reason to assume a sharp threshold exists between the absence and the presence of personhood status, since there is no good reason to think that personhood is the kind of property that emerges wholly and instantaneously. This is not incompatible with a species membership criterion of personhood because, even if it is implausible to think that persons come into existence wholly and instantly, it may still be true that personhood supervenes on human genetic coding or human biology. My significant conclusion was simply that, if punctualism is false, it is misguided to grant or withdraw support for a threshold of personhood based on its apparent decisiveness. And in any case, as I also argued, absolutely no threshold is decisive in the requisite way.

So the very fundamental question about the basic conditions for personhood remains. And if there are convincing reasons to support a species membership criterion, the falsity of punctualism will not matter very much for those who argue that abortion is morally prohibited at every stage of human life. The coming-to-be of persons is incremental and vague at the margins because this is true of the coming into existence of new individual human beings, in the form of zygotes. However, *once* a new human being is clearly on the scene, the species membership criterion of personhood, if correct, would still tell us that almost all abortions past that point are morally wrong.

When the criteria question is thrown back open like this, so are all of the familiar *reductio* problems introduced in chapter 5. We still need some defensible criterion

Arguments about Abortion: Personhood, Morality, and Law. First Edition. Kate Greasley. © K. Greasley 2017. Published 2017 by Oxford University Press.

or criteria of personhood to be able to point to those properties the fading in of which mark the onset of moral personhood. But as soon as we begin this endeavour, the *reductio ad absurdum* problems spring right back. It seems that whichever conditions of personhood one might endorse, counter-examples can be summoned with relative ease. Conscious desires: what about the unconscious, or those bereft of any desires? Rationality: what about infants or the severely cognitively defective? Socialization: what about the permanently ostracized? Human species membership: what about the hypothetical existence of a species of super-intelligent aliens? And so it goes on.

An alternative way of thinking about the beginning of personhood in human beings is captured by the increasingly popular idea that moral considerability strengthens throughout gestation as the fetus develops towards full maturation and birth, when the new human being becomes a fully instantiated person. Indeed, this is the thesis more generally associated with so-called 'gradualist' thinking about abortion ethics and fetal moral status. Some notable contributions have expressed support for the broad proposition that late fetuses are owed more in the way of moral protection and respect than early ones, a notion that also seems to fit well with common intuitions about abortion morality. The kernel of *this* gradualist thesis is that moral status at the beginning of life is not an all-or-nothing affair. Rather, as the fetus matures, its interests and moral rights—including, most importantly, its rights against the pregnant woman—strengthen. Margaret Little describes the idea as follows:

> In short, what a great many people believe is a *graduated* view of embryonic and fetal status: even at early stages of pregnancy, developing human life has an important value worthy of respect; its status grows as it does, increasing gradually until, at some point late in pregnancy, the fetus is deserving of the very strong moral protection due newborns.[1]
>
> Part anticipatory and part achieved, moral status is comprised of a number of interweaving stages each leading to and giving way to the next.[2]

As Little explains it, the moral status of the fetus increasingly consolidates as it matures until, eventually, perhaps very close to birth, its moral importance is practically indistinguishable from that of newborns.[3] In a similar vein, LW Sumner writes that development is the 'most obvious feature of gestation', and that '. . . an adequate view of the fetus must be gradual, differential, and developmental'.[4]

This gradualist thesis is clearly different from the one I adumbrated in the previous two chapters. The gradualism that I juxtaposed with punctualism only holds that there is no sharp, absolute borderline between the absence of personhood status and its

---

[1] Margaret Olivia Little, 'Abortion and the Margins of Personhood' (2008) 39 Rutgers Law Journal 331, 332.

[2] ibid.

[3] Little nonetheless believes that as long as fetal life resides in a woman's body, the legality of abortion cannot be determined by fetal status alone, although this is not taken to be a necessary implication of gradualism but the conclusion to a different argument more in line with the kind I surveyed in chapter 3 (see ibid and Margaret Olivia Little, 'Abortion, Intimacy and the Duty to Gestate' (1999) 2 Ethical Theory and Moral Practice 295).

[4] LW Sumner, 'A Third Way' in Joel Feinberg and Susan Dwyer (eds), *The Problem of Abortion* (3rd edn, Wadsworth Publishing 1997).

attainment. It does not make any claim about the timeframe during which moral status progressively emerges. We can think of this as gradualism in sense 1. Little's gradualism, which we can call gradualism in sense 2, holds that the gradual emergence of personhood status takes place throughout the gestation process, and that the further along the developmental path a fetus is, the more moral status it has amassed. Gradualism in sense 2 clearly implies gradualism in sense 1, but the reverse doesn't hold.

The sense 2 gradualist view of fetal moral status is 'developmental' in that it posits a view of moral status as supervening on post-conception human development. However, it clearly differs from the sorts of developmental accounts which tie personhood to a particular biological or (more often) psychological development, which is believed to make all the difference between the complete absence of full moral rights and their attainment. It is usually an upshot of these kinds of developmental accounts that third trimester fetuses are more morally important than first trimester ones, because the more developed fetuses are believed to have acquired a necessary and sufficient person-making capacity or trait. This is true of David Boonin's suggestion that fetuses become morally considerable beings when their brains are capable of organized cortical brain activity and, hence, basic conscious desires, somewhere between twenty-five and thirty-two weeks of pregnancy.[5] But it does not follow from a threshold developmental account such as Boonin's that gestating human life is, at all times, continuously accruing moral status, the crux of the gradualist (sense 2) view. For Boonin, the fetus is simply not morally considerable *at all* before it acquires organized cortical activity, and is morally considerable afterwards.

As intuitive as the gradualist view may be, however, it does not, on its own, resolve the main puzzles surrounding moral status and the conditions for personhood. The fact that this is so can be brought out by reflecting on one of the most important challenges to gradualist thinking, presented by Joel Feinberg.[6] Considering the proposition that the 'moral weight' of the fetus grows in a way that parallels its physical growth and development, Feinberg underscored a certain logical problem. A more developed fetus is, admittedly, closer to becoming a fully realized person than is a zygote. However, being almost qualified for rights is not the same as being qualified for partial or weak rights. Analogously, he remarked, when, in 1930, Roosevelt was only two years away from becoming President and Jimmy Carter was a six-year-old future President, Roosevelt did not have any more Presidential prerogatives than did Carter. It is not obvious why the mere fact that the later fetus is chronologically closer to becoming a fully realized person means that it is *more* of one—or, in Feinberg's terms, is in possession of stronger rights. Sumner's observation that development is the 'most obvious' feature of gestation may be true, but how does this change fetal moral status?

Pursuant to Feinberg's challenge, a gradualist theory of fetal moral status will need to explain why fetuses are more concrete embodiments of persons the more

---

[5] David Boonin, *A Defense of Abortion* (Cambridge University Press 2003) 115–29.
[6] Joel Feinberg, 'Abortion' in Feinberg, *Freedom and Fulfilment: Philosophical Essays* (Princeton University Press 1994) 54.

they develop throughout gestation, and not only chronologically closer to becoming full-fledged persons. As I defined it, this is exactly what the gradualist thesis 'proper' claims. The defender of gradualism must therefore explain in virtue of *what* a gestating fetus enjoys increasing moral status, the more developed it becomes. This of course leads us straight back into the problem over the criteria for moral status, a problem which gradualism shares with all accounts of personhood at the beginning of life. As with any account of moral status, gradualism must endorse some criteria or criterion of personhood. It must specify those properties that are constitutive of personhood in general, so as to be able to explain the growing moral status of the fetus by reference to those properties *in utero*.

A gradualist account is also forced to confront the traditional problems concerning the criteria of moral status as a result of its need to explain why the boundaries of moral status are conception and birth. Put otherwise, why does the process of becoming a fully realized person begin with conception and end with birth? Why does it not begin later, say, at viability, and end later, say, in early infancy? Alternatively, why ought we to dismiss the possibility that the gradual process of developing moral status ends earlier than birth, somewhere in late gestation? In other words, gradualism cannot simply assume that the timeframe of graduated moral development spans the gestation period from beginning to end. Some argument must be presented as to why this is so, and that argument will, of course, rely on some account of the constitutive features of moral status.

So a gradualist view cannot evade discussion about the conditions of personhood. Moreover, when engaging in this discussion it seems that the gradualist is as much at the mercy of *reductio* counter-attacks as any other theory. In what respect exactly is a fully matured fetus more of a person than an embryo? A number of suggestions might be made: its more advanced human physiology; its higher level of brain activity; its possible sensitivity to pain; or its capacity for independent breathing. But for any given criterion, an interlocutor can raise a counter-example to discredit it in the usual fashion. Are not the physically disabled fully instantiated persons? If so, what does fully developed human anatomy have to do with personhood or the right to life? Few would doubt that human beings suffering from brain damage, or currently only able to survive on life-support, are persons in the philosophical sense. If so, why does consciousness, brain functioning, or viability affect the moral value of human life before birth? The problems associated with adducing a universal criterion for personhood do not just disappear when one adopts a gradualist account of fetal moral status. I want now to dwell a little more on a few recurring *reductio* problems in discussion about the basis of moral status.

7.2 *Reductio* Problems and the Conditions for Personhood

7.2.1 Infanticide, radical cognitive deficiency, and sedation

I begin with the infanticide *reductio*. As we have seen, a number of cognitive capacities-based criteria of personhood exclude fetuses from the range of morally considerable creatures only at the cost of seeming to exclude neonates and young infants as well. Rationality, linguistic ability, self-awareness, or possession of a 'self-concept' are all traits that very early infants seem to lack. Michael Tooley's theory which accords full moral status only to creatures in possession of a 'concept of the self as a continuing subject of experiences' is one clear example of a criterion of person-hood which, it seems, cannot extend full moral protection to neonates.[7] Neonates certainly do not appear to be in possession of self-awareness, and some accounts do not attribute that capacity to infants until a much later stage of development. The same is undeniably true of rationality or language ability. Consequently, when such traits are posited as necessary conditions for personhood, it is difficult to see how one can avoid denying the full moral status of human infants.

Some philosophers have responded to the infanticide *reductio* by encouraging us to think the unthinkable and question whether there are really rational founda-tions for the common belief that human infants have a moral status equal to that of born human beings. At the same time, it has been suggested that there are plenty of pragmatic and moral reasons to refrain from terminating the lives of infants, not-withstanding the fact that they may not possess a strong right to life. Both Michael Tooley and Mary Anne Warren have argued that the apparent moral repugnance of infanticide can be explained by a whole number of considerations that do not depend on it being true that neonates possess the same moral rights as persons.[8] Such reasons are typically consequence-based. They include, among other things: the effect of the neonate's 'emergence into the social world' on other people who may have come to love him or her; the fact that infants whose biological parents cannot raise them are usually wanted by others who can; and the potentially cor-rosive effects that tolerating infanticide may have on other moral norms. This last consideration concerns the potential for moral slippage which looms when human beings so closely resembling (and so close to becoming) fully realized persons are treated as dispensable. Three-month-olds are not all that different from neonates, so perhaps attitudes towards killing *them* cannot remain unaffected when killing newborns is tolerated. One possible solution to this would be of course to stipulate an absolute cut-off point, as Tooley suggests would be appropriate fairly soon after birth, at, for instance, around one week of age. However, I do not believe a clear cut-off neutralizes the present concern about moral slippage, which simply points out that any toleration of infanticide will render it hard to maintain the appropri-ate amount of moral opprobrium towards the termination of slightly older infants. Reasons such as these, it can be suggested, may make it necessary to treat all infants *as if* they have strong moral rights even if they in fact do not.

These sorts of responses to the infanticide problem tend to be unsatisfying for a number of reasons. For one, many people will struggle to relinquish their belief that human infants have an inherent moral status equal to that of more

---

[7] Michael Tooley, 'Abortion and Infanticide' (1972) 2 Philosophy and Public Affairs 37.
[8] See: Tooley (n 7) 64 and Mary Anne Warren, 'The Moral Significance of Birth' (1989) 4 Hypatia 46, 56–8.

developed human beings. For them, defending the prohibition on infanticide for any reason other than this is to defend it for entirely the wrong sorts of reasons. Doubtless there *are* many reasons to refrain from killing young infants, even if they do not possess a strong, natural right to life. But those who are repelled by the very suggestion that such a practice could be permissible do not have these contingent considerations in mind. They may even think that to condemn infanticide for *these* reasons (consumer demand for babies; the close resemblance of neonates to children, etc) is morally perverse.

Warren and Tooley's defences of the general prohibition on infanticide also have the undesirable implication that if only all of these contingent considerations are lacking, there will be no other non-contingent reason left for refraining from infanticide in a particular case. Surely it is easy enough to construct a case in which a neonate is unwanted by anyone and where terminating its life does not risk other negative knock-on effects. Yet the powerful intuition against the permissibility of infanticide seems to apply as much in this case as in any other.

Further to these problems, some of the rationale Tooley and Warren provide for maintaining a general prohibition on infanticide seems to apply equally to late fetuses. Late fetuses also have a distinctly human form, so if this feature counts against destroying neonates, it presumably ought to count against destroying late-term fetuses in similar circumstances. Adoptive future parents will frequently be available for late fetuses as well, and treating late-term fetuses as dispensable might be morally desensitizing in much the same way as is killing neonates.

Christopher Kaczor, in particular, criticizes Warren for failing to see that these putative reasons for abstaining from infanticide apply equally to late fetuses.[9] In fact, Warren does not disregard these equivalences, posing herself the question: 'if protecting infants is such a good idea, then why is it not a good idea to extend the same strong protection to sentient fetuses?'[10] Her answer is that the same consequentialist-type reasons for protecting infants do not apply to late fetuses because of the repercussions of that practice for pregnant women. As she states, 'it is impossible to treat fetuses *in utero* as if they were persons without treating women as if they were something less than persons'.[11] Put differently, Warren's position is that although neither late fetuses *nor* newborns have the qualities which endow them with a fundamental right to life, there is little to be lost and much to be gained in general community welfare through protecting infants, but *not* by extending protection to fetuses, which would cause more harm than good for actual people.

While Warren's position is not actually lacking in coherence, as per Kaczor's critique, many will still find it difficult to accept that the equal protection of infants depends on contingent considerations such as the effect of infanticide on wider society and the desirability of orphaned children. The clear implication is that were it not for the fact that protecting infants is in the public interest, no strong innate right to life would bar the permissibility of infanticide. The problem is not that

---

[9] Christopher Kaczor, *The Ethics of Abortion* (2nd edn, Routledge 2015) 44–5.
[10] Warren (n 8) 58.   [11] ibid 59.

this reasoning fails to differentiate the situation of infants and late fetuses, but that, for many, an explanation of the wrongness of infanticide which is dependent on circumstances and culture will only show that something has gone wrong in the argument; specifically, it makes the impermissibility of infanticide depend on the wrong kind of moral considerations.

Moving on from the infanticide problem, cognitive capacities-based criteria of personhood can also have difficulty accounting for the moral status of the radically cognitively defective—born human beings whose psychological abilities do not meet the threshold of rational functioning or agency laid down by defenders of those criteria. Again, one response to this problem could be to concede that the severely cognitively disabled do not meet the conditions for personhood, although, as is the case with infants, there may still be many reasons, both moral and pragmatic, for valuing their lives. On one view, attributing moral status to such human beings that is superior to that of non-human animals whose psychological capacities are more advanced is just another example of 'speciesism'—the privileging of human species membership for no morally defensible reason. For those who make such claims, it is not usually their view that disabled human beings should be valued any less than they actually are, but rather that we should revise our attitudes towards the non-human animals whose cognitive abilities are equal or superior—primates being a prominent example—and award those animals greater moral protection.[12] Still, it is not easy for many to accept that cognitively deficient human beings lay claim to any less moral status than fully functioning ones, a seemingly unavoidable implication of cognitive theories of personhood. The speciesism problem is of course also a challenge for those who believe that human infants possess higher moral status than non-human animals with the same or higher levels of cognitive functioning.

Sleep and sedation present yet further problems for cognitive criteria of personhood, such as consciousness or the capacity for conscious desires. None of us are conscious during the times when we are asleep, or then able to form any desires, and people in reversible comas lack these traits now and for the indefinite future. If conscious experience, desires, or agency are necessary conditions for personhood, do we lose that moral status while asleep and gain it again upon waking? Do the temporarily comatose lack that status indefinitely? This is known as the 'episodic problem'. There are also those who may lack the desire to live, or any desires at all, due to emotional disturbance, such as a teenager feeling suicidal after a heartbreak. Kaczor provides a different example of someone who achieves the Buddhist ideal of extinguishing all desires. On a theory which makes personhood status dependent on conscious desires or rational functioning, are such people excluded from the moral community? If cognitive-based theories of moral status cannot manage to ascribe personhood status to such people, then many will be reluctant to accept them.

---

[12] cf Jeff McMahan, 'Our Fellow Creatures' (2005) 9 Journal of Ethics 353, 358.

7.2.2 Species membership and potentiality

From all of this it may seem that *only* a human species membership or potentiality-based criterion of personhood status can avoid the various *reductios*. A potentiality theory of moral status can come in more than one form. Most basically, however, potentiality reasoning posits that the correct criterion of moral status is a creature's future potential to become a fully realized person. On this reasoning, it may still be true that personhood requires meeting some threshold of psychological capacities. However, the important quality for full moral status and the right to life is only that of *potential* personhood. The attractiveness of the potentiality criterion lies in the fact that it confers full moral status on both infants and human beings in reversible comas on the basis that, although they do not currently exercise the traits character-istic of personhood, they have the capacity to exercise them in the future.

Michael Tooley has argued that anyone defending the proposition that human beings are persons from conception are in fact forced into a dilemma whereby they must choose between a potentiality basis for moral status or a morally arbitrary, 'speciesist' preference for human species members.[13] If one wishes to avoid a pure species membership criterion, only the potentiality principle can tell us why human infants, let alone fetuses, have full moral standing, since infants seem not to meet the conditions for personhood on any non-speciesist account. Thus Tooley thinks that both the pro-life case and the equal moral status of infants stand or fall on the success of such a principle. Although human fetuses and infants do not possess the psychological capacities sufficient to qualify for personhood (on Tooley's reason-ing), they do possess the *potential* for those capabilities. Only if this potentiality is status-conferring, then, will they be owed a strong right to life.

Plenty has been written about the potentiality principle, which has been widely criticized by many accounts of moral status. I will make only a few points here, mostly relevant to the *reductio* problems that potentiality, or, indeed, anti-potenti-ality, reasoning throws up. To clarify, the potentiality principle ties moral status to facts about a creature's capacity or future potential to realize certain goods or capaci-ties typically associated with personhood, like the capacity for rational thought or the conscious desire for continued life. A potentiality criterion of moral status is therefore able to avoid episodic problems concerning human beings in comas and those with no current desire to live. Such beings still have the capacity for rational thought or conscious desires, and that is what counts. Such theories also have no problem accounting for the moral status of infants, who also possess the relevant potential, even if they do not have the current capabilities of persons.

The price for this, or the pay-off, depending on one's outlook, is that the potential-ity criterion seems to confer equal moral status on human embryos or fetuses, which *also* possess the capacity for future rational thought processes, conscious desires, or whichever other cognitive-based capacities one takes to constitute personhood. The problem here is how to distinguish between the kind of potentiality exhibited

---

[13] Tooley (n 7).

by infants, sleeping people, or the comatose, and that exhibited by embryos and fetuses. Of course, a sleeping or comatose adult may not be currently exercising her capacities for conscious thought, but she has certainly exercised that capability in the past. Moreover, it might be argued that sleeping or comatose adult human beings possess the mental apparatus for the relevant kinds of cognition, even if it is not currently operational, whereas fetuses, certainly up to a late stage, do not. The former beings, we might say, have cognitive capacities that are immediately exercisable, unlike nascent human beings, whose potential is still future and theoretical.

We can think of cases, however, of which this is not true. Take, for instance, someone who is comatose due to temporary brain trauma, and who has the capacity to regain normal cognitive functioning, but only after a period of brain regeneration. Such a person does not have a current or an immediately exercisable capacity for, say, rational thought, self-awareness, or conscious desires. Added to this, it is not clear how a personhood criterion based on 'immediately exercisable' cognitive capacities would accommodate the moral status of neonates or slightly older infants, whose potential for higher thought processes is not immediately exercisable. Whether the immediate/non-immediate distinction draws acceptable boundaries regarding who is in and who outwith the category of persons, we still need some kind of justification for treating the kinds of potentialities differently. Some are understandably sceptical about any such justification. As the philosopher Patrick Lee writes:

What matters is that the difference between the kind of potentiality a human embryo or fetus has (not immediately exercisable) and the kind that a sleeping person has (immediately exercisable) cannot carry the moral weight which proponents of this position load upon it.[14]

For those that endorse it, the potentiality principle is the antidote to cognitive-based criteria of moral status, which exclude too many obviously rights-bearing human beings from the personhood category. It is widely taken to correspond with the conception threshold of moral status, since this is when an individual being with whom we can identify the relevant potential arrives on the scene.

But potentiality criteria of moral status also appear to be subject to *reductios* in being both over- and under-inclusive. One *reductio*, depending on your point of view, is precisely that the potentiality principle puts embryos and fetuses on a par with all born human beings, infants, and adults, in terms of moral status. Thought-experiments like the Embryo Rescue Case show this to be deeply counter-intuitive. As will be remembered, the Embryo Rescue Case asks you to imagine that you are about to flee a burning hospital and have the option of grabbing and rescuing either five human embryos or one fully formed human baby. Most people consider it unthinkable—probably even morally impermissible—to choose to save the embryos rather than the baby, even though they number five and the baby only one. If this intuition is correct, it can only be because the moral status of the baby

---

[14] Patrick Lee, *Abortion and Unborn Human Life* (2nd edn, Catholic University of America Press 2010) 26.

vastly outweighs that of an embryo, such that, even though the embryos are greater in number (and all things being equal, one ought to save the many over the few), saving the baby is the only reasonable course of conduct.[15]

Any persuasive potentiality principle must also advance an intelligible rationale for making potential personhood the condition of moral status. Those charged with the task of formulating such a rationale immediately face a simple problem. This is that it is difficult to see why being a potential person should endow a being with the same moral status as an *actual* person. Being a potential person means that a being is, by definition, not an actual person. Why, then, should such a creature enjoy the rights and status that attends actually realized personhood?

One possible answer to this might be found in the philosopher Don Marquis's 'future like ours' argument in defence of the potentiality principle.[16] Marquis begins his argument against abortion not by asking what features are constitutive of personhood, the typical approach, but by asking instead why it is usually so wrong to kill adult human beings. He answers this by claiming that the essential wrongness of killing adult human persons lies in the deprivation of their future, a future which would be characterized by all of the quintessential goods of human life, such as rational and other higher thought processes. Thus it is that killing a person painlessly in her sleep is no less of a wrong *qua* killing than a brutal murder. The deprivation of a future of value—the core wrong-making factor in killing—is inflicted on the victim regardless of any other features of a killing, such as the pain experienced by the victim.

Marquis's next move is to point out that embryos and fetuses *also* possess a future which will include the goods of distinctly human flourishing—'a future like ours'. Thus, if the essential wrong-making factor in killing *us*, persons, is the deprivation of our future, then killing embryos is just as wrong for exactly the same reason: that it deprives them of the same kind of future.

Marquis's theory seems to entail the equal moral status of embryos, fetuses, and all born human beings, at least when it comes to questions about the permissibility of killing. However, it also seems to bear out the deeply counter-intuitive implication that killing an embryo or a zygote which has just come into existence is the worst kind of killing there is, because it involves inflicting the greatest loss of future (human embryos that will not die *in utero* probably have a lengthier valuable future ahead of them than I have). This seems to prove too much, and to place far too much significance on fertilization as an event of hugely moral import. Could it really be correct that the difference fertilization makes is the difference between no

---

[15] Defenders of the conception threshold have advanced a number of debunking explanations for the common intuition in the Embryo Rescue Case, the conclusion being that the intuition is not incompatible with the view that personhood begins at conception (see Kaczor (n 9) 146 and Robert P George and Christopher Tollefsen, *Embryo: A Defense of Human Life* (Doubleday 2008) 138–42. Since there is not enough space to review those arguments here, I will simply say that I find them to be unconvincing primarily because they fail to dislodge the very compelling notion that the *explanation* for the common conclusion that one ought to save the baby rather than the embryos is that the baby is intrinsically more morally valuable a being than the embryos, and not some other explanation.

[16] Don Marquis, 'Why Abortion is Immoral' (1989) 86 Journal of Philosophy 183.

meaningful loss of life, where two gametes about to fuse are destroyed, and the most serious loss of life that there is?

Potentiality principles of moral status (whether Marquis's version or others) might equally prove too much in some other respects. If the relevant potential is taken to be only theoretical potential—meaning, the future potential to embody distinctly human forms of flourishing *in the right circumstances*, then it appears to confer full moral standing on too many kinds of beings. Jeff McMahan provides an imaginary example in which we discover that dogs have the potential to develop cognitive capacities similar to that of a normal five-year-old, but that this potential can be realized only by subjecting the dog to an intensive regimen of cognitive therapy for the first five years of its life.[17] If we do not think that all dogs, by virtue of this discovery, possess moral status equal to all born human beings, then 'mere potential alone is not sufficient to bring a being within the scope of the constraint'.[18] As McMahan claims, the intuitively sound reaction to this sort of scenario seems to be to say that although all dogs have an interest that their potential is realized, this alone does not grant them any more moral status unless and until it is.

Alternatively, if the criterion of moral status is not theoretical but *actual* potential—in other words, the fact that, if not interfered with, a creature *will* come to acquire higher cognitive functioning or a 'future like ours'—that criterion seems to be overly exclusive. There are some born human beings which do not function rationally, or embody other distinctive forms of human flourishing either actually *or* potentially, such as human beings with radical cognitive deficiencies. Although it seems incorrect to exclude such human beings from the category of persons, it does not look as though mere *potential* personhood, where that potential is of the kind that can and will be realized, is a basis for ascribing them moral status.

The same, of course, can be true of both infants and fetuses, depending only upon their individual prospects. McMahan points out, for example, that viable fetuses which are severely, congenitally, cognitively impaired lack an actually, realizable potential of the relevant kind.[19] The same can be true of severely disabled infants. On the actual potentiality criterion, we apparently get the result that a woman can permissibly have her fetus or infant destroyed if it has no prospect of meeting a certain threshold of cognitive functioning, but not otherwise. Moreover, it will not be an answer to this to state that being a potential person *or* being a born human being with no similar potential *both* suffice individually to qualify for strong moral rights. The entire pay-off of potentiality reasoning is that it is meant to overcome the speciesism objection to a pure species membership criterion of personhood. Suggesting it as merely a second, alternative, sufficient criterion for personhood therefore does nothing to solve the problem in response to which it is introduced.

Certain defenders of the view that personhood begins at conception would likely respond by claiming that I am defining the potentiality principle incorrectly.

---

[17] Jeff McMahan, 'Infanticide' (2007) 19 Utilitas 131, 145.   [18] ibid 145.
[19] ibid 144.

Instead of pertaining to either theoretical or actual potential for certain cognitive capacities, or a certain kind of future, some have suggested that the morally relevant kind of potentiality is the 'radical' capacity for these traits which all human species members possess by virtue of their genetic code, whether they are ever able to realise that capacity or not.[20] According to Kaczor, for instance, all creatures belonging to the natural kind 'human being' have those capacities encoded in their genes, and are thus properly described as 'rational beings', whether or not they are ever able to function rationally. He writes:

> Rational endowment is nothing other than the capacity, ability or disposition (though perhaps not realizable) enjoyed by whole, living beings whose active self-development is aimed towards and whose flourishing consists in freedom and rationality.[21]

In saying that a zygote's 'flourishing consists in freedom and rationality', Kaczor means to say that forms of flourishing and cognitive functioning which typify normal, developed members of the human species (and distinguish us from non-human animals) are the benchmark against which the good of all species members are evaluated, and he elaborates this point elsewhere. For example, the inability to read, or to communicate using language, constitutes an unfortunate lack of flourishing for a ten-year-old child, but not so for a cat. A cat's failure to reach those benchmarks is not deemed lamentable like the child's, precisely because reading and speaking do not constitute typical forms of flourishing *qua* cat. Consequently, Kaczor writes, even though not every human being can communicate, is consciously aware, and so on, 'every single human being is nevertheless properly described as a rational being. Not a potentially rational being, but a currently existing actual rational being.'[22]

To underscore the point, Kaczor provides an analogy. 'To say that the human being *in utero* is not a rational being because he or she is not functioning rationally', he writes, 'makes as much sense as saying that a human being is not male or female unless in the act of successfully reproducing'.[23] He suggests that just as a human being can be biologically male or female regardless of their ability to perform activities specific to their sex (i.e. perform a male or female reproductive role), so a human being who never possesses reasoning ability is still rational. The analogy seems somewhat inapt, if only because reproductive potential does not appear to be integral to any definition of 'male' or 'female'. The core suggestion, though, is that rationality *is* a defining capability of human beings, and that all human beings are therefore latently rational, whether or not they are ever *actually* capable of reasoning.

Arguments such as these have been collectively referred to as 'nature-of-the-kind' arguments about moral status, and I will return to look at them more closely in

---

[20] See, for example, Patrick Lee, 'The Basis of Being a Subject of Rights' in John Keown and Robert P George (eds), *Reason, Morality and Law: The Philosophy of John Finnis* (Oxford University Press 2013) 242. Lee defines creatures which possess the 'radical capacity for rationality' as those 'having a constitution or nature orienting one to active development to the stage where one does perform such actions—as opposed to an immediately exercisable capacity'.
[21] Kaczor (n 9) 106.   [22] ibid 107.   [23] ibid.

due course.[24] For now, the question is whether arguments like this can salvage the potentiality criterion for full moral status. As I see it, they cannot, because they instead *replace* that criterion with something else. A 'radical' potentiality criterion which looks only to whether a creature has the genetic coding of a species that typically exhibits person-like traits might well dodge some problems of over- and under-inclusiveness. For instance, it would not include all of the dogs yet to be equipped with higher cognitive faculties in McMahan's science fiction scenario. And it *would* include infants and the radically cognitively impaired, since such human beings still have the 'radical' capacity for uniquely human cognitive abilities even if they do not, and never can, realize it. However, the new criterion is only able to do this by dropping potentiality as the morally significant feature completely, and endorsing instead a simple species membership criterion of personhood.

Either potentiality (theoretical or actual) matters for moral status, or it does not. If it does, then the various counter-examples which seem to show potentiality reasoning to be over- or under-inclusive are live objections. If it does not, then we are no longer confronted with a recognizable instance of a potentiality-based theory. But once potentiality is dropped out in favour of a pure species membership criterion of moral status, the other horn of Tooley's dilemma closes in. That criterion will amount to mere speciesism unless a convincing theory that ties moral status to human species membership can be offered.

In summary, the potentiality criterion for moral status is highly problematic for much the same reason that psychological criteria seem to be: that it cannot be grounded in a rationale which draws the boundary lines for morally considerable beings in a way that we would deem acceptable. On the other hand, once the independent value of future potential is altogether removed from our determinations of moral status, we do indeed seem stuck with how to explain the moral status of infants or the comatose in a way which does not fall back on a form of speciesism, let alone that of human beings with radical cognitive deficiencies, whom it may seem can be accounted for only by a pure species membership criterion.

At this point, one may want to change tack entirely and propose a bare sentience criterion which accords full moral status to all creatures capable of conscious, sensory experience, regardless of their further cognitive capacities. It might be thought that a bare sentience criterion tracks a middle way between a pure species membership basis for personhood, which seems insufficiently justified, or a psychological criterion, like rationality or agency, which is unpalatably exclusionary. However,

---

[24] Kaczor's reproduction analogy raises plenty of questions all by itself, such as whether we, or indeed all things, are defined by our latent or theoretical, although in actuality inexpressible, characteristics. It is not unthinkable that I could have been a gymnast, although I cannot possibly be one now, and probably never would have been one. Is 'gymnast' one of my defining characteristics? Kaczor may say that it is only those characteristics which human genetic coding makes possible that are definitive of all of us, but this *does* include the characteristic of being a gymnast, being a zookeeper, a linguist, or anything else only human beings can be or be like (psychopathic, for instance). Kaczor will need to explain why, on his understanding of defining characteristics, *all* of the capacities which uniquely human genetics make possible are not defining traits of every species member, or if only some, which ones, and why.

it will be difficult to explain why a bare sentience condition would not accord the same level of moral status to *all* sentient creatures, human and non-human. Most non-human animals, even those that lack sophisticated mental states, are at minimum sentient beings. That is, they are capable of subjective experience: they touch, taste, smell, and feel, and there is something it is like to *be* them. This is as true of birds and mice as it is of humans. A bare sentience condition of personhood would therefore appear to be overly inclusive in its extension of full moral status to such creatures, unless, that is, it is a threshold for moral status limited to human beings. How, though, would one explain this additional species membership condition without once again inviting the speciesism charge?

7.3 Multi-Criterial Approaches

By now I have, hopefully, provided a good idea of how the traditional debate about personhood's conditions proceeds, albeit without offering a solution. We have also seen just how difficult it is to propound a criterion of moral status which evades all of the obvious *reductio ad absurdum* problems, as well as other kinds of counter-arguments.

By the end of any such discussion, supporters of the species membership criterion will be tempted to think that they have come out of it the clear victors. After all, only their favoured criterion of personhood clearly brings *all* human beings—including infants, the comatose, and the radically cognitively defective—within the parameters of full personhood status. And if the pure species membership criterion for personhood is correct, and if embryos and fetuses are human beings, it follows that they too are included in the category of persons.

But this is a hollow victory for proponents of personhood-from-conception, if it is one at all. It is, to begin with, a victory grounded on purely negative virtues. The strongest recommendation for the species membership view comes from the fact that, unlike its capacities-based contenders, it is consistent with the equal moral status of human beings we are not comfortable leaving out of the personhood category. This is a far cry from offering a compelling rationale in defence of the species membership criterion, or answering the 'speciesism' charge. Particularly in light of the obvious conceptual difference between biological humanity and moral personhood (a difference which, I have stressed throughout, cannot be denied), we still require an explanation for *why* personhood supervenes on human genetics. An explanation, that is, which offers more than just satisfying entailments. Moreover, the negative virtues of the species membership criterion do nothing to neutralize its own *reductios*. Could it really be true that the death of a single-celled zygote just moments after conception is tantamount to the death of a five-year-old child? Many will have great difficulty believing this to be true.

It is crucial here not to employ double standards with the epistemic value we place on *reductio* arguments. For example, defenders of the species membership criterion cannot argue that post-conception criteria of personhood must be rejected as soon as they are seen to countenance infanticide, but that the species member-ship criterion does not have to be rejected for its equally implausible suggestion that zygotes are morally equivalent to five-year-old children. Fair play is paramount here. One cannot say only about one's own theory that whatever conclusions fall out of it is simply where the logic leads us, whilst maintaining that patently unac-ceptable implications of rival theories show them to be false. Those who would countenance the moral permissibility of infanticide in the same circumstances we permit abortion also need to be mindful of this when impugning personhood-from-conception accounts for having obviously false implications.

Of course, one's own judgements about the relative plausibility of the various *reductios* will always count for much in discussions like these. It is always open to someone, when confronted with a putative *reductio* of her criterion of personhood, to simply deny that it is indeed a *reductio* and claim that it is instead a correct entail-ment telling us something we deep down already knew to be true. One woman's *reductio* is another woman's thesis-affirming conclusion. Hence, Kaczor, George, and Tollefsen, and other supporters of the species membership criterion do not reject it once it leads them to admit that zygotes are every bit as morally valuable as adult human beings. This is, after all, what they always imagined to be true. Likewise for supporters of theories which lead inescapably to the view that infanti-cide is no different from late abortion. For some people, this is an entirely intuitive implication, and therefore *not* a *reductio* at all.

All of this places some limitations on *reductio* reasoning in argument about per-sonhood. Interlocutors may devote endless time to constructing *reductios* out of one another's theories, but as soon as there is disagreement on whether something *counts* as a *reductio*, it is not obvious where to go from there. It may be feared that, at bottom, *reductio* reasoning just replays deep-seated disagreements in our starting convictions about what can and cannot plausibly count as a person with full moral rights. This limitation does not make *reductio* reasoning pointless in moral argument about abortion. At the very least, summoning counter-examples such as radically cognitively defective persons or thought-experiments such as the Embryo Rescue Case compels discussants to reconsider their theory of moral status in response to its apparent implications, or to deepen or elaborate that theory so as to explain them. Still, at the point at which discussants find themselves conflicted about which entailments really are too counter-intuitive to accept, we may well ask ourselves if there is any way of thinking about moral status which moves the con-stant exchange of counter-examples.

One suggested way of breaking out of this cycle of counter-examples has been to adopt a multi-criterial account of the conditions of personhood. My discussion so far has focussed on the various counter-examples that can be levelled against any one putative criterion of personhood taken to be both necessary and sufficient for full moral status. Some philosophers, however, have eschewed the idea that there is only one core criterion for personhood, favouring instead a 'cluster concept' account of personhood's conditions. Accounts like this propose that personhood does not admit of a strict set of necessary and sufficient conditions, but supervenes on a clus-ter of properties, only an adequate selection of which are required for personhood.

Mary Anne Warren enumerated five such characteristics: 1. consciousness (especially the capacity to feel pain); 2. reasoning ability; 3. self-motivated activity (or, we might say, agency); 4. the capacity to communicate; and 5. a concept of the self.[25] Warren contended that there is no strict formula regarding exactly how many of the five traits an individual must possess, or in which combinations, to warrant an ascription of personhood. The only clear thing, she argued, is that a creature possessing *none* of the traits is not a person. Warren thus rejected the idea that any single property demarcates those creatures which possess full moral standing from those which do not—what she called, 'the single-criterion assumption'.[26]

Reflecting on the previous discussion, it is easy to see that, on its own, each one of Warren's criteria is subject to a counter-example. Is a human being afflicted with a rare disease rendering her incapable of pain sensation thereby not a person? Is someone who becomes paralyzed and incapable of any self-motivated activity stripped, for that reason, of his personhood status? On Warren's account, no one single trait need bear all of the weight. Someone incapable of self-motivated activity could still be a person if, say, he possesses consciousness, reasoning ability, and a concept of the self. A human being who lacks reasoning ability may still be a person if she is conscious, has the capacity to communicate, and is capable of some agency. We might wonder, then, whether a multi-criterial approach such as Warren's, if persuasive, can break us out of the stalemate induced by the countless *reductios*.

Against the cluster concept approach, Kaczor has argued that such a view cannot rescue developmental criteria for personhood from the counter-example problem. He rejects a solution by which a selection of traits which have all been shown to be individually inessential for personhood (by means of counter-examples) could be simply lashed together in a theory which takes moral status to supervene on all of them, although not, *necessarily*, on any of them. Kaczor frames the objection as one which cuts against the gradualist (in sense 2) view of fetal moral status, according to which the fetus strengthens in moral value throughout development. However, it is more fundamentally an argument against any multi-criterial concept of personhood, gradualist or not. Kaczor illustrates the multi-criterial approach by analogy with the construction of a rope.[27] Each individual stage of development from conception to birth is a single thread which is easily broken (by a counter-example which shows it to be over- or under-inclusive). When added together, however, the various 'threads' of development construct a rope which is difficult to split: a sound basis for the attribution of moral status. Taking the rope analogy as a target, he writes:

The weakness of the rope analogy . . . is the comparison of the various arguments in favour of personhood to threads which, though weak taken individually, make an increasingly strong case. For unlike a thread, an argument that is invalid or unsound does not have any 'strength' which could then be added to other arguments, the sum of which would amount to a stronger case for one's view. If, for instance, Tooley were correct that viability, spontaneous

---

[25] Mary Anne Warren, 'On the Moral and Legal Status of Abortion' (1973) 57 The Monist 43.
[26] Warren (n 8) 47.   [27] Kaczor (n 9) 88–9.

movement, and human form do not distinguish mere human beings from persons, then putting viability, spontaneous movement, and human form together would not make the gradualist case any stronger . . . A thread has some strength: a bad argument has none.[28]

But this is a misleading analogy. In effect, it claims that the complex moral quality of being a person cannot supervene on a cluster of simpler properties if it can be shown that they are not individually necessary for personhood. But any number of complex properties seem to be constituted thusly. Let us take, as just one example, the concept of being a friend. The property of being someone's friend appears to supervene on a cluster of base properties none of which is individually essential. The core constitutive features of friendship are qualities like loyalty, regularity of social contact, enjoyable companionship, shared interests or ideology, and mutual care and concern. It would be hard to make the case that any one of these properties is individually essential for friendship; counter-examples could, surely, always be summoned to prove otherwise. Friends can be distant, ideologically antagonistic, no fun to be around—even disloyal, up to a point. When it comes to friendship, this goes to show that a property is not conceptually redundant merely for being inessential. Loyalty is still a constitutive feature of friendship, even if one can adduce a real or hypothetical example of a friend who does not typically behave thus. Doubtless, one can rightly rebuke a treacherous friend for behaving in an unfriendly manner—for failing in his capacity as a friend. This only reinforces the rightful place of loyalty in our cluster concept of friendship, whether or not it is a necessary condition.

Consequently, the entire thrust of the *reductio*-type argument against developmental accounts of personhood might well fail to appreciate that the test for conceptual salience regarding a moral quality such as personhood is not whether or not we can manage to adduce instances of persons that are lacking in the relevant feature, but whether the absence of that feature is a deficiency that is explained by reference to what it means to be a person. Emotional ineptitudes like the inability to empathize, or cognitive ones like the inability to use language or reason, are, as Kaczor rightly says, deficiencies in human beings but not in cats because they amount to the failure to realize characteristics quintessential of persons. This is exactly how we know that they are constitutive elements of personhood.

In fact, the same seems to be true of every putative criterion of personhood on Warren's list. Human beings that lack rationality, agency, communication ability, and so forth may be persons nevertheless, but the failure to realize any of these capacities is without doubt a deficiency relative to what it means to be a person. The only trait of which this does not appear to be true is human species membership. The fact that this is so can be demonstrated by considering the simple 'intelligent alien' hypothetical that we have already encountered elsewhere. Consider a member of an intelligent alien species which resembles typical human beings in all of their emotional, social, and cognitive capacities, with the one difference that in the place of human DNA, there is alien genetic coding. It does not appear that the

---

[28] ibid 89–90.

alien's different biology is any kind of deficiency by reference to what it is to be a person. We would all agree, I believe, that the alien is every bit as much a full instantiation of a person as the typical adult human—that nothing whatsoever is taken away by the pure fact of his different species membership. This seems to establish a good prima facie case for favouring developmental criteria such as that propounded by Warren over the human species membership criterion supported by defenders of personhood-from-conception. On the very same test that shows psychological capabilities to be salient to the concept of a person, human species membership appears to fall down.

7.4 Archetypes and Qualifiers

Having introduced one reason for thinking that our common concept of a person supervenes on a cluster of psychological capacities but not on human species membership, I now want to deepen the argument in favour of such an approach. I made the point above that arguing about personhood only by way of exchanging *reductio ad absurdum* examples has the drawback that it might only replicate deep-seated disagreements about the boundaries of the concept. Perhaps a better starting point might be to look to where we undoubtedly agree and extrapolate the core conditions for personhood from that. But where can any such agreement be found?

One possibility is to begin by focussing on the idea of the *archetypal* person. Although we know that people disagree on what it takes to qualify as a person—the threshold conditions—we can expect broader agreement on what personhood looks like in its fullest instantiation—the person archetype. This question holds out more promise for unearthing common ground between discussants who endorse different basic conditions for personhood, since those who stipulate radically different threshold conditions are still likely to agree about what the archetype, the paradigmatic example of a person, will be like.

As with all of our concepts, the core instantiation of a person can be differentiated from the example at the outer boundaries. There are core and penumbral instances of most things, and not every individual that *qualifies* as a person need be an archetype. Still, if anything about the nature of personhood can be gleaned through thinking about the nature of the archetype, it may form the basis of an argument that appeals to discussants who endorse drastically different qualification conditions. In a similar vein, we can also consider the most uncontroversial examples of things that are non-persons, and look to see what underlies universal agreement in those cases.

The key questions to ask, then, are whether there are any identifiable examples of archetypal persons, and what it is that makes them obvious archetypes. There are, I think, certain kinds of creatures about which it is true that if *they* are not persons, it is not clear what is. This is most obviously true of normally functioning, mature human beings. If someone were to refuse to acknowledge that *this* class of beings at least are persons, one could reasonably accuse him of having no grasp whatsoever of the concept. Equally, there are examples of creatures and objects that could not, on any reckoning, seriously be thought to fall within the concept of a person, like rocks or insects.

In virtue of *what*, then, is the archetype—the normal, fully matured human being—such an uncontroversial example of a person? Why is it that this case commands universal agreement? It seems clear that fully matured, normally functioning human beings are paradigm examples of persons because of certain psychological capacities which they possess: their high level of sentience and conscious experience of the world, capacity for language, intelligent learning and communication with others, reasoning ability, and exercise of intentional action and agency. Typical, mature human beings are able to appreciate and act on reasons, to plan and desire things, and to understand and evaluate their own desires and behaviour, as well as those of others. They also possess a sophisticated concept of the self 'as a subject of continuing experiences', Tooley's core requirement for moral status. If asked to explain why typical mature humans are such uncontroversial examples of persons, these are the kinds of traits to which I believe most people would point.

It will be noticed that the selection of traits I have enumerated is not all that dissimilar from Warren's list. I would, however, make a key addition. As well as cognitive capacities like intelligent learning and reasoning ability, the range of complex emotions enabled by those capacities also, I believe, account for the undisputed personhood of mature humans. Warren omits specific reference to emotional experience in her list of criteria, preferring to focus on cognitive powers. However, I think it apparent that the breadth and depth of emotional experience typical of mature human beings is distinctive of personhood in its own right, and an important part of what explains their status as the least contestable examples of persons. Embarrassment, elation, disappointment, empathy, guilt, relief, exasperation (to name but a few examples) are all sophisticated states of feeling that go far beyond the primitive experience of pleasure or pain. The ability to experience these sophisticated states of emotion strikes me as another capability of the paradigm person. Being a person is not just a question of thinking like a person but of *feeling* like one.[29] To be sure, there are adult human beings who either partly or entirely fail to experience the complex range of emotions that characterize the person archetype. But such complex emotions are germane to the archetype all the same. Psychopaths, who lack empathy, lack a capacity which, although not essential for personhood status, clearly amounts to an impoverishment relative to everything that being a person can and should be. Part of what defines the archetypal person is the possession of a trait which the psychopathic individual lacks.

---

[29] It might be pointed out that many non-human animals also experience emotion to a considerable degree, particularly the higher mammals. They can panic, become aggressive, get excited, and, in some cases, mourn. And we are surely likely to underestimate the depth of emotional experience of which non-human animals are capable. My argument is not that fully matured humans are unique in the basic capacity to experience emotion (I do not even wish to here rule out the possibility that some non-human animals *are* persons), but that the archetypal person is partly identified as such through the diversity and depth of her emotional repertoire. Even so, certain emotions like nostalgia, sentimentality, and shame do seem to be elusive in the rest of the animal kingdom, although many kinds of emotional states are more common.

Conversely, as soon as we reflect on why it is preposterous to the point of the conceptually incoherent to imagine that rocks or insects could possibly be persons— why it is that they are not even contestable, borderline cases—I think it abundantly clear that it is because they lack *any* of the traits outlined above. It appears to follow from these reflections that our concept of a person must at least be rooted in capacities such as these, even if its inclusion criteria stretches beyond them. As with most classifications, there are archetypes and there are qualifiers. We have not here established that fetuses (or indeed infants) could not be qualifiers. But reflecting on what the archetype is like, and what it is that *makes* something an archetype, nevertheless provides us with an insight into the core constitutive features of a person—the necessary starting point from which to think about qualification criteria.

An objection might be raised at this point. It might be replied that a typical, mature human being is an archetypal person for the plain reason that we all happen to agree in her case, as we all just happen to agree that insects are *not* persons. Yet, depending on one's views about the nature of a person, one need not agree that the fully matured human is more of a fully instantiated case of a person than other examples. In particular, a defender of the species membership criterion may insist that the zygote is *as paradigmatic an example* of a person as a mature human species member, and that the fact that there is widespread agreement only in the latter case is just a function of the fact that many hold to erroneous criteria for personhood. On this view, the mere fact that there is disagreement about the fetus does not make it a borderline case of a person—something which could at most be a qualifier, but never an archetype. The disagreement is, rather, between those who view the fetus as firmly outwith the category of persons and those who take it to be *as* central a case as any other, in light of its human species membership. For those holding the latter view, disagreement about the fetus does not make it any less a clear case of a person.

I struggle, however, to see how defenders of the species membership criterion could reject the notion that a fully matured, normally functioning human being is a paradigm example of a person, and is such a paradigm because of her developmental capacities. This is especially difficult to accept when considering our hypothetical alien above, where everything distinctive of paradigmatic persons is retained *except* human genetic makeup. In fact, a particular problem for such theorists arises from the fact that their very defence of species membership as *the* core constitutive feature of personhood proceeds only by appealing to the developmental capabilities that typical, mature members of the human species possess.

So-called 'nature-of-the-kind' arguments about moral status define the category of persons as those that are related in a particular way to a further category of beings who are paradigm persons. As McMahan describes them, such accounts argue that all human beings have a status higher than any animal 'by virtue of being members of a species whose nature, as determined by what is characteristic of its normal or typical members, is to possess certain status-conferring intrinsic properties'.[30]

---

[30] McMahan (n 12) 356.

Kaczor's own rendition of this argument, what he terms the 'flourishing like ours' account, claims that all creatures whose flourishing would consist in the cognitive capabilities typical of mature humans are for that reason in possession of the same strong moral rights owed to typical mature humans.[31] Being unable to read, or reason, or speak is a 'painful handicap' for a girl but not for a dog, because it is a failure to realize the abilities that would amount to flourishing *for her*. Kaczor argues that all individuals who have a 'flourishing like ours'—by which he means, like typical, mature human beings—'are individuals who have the right to life, and that, since all human beings have the genetic orientation towards this kind of flourishing, this includes all human beings from conception.[32]

On Kaczor's account, then, the 'qualifiers' (all human beings that count as persons because of their species membership) *are* defined by relation to an archetype: a typical, mature human being, flourishing in quintessentially person-like ways. It is undeniable, then, that the archetypal traits of personhood, which I have defined by way of both cognitive and emotional capacities, are the starting point for the species membership view of personhood—and indeed, its defenders do not deny it. The question for us is whether there is any defensible basis for extending the category of persons out from the archetypal case to every creature related to it in this precise way: that it is a member of a species the typical, mature members of which are clearly persons.

McMahan has attacked the nature-of-the-kind argument for presupposing, against its own conclusion, that 'the essential properties for membership in the human species are not themselves status-conferring'.[33] Those supporting the argument are, he suggests, in something of a bind. For, if human biology itself were sufficient for personhood, then there would be no need for them to argue, as they do, that 'all human beings have a higher status than any animal by virtue of belonging to a kind whose normal or typical members have certain evidently or recognizably status-conferring intrinsic properties'.[34] Instead, all human beings would have that moral status no matter what normal, mature members were like. The very fact, then, that such proponents need even appeal to the typical traits of mature members in their theorizing amounts to an admission that there is nothing intrinsically valuable about human species membership alone. Put more succinctly: if the cognitive capacities of typical humans is the thing which makes human species membership matter morally, why are those capacities not the basis for moral status, rather than human species membership?

McMahan also thinks there is a flaw in the logic by which we ascribe moral status to some human beings that derives from the status of other members of their species. As we have already seen to some degree, this derivative moral status is sometimes defended on the ground that everything belonging to the human species has the same basic nature, captured in a natural, genetic orientation towards rationality and other higher cognitive powers. But McMahan counters that one cannot simply

---

[31] Kaczor (n 9) 124. [32] ibid 126. [33] McMahan (n 12) 357. [34] ibid 356.

impute characteristics into an individual species member's nature in this way. He argues:

The morally significant properties characteristic of a kind do not get to be a part of an individual's nature simply because that individual possesses the closely but contingently correlated properties that are essential to membership in the kind. Properties that are inessential to membership in the kind do not define the nature of the kind, even if they are characteristic or typical.[35]

For McMahan, the nature-of-the-kind argument fails because it cannot bridge the logical gap between the morally significant properties that are characteristic of an individual's kind and morally significant properties that are part of the nature of every individual member of that kind. If typically person-like characteristics are not essential features of all human beings, then how is it that they are part of the nature of all human beings?

As McMahan also points out, 'nature-of-the-kind' arguments are far more appealing when they 'level up' moral status than when they 'level down'. Awarding individuals the moral status of typical members of their species is appealing when it implies that radically cognitively defective human beings ought to be given full moral standing, but far less so where it implies, for example, that a uniquely intelligent chimpanzee who, through conditioning and training, has managed to attain the IQ of a ten-year-old child, possesses only the same moral status as typical chimpanzees.

McMahan's rebuttal of the nature-of-the-kind argument is compelling. But so too is the notion that the category of morally protected beings extends beyond archetypal persons to those related to them in a particular way. Surely infants or the radically cognitively disabled are *qualifiers* for personhood even if they are not archetypes. If moral status does not extend out in this kind of way, it seems that we will indeed struggle to include such individuals within the class of persons. If embracing a 'nature-of-the-kind' theory, however, we would instead have to consider why fetuses and embryos do not equally qualify for strong moral rights, though they are by no means person archetypes.

In an article which partly reflects the nature-of-the-kind view, Shelly Kagan has argued that our common intuitions seem to support the belief that rights-holding beings are those which, in some intelligible way, *could* have been persons in the paradigmatic sense.[36] Kagan terms this view 'modal personism'. He argues that most of us are in fact committed to 'modal personism' in that we count as especially important the interests not only of persons (in the archetypal sense) but also of those who are not and perhaps never will be persons, so long as it seems to us that they *could have been* persons. Being a member of a species the typical adult members of which are persons is one clear way for a creature to be a modal person, on Kagan's reckoning. It matters to us that a severely cognitively impaired human being is a member of a typical 'person species' (Homo sapiens) because it enables us to see her

---

[35] ibid 358.
[36] Shelly Kagan, 'What's Wrong with Speciesism?' (2016) 33 Journal of Applied Philosophy 1.

as someone who might have been a person had she not suffered the misfortune of being so impaired. Kagan is determined to stress that the 'modal personism' view is not open to the speciesism charge, since it does not privilege the human race per se. What matters, on Kagan's account, is not that a creature is a human being, but that it is a member of a person species, and the 'metaphysical' fact which follows from this that it 'could' have been a person. It is consistent with this theory that there are non-human person species, and hence non-human persons *and* modal persons. The human race is just, perhaps, the only known, or only clear, case.

Furthermore, it is not an implication of modal personism that any interest possessed by a member of a 'person species' counts for more than any different interest possessed by an individual lacking that quality. This is not true of paradigm persons either. If I am more morally considerable than a cat, it does not follow that my interest in getting a hot cup of coffee this instant trumps a cat's interest in being free from torture. Kagan's suggestion is only that all other things being equal, modal persons count for more than non-persons. Thus, a cognitively impaired human's interest in being free from pain would trump the exact same interest of a chimpanzee whose cognitive abilities are exactly the same (assuming that chimpanzee is not a person species). Kagan adds the caveat that *actual* personhood remains, on this theory, a sufficient condition for moral rights.[37] Hence, a creature which possesses all of the core qualities of a person (is intelligent, self-reflective, and so on), is not stripped of her personhood because she does not belong to a person species. A cat injected with a magical serum which enables it to talk and reason is a person, despite not belonging to a person species.

Kagan's 'modal personhood' proposal bears clear similarities to Kaczor's 'flourishing like ours' basis for moral status, in that it looks to everything that a creature's species membership suggests it can and should be when determining its moral standing. Kagan believes that our common intuitions support the conclusion that actual personhood counts for more than modal personhood—hence, the death or the pain of a person counts more than that of a modal person. The important element of modal personism is only that 'the death of a modal person counts more—is worse—than the death of a mere animal with equivalent mental capacities'.[38]

But Kagan's proposal raises yet further questions. Kagan is clear about the fact that the 'modal personism' theory is meant only to expound a common intuition about moral status, rather than to explain and justify that intuition. And there are plenty of questions arising out of the very notion of a 'modal person' and exactly what counts as a creature which 'could have' been a person in the relevant way. Why does this include only members of a person *species*, for example, and not members of other kinds of groups the typical members of which are persons (take, for instance, a tortoise who, as a college pet, is made an official member of a college the typical members of which are persons)? Kagan's answer to this is that, differently from membership in other kinds of groups, membership of a person species

---

[37] ibid 19.   [38] ibid.

is salient to the question whether or not an individual could have been a person. It is species membership, rather than anything else, which defines what one 'could have been'.

Depending on how this idea is unpacked, though, perhaps not *all* human beings are modal persons. We might think, for instance, that all human beings are modal persons because they carry the genetic coding for personhood, even if that coding is, for some reason, unexpressed. But human beings whose radical cognitive impairments are owed to congenital defects appear to lack that genetic coding. Perhaps modal personhood is a quality of all creatures that, we might say, *could have had* the genetic basis for personhood. But again, it is difficult to see how one might elaborate the relevant sense of 'could' without inviting more and more creatures into the category of modal persons. These are just some of the answers we might need a fully fleshed-out theory of modal personhood to provide.

Even, however, if something like the 'flourishing like ours' account or modal personism were correct, it is far from clear that gestating human beings qualify for higher moral status according to their terms. In particular, it could be argued that fetuses are not creatures which 'could have been' persons in the same way that radically cognitively impaired human beings could have been. Their relation to the person archetype is different. For one, it is clear that fetuses *do not* have a 'flourishing like ours'. Granted, they are members of species the typical, mature members of which have a flourishing which includes the distinct capacities associated with personhood. But Kaczor does not adequately explain why that same flourishing ought to be imputed to embryos and fetuses. On no sensible account can fetuses be said to be 'failing to flourish' by being unable to read, write, or speak, since none of these things are yardsticks for flourishing *qua* human fetus. Unborn humans *always* lack those distinctive person-like characteristics. Quite unlike severely disabled human beings, the inability of a fetus to communicate is not a painful disadvantage but rather par for the course of being a fetus. There is a notable asymmetry, therefore, in how Kaczor's particular criterion of moral standing applies to the cognitively defective, mature human being, and how it applies to the the typical, immature one. Only in the case of mature humans does the failure to achieve certain capacities equate to a failure to flourish as a member of her species. Continuing to survive and develop normally are the only criteria for flourishing in the womb. It is true then that a human fetus does *have* a flourishing, and that this entails continuing to survive. But as much is true of all living creatures.

Likewise, we might ask in what sense fetuses are creatures that 'could have been' persons for the purposes of Kagan's modal personism. We cannot say that the human embryo or fetus is a creature which *could have been* a person if not subjected to some misfortune. If it survives (presuming a bodily criterion of numerical identity), it *could become* a person. The question is whether this has the same moral force on Kagan's account. My inkling that it has not derives from my sense that it is morally salient on Kagan's theory that the modal person could *currently* be a person in a counter-factual where she did not suffer some clear misfortune. In this respect, the radically cognitively defective are differently situated. We can conceive of counter-factuals in which someone afflicted with a severe cognitive impairment was not so afflicted. But there is no way to imagine that a fetus might currently be a thinking, communicating person. The rub, of course, is that neonates are like fetuses in this regard, not like the radically cognitively impaired.

7.5 Human Embodiment

So far, I have suggested that reflection on the nature of person archetypes steers us towards the view that the core constitutive features of personhood are developed psychological and emotional capacities. But not every individual who qualifies for personhood need exhibit all such characteristics to their greatest extent. If personhood is the sort of cluster concept which Warren describes, then it should suffice to qualify if an individual displays enough of the salient characteristics to the requisite degree. Someone who is only barely rational and communicative could still comfortably fit our common concept of a person without fully realizing all of the personhood-making capacities.

To tarry a moment on this last point, a big issue in discussion about the moral status of the radically cognitively impaired concerns the charge, no doubt justified, that those of us who have little close experience with such people can be profoundly unaware of the many ways in which they are able to share in quintessentially personal, human life, notwithstanding their disabilities. One lesson from these sorts of critiques is that the cognitively impaired human being who cannot relate to others on levels higher than that of an ape might very rarely, if ever, be a reality. Thus it is that writers about cognitive disability such as Eva Kittay, whose own daughter suffers from severe mental disabilities, are often eager to enlighten us on the minutiae of everyday life with such persons and the myriad ways in which they can and do interact with other human beings on an interpersonal plane far above that which is possible for non-human animals.[39]

In reality, then, there may be hardly any mentally disabled human beings whose cognitive abilities fall below the threshold which characterizes persons on the standard developmental account (with the obvious exception of the unconscious—a different kind of case). There are surely some, though. 'Nature-of-the-kind' accounts of moral status have the appealing implication that even a human being whose cognitive abilities do not surpass those of the typical chimp are nonetheless entitled to the same level of moral respect as normal human beings, simply by virtue of being related to them in the right way. But when the nature of that relation is understood as pure human species membership, it appears to confer the moral status of persons on embryos and zygotes as well.

As we have seen, much of the thinking behind nature-of-the-kind arguments concerns the idea that we ought to accord elevated moral status to creatures that *could have been* persons or who share our 'flourishing' in the sense that their failure

---

[39] cf Eva Kittay, 'The Personal Is Philosophical Is Political: A Philosopher and Mother of a Cognitively Disabled Person Sends Notes from the Battlefield' (2009) 40 *Metaphilosophy* 606.

to act like persons is a result of misfortunes to which we might have fallen prey. I argued that pre-born human beings do not seem to qualify for derivative moral status on this basis, since it does not seem true of them to say that they share our forms of flourishing. It is incoherent to think of a zygote or an embryo as something that *could have been* a person and is in some way failing to flourish by not being one. But let us think further about why this is the case. Why does the idea that fetuses are creatures that 'could have been' persons (or 'modal persons', if using Kagan's terminology) lack intelligibility?

One suggestion as to why embryos and fetuses are disqualified from the category of modal persons is that they lack the *embodied form* that archetypal persons belonging to their person-species take. The developed, embodied form of mature human beings is a clear pre-requisite for everything that is valuable and distinctive about human life. The idea that human embodiment, as opposed to human species membership, is salient to the 'nature-of-the-kind' intuition and 'modal personism' is therefore worth considering. If so, it may help to vindicate the basic gradualist (in sense 2) intuition that pre-born human beings are owed increasing moral respect as they develop *in utero*. All fetuses may be individual, genetically complete human organisms, but later fetuses possess far more human embodiment than do earlier ones—that is, they share more of the human form. If there is anything of moral import attaching to the acquisition of embodied humanity, then, this could reveal at least one reason for regarding earlier and later developed fetuses differently.

Some philosophers have sought to elucidate the significance of specifically *human* embodiment by appealing to the idea of what it is to be a 'fellow creature' of fully developed human beings. Stephen Mulhall, for example, attempts to illustrate the ways in which human embodiment is crucial to distinctive human life by engaging with a theoretical example of Jeff McMahan's concerning a dog with human levels of intelligence.[40] McMahan's problem, simply put, is why the dog ought not to be treated with the same moral considerability as human beings with equal cognitive abilities, unless our criterion of moral standing is plain speciesist. However, although the 'Superdog' possesses the psychological capacities of a typical human being, Mulhall worries that the thought-experiment fails to account for the numerous ways in which the dog's different embodiment would preclude human beings from treating him *as* a person, and regarding him the same way they regard each other.

While McMahan exhorts us to 'put aside' the contingent problems that the dog would be a freak in human society, unable to find a suitable partner, or to integrate into the lives of other persons, Mulhall does not find these considerations so easy to stipulate away. Without the possibility of sharing in the common life distinctive of human beings—of assimilating into a community, or having personal

---

[40] Stephen Mulhall, 'Fearful Thoughts' (2002) London Review of Books, http://jeffersonmcmahan. com/wp-content/uploads/2012/11/London-Review-of-Books.pdf (last accessed 28 March 2014.)

relationships—he questions what sense there would be in considering the dog a person. He writes:

Would a human being, deprived of any acceptable mate and regarded as a freak by his fellows, be faced with merely contingent problems that would leave his capacity to conceive of himself as a person essentially unaffected? What interpersonal relations (of friendship, family, gossip, common hobbies and interests) would be conceivable for our Superdog? And in their absence, what would the sense be of calling it a person nonetheless? I don't say that there could be no sense in doing so. I say only that the sense it would have is not the sense it has when human beings acknowledge one another as persons.[41]

While the Superdog may be more on the level with us cognitively than some impaired human beings, Mulhall believes his canine embodiment would exclude him in many ways from sharing in the common life distinctive of human beings, and that this matters for our moral relations. Conversely, even human beings that are radically cognitively defective are able to engage in many aspects of that 'distinctive form of common life' from which the Superdog is barred. Their human form opens up many ways for them to be brought into fellowship with the rest of us, notwithstanding their limited capacities. As Mulhall sees it, 'the embodied common life open to distinctively human creatures' provides the necessary context for our concept of personhood. He continues:

To see another as a human being is to see her as a fellow-creature – another being whose embodiment embeds her in a distinctive form of common life with language and culture, and whose existence constitutes a particular kind of claim on us. We do not strive (when we do strive) to treat human infants and children, the senile and the severely disabled as fully human because we mistakenly attribute capacities to them which they lack, or because we are blind to the merely biological significance of a species boundary. We do it (when we do) because they are fellow human beings, embodied creatures who will come to share, or have already shared, in our common life, or whose inability to do so is a result of the shocks and ills to which all human flesh and blood is heir – because there but for the grace of God go I.[42]

Mulhall notes that the inability of the severely mentally handicapped to reflect, communicate, and so on, owes only to the 'shocks and ills' that can blight any human life. Put otherwise, there is a sense in which *we might be them* (an important aspect of Kagan's modal personism) in a way that is presumably not true of the Superdog. *Their* fortunes and misfortunes reflect those of our own, and they are our 'fellow creatures' in being subject to the same 'uncanny fate' that characterizes human flourishing or floundering.[43]

In a similar vein, Cora Diamond has sought to draw attention in her work to the various ways in which our practices and intuitions lend support to the view that the morally appropriate treatment of individuals (including by those unrelated to them) is coloured by far more than their particular psychological capacities or interests.[44] As a prime example, she points out that eating human corpses is almost universally (and cross-culturally) considered morally perverse,

---

[41] ibid 5.   [42] ibid 5.   [43] ibid 6.
[44] Cora Diamond, 'Eating Meat and Eating People' (1978) 53 Philosophy 465.

despite the fact that dead human bodies clearly have no interests or moral rights. As she writes, 'We do not eat our dead, even when they have died in automobile accidents or been struck by lightning, and their flesh might be first class.' Neither, she notes, do we eat amputated limbs, even though doing so would not harm anyone. Diamond moreover points out that the fact that we perform funeral services for newborn babies but not for puppies has nothing to do with the superior psychological capacities of the babies. And we do not refrain from eating our pets only because we recognize that they have some interest in not being so treated (interests which animals that are on the dinner table can share), but because we recognize that a pet is not something to eat. She writes: 'There is not a class of beings, pets, whose nature, whose capacities, are such that we owe it to them to treat them in these ways'.[45] As with pets, she says, it is not respect for the interests of human beings, rooted in their psychological capacities, which explains why we do not eat human corpses. These attitudes and practices would be unreasonable if the morality of our treatment of other creatures were governed solely by their individual psychological capacities.[46]

Mulhall and Diamond's accounts seek to explicate, among other things, the importance of simply being human for the morally proper treatment of others. The responses will likely come thick and fast that such accounts ultimately boil down to a rather weak defence of speciesism. Among a roster of objections to Mulhall and Diamond specifically, McMahan points out that some non-human animals such as dogs can be 'fellow creatures' of ours to a considerable degree, and are even capable of sharing in our distinctive common life to a greater extent than some radically cognitively defective human beings.[47] (For example, he says, there is a 'widespread practice within our common life involving cohabitation and mutual devotion between human beings and their pets'.)[48] Humans with radical cognitive deficiencies may still be capable of 'minimal forms of participation' in our common life, but then so too are some highly developed animals. And psychopathic human beings, incapable of empathy, may be *less* able to enter into emotional intimacy with other humans than some animals can. Some human animals share our common life not only by engaging in personal relations but also by performing some function in human society, such as guide dogs. McMahan asks why Mulhall's framework does not entail that animals which participate in our common life in such ways 'assert a stronger claim on us' than some human beings 'whose participation is necessarily more modest'.[49] In essence, the question for McMahan is still whether human embodiment per se is a morally relevant feature.

---

[45] ibid 469.

[46] To be clear, it is not the claim of so-called 'moral individualists'—who argue that it is one's individual features rather than group memberships which determines one's proper moral treatment—that nothing else can bear on the reasons we have to treat a particular being one way rather than another. McMahan, for instance, readily agrees that our personal relations to a particular being can rightly affect the duties we owe to that individual (McMahan, n 12). It is rather McMahan's claim (and the claim of others who take the same view) that individual psychological capacities alone determine how it is correct for *anyone* to treat a creature with those capacities.

[47] McMahan (n 12) 363–4.   [48] ibid 364.   [49] ibid 365.

It is important to make the point here (not neglected by McMahan) that accounts such as Diamond's and Mulhall's are not attempts to show that only human beings are morally considerable, or indeed that our harsh treatment of non-human animals is justified. In fact, both authors believe that the same considerations underpinning the significance of our common humanity also better explicate the reasons we have to treat animals better than we do. Diamond, for example, does not use her lesson about eating people in defence of omnivorism. Instead, she believes that the wrongness of killing animals for food can best be drawn out by the same kinds of reflections that show cannibalism to be so unthinkable: that like us and like our pets, non-human animals are, perhaps, not things to be eaten. Mulhall argues that there are plenty of respects in which non-human animals are also our 'fellow creatures', and that thinking of them as such can help to animate much of what is wrong with treating them barbarically. In many ways, he says, nonhuman animals share 'our common fate'. 'They too are needy, dependent, subject to birth, sexuality and death, vulnerable to pain and fear . . . '[50] The very fact that they share with us so many vulnerabilities and common experiences is, for Mulhall, reason enough not to treat them brutally, regardless of their psychological capacities.

In a recent book which echoes some of these thoughts, Alice Crary has also tried to demonstrate how approaches to moral status which look solely to a creature's individual psychological capacities—what has been termed 'moral individualism'—can miss important aspects of the ethical treatment of animals.[51] Crary uses numerous examples to illustrate the point. One example she gives is of a group of children using a brain-dead rabbit as a dart board.[52] Another real life example, borrowed from Cora Diamond, is the behaviour of researchers at the University of Pennsylvania who were revealed in a secret video to have mocked and ridiculed their injured baboon subjects. As Crary asks: 'mightn't we say . . . that these researchers exhibited a form of disrespect to the baboons that wasn't somehow mitigated by the fact that it was lost on the baboons themselves?'[53] Crary's important point here is that an ethic of animal treatment which focuses only on individual capacities will fail to capture the 'source of our conviction' that such behaviours are 'insulting and wrong'.[54] Animals too, then, may merit a certain kind of respect in virtue of their form of embodiment—by merely being an animal of a certain kind. Perhaps it is morally perverse to perform the same lab experiments on a gorilla which we might permissibly perform on rats, even if this *particular* gorilla's cognitive capacities are no more sophisticated than that of rats.

Crary tries to show, then, that just as the mere fact of being human can inform the morally proper treatment of an individual regardless of his or her capacities, so too can the mere fact of being a dog, or being a chimp. She develops this thesis further with the use of literary examples. One is a short story by Raymond Carver entitled 'So Much Water So Close to Home', about a woman who hears the

---

[50] Mulhall (n 40) 5.
[51] Alice Crary, *Inside Ethics: On the Demands of Moral Thought* (Harvard University Press 2016).
[52] ibid 132.   [53] ibid.   [54] ibid 134.

disturbing revelation that her husband and his friends had allowed the naked body of a recently deceased young woman to remain floating in a stream for three days so as not to cancel their fishing trip in order to inform the police.[55] The protagonist's dismay comes partly from the fact that she views the body of the woman not as a mere object, but as 'the mortal remains of a person to whom things mattered'.[56] Toward a similar end, Crary considers a passage in JM Coetzee's novel *Disgrace*. Here, the main character is a man who spends time working at an animal clinic and is asked to dispose of the corpses of dogs that have been euthanized there.[57] After increasingly identifying with the dogs in their final stages of life, the man refuses to simply leave their corpses at the dump along with the rest of the garbage until they can be incinerated. Crary wants to suggest that just as an understanding of what is important in human life can determine the morally respectful treatment of a human corpse—regardless of its absent capacities—so too can sensitivity to what matters in a dog's life inform the ethically correct attitude towards dog corpses, or indeed, mentally impaired dogs.[58]

Crary's reflections on these literary and real-life anecdotes are offered up as a challenge to moral individualism, which, on her description, is the 'proposal to ground human moral standing in individual attributes'.[59] Moral individualism, on Crary's view, is liable to lead us astray not just when it comes to the appropriate treatment of human beings, but also of non-human animals. She writes:

> If we are disturbed by the idea that human beings only merit moral consideration insofar as they have such-and-such individual characteristics, then we may equally well be disturbed by the idea that animals only merit moral consideration insofar as they have such-and-such individual characteristics.[60]

Insofar as her reflections are intended to be ammunition against the view that moral standing is rooted in cognitive capacities, one can imagine the nature of the reply along similar lines to McMahan's reply to Mulhall. The account, it might be charged, still appears speciesist if it isolates species membership alone as the most morally significant characteristic of an individual creature. It seems to follow from

---

[55] ibid 146.   [56] ibid 148.   [57] ibid 155–6.

[58] It would be remiss not to mention the fact that much of the dispute philosophers like Crary have with accounts that tie moral status to individual psychological capacities alone is a methodological one about the correct way to reason about such matters. Such philosophers use argument about the moral status of animals as a demonstration in a much broader argument about what counts as valid moral thinking and about the moral force of literature. At the crux of Mulhall's own argument is the claim that the moral relevance of what it means to be human is simply part of our concept of a person, without which the concept loses its meaning. As he says, 'our concept of a person is an outgrowth or aspect of our concept of a human being', which is not merely a biological concept, but includes everything that is distinctive about human life. His claim, in McMahan's words, is that 'failure to understand the significance of our common humanity . . . is a failure to understand the concept of a human being'. Since I do not wish to adjudicate on these aspects of the debate, I am sidelining them in my discussion here (much, I fear, to the chagrin of the philosophers whose work I am discussing). It is important to emphasize, though, that a proper consideration of these views on moral status must give serious attention to the challenges they pose to moral individualists' 'fundamental theoretical framework' (see Crary (n 51) 149, n81).

[59] Crary (n 51) 130.   [60] ibid 131.

her analysis that all humans are to be treated in a way appropriate for typically functioning humans, dogs in a way appropriate for typically functioning dogs, and so on, regardless of their individual degrees of awareness and cognitive capabilities. The obvious reply will press further as to what it is precisely about human species membership that warrants a particular level of moral status. If the further explanation cites a quality or capability which is usually facilitated by human embodiment (like common fellowship with the rest of us), the reply will be that it is *not* in fact human species membership which is status-conferring, but something else, and that the something else can, in principle, vary across species (to wit: some dogs can enter into more fellowship with us than can some humans). If, on the other hand, no further quality or capacity linked to human embodiment is cited, the argument will just appear to reflect species-based prejudice.

This persistent defence of moral individualism is difficult to answer. However, perhaps we do not need to accept reflections such as Crary's and Diamond's as a refutation of capacities-based theories of moral status in order to draw out of them some important conclusions about the moral significance of human embodiment. Let us grant that such arguments do not show human embodment per se to be status-conferring. There is good reason to be sceptical of this if we cannot resist the notion that the core constitutive features of moral status are emotional and psychological, which, I have suggested, is indeed difficult to reject. Nevertheless, the discussions above might still expound a number of ways in which the possession of human embodiment can rightly inform the attitudes we hold towards individual human beings.

We can consider again Cora Diamond's observation about our treatment of dead human bodies. Diamond's suggestion there was not that dead human bodies are persons, but that the way we regard them bears out the belief that some moral significance attaches to the human form, such would make eating human corpses morally perverse in a way that eating the bodies of non-human animals is not, even if omnivorism is not justified. As these observations can be used to show, individual moral status is not the only thing relevant to questions about the morally appropriate treatment of creatures, living or dead. If the moral imperative to treat dead human bodies with respect has nothing to do with their psychological capacities or inviolable rights, this opens up the possibility that there are many ways in which a human being's form of embodiment partly determines her morally proper treatment. These sorts of considerations sometimes rise to the surface in discussions about harmless wrongdoing, such as the rape of patients in permanently vegetative states, with no damaging after-effects or possibility of discovery. Our revulsion at such behaviour has nothing to do with the victim's subjective experience of pain or humiliation as a result of the violation, but far more to do with the moral indignity to which she is nevertheless subjected given that she is a human being, and not a mere thing.

Even, then, if we cannot escape the conclusion that the core constitutive features of personhood are cognitive and emotional, the possession of human embodiment seems to retain some moral importance in the proper treatment of others. Much of this may well have to do with the centrality of human embodiment for our own personal life. Perhaps it is simply impossible for us to treat the human body itself as a valueless shell whilst demonstrating the right kind of moral consideration for all human beings. But another important dimension, central to the accounts considered above, may be the moral aberration involved in failing to see in a creature everything that she can and should have been, and what, given her form of embodiment, would constitute a life going well. As many of our practices and attitudes suggest, demonstrating the right kind of sensitivity to these features can require us to treat individuals in ways which go beyond responding to their capacities and interests alone. The disrespectful treatment of the human form, even when completely bereft of any interests or conscious experience (as when the victors in war dance on the bodies of their enemies), is distressing to a large degree because it seems so incompatible with appreciating everything that is valuable in a good human life.

Finally, what bearing does all of this have on the standing of fetuses? Unlike human beings with radical cognitive deficiencies, fetuses and embryos *lack* much of our human embodiment. Certainly, the earlier gestated the fetus, the less it is an example of an embodied human being. Sharing only some of our human embodiment, it also seems less true to say of fetuses that they are vulnerable to the same 'shocks and ills' as are we. As I noted above, flourishing *qua* fetus is very different from flourishing *qua* fully matured human being. Like mature humans, fetuses may live or die, but the similarity in what their thriving consists in ends there. It is not the case that a fetus *would* be in possession of the capacities and characteristics distinctive of human flourishing but for some calamity or misfortune. This is no truer of human fetuses than it is of rabbits or frogs. It makes very little sense to think of a zygote: 'there but for the grace of God go I', the way that we are moved to think of cognitively impaired human beings. The human fetus's radically immature embodiment precludes it from being fully the sort of creature whose good and ill reflects that of our own.

However, the gestating fetus does possess some, and increasingly more, human embodiment. At the very beginning of this chapter, I drew attention to the common intuition that a fetus accrues moral status as it develops *in utero*—what I called gradualism in sense 2. The main problem for this kind of gradualist theory is that of stipulating the characteristics in respect of which the fetus gains moral importance. This is a special problem for anyone who takes personhood status to supervene on cognitive capacities such as reasoning ability, communication ability, and so on. For gestating human beings do not become *more* rational, communicative, etc, as gestation progresses. They do not possess these characteristics at all. The question remained then as to how the gradualist scale of moral status before birth is explained.

Many writers on abortion ethics take it as granted that fetuses do gain some minimal levels of sentience throughout gestation—responsiveness to light, touch, auditory ability, and so on. As Warren pointed out, however, the degree of sentience evidenced by fetuses even in late gestation does not surpass that possessed by a whole range of non-human animals, including mice.[61] Forms of basic sentience such as these, and,

---

[61] Warren (n 8) 50.

indeed, even the minimal forms of consciousness of which some take late fetuses to be capable, do not appear central to our concept of a person, even if they are necessary preconditions for anything which might be a person.

But if it is correct to attach some moral significance to human embodiment in itself, the thought may provide some underpinning for the basic gradualist notion that earlier and late fetuses are dissimilar in at least one meaningful respect. Late fetuses do not bear out the constitutive features of personhood any more than embryos do, even if they are more sentient. But they do possess a great deal more of human embodiment. While a zygote possesses hardly more than the genetic coding for a human being, a late-term fetus embodies much of its actual human form. The process of attaining human embodiment is a continual and gradual process which spans the whole of gestation. Although the precursors to many parts of human anatomy are in place early on in gestation, biological structures such as organs do not come into existence all at once, one after the other. Rather, they continue to develop and gain layers of complexity all the way into the third trimester. Harold Morowitz and James Trefil described the process in the following way:

The best way to think of this type of organ development is to compare the fetus to a building under construction. Once the outer walls and roof are up, a building looks pretty much completed. In fact, there is an enormous amount of work to be done as electricians, plumbers, painters and others convert the basic outline of the building into the final product. In the same way, the final two trimesters of pregnancy involve the development of the fine structure of the internal organs of the fetus.[62]

The most complex organ of all, the brain, follows the same pattern of incremental development. They write:

Building the brain, in other words, is like building a house. First, the general structure is assembled—the walls are raised, the roof completed, and so on. Only after this work has been finished do we go on to filling in the details. The brain simply does not develop so that at some point you have half a complete organ, then three fourths, and so on. The brain isn't completed until the finishing work is done.[63]

The authors are at pains to point out that the two-month embryo is not a miniature human being that simply grows 'proportionately larger' until birth.[64] The embryo is more like a faint tracing that becomes gradually more elaborated with detail and substance during the rest of gestation. The kidneys, for example, need, throughout gestation, to develop the 'one to three million tubules' responsible for collecting waste and delivering it to the bladder. As Morowitz and Trefil write, 'it simply takes time for all this detailed structure to form'.[65]

The fetus thus becomes more of an embodied human being all throughout the process of gestation. And, while that form of embodiment is not a constitutive feature of personhood status, the notion that late fetuses warrant greater moral respect,

---

[62] Harold J Morowitz and James S Trefil, *The Facts of Life: Science and the Abortion Controversy* (Oxford University Press 1992) 88.
[63] ibid 116.   [64] ibid 85.   [65] ibid 88.

or that late abortion entails a more serious loss, can be made intelligible if Crary and Diamond are correct that individual capacities are not the only things which appropriately inform our attitudes to other creatures.

Just as with Crary's examples, we might judge that the flippant or brutal treatment of recognizably embodied human beings is disquieting in large part because of the disrespect that it manifests for a creature of a certain kind, that is, assuming a certain form—*our* form—despite the fact that her psychological capacities are no more developed than that of a lower mammal. Callous attitudes towards partially or nearly fully formed human beings could be disturbing in much the same way as was the behaviour of the scientists who mocked their baboon subjects.

According the fetus greater moral respect on account of its growing embodiment might not, on its own, yield any obvious implications about the permissibility of abortion—including late abortion—where the strong interests of persons (pregnant women) are at stake. While Diamond and Crary underscore the moral imperative to treat even dead human bodies respectfully, neither argue that this holds at the cost of sacrificing the most significant life interests of actual persons. Thus Diamond does not condemn the cannibalism of already dead human beings in emergency situations. However, the moral importance of respecting the human form can make rational sense of the common aversion towards very late abortion, and unease about abortive procedures which proceed by violently attacking the bodily integrity of the fetus, even if such abortions can be morally permissible.

Our moral sensibilities rightly react against the treatment of developed fetuses as negligible blobs of matter not because we mistake them for persons, but because we share in the belief, expressed various ways, that the morally appropriate treatment of creatures is informed not only by their individual capacities, but also, in many cases, by their mode of embodiment. This is what I take to be the kernel of truth in the gradualist view of fetal moral status.

8

Human Equality and the Significance of Birth

8.1 The Equality Problem and the Threshold Problem

In the previous chapter, I argued that the core constitutive features in our concept of a person are the sorts of sophisticated emotional and psychological capabilities typical of mature human beings. While there might exist no strict set of necessary and sufficient conditions for personhood status, it is capacities of this nature which, I argued, are central to what it means to be a person. However, I also offered an argument as to why there may be good reason to regard later abortion as more sobering than abortion at earlier stages, grounded in the idea that pure human embodiment can matter for the morally appropriate treatment of individuals, regardless of their capacities. My conclusions thus broadly supported gradualist moral intuitions about abortion, although not in the typical way. Since I still take personhood status to supervene on the acquisition of a cluster of higher psychological and emotional capacities, none of which obtain before birth, I do not endorse the sort of gradualism which ascribes the fetus greater degrees of personhood status as gestation progresses. However, I contended that we nevertheless have good reason to treat more fully developed fetuses with greater moral respect, and not like pure masses of tissue, and that the basic gradualist intuition is thus rationally defensible.

If I am right about all of this, two important questions still remain. One has to do with the difference between abortion and infanticide. The other has to do with the moral equality of all human beings. I contend that our concept of a person is grounded in sophisticated psychological and emotional capacities. However, it is clear that these traits themselves admit of degrees. That is to say, not even all *born* human beings bear out these capacities to exactly the same extent. This seems to be true whether the capacity we are considering is rationality, agency, language ability, empathy, sensitivity, or any other developmental characteristic which we think part of the concept of a person.

Human beings can possess these qualities in drastically different measures. And, of course, some are absent entirely from infants and the radically cognitively disabled. The upshot is that developmental accounts of personhood appear tough to square with the view that all human beings possess equal moral status. For some, this is an insurmountable obstacle for any theory which takes personhood to supervene on acquired characteristics or traits. If moral status depends on graduated characteristics, how can one avoid the implication that some born human beings

Arguments about Abortion: Personhood, Morality, and Law. First Edition. Kate Greasley. © K. Greasley 2017. Published 2017 by Oxford University Press.

are more fully realized persons than others? Robert P George and Christopher Tollefsen explain the problem as follows:

The acquired qualities that could be proposed as criteria of personhood come in varying and continuous degrees. There are, in fact, an infinite number of degrees of the development of the basic natural capacities for self-consciousness, intelligence or rationality. So if human beings are worthy of full moral respect (as subjects of rights) only because of such qualities, and not because of the kind of being they are, then, since such qualities come in varying degrees, no account could be given of why basic rights are not possessed by human beings in varying degrees. The proposition that all human beings are created equal would be relegated to the status of a myth – a noble (or, perhaps, not-so-noble) lie.[1]

They develop the objection at a later point:

We most certainly do not think that especially magnificent human beings, such as Michael Jordan or Albert Einstein, are of greater fundamental and inherent worth and dignity than human beings who are physically frail, or mentally impaired, or even just physically immature. We would not tolerate the killing of a retarded child, or a person suffering from, say, brain cancer, in order to harvest transplantable organs to save Jordan or Einstein.[2]

According to George and Tollefsen, this equality problem is a fatal flaw of all developmental theories of personhood. The problem might be thought to pose a serious challenge to the view that personhood has anything whatsoever to do with characteristics like rationality or communicative ability, which admit of degrees. Since all of these properties are scalar, how can any account that seeks to analyse personhood in terms of them account for the moral equality of born human beings?

It is important to understand how the equality problem differs from the threshold problem examined in chapter 5. The threshold, or 'cut-off', problem challenged putative thresholds of personhood on the ground that they could not be nonarbitrarily distinguished from earlier or later points on the continuum of human development. The equality problem, somewhat differently, contests the relevance to personhood of *any* property that can be shown to admit of gradations in born human beings. George and Tollefsen believe that the equality problem steers us towards accepting species membership as the sole criterion of personhood, since it alone seems compatible with basic human equality. Unlike everything else, the property of 'being a conceived human organism' is not one that obtains in different amounts across all human beings.

The human equality issue blends into a further problem concerning the threshold for full personhood status. Although fetuses (even late-term ones) instantiate none of personhood's constitutive properties, the gradualist view I have endorsed nevertheless gives us reason to accord them some moral respect on account of their burgeoning human embodiment. But the objection will arise quickly that newborn human infants do not manifest any more 'person-like' traits than do

---

[1] Robert P George and Christopher Tollefsen, *Embryo: A Defense of Human Life* (Doubleday 2008) 121.
[2] ibid 178.

late-term fetuses (they are no more rational, reflective, etc), and that they too are immature versions of embodied human beings. The question remains, then, as to why infants ought to be awarded any more moral respect than late-term fetuses, and why infanticide cannot be permitted in circumstances where late abortion would be.

In response to these problems, the defender of the developmental view of person-hood will presumably want to say that personhood is fully realized and equal across human beings once a certain threshold is passed. But how do we explain that? And why should that threshold be birth? At this point, the familiar objections about the moral arbitrariness of birth are likely to resurface. Since there appears to be no 'intrinsic' change from late gestation to birth, we will want to know why birth ought to mark the beginning of full and equal personhood.

8.2 Personhood as a 'Range Property'

One way to understand the claim that personhood is fully realized and equally pos-sessed by all human beings past a minimum threshold is to think of it as having the character of a 'range property'. The term 'range property' was coined by John Rawls to describe a certain feature of some concepts.[3] For instance, when considering the category of beings to whom the 'constraints of justice' apply, Rawls believed that the sufficient condition for being in that category is the capacity for moral personality. However, he acknowledged a possible problem with this criterion. In essence, this was the equality problem I laid out above. Although human beings in general meet the condition, (as he explains, 'there is no race or recognised group of human beings that lacks this attribute'[4]), there are of course some individuals who fail entirely to realize that capacity, or who realize it only to a minimal degree, perhaps as a conse-quence of some unfortunate defect or deprivation.

Nevertheless, Rawls believed that grounding human equality on variable 'natu-ral capacities' could be consistent with a commitment to basic human equality. While a 'natural' (meaning, capacities-centered) basis for equality may be needed to identify the morally important class, Rawls argued that a correct conception of justice does not permit fine-tuning the amount of moral protection to a subject's individual capacities, once a minimum threshold is crossed. Rather, 'once a certain minimum is met', he claimed, a person is entitled to equal liberty on a par with everyone else'[5]. He explained further:

All we have to do is to select a range property (as I shall say) and to give equal justice to those meeting its conditions. For example, the range of being in the interior of the unit circle is a range property of points in the plane. All points inside this circle have this property although their coordinates vary within a certain range. And they equally have this property, since no point interior to a circle is more or less interior to it than any other interior point.[6]

[3] John Rawls, *A Theory of Justice* (Original edn, Belknap Press 2005), 508.
[4] ibid 506.   [5] ibid.   [6] ibid 508.

The crux of the range property analysis is that once the boundaries of the range are specified, every example within it is regarded as being an equal instantiation of the property, whether it is at the centre of the range or right at the boundary-line. Jeremy Waldron further explains the nature of a range property with the use of a juridical analogy:

Consider the legal or administrative characteristic which a town might have of *being in New Jersey* (e.g. as opposed to being in New York or being in Pennsylvania). Though the city of Princeton is in the heart of New Jersey, well away from the state line, and Hoboken is just over the river from New York, right on the boundary, still Princeton and Hoboken are both *in New Jersey*, and they are both in New Jersey *to the same extent*, so far as the law is concerned. One could point to the scalar geographical difference between them and for various reasons that might be important; but jurisdictionally it is irrelevant. *Being in New Jersey*, then, is a range property, ranging over all the points within the boundaries of the state.[7]

As far as the administrative law is concerned, just where Princeton is located in New Jersey is irrelevant: 'that it is *within the range* is all we need to know'.[8] Our judgements about moral personhood suggest that we regard it in much the same way. Embracing the 'range property' approach to personhood does not mean that we should remain blind to differences in degree at all times and for all purposes. There are many sound reasons for the law, especially, to respond to differences in rational functioning, independent agency, and other capacities, in its treatment of human beings. Children need to be assigned guardians, because they are not mature enough to care for themselves. The mentally incompetent cannot give valid legal consent to medical procedures, because of the limits of their understanding, or be held accountable for crimes, because of their lack of agency. The law makes wards of those who, owing to a dearth in one or many of the paradigmatic person-like qualities, cannot live independently. And it bars the immature from some potentially dangerous activities: teenagers cannot make foreign policy, or operate dangerous machinery.

There may be all sorts of contexts, then, in which scalar differences are important. But on the 'range property' approach, there is one respect in which these differences do not make a difference: the property of being a full, rights-holding person. If personhood is a range property, then all humans within its range are persons equally, however much or little they instantiate its base properties. As far as inclusion in the category of persons is concerned, the switch is either on or off.

But how is the range property analysis of personhood to be defended? One might wonder if the range property view is not just an attempt to have it both ways - to claim that personhood is a binary property *and* that it supervenes on scalar properties. Defenders of the species membership criterion of personhood might well retort that this kind of thinking about personhood is simply indefensible. If personhood is correctly analysed in terms of rationality, self-awareness, emotional sensitivity, and

---

[7] Jeremy Waldron, *God, Locke, and Equality: Christian Foundations of John Locke's Political Thought* (Cambridge University Press 2002) 77.
[8] ibid 78.

so forth, then how could it fail to diminish or increase with the strength of those traits? If, instead, our commitment to human equality leaves us unable to relinquish the binary view of personhood, then perhaps we must reconsider the possibility that it supervenes on a property which is *not* graduated across born human beings, like human species membership.

Another pressing question is how we are to draw the boundaries of the range property. On the range property account, all individuals past a minimum threshold count as persons to the same extent; they are all equally within the circle. But what exactly is that minimum? The working assumption, of course, is that it is birth. But it is not obvious why birth, rather than some earlier or later threshold, should mark entry into the range of persons. Rawls recognized that 'the required minimum may often prove troublesome'.[9] Here, that trouble is the potential resuscitation of the abortion–infanticide issue. Of all the boundary-lines that could be chosen, why passage through the vaginal canal?

The beginning of a defence for the range property approach might be hinted at in Waldron's suggestion that where range properties are at issue, there is an 'interest' which 'drives us away from scalar differentiations'.[10] In the New Jersey example, that interest is 'constitutional and administrative'. He writes:

Relative to the interest driving the specification of the range property, the precise location of the entity on the scale is uninteresting. That it is *within* the range is all we need to know. Without such an interest, of course a range property seems merely arbitrary. One might stipulate it. But it would be hard to see the point . . . *the interest shapes the range property and makes it intelligible.*[11]

It is not hard to imagine what possible legal or pragmatic interests there could be in understanding personhood as a range property. There is a serious need for legal bivalence about personhood status in any individual case. The reasons for the law to regard personhood status as absolute may be many. They include: avoidance of the harmful symbolic significance of sub-classifications; the maintenance of social cohesion; the prophylactic interest in avoiding unjust or callous treatment of marginalized groups and the disintegration of a common citizenship which might result from hierarchies of personhood status. It is nothing short of unthinkable that the law should deal with personhood as anything other than an absolute property.

But the objection is likely to arise that these are merely pragmatic or instrumental reasons for treating all human beings within a certain range as equal in moral status. Even if human equality under the law is practically necessary for human life as we know it, it might be argued that a purely contingent basis for moral equality fails to properly address the equality problem. For that, one must be able to produce a non-instrumental reason why all human beings within a range are in fact persons equally. As Margaret Little contends, any theory on which the equality of mentally impaired human beings is a matter of 'polite extension' seems to be 'a limited theory indeed'.[12]

---

[9] Rawls (n 3) 509.   [10] Waldron (n 7) 78.   [11] ibid. My emphasis.
[12] Margaret Little, 'Abortion and the Margins of Personhood' (2008) 39 Rutgers Law Journal 336.

We should, I think, be cautious of supposing that all pragmatic or instrumental considerations are necessarily non-moral ones, or that contingent worries cannot feature in moral assessments. Some instruments are of a very special kind. Maintaining a coarse-grained approach to gradations across human beings for the purposes of ascribing basic moral status might be an attitude that is absolutely critical to human life and what is valuable within it. Given this, it would be distorting to claim that the range property analysis lacks a compelling justification because it is a 'merely' contingent necessity. Further to this, though, the 'merely instrumental' objection might fail to account for very particular ways in which the maintenance of human equality within a range is a genuinely moral, not only practical, necessity. More needs to be said to explicate that moral necessity. Taking our cue from Waldron, it seems what we must look for is a general moral interest that drives the range property analysis and 'makes it intelligible'.

8.3 'Opacity Respect'

We might worry that there is a problem of circularity in claiming that there is a moral interest driving the specification of 'person' as range property. Surely such a moral interest exists only if all human beings within the range really *are* morally equal. But this is exactly what an account that grounds personhood on graduated characteristics seems to deny.

In a discussion about the basis of human equality, Ian Carter considers this challenge as it applies to the range property solution.[13] The problem, Carter explains, is that of showing why we should concentrate on the range property itself, rather than on the more basic scalar properties. We require, he says, some 'independent moral reason for focusing on the range property', a reason that, to avoid circularity, must be independent from any prior commitment to equality.[14]

Carter suggests that a moral reason of this nature can be found in the necessity for what he terms *evaluative abstinence*, meaning, 'a refusal to evaluate persons' varying capacities', relative to their classification *as* persons.[15] The need for evaluative abstinence stems from the conditions of showing respect for human dignity. Showing respect for persons, he argues, involves adopting a certain perspective, one which avoids looking at their variable qualities and capacities when assigning them basic moral respect. He writes:

Respect, on this alternative interpretation, is a substantive moral attitude that involves abstaining from looking behind the exteriors people present to us as moral agents. More precisely, while we may see behind these exteriors (for to do so is often unavoidable), if and when we do perceive people's varying agential capacities we refuse to let such perceptions count as among the reasons motivating our treatment of those people.[16]

---

[13] Ian Carter, 'Respect and the Basis of Equality' (2011) 121 Ethics 538.   [14] ibid 550.
[15] ibid.   [16] ibid 551.

On Carter's view, respect for human dignity requires maintaining a kind of blindness towards individuals' varying capacities. It requires, in his words, treating them as 'opaque' in many respects. The outward dignity of a person is, he argues, compromised by a certain kind of appraisal by others. Humans lose that dignity when they are 'inappropriately *exposed*', which is when they are evaluated in respect of features which ought not to be evaluated in the given context.[17] The realization of outward dignity requires, he argues, 'a degree of concealment' in the way of inaccessibility to features that pertain to particular agential capacities.[18] Carter terms this external perspective 'opacity respect'. He claims that opacity respect is the appropriate attitude to adopt above a certain absolute minimum possession of the relevant capacities. Opacity, we might say, is instrumentally indispensible to sustaining the sort of relations that Carter thinks of as inherently morally valuable: relations in which the community of persons treat each other with dignity.

Carter makes clear that the importance of evaluative abstinence does not render all engagements in internal evaluations of others inappropriate. Some such evaluations are apposite when people occupy certain roles. 'I can', he explains, 'assess a person's intellectual capacities as insofar as I relate to her as a professor'.[19] Likewise, it is not inappropriate when medics and psychologists assess our physical and mental capacities. Human dignity does not require total blindness to each other's differences in all contexts. But it requires the refusal to focus on many of them in many contexts, and especially insofar as we relate to each other as morally considerable persons.

Thus, respect for persons and their outward dignity grounds a moral need to treat personhood as a range property. Carter's analysis explains why, above an absolute minimum, 'opacity respect' necessitates a range property analysis, under which interpersonal variations in person-relevant capacities do not affect the equal moral status of individuals within the range. These reasons to treat personhood as a binary category above a minimum threshold are not merely instrumental, but morally essential for maintaining the kind of relations between persons that we deem valuable. To be a person is to be the sort of being whose specific cognitive or emotional capacities are irrelevant for the basic appraisal of her standing as a creature worthy of the strongest moral protection. This same idea is, of course, embedded in the philosophy of those who support conception as the qualification threshold for personhood. Proponents of the conception threshold also treat personhood as a binary property within a specified range. Where they differ from others is in how they specify the boundaries of that range.

8.4 The Edge of the Range

Let us suppose then that we have hit upon a moral interest driving the specification of personhood as a range property. A difficult question still remains. What is

---

[17] ibid 555.   [18] ibid 556.   [19] ibid 557.

that absolute minimum threshold above which the range property specification applies? In most discussions about human equality, as I noted, it is assumed that the boundary-line is birth. But why does 'opacity respect' begin here, not sooner or later? Presumably, the interest driving the need to specify a range does not necessarily specify *how* that range ought to be marked out. Carter presents a persuasive argument for regarding personhood as a binary property above a minimum threshold, but it is not yet clear why that threshold could not be conception, viability, or some time during infancy, rather than birth.

As I have said, defenders of the species membership criterion for personhood share the 'range property' intuition, but take that range to be bounded by genetic humanity rather than birth. Should opacity respect not include fetuses, along with born human beings? The species membership argument might be helped along here by the popular claim that there is no morally significant difference between a very late fetus and a neonate that could explain or justify placing personhood's minimum threshold at birth.

The question then turns to the reasons which exist for stipulating the threshold in one place rather than another. To stipulate it at conception seems unsatisfactory given just how far away such organisms are from the sort of creatures that exemplify the base properties of personhood. Of course, wherever the threshold for full moral status is placed will be arbitrary in at least the sorites sense. This cannot be avoided. But there is no requirement to avoid that kind of arbitrariness unless one thinks that the threshold must aim at correspondence with a sudden metaphysical leap into personhood—a suggestion that I have argued lacks credibility.

When it comes to the law in particular, Timothy Endicott has set out some of the reasons why vagueness surrounding legal thresholds cannot be completely eliminated.[20] In fact, he argues, it is not clearly the case that vagueness entails a deficit in rule of law standards, or leads to arbitrariness in the pejorative sense. Endicott distinguishes four different forms of arbitrariness in governance. The law can be arbitrary when it: 1. 'gives effect to the unconstrained will of the rulers'; 2. does not treat like cases alike; 3. is unpredictable; or 4. when its provisions depart from what Endicott calls 'the reason of the law', by which he means the principles contained within the law.

Endicott's main point is that it is impossible for the law to perfectly uphold all of these standards. Moreover, much of the time, reducing arbitrariness in some respects may only increase it in others. For instance, making laws more precise, and hence more predictable, might require departing from the reason behind the law. He gives the example of a time limit of precisely seven months for the prosecution of serious criminal offences. A strict seven-month cut-off would result in permitting some prosecutions which, according to the rationale for the limitation, should really not be permitted, and precluding some that ought to be. This is an inevitable result of there being no meaningful difference between cases immediately on one side of the line or the other.

---

[20] Timothy Endicott, 'The Impossibility of the Rule of Law' (1999) 19 Oxford Journal of Legal Studies 1.

A precise legal threshold of personhood is not arbitrary in any of the senses one to three. But increasing precision can increase arbitrariness in the fourth sense by stipulating boundary-lines which 'do not reflect the reasons on which such a law ought to be based', like the reasons for or against prosecuting a crime.[21] The more precise a boundary is, the less likely that one can adduce a legal reason for placing the line right there. Increasing precision can require determinations to be made between adjacent points when there is no 'reason of law' for choosing between them. Given the sorites problem, it might be argued that every legal threshold is arbitrary in this fourth sense. No threshold can be non-arbitrarily distinguished from its very closest neighbouring points using principles of law.

So a legal threshold of personhood is not unacceptably arbitrary merely because it is sorites-susceptible. It may depart from the rule of law in being *too* precise to follow or to consistently enforce, or, indeed, too vague. This sets down some basic standards of clarity and practical usability for the legal threshold of personhood. A law which stipulates the beginning of personhood down to the millisecond will not be a good guide for conduct, even if it can just about be followed.

Some favour birth as a legal threshold for precisely these kinds of reasons: birth is a highly visible event, it is not speculative, and it is an easy guideline with which to comply. Other milestones, both post- and ante-natal, are somewhat less transparent and much easier to mistake or conflate with earlier and later developments, such as the acquisition of viability *in utero*, or of self-awareness post-birth. As Endicott helps to explain, considerations like clarity are not extra-legal, given that the need for clear resolution is itself a concern of the law. The only condition on the stipulated threshold is that it is within the range of acceptable solutions.

According to Endicott's standard, therefore, the only question we need ask is whether there is a decisive reason *against* stipulating birth as the threshold of fully realized personhood. Not only do I think that no such reason against birth as a legal resolution exists; there are, moreover, compelling reasons in favour of equating birth with the entry into the personhood range. Those reasons derive from the birth threshold's practical workability and its importance for some of the basic conditions of personhood.

8.5 From Womb to World

The utter triviality of birth for the moral status of an emerging human being is a long-standing claim in academic discussion about abortion, as we are by now well aware. In one iteration of that view, LW Sumner categorically dismisses the relevance of birth to moral status in the following terms:

Birth is a shallow and arbitrary criterion of moral standing, and there seems to be no way of connecting it to a deeper account. In most respects, the infant shortly after birth has the

---

[21] ibid 8.

same natural characteristics (is the same kind of creature) as a fetus shortly before birth; the same size, shape, internal constitution, species membership, capacities, level of consciousness and so forth. Biologically, a full-term infant resembles a fetus much more than it resembles a zygote or an embryo.[22]

Similarly, Jeff McMahan has challenged the moral distinction between infants and viable fetuses, questioning how the law can, with moral consistency, permit the abortion of fetuses at twenty weeks' gestation but not the infanticide of babies born prematurely at the same gestational age.[23] The problem of consistency, he claims, is raised by the fact that there is no 'intrinsic' difference between the two, only the 'extrinsic' difference of location. One manifestation of this inconsistency, he highlights, is that people will often accept the legitimacy of late abortion for reasons of fetal abnormality, like Down's Syndrome, while balking at the very suggestion of infanticide for the same reasons.[24]

I have argued so far that there is a moral interest in specifying personhood as a range property, stemming from the necessity for what Ian Carter calls opacity respect. I have also pointed out that settling on a threshold into that range by means of stipulation can be a legal end in itself. As Endicott explains, all legal resolution by stipulation entails a certain kind of arbitrariness, in that there will be no *principled* reason to place the boundary-line where it is and not a fraction to either side. Thinking again about the kind of moral arbitrariness to which McMahan alludes, let us accept, for now, that there is no significant moral distinction between human beings of the same gestational age that are on either side of the vaginal canal. The legal interests in stipulation—practical resolution, and the elimination of other forms of arbitrariness, like unpredictability and the different treatment of like cases—are, however, unaffected by this. As Endicott says, the only questions one need ask about a candidate threshold are whether it falls within the range of acceptable boundary-lines and whether there is any decisive reason *against* placing the threshold there. The fact that no principled distinction can be drawn between full-term fetuses and neonates, if that is true, cannot count as such a reason, since that only implicates the kind of arbitrariness that goes hand in hand with stipulation at any point.

Still, one might hope to see reasons of at least some kind for stipulating birth as the threshold for legal personhood, namely, reasons to favour it over other thresholds within an acceptable margin. I think that reasons of this kind are in fact forthcoming. As I hope to illustrate, birth is a particularly appropriate minimum threshold for entry into personhood's range for reasons having to do with the procedural interests in stipulation (certainty, consistency, and so on) and the essential preconditions for fully realized personhood.

[22] LW Sumner, *Abortion and Moral Theory* (Princeton University Press 1981) 53.
[23] Jeff McMahan, 'Infanticide and Moral Consistency' (2013) 39 Journal of Medical Ethics 273.
[24] For a simple restatement of this line of thought, see Alberto Giubilini and Francesca Minerva, 'After-Birth Abortion. Why Should the Baby Live?' (2013) 39 Journal of Medical Ethics 261.

8.5.1 Intrinsic and extrinsic qualities

I first want to pause a little over the claim that there is no 'intrinsic' difference between neonates and full-term fetuses. In the service of declaring birth morally insignificant, discussants typically emphasize the biological comparability of the late-term fetus and neonate. But this claim alone is liable to be exaggerated or simplified. In fact, many significant biological and behavioural state changes are triggered at birth. These include a number of biological adaptations which need to take place to enable a newborn to breathe in air for the first time. One such adaptation is the clearing of fluid from the lungs to allow them to inflate and draw in breath. Other significant adaptations include changes in the circulatory system, the activation of new enzyme systems, the digestive system, and the release of hormones to regulate temperature outside of the womb—to name just a few. In an explanation of the transition from intrauterine to extrauterine life, Noah Hillman *et al* describe that transition as 'the most complex adaptation that occurs in human experience'.[25] Birth is a dramatic biological event.

Upon emergence into the world, a new baby also exhibits radical behavioural state transitions, most notably: crying for the first time; heightened wakefulness and reactivity, and increased responsiveness to environmental stimuli like noise, light, and touch.[26] Some experiments have documented the capacity for neonates to imitate other people's facial expressions as early as forty-two minutes after birth, which is taken to indicate a primitive form of self-consciousness.[27]

It is simply false to claim, then, as some do, that the late fetus and the newborn share all of their properties except for their respective locations in the womb and in the world. Birth triggers this very same catalogue of changes in viable preterm neonates regardless of gestational age, although some of the developments will of course be stunted if the human being is too premature. Viable preterm infants undergo the same biological adaptations necessary for extrauterine life upon expulsion from the womb as do full-term ones. They too cry and breathe, and engage in limited inter-subjective interactions, such as responding to touch and sound.[28]

---

[25] Noah H Hillman, Suhas G Kallapur, and Alan H Jobe, 'Physiology of Transition from Intrauterine to Extrauterine Life' (2012) 39 Clinics in Perinatology 769, 769.

[26] Lynna Littleton and Joan Engebretson, *Maternity Nursing Care* (Thomson 2005) 757.

[27] José Luis Bermúdez, 'The Moral Significance of Birth' (1996) 106 Ethics 378, 398. See also, AN Melttzoff and MK Moore, 'Imitation of Facial and Manual Gestures by Human Neonates' (1977) 198 Science 75, and AN Meltzoff and MK Moore, 'Newborn Infants Imitate Adult Facial Gestures' (1983) 54 Child Development 702. In the process of challenging the view that a change in 'spatial position' is all that birth amounts to for the new human being, José Bermúdez drew attention to a series of experiments revealing that the ability to imitate facial expressions such as tongue protrusion obtained extremely quickly after birth, at an average age of thirty-two hours, and a lower limit of only forty-two minutes post-birth. Bermúdez argues that the capacity for facial imitation requires at least a primitive understanding of the difference between self and other, a rudimentary form of self-consciousness that full-term fetuses do not possess (see also Achas Burin, 'Beyond Pragmatism: Defending the Bright-Line of Birth' (2014) 22 Medical Law Review 494, 500–504).

[28] See: Colm PF O'Donnell and others, 'Crying and Breathing by Extremely Preterm Infants Immediately After Birth' (2010) 157 The Journal of Pediatrics 846, and Carol O Eckerman and others, 'Premature Newborns as Social Partners Before Term Age' (1994) 17 Infant Behaviour and

Is it so obvious that these kinds of physiological and behavioural state changes could not be intrinsic changes? Of course, this all depends on what exactly is meant by 'intrinsic'. If 'intrinsic' is taken to be merely interchangeable with 'morally significant', then sceptics about the significance of birth would presumably argue that birth does not mark an intrinsic change because it does not occasion any of the developments in cognition or consciousness which they take to be the only features relevant to moral status. It is important to be watchful here of the potential for such accounts to smuggle in a psychological capacities-based view of personhood's constitutive properties under the cover of the intrinsic–extrinsic distinction. It cannot be a foregone conclusion that intrinsic properties are only ever mental ones. This is what anyone committed to a psychological capacities account of moral status must establish independently. Thus, one cannot deploy the intrinsic–extrinsic distinction against the birth threshold before one explains what, on one's accounting, makes a feature intrinsic or extrinsic, and why the features one picks out as intrinsic are the only morally relevant ones. Unless we are sure that biological, relational, or location-based properties could never be morally significant, the intrinsic–extrinsic distinction will not entail a powerful a dismissal of the birth threshold. I have, of course, already endorsed the account which grounds the concept of a person in core psychological and emotional capacities. But this is not, to my mind, inconsistent with attributing some moral significance to birth—the kind of significance that might explain and defend identifying the threshold of personhood status with the birth event, given that such a threshold must be stipulated. For this, we need only be convinced that birth is in some way morally salient, enough that we might justify preferring it over other potentially reasonable entry points.

What does it mean to say, then, that the changes occasioned by birth are *merely* extrinsic? Some may want to dismiss them as such for the sole reason that they are precipitated by an event. But it is clearly not true that morally significant 'intrinsic' changes cannot be brought about by other changes in the world. That rendering of the intrinsic–extrinsic distinction could not possibly be correct. This can be shown by harnessing an example considered in the previous chapter, of a Superdog who, as a result of being subjected to intensive treatment, has acquired the cognitive capacities of a normal adult human being. It is not right to suggest that because the change in the dog's capacities depends on the circumstantial (or 'extrinsic') fact of having been selected for conditioning treatment, it is thereby not an intrinsic change. Clearly, intrinsic changes supervene in all sorts of ways on extrinsic ones.

The fact of having been born can certainly be extrinsic in a way, since it can depend on circumstantial factors not having to do with the nature of the early human being, including any of the circumstances that trigger labour. Nevertheless, the usual causal factor triggering birth is the maturity of the fetus, which is an intrinsic feature so far as an individual's biological traits can count as intrinsic. The reply to this by those who are sceptical about the moral significance of birth is likely

Development 55, in which the authors note that 'well before term age', newborns in face-to-face interactions responded to 'motherese' (baby talk) with 'increased visual attention' and to tactile stimulation with 'increased signs of distress and/or avoidance' (at 66).

to be that the kinds of changes occasioned by birth—adaption to the extrauterine environment, and the beginning of interaction and intersubjectivity—are simply irrelevant to moral status, biological or not. Even if it is true that intrinsic properties often depend on extrinsic ones, or that some intrinsic changes invariably take place at birth, the defender of the birth threshold must still show that these changes are intrinsic in the sense of being morally significant, not just in the sense of being internal to the individual rather than circumstantial. This is exactly what anyone who thinks that birth is utterly morally arbitrary believes cannot be shown. None of these changes, it will be argued, has anything to with what it means to be a person and to possess strong moral rights.

But it is not true that birth is irrelevant to the possession of those traits that constitute personhood status on the capacities-based view. For one, entrance into the extrauterine world is a necessary precondition for any of the higher cognitive abilities constitutive of fully realized personhood on those accounts. Some psychologists have even suggested that it is a basic precondition for consciousness itself.

While it does not possess anything like the spectrum of cognitive capacities paradigmatic of personhood, the neonate's emergence into the world introduces it to a mass of content for mental processing: the sights, smells, sounds, and feel of the world. The psychologist Stuart Derbyshire contends that exposure to this content is essential for developing conscious experience, memory, and emotion.[29] Considering this relationship between exposure to content and mental states in the context of the fetal pain debate, he writes:

Before infants can think about objects or events, or experience sensations and emotion, the contents of thought must have an independent existence in their mind. This is something that is achieved through continued brain development in conjunction with discoveries made in action and in patterns of mutual adjustment and interactions with a caregiver . . .

When a primary caregiver points to a spot on the body and asks 'does that hurt?' he or she is providing content and enabling an internal discrimination and with it experience. This type of interaction provides content and symbols that allow infants to locate and anchor emotions and sensations. It is in this way that infants can arrive at a particular state of being in their own mind.[30]

One of Derbyshire's main claims is that the content of the world provides the essential material for conscious thought and experience. In the womb, the fetus is cut-off from this content. Cocooned in the uterine environment, it lacks the stuff of both conscious experience and, Derbyshire argues, sensory reaction. Emergence into the world thus brings with it the objects of thought and experience. This new exposure to content is reflected in the neonate's mental state immediately after birth, when it experiences a period of intensely heightened alertness, interacting with and processing the world and everything in it.[31]

This is sharply contrasted by the 'sleepier' states of fetuses of the same or later gestational age.[32] As Derbyshire explains further, only when being presented with

---

[29] Stuart Derbyshire, 'Can Fetuses Feel Pain?' (2006) 332 British Medical Journal 909.
[30] ibid 911. [31] ibid 910. [32] ibid.

content can young infants begin to develop representational memory (what he calls, the 'building blocks of consciousness') by 'tagging' as 'something' 'all the objects, emotions, and sensations that appear or are felt', enabling, among other things, the subjective experience of pain—the 'ow!' reflex.[33] Like other mental processes, Derbyshire's conclusion is that the subjective experience of pain depends on the post-birth environment that makes all experiential discrimination possible.

According to some, then, emergence into the world marks the beginning of a human's exposure to the objects of mental experience and enables the discriminations necessary for conscious self-awareness and the basic understanding of where we end and everything else begins. It could be argued that embodiment in the world is a precondition for another capacity central to our concept of a person: the capacity for individual agency. Embodied presence in the world is integral to becoming an agent within it. Joseph Raz has argued that only through engagement with the world can human beings learn how to act so as to produce effects.[34] Through lived experience, we come to understand how to manipulate our environment so as to become a force within it. We learn this by testing our skills, learning how to calculate risk, and 'assessing what is likely or unlikely to happen in the normal course of events'.[35] As Raz elaborates, learning how to perform even the most basic of actions requires a certain amount of understanding the world as it is:

Unless I can trust the chair to carry my weight, the ground not to give way when I move across it, the plate on the table not to be stuck to the table when I reach for it, and to maintain rigidity and balance when I hold it, and so on, I cannot perform even the simplest act.[36]

Raz explains that learning how to perform actions is often concurrent with the acting itself; we learn how to affect our environment simply through doing so, and we learn how and when to exercise our skills through trial and error. Ultimately, it is only this kind of engagement with the world that enables persons to act *at all*, and hence mould their personal identity. Consequently, Raz suggests, someone who never engages with the world and only ever performs mental acts (who might be, for instance, kept alive through intravenous feeding)—who is, in other words, utterly passive—would live what seems to us to be a 'stunted and pointless' life. Raz seems to suggest that such a person would not be an agent at all, able to carve out a life narrative for himself. For this, one must be capable of *doing things* in the world.

If engagement with the world is inextricably bound up with our becoming agents, it seems that emergence *into* that world, far from being a mere change of location, marks the beginning of the early human being's path to agency. Although

---

[33] ibid 911.   [34] Joseph Raz, 'Being in the World' (2010) 23 Ratio 433.
[35] Joseph Raz, 'Agency and Luck' in Ulrike Heuer and Gerald Lang (eds), *Luck, Value, and Commitment: Themes From the Ethics of Bernard Williams* (Oxford University Press 2012) http://papers.ssrn.com/sol3/papers.cfm?abstract_id=1487552, 15 (last accessed 15 October 2016).
[36] Raz (n 34) 439.

a neonate is hardly an agent, birth is when it begins the concurrent process of understanding the world and learning how to act within it.[37] This is so because it marks the very beginning of a human being's exposure to the world in which she must learn how to act.

If agency in the world and conscious experience (including, especially, awareness of oneself as an individual subject) are important constitutive features of personhood, birth is a watershed development in the life of the early human being. It may be objected, however, that birth is still only a precondition for such capabilities. It is not typically thought that neonates are, by virtue of having *just* been born, in greater possession of these capabilities than are late-term fetuses. While it may now exist in the essential context for developing conscious awareness and learning how to be an agent, a baby seconds after birth is not, at that moment, more of an agent or a subject of consciousness than a fetus seconds prior to birth. Because of this, it could be argued that birth is still a morally arbitrary threshold for full moral status.

However, following on from my argument above, this objection fails to properly apprehend what counts as a good reason to stipulate the legal threshold of personhood at birth, and what sort of arbitrariness that stipulation needs to avoid. I have already pointed out that any stipulated threshold for fully realized personhood will be arbitrary to the extent that nothing metaphysically transformative will have taken place directly on either side of the threshold. This arbitrariness is unavoidable. We have seen, however, that resolution through stipulation is a principled reason in itself, and that there is a moral interest for specifying personhood as all-or-nothing past a minimum threshold. Assuming, then, that birth is within the range of acceptable minimum thresholds for personhood, we only need reason to regard it as an especially significant development for the moral status of the early human being, such as could explain and defend choosing it over other acceptable thresholds.

8.5.2 Embodiment in the world

I have yet to consider the most obvious change brought about by birth: physical separation from the pregnant woman. Unlike the preconditions for self-consciousness and agency that I discussed above, this change *is* an immediate difference between late fetuses and neonates on the other side of birth. As soon as it is born, the neonate immediately possesses something it previously lacked, this being separate embodiment in the world. Is that a purely 'extrinsic' property?

Insofar as physical separation of the fetus from the woman can depend on things not having to do with the individual features of the fetus, such as a freak incident triggering premature labour, it could be considered an extrinsic property. But then,

---

[37] See also Burin (n 27) 507, where she writes: 'We want to influence or affect the world in our everyday lives, and we do this by interpreting it and acting in it. There is a constant dyad between it and us.'

almost any property can be extrinsic in this kind of way. The neonate's physical separation is also an *intrinsic* feature in the sense that it is a physiological feature internal to the new human being. But is it a morally significant intrinsic feature?

A foreseeable objection to the suggestion that separate embodiment is morally significant is that an individual who is physically attached to someone else can undoubtedly still be a person, as Thomson's violinist demonstrates. In that thought-experiment, there is no doubt about the violinist's full moral status merely because he is attached to another's body; this is what makes the case an apt control test for the moral relevance of bodily dependence on another.

As Thomson's argument tried to show, facts that are in one way 'extrinsic', like the fact of your being attached to another person's body, could also be morally significant, affecting your rights against that person, like the right not to be killed by them or to continue getting bodily support at their expense. The fact that the violinist finds himself attached to your body and incapable of surviving in any other way is an extrinsic feature of his in that it is situational, yet so are many facts that can determine an individual's right to life. One thought-experiment in moral philosophy I mentioned in chapter 3 concerned a large man blocking the mouth of the cave in which other people are trapped and which is quickly filling up with water. As we saw there, some hold the view that if there is no other route to salvation, those trapped are permitted to blow up the large man in order to escape. This of course means that the large man's right to life is conditioned by situational facts: the fact that he is (albeit blamelessly) blocking the mouth of a cave in which others are trapped; the fact that the cave is filling up with water, the fact that there is no other avenue of escape, and so on.

So Thomson was not wrong to think that a situational fact could affect a person's right to life. I argued that Thomson was nevertheless wrong in her particular claims about abortion. That is, if we really believe that the fetus is a fully realized person, we cannot show, using general moral and legal principles, that abortion is almost always permissible. But in chapters 2 and 3 we also learned just how difficult it is to maintain, for the sake of argument, the presumption that the fetus is fully a person whilst being entirely enclosed within the womb. As Margaret Little points out, imagining persons *like this* seems to stretch our concept of a person possibly beyond recognition.

The difficulties we encounter when trying to imagine persons that are enclosed in another's body indicate to me that separate embodiment in the world plays some part in our concept of a person. At the very least, a lack of individual embodiment seems to constitute a diminution of one's personhood. This can be brought out by looking to Stephen Mulhall's analysis of a real-life case of conjoined sisters, Abigail and Brittany Hensel, who, conjoined below the neck, share a significant proportion of their body. Mulhall's comments about the twins come as a response to McMahan's claims that, in such a case, no one can doubt that they are 'separate and distinct little girls', each one having an independent mental life and personality, despite sharing a physical body.[38] In reply, Mulhall underscores the myriad

---

[38] This consideration is intended to go in favour of McMahan's 'embodied mind' account of personal identity, according to which we persist as the same person over time as long a certain part of

ways in which the girls' shared embodiment precludes them from living the kind of life distinctive of persons. For example, the 'rootedness' of their biographical lives in 'common flesh' means that neither twin can ever play with other children on her own, have a private conversation with her mother, or go out alone with a boyfriend.[39] This does not mean that neither twin should be regarded as a person in her own right, and Mulhall does not suggest this. But we might accurately say that the twins' wealth of togetherness, caused by their physical union, gives rise to a serious deficiency in their ability to live fully as persons. Perhaps, then, as Mulhall writes, a 'sense of the separateness of persons' is embedded into our concept of personhood.[40]

The fetus's lack of individuated embodiment is far more extreme than that of the Hensel twins. Despite sharing a physical frame in very thoroughgoing ways, the conjoined twins do both have an embodiment in the world of other human beings. They can interact with that world and with other people as individuals, and produce some effects in it. If nothing else, they can communicate as individuals and express personal identities. None of this is true of the fetus. We can imagine being presented with a different pair of conjoined twins, one of which is completely enclosed within the other whilst still, somehow, being biologically sustained and in possession of a mental life. Unlike what appears true of the Hensel twins, I imagine that here many people will find themselves doubting whether it is really correct to identify two individual persons at all. This is a good indication of the importance of physical individuation for our common concept of a person, and of its limits. Although it is easy to think of persons that are, in some significant ways, in a situation of bodily enmeshment with others, there is a level of enmeshment beyond which much of the meaning of personhood seems to be lost.

In this respect, the fetus and the neonate are indeed differently positioned, despite the fact that whether or not they are so positioned depends on the fact of birth and everything that occasions it or delays it. Before it emerges into the world, the fetus cannot partake in interpersonal relations of any kind, communicate with the wider world, or respond primitively to other human beings, as can the neonate. Enclosed entirely within the body of another, the fetus has a solipsistic kind of existence whereby it is hidden and sealed off from other human beings and whereby they, in turn, are sealed off from it. This enclosure forestalls the fetus's engagement with the world of other persons as an individual member of their community, as well as its ability to express agency in the world. Although we can feel and see signs of its existence, and the fetus itself might respond to some stimuli that originate in the outside world—sounds, taste, movements, etc—that engagement is at all times mediated through the body of the pregnant woman.[41]

---

our brain survives. See Jeff McMahan, *The Ethics of Killing: Problems at the Margins of Life* (Oxford University Press 2002).

[39] Stephen Mulhall, 'Fearful Thoughts' London Review of Books 24 (2002) 16–18.
[40] ibid.
[41] For a good development of this point, and of the fact that the distinction between being in the world and being in womb subsists despite permeable boundaries, see Burin (n 27) 514–15.

The fetus is, in important ways, set apart from the world of common humanity. It is only upon emergence into that common world at birth that other humans can fully *treat* it as a fellow person—can directly see it, touch it, speak to it, assess and respond to its needs or confer benefits upon it, without going through the body of the pregnant woman.

Just as Mulhall said of the intelligent Superdog, it is difficult to see the sense in calling the developed fetus a person when it is so set apart from the context of shared human culture in which personhood as we know it is expressed. One might argue that the fetus is much further outside of that shared life than is the Superdog, since it cannot so much as exercise simple agency in the world. Its effects on the body of the pregnant woman are the only direct effects in the world it is able to produce. Newborns, by contrast, possess the separate embodiment that is necessary to fully partake in shared human life, and necessary for other humans to relate to them as fully fellow creatures. Other human beings can soothe a newborn, teach it, talk to it, and try to ascertain its wants. In short, they can treat it as one of them in ways that are only made possible by direct engagement with a creature as a separately embodied being.

Mulhall does not consider the fact that the fetus's enclosure in the womb seals it off from embodied human life not only partially but completely. Rather, he implies that, as with infants and the severely cognitively disabled, the ability to see in fetuses our own human embodiment is a reason to regard them as fellow creatures in the fullest sense, and to draw them into the fold rather than marginalize them. In the previous chapter, I argued that the burgeoning human embodiment of the gestating fetus is a reason to accord the fetus greater moral respect as it develops throughout gestation. Even late in gestation, however, fetuses differ starkly from both infants and the radically cognitively disabled in one respect that Mulhall deems pre-eminent. They lack the separate, physical presence in the world essential for sharing in embodied human life.

To be clear, the argument here is not that separate embodiment in the world is a condition for personhood status. Whether or not that is true, we do not have to decide on it for my purposes here. Pursuant to the 'range property' argument, I have only been outlining some reasons why birth is a particularly appropriate threshold at which to stipulate the beginning of fully realized personhood according to law, given that stipulation is, in all events, unavoidable. Against the conventional view that birth is completely morally arbitrary, I suggested that the transition from the womb to the extrauterine environment is a meaningful event in the life of a new human being. The many physical transformations occasioned by birth are not 'merely' extrinsic. Moreover, reflection upon the importance of separate embodiment in the world for distinctively personal life reveals the ways in which birth, far from being meaningless, places a new human being in the context within which the capacities of personhood are made possible. These strike me as good enough reasons to settle on birth as the threshold of legal personhood, assuming that it lies within the range of acceptable answers.

8.6 Conclusion

Let me now briefly retrace the argument about human equality and the significance of birth. It is comprised of two main stages. I first stated an argument for a basic threshold beyond which the differences between the cognitive or emotional capacities holding between human beings are not to be recognized for most purposes. It is morally critical that there is a point beyond which personhood, in its extra-legal and legal sense, is absolute.

I next presented an argument about what that threshold ought to be. I first pointed out that within an acceptable range of thresholds, the law's interest in resolution by stipulation means that the only applicable standard in picking an exact threshold is that there is no conclusive reason *against* settling upon it. However, I argued that there is particularly good reason to place that minimum threshold at birth, owing to the significance of separate physical embodiment for cultivating the core constitutive properties of personhood. Birth is a cataclysmic event in the life of a new human being because it propels the fetus into the context in which it can begin learning how to act in the world and be brought into membership with other human beings. Because of this, I contested the widely held belief that birth is a trivial, merely circumstantial change.

The range property analysis of personhood does not demand total blindness to variations in capacities between different human beings. We might, for instance, acknowledge that it is not in the best interests of a permanently comatose patient to have his life artificially prolonged, given that there are such significant elements of human life that he can no longer realize. It stated only that relative to the property of being a person, all living human beings post-birth are to be treated as equal within the range. Conversely, treating personhood as a range property from birth does not demand blindness to the *similarities* between late fetuses and neonates, which remain very close to one another on the continuum of human development. It may well be appropriate to respond to this closeness by according the late fetus a degree of moral standing, as the gradualist thesis holds. However, the closeness of late fetuses to neonates on the developmental scale is not an objection to the birth threshold. Both the moral interest driving the need to stipulate that threshold and the case for tying it to birth are unaffected by the many resemblances between early human beings either side of birth.

PART III

PRINCIPLE AND PRAGMATISM

9

Regulating Abortion

Part I of this book argued that whether or not the fetus is rightly considered a person is central to the moral and legal appraisal of abortion. Part II embarked on a sustained analysis of a number of arguments about the threshold of moral personhood and the constitutive properties of a person. I concluded that although the concept of a person has at its core the kinds of higher psychological and emotional capabilities typical of mature human beings, our practices and intuitions tend to attribute some moral meaning to the possession of human embodiment. In the context of abortion, this could explain why abortion is correctly considered a more morally sobering affair the later in gestation it occurs—a common view among liberals and conservatives alike.

I also argued that there are strong moral interests driving the treatment of personhood as a 'range property'. In short, there is a moral necessity in treating personhood, especially according to law, as all or nothing within a specified range. I finally argued that there are good reasons to stipulate birth as the threshold for fully realized personhood. Whilst acknowledging that the emergence of personhood is, in truth, a continuum admitting of no sharp borderline, I drew attention to a number of ways in which birth can be considered a meaningful event in the life of the early human being, and an apt threshold with which to identify the attainment of full personhood status, given that such a threshold must be stipulated.

What does all this mean for the legal regulation of abortion? The answer to this question, which is not immediately apparent, is the focus of this chapter. Let me state at the outset that it is unlikely any detailed schema of abortion regulation follows directly from my conclusions in Parts I and II. Instead, I want to suggest a few ways in which those conclusions might inform a good law of abortion or answer common arguments made in the realm of abortion regulation. I begin by surveying the various forms of abortion regulation that are on the table.

9.1 Modes of Regulation

When it comes to deciding upon the general structure of abortion regulation, the law has a whole menu of options from which to choose. Abortion can be criminalized in its entirety, or decriminalized only where specific circumstances are made out, as it is under the Abortion Act 1967 in England, Wales,

Arguments about Abortion: Personhood, Morality, and Law. First Edition. Kate Greasley. © K. Greasley 2017. Published 2017 by Oxford University Press.

and Scotland. The British legislation, introduced in order to legalize abortions deemed socially acceptable, operates by providing exceptions to default criminal liability for abortion where certain specified grounds are attested to by two doctors. Those grounds become stricter once the pregnancy has surpassed its twenty-fourth week.

A law of abortion which begins with default criminal liability and carves out exceptions can make those exceptions narrow or broad, numerous or few. Moreover, a lot depends on how much is open to interpretation. Some would argue that the liberal construction by medical professionals of ground 1(1)(a) of the Abortion Act in the years since its enactment has resulted in something close to 'abortion on demand' before twenty-four weeks of pregnancy. The ground provides that no one shall be criminally liable for an abortion where two registered practitioners form the good faith opinion that continuing the pregnancy poses a risk to a woman's 'physical or mental health', 'greater than if the pregnancy were terminated'.[1] As it happens, medical professionals in Britain have interpreted this ground widely and do not, for example, insist on demonstrable proof that continued pregnancy will cause a woman clinical depression or another medically recognized psychiatric condition before agreeing that a 'mental health' ground is made out. But it is easy to see how things might be very different. By placing the interpretive and decision-making power in the hands of medical professionals, the Abortion Act effectively made the medical profession the gatekeepers of legal abortion in Britain.[2] While this has resulted in a fairly permissive abortion practice today, a significant shift in medical opinion about abortion morality is all that it would take to completely overhaul this open practice.

A different kind of permissive abortion law might regulate only the medical procedures used in abortion to ensure standards of health and safety, leaving the decision to terminate entirely to women, either independently or in consultation with their doctors. This, in effect, would be to repeal all abortion law entirely, leaving the practice subject only to the general standards of care applicable to all medical practice. It would be to adopt a policy of complete non-interference with respect to abortion provision.

Differently again, access to abortion could be construed as a constitutional or human right within a legal system, or necessary for the fulfilment of some broader right, such as the right to privacy or procreative control. This, in essence, is the legal position on abortion in the United States as declared in the landmark decision *Roe v Wade* in 1973. In this alternative, the law does interfere, but on behalf of those who wish to obtain abortions. It might do so by placing principled legal limits on the kinds of restrictions on abortion that can be constitutionally valid, as in the US system, or, even, by making safe abortion provision a state obligation, something which *Roe v Wade* did not do.

---

[1] Abortion Act 1967, s 1(1)(a).
[2] See generally, Sally Sheldon, *Beyond Control: Medical Power, Women and Abortion Law* (Pluto Press 1997).

An important point to make here is that jurisdictions adopting very different structures of regulation might not necessarily differ all that much in terms of the practical availability of abortion. The comparative accessibility of abortion under markedly different regulatory regimes could even be the opposite of that which we expect. In Britain, as I said, abortion is a criminal offence unless one of the grounds in the Abortion Act applies. In the United States, on the other hand, the starting point is that the right to termination is a protected constitutional right. Nevertheless, abortion is more reliably accessible in Britain than it is in many parts of the United States. This owes largely to the fact that individual states are under no legal obligation to provide abortion services, even though the liberty to terminate is protected under the Constitution. This leaves practical abortion access highly dependent on the wishes, and, hence, ideology, of each individual state, many of which are far more antagonistic to abortion practice than is generally true of Britain. In the United States, the substantive right to abortion is therefore largely dependent on geography.

This brings into the foreground the important difference between the substantive freedom to obtain an abortion and a bare legal liberty to abort, where abortion is merely decriminalized but not provided for. Whether or not the abortion 'right' is formally recognized, one clear condition for the substantive freedom to abort is state provision of abortion through funding or services. Repeal of all abortion laws will not produce meaningful reproductive freedom if the only abortion services available are expensive or far away—or rather, that freedom will only exist for a select few. State funding of legal abortions in Britain (many abortions are funded by the National Health Service) probably does far more to facilitate abortion access than the default criminalization of abortion does to hinder it. Since *Roe*, the question of state and federal funding for abortions has been a key battleground of abortion politics in the United States, with the Supreme Court demonstrating unwillingness to read into the right to termination a positive obligation on governments to provide it. This was seen most unequivocally in the 1983 decision *Harris v McRae*, when the Court upheld the constitutionality of the 1977 Hyde Amendment which barred the use of US Medicaid funds for abortions, except where the woman's life is in danger or in cases of rape or incest.[3]

The restriction on the substantive freedom to abort in the United States has also been greatly compounded by the fact that the central ruling in *Roe v Wade* (that a woman has a fundamental right to termination of pregnancy) was subsequently held to be compatible with a large number of state-level restrictions on abortion access. This is because the Supreme Court in *Roe* did not recognize an *unqualified* right to an abortion. Rather, it held that states could have a legitimate interest in 'protecting potential life', and that they were entitled to restrict abortion where that interest

---

[3] *Harris v McRae* 448 US 297 (1980). The Court ruled that the Hyde Amendment was constitutional because it did not place an obstacle in the way of a woman who wanted a termination, but instead just encouraged an alternative choice. On the matter of public funding for abortion provision, see also: *Beal v Doe* 432 US 438 (1977); *Maher v Roe* 432 US 464 (1977); and *Webster v Reproductive Health Services* 492 US 490 (1989).

becomes 'compelling'. The *Roe* Court determined that the interest in protecting fetal life did not become compelling until the third trimester of pregnancy, when the fetus is capable of living independently from the pregnant woman. Thus, states were permitted to proscribe abortion in the third trimester of pregnancy, when the fetus was presumed to be viable, except where abortion was necessary to preserve the health and life of the pregnant woman. The Court also held that states could cite a legitimate interest in enacting restrictions for the protection of the health and safety of pregnant women, although this interest did not become 'compelling' until the second trimester. Abortion restrictions in the second trimester were therefore also constitutionally valid, but only if they were in the service of protecting women's health. In the *first* trimester, where no compelling state interest in restrictions could be adduced, it was held that women must be free to make abortion decisions in consultation with their doctors and without state restrictions—although, as was clarified in *Roe*'s companion case *Doe v Bolton*,[4] this did not amount to a constitutional right to 'abortion on demand'.

The 'trimester framework' for constitutional review of abortion regulation established in *Roe* was notably replaced in 1992 by the decision in *Planned Parenthood of Southeastern Pennsylvania v Casey*.[5] The *Casey* decision affirmed *Roe*'s central ruling that the right to a termination could be construed out of the constitutional right to privacy under the Ninth and Fourteenth Amendments, but replaced the trimester framework with a different structure of constitutional scrutiny, one which required only that state restriction of abortion prior to fetal viability did not place an 'undue burden' on a woman's right to procreative autonomy through the imposition of a 'substantial obstacle' to abortion access. Like *Roe*, *Casey* underscored fetal viability as the threshold beyond which the state's interest in protecting fetal life became 'compelling', and at which point states were therefore at liberty to prohibit abortion, so long as they provided exceptions where the health or life of the pregnant woman was at risk.

The abortion right in the United States is therefore far from unqualified. Since the *Roe* decision, the Supreme Court has upheld the legal validity of an array of state restrictions on abortion provision, including in the *Casey* decision itself. There, the Court upheld pre-abortion mandatory waiting periods, counselling requirements, and parental consent requirements for minors contained in the Pennsylvania law under consideration, invalidating only a spousal notification requirement which it deemed placed an 'undue burden' on women seeking abortion. Since then, the Court has upheld the constitutionality of further state regulations and, in *Gonzales v Carhart*, a near-absolute federal ban on 'partial-birth abortion', the extremely controversial method of late abortion during which the fetus is partially extracted from the uterus before being killed and fully extracted (briefly described in chapter 2).[6] Decisions such as these have had the effect of scaling back the abortion right established in *Roe* in many states.

---

[4] *Doe v Bolton* 410 US 179 (1973).
[5] *Planned Parenthood of Southeastern Pennsylvania v Casey* 505 US 833 (1992).
[6] See *Gonzales v Carhart* 550 US 124 (2007).

More recently, numerous state legislatures have managed to significantly restrict access to abortion by enacting what have come to be known as Targeted Regulation of Abortion Providers (TRAP) laws—extremely onerous licensing requirements that have resulted in the shutting down of many abortion clinics. Examples of TRAP law regulations include mandatory minimum hall widths that are the same as are required for hospitals, formal associations with hospitals that are often difficult to obtain, practitioner accreditation requirements beyond the level of skill required for performing abortions, and a whole number of facility standards based on those for hospitals and emergency rooms, the attainment of which would be effectively bankrupting for abortion clinics. In the recent case *Whole Woman's Health v Hellerstedt*, the Supreme Court struck down two such provisions in one of Texas's TRAP laws that had resulted in the closure of numerous clinics.[7] It was held that the requirements placed an undue burden on women seeking abortions, in breach of the *Casey* standard, by operating in effect to close down Texas abortion clinics and force women instead to travel hundreds of miles in order to obtain an abortion from the clinics left open, or even to go out of state.

In a similar vein, so-called 'informed consent' or women's 'right to know' laws have had the effect of restricting the ease of abortion access. Provisions of the kind typically include mandatory pre-abortion ultrasound scanning and information requirements that attempt to dissuade women out of choosing abortion by requiring medical staff to show them and/or describe to them the anatomy of their fetus, under the aegis of 'informed consent' to the abortion procedure.[8] Some 'right to know' laws have been struck down by state constitutional courts, although the mandatory ultrasound requirements have yet to be subject to constitutional review by the US Supreme Court.

Contrasting the British and US contexts clearly demonstrates that the availability of abortion in a jurisdiction depends on far more than the basic structure of abortion regulation. Despite the default criminalization of abortion in Britain, convictions for abortions performed are almost non-existent,[9] and abortion is easily accessible, especially before twenty-four weeks, owing to the liberal interpretation of the Abortion Act by the medical profession. In the United States, by contrast, abortion access continues to be patchy, and practically non-existent in some states, despite the constitutionalization of abortion rights.

Considering this contrast, supporters of abortion rights might understandably find themselves unsure about which regulatory framework is most conducive to

---

[7] *Whole Woman's Health v Hellerstedt* 579 US ___ (2016).

[8] For a good description of different state versions of the law, see Carol Sanger, 'Seeing and Believing: Mandatory Ultrasound and the Path to a Protected Choice' (2008) 56 UCLA Law Review 351. Some states require the provider to show and describe the image; others provide that she may decline to see or look away, though her decision to do so must be recorded. The Texas version of the law requires the practitioner to make the fetus's heartbeat audible to the pregnant woman.

[9] One notable exception is *R v Smith* [1974] 1 All ER 376, where a doctor was convicted of illegally performing an abortion after the jury found that he had not acted in good faith to preserve the health of the woman. The evidence in the case suggested that the doctor had made no examination of the patient or inquired into her personal history or situation. It was also unclear whether the doctor who had given the second opinion had examined the patient.

reproductive choice. Political temperature can determine far more than formal abortion law, and the optimal regulatory framework for securing the substantive abortion right will likely be jurisdiction-specific.

9.2 Moral Conclusions and Legal Regulation

Needless to say, regulating abortion is not the same as moralizing about it. Between morally permissible abortion practice and morally defensible regulation, there are any number of considerations to weigh in, not the least the fact that the law is rarely perfectly complied with, and in this area in particular. One sceptical worry might be that once all of the relevant factors are accounted for, hardly any role will be left for our thinking about fetal moral status when deciding on the correct legal framework for abortion.

A gap between what morality condones and what the law ought to permit can arise in more than one way. One way is where abortion regulation flies in the face of pragmatism—if, all things considered, enforcing morally proper abortion practice is counter-productive, if it merely augments overall harm done, or if it simply makes no difference, in which case it is inexpedient. This might be the case if, for instance, coercively removing abortion options does not reduce or discourage unacceptable abortion practice, but only fuels demand for unprofessional and unsafe practitioners, endangering women's health and lives. This is the well-rehearsed 'back-street abortion' argument.

The 'back-street abortion' argument claims, in short, that since abortion practice will go on whether it is prohibited by law or not, and since illegal abortion is more dangerous for women than legally and medically regulated abortion, we should eschew abortion prohibitions *whether or not abortion is morally permissible.* The prohibition serves no purpose except to create needless risk of harm to women, who are likely to turn, in desperation, to unsafe 'back-street' abortionists. The historical prevalence of illegal and hazardous abortion in the United Kingdom and in the United States prior to the liberalization of their respective abortion laws is often presented as evidence of the extreme imprudence of banning abortion, whatever its moral character.[10]

We should bear in mind that the back-street abortion argument does not apply exclusively to a blanket prohibition. Rather, it might be unleashed against any specific abortion restriction. For instance, someone might claim that prohibiting 'late' abortion (say, post-twenty-four weeks) would only lead scores of women intent on procuring abortion late in pregnancy to find amateur means of doing

---

[10] For a detailed account of the widespread practice of illegal abortion in the United States before *Roe v Wade* see, generally, Carole E Joffe, *Doctors of Conscience: The Struggle to Provide Abortion Before and After Roe v. Wade* (Beacon Press 1995). As Joffe illustrates, it was disproportionately poor and socially unconnected women who had to take their chances with the unsanitary and unprofessional back-street abortionists, or 'butchers', whilst socially privileged women could often locate a qualified obstetrician-gynaecologist to perform the procedure safely and in secret.

so—including self-performed abortion. Hence, even if we believed that abortion only becomes morally impermissible past some late stage of pregnancy, the argument from counter-productivity might still be used to oppose legal restrictions on late abortion.

The back-street abortion argument strikes many people as convincing. If attempting to prevent abortion through illegality (if and where it ideally would be prevented) is futile in any event, minimizing the harm to women that prohibition would only cause might appear to be the morally optimal policy. To start with, however, the inefficaciousness of abortion prohibitions can be exaggerated in some versions of the argument. Whilst it is true that criminal abortion laws will never deter all abortion, law abidance is a concern for enough people, I think, that we can presume a prohibition would appreciably reduce the number of abortions otherwise performed.[11] Not everyone will be willing to break the law to obtain an abortion. Moreover, the fact that a criminal prohibition will not deter all malfeasance is not generally accepted as a reason to dispose of a prohibition where the conduct *is* regarded as truly immoral and harmful. The fact that some theft, rape, and murder will always take place in spite of criminal prohibitions is not a good argument for the repeal of our theft, rape, or murder laws. There is no efficacy condition of absolute deterrence attaching to legal prohibitions on homicide, or indeed on any other offences against the person, and potential perpetrators of crimes involving harm to others cannot expect for the law to be guided by foresight of their recalcitrance and possible self jeopardy when framing its prohibitions.

That is just one indication that the success of the back-street abortion argument depends on our other moral commitments regarding abortion. The main argument, we saw, is not just that many women will be undeterred by prohibitions, but that the illegality of all abortion procedures will mean that many of them will come to harm, as they did in the days before the widespread legalization of abortion in the 1960s (in Britain) and 1970s (in the United States). But it seems to me that the force of this argument against abortion regulation critically depends on the belief that fetuses are not fully realized persons. This can be brought out with an imaginary example. Take a society in which ritual child sacrifice is routinely practiced by a certain group of people. In this society, those engaging in the ritual sacrifice usually do so under a certain amount of social pressure, and in the belief that a deity will punish them if they do not partake. Consequently, outlawing the

---

[11] As well as the sheer normative force of the law, which still resonates with many, registered obstetrician-gynaecologists have plenty to lose through disobedience, even if their patients do not. Added to this must be the reticence of some, at least, to subject themselves to unregulated abortion care for fear of the enhanced risks. The general deterrent effect of illegality is especially potent where it is instrumental to creating a moral stigma around a practice, which often it can be (consider the stigmatizing effect of the prohibition on various drugs, or the banning of smoking in public places). The decision to not only restrict or prohibit a practice, but to actively stigmatize it as well, is among the regulatory choices that governments can make, and a choice that can tend towards greater compliance with prohibitions. Lastly, the relative inaccessibility and inconvenience of abortion that its illegality would entail is also sure to deter a large number, even if it would not inhibit the attempts of those most determined to end their pregnancies.

practice will not extinguish it, but only lead those involved to carry it out in secret, but with the side-effect of creating a danger for the practitioners, for let us suppose that the ritual killings involve hazardous procedures which, if not performed by regulated professionals, will threaten the health and life of all those involved.

I presume most people would agree that even if outlawing the practice would not prevent it from taking place, and would almost certainly result in additional injuries to those performing it, conscionable lawmakers would ban the practice all the same and simply hope to enforce the ban as best they could. If this is indeed correct, the thought-experiment reveals that the inevitability of some non-compliance and consequent jeopardy to women's health are not considerations strong enough to defend the legality of abortion if it amounts to unjustified homicide. This in turn shows that our independent conclusions about the moral status of the fetus are relevant even to the back-street abortion argument against abortion restrictions.

Another gap between abortion morality and appropriate regulation might arise from a principle of justified toleration of morally suboptimal conduct. Not all immoral conduct is apt for legal prohibition (most people do not, for example, wish to outlaw all lying, or infidelity). Liberal political values require that some margin of error be left for us to make morally dubious choices. Perhaps this includes morally dubious reproductive choices. Like the back-street abortion argument, however, the justified toleration argument does not go through if and when abortion is considered to be an instance of justified homicide. The law does not and cannot consign homicide to the realm of private morality. This means that the toleration argument will not hold sway for anyone who believes that the fetus is morally on a par with human children or adults.

Next, it is sensible to think that some degree of efficacy is a basic condition for acceptable legal regulation, especially for prohibitions. If that is correct, then it is relevant question whether a law which proscribes only patently immoral abortions will have much of an impact on behaviour, given the general operation of self-censure. The undesirability of 'late' abortion is widely recognized by women in England and Wales without the help of the law, as is illustrated by the comparatively low rate of terminations taking place after twenty-four weeks of pregnancy: in 2014, 92 per cent of terminations were carried out at under thirteen weeks, with only 2 per cent carried out at over twenty weeks, and one tenth of one per cent after twenty-four weeks.[12] The example of a woman who aborts a late pregnancy for a frivolous reason like safeguarding a holiday may be unsettling, but it is also quite farfetched; these are not abortion scenarios the law is typically needed to prevent.

---

[12] Department of Health, *Abortion Statistics, England and Wales: 2014* (June 2015). The British Pregnancy Advisory Service (BPAS), England and Wales's largest provider of post-twenty-week abortions, receives around only 100 requests a year for abortion beyond the twenty-four-week threshold, which have to be turned down. As BPAS reports, the figures for abortions carried out between twenty and twenty-four weeks are already low. This suggests that women on the whole are extremely reluctant to request abortions for developed pregnancies, and that where they do so, they perceive the need to abort to be fairly urgent (see British Pregnancy Advisory Service, 'Abortion: A Briefing Document on Why Access to Late Abortions Needs to be Defended' http://www.prochoiceforum.org.uk/ocrabort-law9.php (last accessed 15 October 2015)).

A relevant question here is not just whether the legal permissions tally with the moral ones, but whether restrictions are worth their cost, and one important factor in assessing this is whether the difference to reproductive behaviour they will actually make is worth the added risks they will impose on those who are willing to flout them. This is only assuming, though, pursuant to the above, that abortion, even when immoral, is not the wrong of unjustified homicide.

A further consideration might be whether regulation is able to fulfil a worthwhile expressive value, even if its effect on the abortions actually carried out is negligible. Perhaps, it could be argued, the default criminalization of abortion or the requirement that women state grounds for termination, such as is in place in the British regulatory framework, plays an important communicative role in underscoring the moral value of the fetus and the moral seriousness of the abortion decision. Indeed, regulation might well fulfil that function even where, in practice, it amounts to little more than a rubberstamp system. Part of that value, someone might suggest, lies in simply signposting the moral gravity of the abortion decision to the woman herself and encouraging her appreciation of its seriousness.

Even if this communicative function is a legitimate legislative aim, however, that expressive value will still need to be balanced against the intrusiveness and burdensomeness to women that regulation entails. This is especially true in a framework like that of the United States, in which the choice to terminate pregnancy is a protected constitutional right. Calculations such as this would also need to take account of the intrusiveness of regulation in light of its standard interpretation. In the British context, for example, the fairly liberal interpretation of ground 1(1)(a) means that a ground for abortion can usually be adduced before twenty-four weeks of pregnancy. However, the medical profession's—and to some extent, the courts'—interpretation of other provisions in the Abortion Act has resulted in the imposition of some non-negligible burdens on women seeking out early termination. This has been especially true of provisions pertaining to where abortions can be carried out, and the extent to which adequately trained nurses, rather than doctors, can perform simple abortion procedures.[13]

Balancing the symbolic value of the need to state statutory grounds for abortion against its burdens also requires one to take account of the fact that all reproductive decisions are by their very nature serious, regardless of the individual reasons for which a woman desires a termination. All abortions are carried out for at least the reason that the pregnant woman does not wish to become a parent, or to carry and then give up her biological child. Whatever the circumstances motivating those wishes (whether they stem from financial or relational insecurity, the wish not to interrupt one's life plans, or the simple belief that one would not relish being a parent), responsibility for a new child is a radical enough development in anyone's life that to become a parent against one's will at any time is always fairly serious. Thus, there *is* always a reason behind abortion, and that reason is hardly ever (if

---

[13] See, for example, *British Pregnancy Advisory Service v Secretary of State for Health* [2011] EWHC 235 (Admin).

ever) trivial, because the plain wish not to bring a new child into the world is not trivial. This may call into question the notion that formal regulation is ever needed to impress on women the gravity of the abortion decision.

Lastly, a gap between the legal regulation of abortion and the morality of abortion can arise from the constraints of the rule of law. The law cannot declare that there is a grey area during which personhood emerges, and leave it at that. It cannot state that abortion is more serious the later in pregnancy it occurs, but refuse to lay down specific rules. The law must offer guidance on abortion that is capable of being followed, that is clear, predictable, prospective, treats like cases alike, and so on. As we saw in the last chapter, providing practical resolution for some threshold problems is part of the purpose of the law. The rule of law's standards thus imports considerations into the regulation of abortion that do not exist in abortion morality.

9.3 Legal Goals and Legal Constraints

As we know, then, adjustments always have to be made when translating moral conclusions into legal norms. But scepticism about the legal implications of my analysis in Part II might be of an even more thoroughgoing nature. One might wonder, for example, what the implications are of believing that the fetus is owed *some* moral respect on account of its growing human embodiment, even though it does not instantiate any of the core features of a person. Or of the fact that there is no non-arbitrarily distinguishable 'moment' at which it is reasonable to believe a fully rights-holding entity arrives on the scene. One possible concern is that these contentions are too philosophically inert to yield clear conclusions about when abortion is and is not acceptable, such that could provide even the starting point for a legal framework. In most of what remains here, I want to suggest just a few possible ways that my analysis in both Parts I and II might inform the legal regulation of abortion, bearing in mind that the usual gaps between morally ideal behaviour and justified legal regulation must always be considered.

9.3.1 Proportional moral gravity

One of my conclusions in Part II was that the moral significance of human embodiment underpins the basic gradualist intuition that abortion is a more serious affair the later in gestation it occurs, as pregnancy progresses and the fetus becomes more of an embodied human being. In short, it is intelligible to treat late abortion as involving a more serious loss of value than early abortion, notwithstanding the fact that even a late fetus does not possess any of the core constitutive features of personhood. If this is right, the law may have a prima facie reason to reflect this gradualist-leaning ethic through its abortion regulation. This could be communicated in a number of ways, and not only, or necessarily, by placing greater restrictions on abortions carried out later on in pregnancy. At the very least, the increasing embodiment of the fetus provides the law with a reason, in addition to concerns for women's health, to encourage early abortion over late abortion, and to abjure procedural requirements like mandatory waiting times, enforced counselling, and mandatory ultrasound if their net effect is only to delay abortions which will nevertheless take place.[14]

Where abortion regulation is in place, demonstrating respect for human embodiment may require nothing more than that early and late abortions are broadly differentiated in a legal framework. A more complicated abortion law, fine-tuned to multiple phases of fetal development, may come at the expense of being too difficult to follow and undermining clarity in the law (particularly so given that dating pregnancies always involves a margin of error), without adding much in terms of vindicating the gradualist outlook.

Reflection on the moral significance of both human embodiment and separate embodiment in the world can also have implications for the use of viability as a milestone in abortion regulation. The standard of constitutional review of abortion restrictions endorsed in *Casey* and the permissions of the Abortion Act in Britain are alike in treating viability as a pivotal milestone for the purposes of the law. As we saw, the *Casey* requirement that abortion restrictions not impose an 'undue burden' on women seeking abortions applies only before the threshold of viability, with states being free to prohibit abortion post-viability so long as they allow for exceptions where the pregnancy threatens the woman's life or health. Similarly, the British legislation places emphasis on the importance of viability by requiring more serious grounds for abortion after the lower threshold of viability which, when the Act was last amended, was thought to equate to twenty-four weeks of pregnancy.

In the conventional philosophical debate about personhood, we saw, viability is usually dismissed as tracking features that are inessential for personhood, such as independent breathing or living ability. However, where viability is taken to signify the current ability to live as a separately embodied being, then it may well track a development that is pertinent in our thinking about moral status. Viable fetuses are not yet in our world, but they are the sorts of beings which, if safely extracted rather than aborted, are capable of existing among us and of being included in distinctive human life. (At least, this is so where 'viability' denotes the point at which a human being is capable of living independently in the world and not the point at which extraordinary medical efforts can keep a child alive for a very short time only, in a state of severe dysfunction.) Defending the use of viability as a regulatory milestone need not imply the claim that independent living ability is a universal condition for personhood, but only that separate embodiment in the world is salient in our common understanding of personhood. If there is reason enough to endorse a time-limited abortion law, then pointing to this salience could justify incorporating the viability threshold into a legal framework.

---

[14] For an explanation of another key procedural obstacle to early abortion contained in the provisions of the Abortion Act which requires that all abortion 'treatment' be carried out on medical premises, see Kate Greasley, 'Medical Abortion and the "Golden Rule" of Statutory Interpretation' (2011) 19 Medical Law Review 314.

9.3.2 Upper limits

I turn now to the question of upper time limits for legally permissible abortion practice, the main regulatory question in which I believe most people are interested. Should there be an absolute cut-off for abortion? And if so, when should that be? Disappointingly, my arguments in Parts I and II do not provide a definitive answer to this question. I argued that the constitutive traits of personhood emerge gradually in human beings, but that there is nonetheless good reason to recognize the value in growing human embodiment, including in the womb, and that, as a matter of moral necessity, personhood must be regarded as all or nothing past a minimum threshold. I also argued that there are compelling reasons to recognize birth as that threshold past which the moral status of humans is full and absolute. But a range of absolute cut-off points for abortion could be consistent with these claims. Here, then, I will focus only on what my arguments do clearly suggest on the matter of upper limits, both in terms of the kinds of constraints they place on legal cut-off points and criticisms of abortion law which they might be used to counter.

The ubiquitous 'arbitrariness' complaint against any absolute cut-off is one criticism which, by now, we should be able to dismiss fairly quickly. Whether it is the absolute upper limit or the 'working gestational limit' (such as the twenty-four-week limit under the Abortion Act 1967) that is in question, this 'arbitrariness' complaint against legal line-drawing is not a sustainable criticism of any threshold where the arbitrariness impugned is that of the sorites kind. Not only does that complaint neglect the fact that resolution by clear stipulation is a function of the law, it also implies something about the nature of personhood which I argued there was little reason to believe, and good reason to disbelieve. It implies that the beginning of personhood is a sharp borderline, or, what I called the 'punctualist' thesis. I argued that, particularly given the falsity of punctualism, the inability to non-arbitrarily distinguish a twenty-four-week fetus from a fetus at twenty-three weeks and six days is not a reason to lower an abortion limit.

It is clearly incumbent on the law to stipulate a threshold of fully recognized personhood. I argued that birth is a particularly appropriate threshold for the law to use, owing to the significance of separate embodiment in the world for everything it means to be a person. Birth also has the legal virtues of clarity and recognizability. It has a universal social salience, high visibility, and unmistakability that make it especially suitable as a legal boundary-line. The birth threshold is not susceptible to reckless or negligent errors or accidents, and hence also does not encourage the kind of defensive or cautionary practices by healthcare professionals that might threaten to scale back abortion access far behind the permissions of the law were the threshold to be placed somewhere in gestation. Birth is not a matter of speculation, diagnosis, or disagreement. Settling on birth as an absolute cut-off allows for no ignorance of the upper limit, especially given the widespread cultural use of birth as an unequivocal marker of fully realized personhood outside of the law. Although there is still widespread disagreement about the fetus, it is universally understood that newborns are members of the human community, and, indeed, they are immediately treated as such: they are washed, wrapped up, embraced, and (usually) named, all within minutes of emerging from the womb. The extra-legal significance of birth is an added virtue of birth as a legal cut-off, since it leaves scant room for ambiguity, confusion, or ignorance.

But stipulating birth as the threshold for legal personhood status is not inconsistent with drawing an upper limit on abortion sometime *before* birth. Neither British nor American law recognizes the personhood of the early human being before it is born. But even if it is not equated with homicide, some might think there are compelling reasons to protect the life of the late fetus with an upper limit on abortions performed in late pregnancy in all but perhaps the most dire circumstances. The argument for an upper limit might be bolstered by the fluidity of human development and the close resemblance of late fetuses and neonates. It is not wholly unacceptable, on my account, to impose near-absolute cut-off some time before birth. The question, again, is simply what that upper limit would need to be like. First and foremost, it must be administrable. It is a rule of law requirement that there be a clear and practicable boundary-line for abortion, a boundary that is completely perceptible, that is enforceable, that treats like cases alike, that is supported by reason to the extent that it is within the range of reasonable cut-off points, and that there is no conclusive reason against adopting. This said, is not incumbent on lawmakers to provide reasons why the threshold is preferable to its closest neighbouring points. Not only is this obligation in tension with the aim of practical resolution as an end in itself, it falsely assumes that there exists, either biologically or morally, a non-arbitrary threshold of the kind.

9.3.3 Late abortion and fetal pain

Wherever an upper limit for abortion is placed, many people believe that the late-term fetus is worthy of a serious amount of moral consideration. Abortions that are regarded as 'late-term' continue to be especially contested in abortion law and ethics. Those generally opposed to abortion rights reserve a special horror and moral opprobrium for abortions carried out late in pregnancy. And those that are generally in favour of abortion rights often still express some measure of discomfort about them.[15] These attitudes are intelligible on the view that greater moral respect for late fetuses is appropriate in virtue of their human embodiment. Late-term fetuses are not merely closer to becoming persons, they share far more of our form of embodiment than do early ones.

Focusing on this shared embodiment can, I think, illuminate much of what is unsettling about aborting very developed fetuses regardless of their status as persons, or, even, of their capacity for pain experience. Concern about fetal pain

[15] 'Late' is obviously a relative term, and in the context of the abortion debate an evaluative one too, for it is usually taken to denote the time from which abortion is considerably sobering, even if still justifiable. While there is therefore some disagreement as to what 'late' here really means, I will take it largely to mean late second to third trimester abortions when the fetus is at least twenty weeks gestated.

during late abortion was a key focus of the US Congress's reasoning when passing the Partial-Birth Abortion Ban Act 2003, which prohibited the controversial 'dilation and extraction' abortion method. The text of the 2003 Act set out the congressional 'findings' that:

It is a medical fact . . . that unborn infants at this ['late'] stage can feel pain when subjected to painful stimuli and that their perception of this pain is even more intense than that of newborn infants and older children when subjected to the same stimuli.

Thus, during a partial-birth abortion procedure, the child will fully experience the pain associated with piercing his or her skull and sucking out his or her brain.[16]

Contrary to the congressional findings, medical and scientific opinion is in fact quite agnostic about fetal capacity for pain experience.[17] Disagreement about fetal pain stems from the fact that pain is not just a physiological response to stimuli, but also a subjective psychological experience. According to some psychologists, pain *experience* cannot be directly inferred from the presence of sensory pathways or stress hormones (purely physical pain responses) alone, because the contents of that subjective experience require more than travelling neurons; they require self-consciousness.[18]

But the divisiveness of late abortion does not, I think, only have to do with the possibility of fetal pain. For one, it is unlikely that those who focus so much effort on the eradication of late abortion would be altogether placated by legal requirements to anesthetize fetuses, or to kill them painlessly with a heart-stopping lethal injection ahead of performing the abortion. Late abortion is especially troubling to many because when they look at developed fetuses, they see babies. Once appreciating this, we might understand why the partial-birth abortion procedure is so widely reviled irrespective of the question of fetal pain. Dilation and extraction involves the sort of attack on the body of a fetus that if directed at a baby, anaesthetized or not, would be horrifying. The anatomical closeness of the two makes it difficult to retain the horror reaction in the case of the baby but not of the fetus which shares so much of its form of embodiment. It is an exacerbating factor that the aggressive part of the procedure is carried out when the fetus is already in the process of emerging from the womb, or what *would* constitute that process, were it not killed before it fully emerges. There is an attitudinal difficulty with identifying neonates as fully within the range of persons from the time that they are born—which, I have argued, we have very good reason to do—whilst remaining wholly indifferent to very late-term fetuses.

If being embodied in the world is a precondition for personhood, partial-birth abortion is also a special case because it takes place right on the borderline: between

---

[16] Partial Birth Abortion Ban Act 2003, s 2.

[17] In 2007, a House of Commons Select Committee set up to investigate scientific developments relating to the Abortion Act concluded, after hearing a number of submissions, that 'while the evidence suggests that foetuses have physiological reactions to noxious stimuli, it does not indicate that pain is consciously felt, especially not below the current upper gestational limit of abortion [24 weeks]' (House of Commons Science and Technology Committee, 25).

[18] See Stuart Derbyshire, 'Can Fetuses Feel Pain?' (2006) 332 British Medical Journal 909.

the fetus occupying the isolated world of the womb and the world of fellow human beings. The dilation and extraction method destroys the fetus *as it* enters our world, just as it begins to gain its individual embodiment. If this separate embodiment is no 'merely extrinsic' development, as I have suggested it is not, then the location of the partial-birth procedure right on the line between womb and world will reasonably add to our consternation about it.

Partial-birth abortion might also be thought to threaten the clarity of birth as the threshold for legal personhood because it demands a sharper legal definition of where that borderline lies. Has the baby been born once the head has passed, the head and the shoulders, or not until it has emerged past the naval? Jeff McMahan criticizes the Partial-Birth Abortion Ban Act for its 'absurd' exactitude on this matter.[19] The Act prohibits the killing of a fetus once 'the entire fetal head is outside the body of the mother, or, in the case of breech presentation, any part of the fetal trunk past the navel is outside the body of the mother'. The absurdity, McMahan thinks, lies in the fact that 'if an 8th of an inch less of the abdomen is exposed, the act of killing is constitutionally protected'.[20]

If partial-birth procedures are to be regulated, this level of exactitude cannot easily be avoided. As we have seen, it is not a legitimate criticism of any abortion law that it stipulates a threshold which cannot be morally distinguished from the closest neighbouring points. This is an unavoidable feature of any legal threshold. Moreover, the ability to follow a law banning abortion procedures that take place partly outside of the womb may well depend on a high level of exactness about what constitutes such a procedure.

Still, a law stipulated *too* precisely may lack effective guiding force. It is easier to follow the rule that human beings are absolutely protected from birth than a rule which stipulates how many inches of human body must emerge before that protection is in force, still less a law which stipulates down to the centimetres or millimetres. And the later in the process of emergence that threshold is placed, the less unequivocal we may think the law's endorsement of birth as the benchmark for personhood is able to be. Considering this, the law could have further reason to express disapproval for the partial-birth method and a preference for less borderline alternatives, notwithstanding the fact that such alternatives may involve no less violent an attack on the body of the fetus.[21]

There is more to think about, however, when it comes to the question of outlawing the partial-birth method. This includes the fact that the method can often be the medically safer option for women undergoing late abortion, and the fact that where other late abortion procedures are *not* banned, the prohibition of the

---

[19] Jeff McMahan, 'Infanticide and Moral Consistency' (2013) 39 Journal of Medical Ethics 273.
[20] ibid.
[21] In her dissenting judgment in *Gonzales* (the Supreme Court decision which upheld the constitutionality of the 2003 Act), Ruth Bader Ginsburg drew attention to the fact that the banned, extraction method of abortion was no less gruesome than the unbanned alternative for late abortion: dilation and evacuation, effectively by fetal dismemberment (*Gonzales v Carhart* 550 US 124 (2007)). Ginsburg clearly did not regard the fact that in the extraction method the fetus is killed in the transition from the uterus to the outside world as being of any significance.

partial-birth procedure is not in the interests of preserving fetal life.[22] Ruth Bader Ginsburg regarded this second consideration as persuasive when delivering her judgment in *Gonzales v Carhart*, the US Supreme Court decision that upheld the constitutionality of the Partial-Birth Abortion Ban Act 2003. In her dissenting opinion, it counted against the ban that while the extraction method could often be in the interests of preserving women's health, banning the procedure was not in the interests of saving fetal life, since alternative methods of late abortion were still available. While the value in demonsrating moral respect for human embodiment is, on my account, a reason for the law to discourage or prohibit very late abortion procedures, that reason may yet be overridden by other considerations, particularly when the pregnant woman's interest in obtaining an abortion is considerable, and what is gained through prohibition negligible.

9.4 Lower Limits and the 'Right' to Abortion

People spend a great deal of time debating the upper limits of abortion. But considerably less time is devoted to thinking about at what point abortion regulation should even kick in—that is, the lower limits of abortion law. I think that it follows from my arguments in Part II that the case for regulating abortion towards the earlier end of pregnancy is considerably weak, except insomuch as is reasonably necessary to ensure the health and safety of women undergoing the procedure. The embryo lacks any of the constitutive traits of personhood. It also possesses very little in the way of human embodiment. Unlike in later pregnancy, therefore, there are no compelling moral reasons to grant at least some protection to the fetus on account of its shared human form, or to discourage abortions that involve the violent destruction of that form. Moreover, since there is no morally transformative 'moment' either of conception or within conception, there is no important moral difference between very early abortion and contraception. The continuum of development from the beginning of the process of conception through to early pregnancy is nowhere punctuated by the arrival of a new, rights-holding being. Thus there is no reason based on moral status for regulating very early abortion in a way fundamentally different from the regulation of contraception.

When we consider these conclusions alongside the significant interests women have in procreative control, the bodily burdens of pregnancy, and the necessity of procreative control for sex equality, the result is that the burden of defence falls squarely on the proponents of regulation in early pregnancy. This lends considerable support for a framework which establishes a general legal right to abortion at least up to a certain gestational point. As opposed to mere abortion permissions,

---

[22] See ibid. Contrary to the congressional findings, which flatly denied the possible medical advantages of partial-birth abortion over other methods, Ginsburg relayed the wealth of scientific evidence that the procedure can be the considerably safer form of late abortion, arguing that the 2003 ban was therefore unconstitutional in failing to provide for a 'health exception', as she points out, directly contrary to the Supreme Court precedents in *Stenberg v Carhart* (530 US 914 (2000)) and *Casey*.

such as are found within British law, a recognized legal *right* to abortion, even if qualified, would mean that it is abortion regulation, not abortion practice, that first and foremost must answer to the law. This was of course the broad position adopted in the United States by *Roe* and later confirmed by *Casey*. Having recognized that American women enjoy a constitutional right to terminate a pregnancy as part of the broader right to 'privacy', the result of these decisions was to set up a standard of constitutional review which all state abortion regulations must pass. As we have seen, the modified *Casey* test required that restrictions, even in pursuit of a 'legitimate aim', such as the protection of women's health or of fetal life, must not place an 'undue burden' on women seeking abortions by putting a 'substantial obstacle' to abortion in their paths.

The question of what does indeed amount to an 'undue burden' under the *Casey* test naturally implicates broader questions about exactly how abortion restrictions ought to be scrutinized once a fundamental right to abort, time-limited or otherwise, is established. Generally speaking, the first stage of the test for a justified infringement of fundamental rights is that the measure is in pursuit of a legitimate aim and is rationally connected to that aim. In other words, assuming that protection of women's health is a legitimate aim of abortion regulation, it would still need to be demonstrated that the regulation in question *does in fact* contribute to making abortion safer, and that it is not inefficacious, futile, or counter-productive. The Supreme Court of the United States demonstrated the importance of the rational connection test in the recent *Hellerstedt* decision when carefully scrutinizing and rejecting Texas's claims that its TRAP law requirements were necessary for safeguarding women's health. Delivering the majority judgment, Justice Breyer underscored the fact that, when asked, Texas had not been able to produce a single case in which its new requirements had actually ensured a better health outcome for a woman.[23]

As another example, a robust 'rational connection' condition might also require that legal measures purporting to protect the fetus (if and where that is deemed a legitimate aim) are actually in the service of saving fetal life, and do not function merely to make abortion more cumbersome or unpleasant for women undergoing it.

But it is often thought that the terms for breaching fundamental legal rights also encompass a proportionality condition, that is to say, the gains made in pursuit of the legitimate aim must be *worth* the level of infringement of the right. In a recent volume, Verónica Undurraga has championed the use of proportionality reasoning in the constitutional review of abortion law—a standard of constitutional scrutiny that has been notably missing from many of the most significant judicial decisions on abortion.[24] As Undurraga rightly states, proportionality review of abortion regulation 'requires judges to order the questions they must address in consecutive stages and encourages them to reflect on substantive issues

---

[23] *Whole Woman's Health* (n 7) 28.
[24] Verónica Undurraga, 'Proportionality in the Constitutional Review of Abortion Law' in Rebecca Cook, Bernard Dickens, and Joanna Erdman (eds), *Abortion Law in Transnational Perspective: Cases and Controversies* (University of Pennsylvania Press 2014).

too often neglected in abortion adjudication'. These 'substantive issues' include questions such as whether criminalization is in fact effective in protecting unborn human life, whether there are alternative means of protection less onerous for women than criminalization, and whether the costs of abortion restrictions for women are worth the net gain in protection of fetal life—what Undurraga calls the 'strict proportionality test'. It is this third limb of the test which calls for the greatest exercise of judgement, requiring, for example, a weighing of the benefits of regulation for the protection of fetal life against their negative impact on the lives of women. As she elaborates, 'in the final stage of the analysis, courts must assess the law on balance: asking whether the protection it affords unborn life is worth the sacrifice it demands of women'.[25]

A standard of constitutional scrutiny of abortion regulation which encompasses proportionality considerations should require, therefore, that the burdensomeness of abortion restrictions which aim to protect fetal life are always balanced against the amount of fetal life they actually have the propensity to save. The limitation must make *enough* of a difference to be proportionate. A legal policy of mandated pre-abortion counselling designed to dissuade women out of having an abortion might not meet this standard of scrutiny if it significantly stalls thousands of women trying to access abortion every year, whilst only successfully discouraging one or two. Likewise, a ban on a particular method of abortion could fail to meet the standard of proportionality if the likely result is only that most of the fetuses which would have been terminated under one method are terminated under another, and if the increased riskiness for women of the alternative procedure is not negligible.

One helpful question for a proportionality assessment of abortion restrictions designed to protect the health and safety of women is to ask whether the regulations mirror those that are required for other medical procedures of a similar nature and complexity. For instance, if the regulation requires disclosure to the woman of all possible risks associated with abortion, are the same disclosures required of all procedures presenting a comparable level of risk? If it is seriously unlikely that such measures would be put in place with regard to similar procedures, this will be a good indication that the measures do not enhance health and safety in a proportionate way. A provision which requires abortion clinics to maintain hospital-standard hall widths will be grossly disproportionate if the contribution to health and safety is minimal, is widely in excess of the health and safety standards for similar medical procedures, and in effect disenfranchises countless women of the abortion right.

Furthermore, on a strict proportionality standard of review, mandatory waiting periods for abortion or mandatory ultrasound provisions could be deemed invalid for being disproportionate even if they do not place a 'substantial' obstacle in the way of women seeking abortion. It will be enough that a provision imposes *some* burden that cannot be reasonably justified by the gains. Strict proportionality review is, in essence, a balancing exercise. Consequently, no regulation will automatically pass the test in virtue of the facts that it furthers some amount of

---

[25] ibid 95.

legitimate aim and that the restriction of the right is not too severe. In any assessment, everything will still depend on how the legitimate gains match up to the imposition, assuming, that is, that a firm relationship between the legal measure and the intended outcomes can be established.

Taking abortion seriously as a fundamental right therefore requires a legal framework that both places the burden of justification squarely on advocates of abortion restrictions and embraces a proportionality standard of review which looks to the efficacy and the effect of regulation, not only the legitimacy of its stated aims. In this analysis, brute fact-finding and evidence concerning the practical impact of regulatory provisions will assume a huge importance. The Supreme Court's decision in *Hellerstedt* is notable for the significance it attributed to such details, drawing on specific evidence about the effects of Texas's 'HB2' ('TRAP') law. Those details concerned both the provisions' realistic contribution to women's health and the extent to which they hampered the abortion right. Consequently, the standard of review engaged represented an important step in the right direction for abortion rights protection in the United States.

10

Selective Abortion
Sex and Disability

10.1 'Hard Cases'

Some abortions of a very particular nature have presented unique difficulties in abortion ethics and policy. These are so-called 'selective' abortions. Selective abortions are characterized by the fact that they are carried out not in order to avoid pregnancy or parenthood per se, but to prevent the birth of child with a particular, unwanted, characteristic. The two characteristics I focus on here are sex and disability. Not only are selective abortions on the basis of sex and disability the most politically relevant kinds (since other characteristics either are not typically tested for or cannot be detected during pregnancy), moral attitudes towards them have also been harnessed in interesting ways in the wider battle over abortion rights. Sex selective abortions (SSA) and what I will call 'fetal abnormality abortions' (FAA) are therefore worthy of special attention.

SSA and FAA are alike in that both have been propounded as examples of 'hard cases' of abortion by one side of the abortion debate for the other. Fetal abnormality abortion is commonly presented as a hard case for those who oppose abortion rights, since even those who support significant restrictions on abortion may, we think, find it difficult to justify abortion prohibitions in circumstances where fetal abnormality will result in the birth of a seriously disabled child. Conversely, SSA has been characterized as a hard case for those that are generally supportive of abortion rights. Abortions carried out because of the sex of the fetus are widely perceived to be morally repugnant and indefensible even by those who defend the morality of abortion in general. As we will see in more detail, the problematic nature of SSA has much to do with its connection to wider problems of 'gendercide' and sex inequality.

On the conventional view, then, FAA is a hard case for opponents of abortion rights, and SSA is a hard case for supporters of them. This conventional view that FAAs are among the most morally defensible kind of abortion and SSA among the least morally defensible is reflected both in regulation and in public abortion debate. The British Abortion Act of 1967 provides for an individual ground of abortion where there is a 'substantial risk' that the child born would suffer from a 'serious handicap'—what is typically known as the 'disability ground' for abortion.[1]

---

[1] Abortion Act 1967, s 1(1)(d).

Arguments about Abortion: Personhood, Morality, and Law. First Edition. Kate Greasley. © K. Greasley 2017. Published 2017 by Oxford University Press.

The disability ground is not time-limited. Aborting defective fetuses is legally permissible all the way up to birth. The ground is therefore grouped with 'grave risk of permanent physical or mental injury' and risk to life of the pregnant woman as one of the only permissible grounds for abortions post-twenty-four weeks of pregnancy.

The implication of this is very clear. The statute communicates the common view that fetal abnormality is a special justification for abortions at a stage too late to be ordinarily permitted. This view is shared even by many people that are hostile towards abortion rights across the board. In this respect, popular opinion about FAA bears similarities with opinion about abortions carried out where pregnancy is the result of rape. Calls for reform of Ireland's restrictive abortion regulation, which currently allows abortion only to prevent risk to the pregnant woman's life, have centred on fetal abnormality as one of the few conditions under which the law should be liberalized.[2] And Sally Sheldon and Steven Wilkinson have noted that opinion polls in Britain 'have consistently found that people consider termination more acceptable in the presence of a disability'.[3]

In stark contrast, a British newspaper sting operation which claimed, in 2012, to reveal evidence of abortion clinics' willingness to carry out SSA was met with widespread consternation and calls for a tightening of the law.[4] In the wake of the alleged scandal, the Health Secretary ordered a mass inspection of abortion clinics to determine the extent to which sex selection was practiced in abortion clinics, and politicians debated introducing amendments into the Abortion Act to explicitly outlaw abortion for reasons of fetal sex.[5]

SSA and FAA hence sit on completely different ends of the spectrum of conventional abortion morality, despite sharing a striking feature which is not true of abortion generally. This feature is, of course, their selectiveness. In selective abortion, it is a *specific* fetus that is being terminated because of a characteristic it possesses. But while this discriminating aspect seems to render abortion *more* reasonable (in

---

[2] See Fiona de Londras, 'Constitutionalizing Fetal Rights: A Salutary Tale from Ireland' (2015) 22 Michigan Journal of Gender and the Law 243, 248, 280. De Londras chronicles that an *Irish Times*/Ipsos MORI poll held in October 2014 revealed that 68 per cent of those surveyed were in favour of holding a referendum on whether to allow abortion in cases of rape and fatal fetal abnormality.

[3] Sally Sheldon and Steven Wilkinson, 'Termination of Pregnancy for reason of foetal disability: Are there grounds for a special exception in the Law?' (2001) 9 Medical Law Review 85.

[4] Holly Watt, Claire Newell, Zahra Khimji, 'Available on demand—an abortion if it's a boy you wanted', *Daily Telegraph*, 23 February 2012, 4–5 http://www.telegraph.co.uk/news/health/news/9099925/Abortioninvestigation-Available-ondemand-an-abortion-if-its-a-boy-you-wanted.html (last accessed 15 October 2016).

[5] See Kate Greasley, 'Is Sex-Selective Abortion Against the Law?' (2016) Oxford Journal of Legal Studies (online first, http://ojls.oxfordjournals.org/content/early/2015/11/26/ojls.gqv031.abstract). Although the Abortion Act does not provide a specific ground for sex selective termination, there is a legal argument to be made that an abortion carried out upon revelation of the fetus's sex can nevertheless be lawful if two doctors believe, in good faith, that the sex of the fetus means that the pregnancy places the woman's physical or mental health at risk, pursuant to ground 1(1)(a). Part of the backlash from the sting operation included calls to amend the law so as to exclude this interpretation of the statute. See also Ellie Lee, 'Recent Myths and Misunderstandings about Abortion Law', in British Pregnancy Advisory Service document, 'Britain's Abortion Law: What it Says and Why' (2012), 10–13 and Emily Jackson, 'The Legality of Abortion for Fetal Sex', in the same volume, 19–21. http://www.reproductivereview.org/images/uploads/Britains_abortion_law.pdf (last accessed 15 October 2016).

the eyes of most) in the case of fetal abnormality, it has the opposite effect when it comes to sex selection. In the latter case, the fact that the pregnancy would be wanted but for a particular characteristic belonging to the fetus seems to make the abortion far more morally problematic than it would be otherwise.

The fact that moderate sensibilities support the view of FAA as paradigmatically 'good' abortions and SSA as paradigmatically 'bad' ones make both cases useful rallying points in the wider discussion about the morality of abortion. In the academic discourse, supporters and opponents of abortion rights both seek to gain an argumentative advantage by attempting to show that their opponents' positions cannot consistently be brought into line with moderate sensibilities about either SSA or FAA. Defenders of abortion choice are charged with being unable to explain why we should make an exception of SSA and prohibit it specifically. Conversely, the broad anti-abortion position will seem, to many, to be considerably weakened if it cannot allow for exceptions even in the event of serious fetal abnormality.

The most robust line of defence from either side would be to argue, counterintuitively, that that selective abortion on grounds of sex or disability are not in fact hard cases. Thus, defenders of abortion rights may be moved to argue that sex selection is as permissible as any other kind of abortion and raises no special problems. Equally, opponents of abortion rights might be tempted to argue that fetal abnormality does not render abortion any more morally permissible than it is generally—that *it* is not a special case.

Because of the resistance these replies are likely to face, the more appealing approach might be for each side to explain why the problem case of selective abortion can be treated as an exception to a general moral or legal position. This will require explaining how the exception can be made consistently, without compromising anything in the wider argument. One question of interest to me here is to what extent this is possible. In other words, can exceptions be made in either case that are not of the sort which undermine the general case for or against abortion rights? Another question I wish to attend to is what the arguments concerning our proper attitudes to the one kind of selective abortion imply about the acceptability of the other kind. If it is permissible to selectively terminate on the grounds of fetal abnormality, why not also on the grounds of fetal sex? Or, if sex selection abortion ought to be banned, why not also abortions that select against disability? In order to better examine these problems, let us look more closely at some specific issues arising out of sex selective and fetal abnormality abortion.

10.2 Sex Selective Abortion

At the outset of any discussion about sex selective termination, it is important to be clear about exactly which abortions warrant the description 'sex selective'. It is clear to me that most discussions of this topic do not mean to restrict that description to abortions that are carried out because of sheer prejudice or sexism against one sex harboured by the pregnant woman. Indeed, defined this way, I think we would be hard pushed to find many instances at all of SSA requests. Abortion, particularly past the point of sex detection, is attended by all kinds of non-negligible costs. It is at the very least a serious inconvenience, and more often physically and emotionally unpleasant. For many, it is financially costly. All of this makes it extremely unlikely that many women will go to the fairly drastic measure of having an abortion out of a simple preference to bear a child of one sex rather than another.[6] There is therefore a credible assumption that in almost any case where fetal sex is pertinent to an abortion request, some more serious interest of future wellbeing is at stake that is tied to or explained by the sex of the future child. We might take the following examples:

> Woman A discovers that her fetus is female. She requests an abortion, reasonably believing that her entire extended family will shun her if she does not have a boy.

> Woman B discovers that her fetus is female. She knows that if she gives birth to a girl, she will come under pressure to have more children so as to have a boy. She feels that she already cannot cope with the children she has.

> Woman C discovers that her fetus is female. The financial ramifications of having another girl rather than a boy in her culture mean that she and her husband are likely to be left destitute in their old age if they have girls rather than boys. She therefore requests an abortion.

These are all 'sex selective' abortions in that they are abortions which would not have been requested but for knowledge of the fetus's sex, but they are not abortions requested because of a pregnant woman's personal prejudice against girls. I think that most people intend the term 'SSA' to apply to such cases, meaning that they intend it to apply to any abortion in which fetal sex is an essential part of the picture. This is despite the fact that, in each case, it is clear that the fetus's sex is only one circumstance which, when combined with others, (such as the foreseeable behaviour of family members and the cultural implications of giving birth to girls) propels the abortion request. Indeed, whether abortions such as these are categorized as SSA is, in one clear way, a matter of choosing between descriptions. For instance, we might just as well call Woman C's abortion a 'financial preservation' abortion, naming it after the interest sought to be protected by the abortion (as in 'risk to life' abortion), rather than after one of the conditions which, when combined with others, places that interest in jeopardy (the fetus's sex).

Needless to say, there is widespread moral ambivalence about all abortion for which fetal sex forms part of the explanation. Importantly, this moral ambivalence seems to span the abortion divide. Many of those that are otherwise staunchly committed to abortion rights still often feel moral disquiet about the idea that a fetus would be aborted because of its sex. This common disquiet about sex selection makes for a useful discussion point for opponents of all abortion. Christopher Kaczor, for

---

[6] It is far more plausible to think that women might avail themselves of less costly methods of sex selection, such as selection of embryos for pre-implantation in fertility treatment, in order to secure a simple sex preference.

example, tries to harness the sex selection issue against permissive abortion ethics in general. He writes:

If abortion does not kill a human person, if abortion is, as Warren for instance claims, no more serious than killing a guppy, then abortion of a human because of gender would be permissible.[7]

Kaczor's key argument is that no one can defend abortion generally whilst making an exception for SSA, which many would presumably to want to do. He claims that most arguments against SSA only succeed on the 'implicit assumption that a human fetus is a being due moral respect'. But if this is true, he claims, then all abortion, not just SSA, is morally objectionable.[8]

The problem of sex selection can look particularly pointed for those who seek to defend abortion rights on feminist or sex equality grounds. This is because SSA and moral opposition to it is inextricably linked with the worldwide problem of so-called 'gendercide' or 'femicide'.[9] It can hardly be denied that where sex selection is widely practiced, it is overwhelmingly used to select against females. China and India are, of course, the standout examples, where, along with infanticide, selective abortion is used as a means of eliminating females, for obvious cultural reasons.[10] Inasmuch as SSA is inseparable from the practice of 'femicide', it seems to pose a serious problem for feminist defenders of legal abortion. How could those discussants defend a practice which terminates the lives of female fetuses *because they are female*, which reduces the number of women existing in the world, and which seems to be both a symptom of the devaluation of women and, potentially, to contribute to it?

All of this seems to leave liberal and feminist supporters of abortion rights in a bit of a bind. If they endorse the popular view that sex selection is morally repugnant and ought to be illegal, they compromise their general position that reproductive control through abortion is both morally permissible and an essential requirement of sex equality. In particular, they would be forced to give up the claim that abortion should be available to all pregnant women as of right, whatever their reasons. But the alternative approach of defending the availability of SSA will seem to be a significant own goal, especially for those who defend abortion rights on feminist grounds. Since we cannot deny the reality that SSA is predominantly used to select against females, they may find themselves defending a practice which functions to entrench sex inequality in all manner of ways.

Shifting to the anti-abortion side, the question may well be asked whether there is some measure of inconsistency about the special level of interest in SSA displayed by opponents of abortion choice, and in the suggestion, by that camp, that SSA is

---

[7] Christopher Kaczor, *The Ethics of Abortion* (2nd edn, Routledge 2015) 211. [8] ibid.
[9] See 'Gendercide: The Worldwide War on Baby Girls' *The Economist* (4 March 2010). The term 'gendercide' was coined by Mary Anne Warren in her 1985 book: Mary Anne Warren, *Gendercide: The Implications of Sex Selection* (Rowman and Allanheld 1985).
[10] See, for example, Sital Kalantry, 'Sex Selection in the United States and India: A Contextualist Feminist Approach' [2013] UCLA Journal of International Law and Foreign Affairs 61.

especially morally repugnant. Against the background assumption that the fetus has a strong right to life, why is SSA any morally worse than any other kind of abortion? If abortion really amounts to unjustified homicide, as many philosophical opponents of abortion claim that it does, then it hard to see why the individual reasons behind an abortion would make a difference to its moral permissibility, except in the very exceptional circumstances when abortion meets the conditions for justified homicide (outlined in chapter 3). An unjustified homicide that is non-sexist is no more morally permissible than one which targets the victim because of her sex. This gives rise to a puzzle about why opponents of abortion would regard SSA as any worse than abortion for all kinds of other reasons, as their special focus on the issue implies.

Of course, it is open to opponents of abortion to answer that they do *not* regard sex selection as morally worse than abortion for any other reason, such as that the pregnant women simply does not wish to have a child at this point in her life. But this admission will make it harder to harness common judgements about the special moral objectionableness of sex selection in argument for the general immorality of abortion.

In fact, I think that ideological opponents of abortion can offer an explanation for why sex selection is especially troubling, even in light of their general opposition to abortion based on the moral status of the fetus. That explanation could proceed by analogy with aggravated assaults. *Qua* homicide, all unjustified homicides are equal so far as they are in being morally impermissible. Nevertheless, whilst holding to the 'equal impermissibility' view, one can still acknowledge that homicides motivated by racism, sexism, or homophobia are uniquely disturbing and worthy of special consideration, and, especially, public policy attention, for all sorts of reasons. This does not imply that non-aggravated homicide—where no such characteristics influenced the assailant's motivations—is any less harmful to the victim or any more permissible an action. Perhaps an opponent of abortion can apply a similar analysis to SSA and liken it to a kind of aggravated assault based on the victim's sex. An analogy with aggravated assault would enable opponents of abortion to continue to underscore the uniquely morally disturbing elements of SSA whilst maintaining their broad commitment to the moral impermissibility of almost all abortion.

On the face of it then, it appears that the burden of explanation regarding sex selective termination still rests with the philosophical defender of abortion, not the opponent. The challenge is how to explain the apparent wrongness of SSA without committing oneself to any claims which entail the moral impermissibility of all abortion, such as the claim that the fetus has a strong right to life.

10.3 Fetal Abnormality Abortion

As we have noted, abortion for serious fetal abnormality is typically regarded as more readily defensible than other kinds of abortion. This is particularly true of fatal fetal abnormalities, where the new human being has no prospect of sustained life after birth in any event, and where there is therefore very little to be gained, in terms of protecting life, by prohibiting abortion. Many that are otherwise opposed to abortion permissions will wish to make concessions in such circumstances. However, on the assumption that abortion is wrong because it amounts to unjustified homicide, it is difficult to explain how a concession for fetal abnormality can be made, even where the fetal defect is fatal.

Kaczor makes this point in relation to Down's Syndrome, a milder fetal abnormality for which many abortions are performed.[11] In Britain, prenatal screening for Down's Syndrome is routinely carried out, often resulting in termination of pregnancy when the syndrome is detected. Kaczor makes the sound point that if one takes the moral status of the fetus to be on a par with born infants, terminating for Down's Syndrome would surely be morally prohibited, along with most other abortions. We could not accept the practice of terminating the lives of Down's Syndrome babies and children on the basis of their genetic abnormality. If the fetus merits equal moral status, it follows that the termination of fetuses with this genetic condition is every bit as morally impermissible.

No doubt, a practice of selectively terminating Down's Syndrome human beings post-birth would be regarded as horrifyingly barbaric.[12] Moreover, our strong moral reactions against such a practice would only be intensified, not mollified, by the fact that the children were being terminated *because* of their disability. Kaczor's point here is simply that once someone assumes the moral parity of fetuses and born human beings, the cornerstone of most philosophical opposition to abortion, our moral reactions to the idea of terminating genetically abnormal human beings ought to be consistent either side of birth.

One possible argument in favour of a special concession for FAA invokes the value of fetal interests. Someone might claim, that is, that even if the fetus's moral status is equal to that of a person, the fetus may well have interests, rooted in its own wellbeing, in not being born and living a life burdened with disability. However, this claim will simply not be true in the vast majority of cases. The fetal interests argument as I have outlined it essentially claims that it can sometimes be better for persons to die than to endure more life in certain states. We may well accept that there is a threshold of suffering past which this is true—that is, a state of being so intolerable that it amounts to a life not worth living. But only a rare few disabilities and syndromes detectable before birth would ever meet that threshold. Down's Syndrome is in fact a very good example of an abnormality entirely compatible with a good, happy, and fulfilling life.[13] Given that life with Down's Syndrome fails to come anywhere close to the threshold of a life not worth living, one cannot justify the termination of Down's Syndrome fetuses by appeal to the interests of the fetus in avoiding continued life. The same is true of a vast number of diseases and

[11] Kaczor (n 7) 191–2.
[12] At the same time, it is worth noting that selective non-treatment of seriously disabled babies, resulting in their death, is often employed in circumstances in which the non-treatment of healthy babies would be medically unthinkable. For an interesting example see Jeff McMahan, 'Infanticide and Moral Consistency' (2013) 39 Journal of Medical Ethics 274–5.
[13] See ibid.

disabilities the avoidance of which may well motivate selective abortion, such as cystic fibrosis or cerebral palsy. Only with respect to extremely debilitating and rare diseases could the suffering involved in life be so acute that it is plausible to suggest that an individual would be better off having that life ended before birth.

More importantly, though, a discussant who ordinarily equates abortion with homicide will not be able to consistently argue that abortion is permissible in the interests of the fetus so as to avoid burdens which would not justify terminating the lives of born human beings, particularly when death is not even at their behest. What is at issue here are the conditions on morally permissible mercy killing. Even in extreme conditions where we would be tempted to conclude that an individual's suffering strips her of a life worth living, it does not follow that we are entitled to engage in unrequested euthanasia. The abortion opponent will therefore face a consistency problem if she wishes to allow for the merciful killing of abnormal fetuses for reasons which would not justify involuntarily euthanizing born human beings.

The interests of the potential parents in avoiding the burdens of raising a disabled child are equally incapable of justifying FAA on the assumption that the fetus is a person. Again, if the same consideration could not be used to defend the infanticide of disabled children, which it surely cannot, then the abortion opponent cannot invoke the special burdensomeness of caring for disabled children to defend concessions for FAA.[14]

Many opponents of abortion rights will happily accept these conclusions. Like Kaczor, they might be satisfied to claim that FAA is no more morally acceptable than abortions for more prosaic reasons, like the wish not to derail life plans. On this view, FAA is simply not an exceptional case when it comes to the moral permissibility of abortion, although it might be supposed that the choice to abort in the face of such serious future burdens renders the decision more excusable than it is in other circumstances.

This conclusion will of course run counter to popular morality, which takes FAA to be better justified than many other kinds of abortion. Moreover, on the view that abortion amounts to homicide, it seems to follow that even termination for a *fatal* fetal abnormality, where the fetus cannot survive for long after birth, is not justified—an even more counter-intuitive conclusion. We can consider, for one example, anencephaly, a severe prenatal defect which results in the early human being, if it survives all the way to birth, lacking a higher brain. Infants with anencephaly possess the lower brain parts responsible for certain kinds of unconscious regulation, like breathing, but not the cerebral cortex necessary for conscious awareness. Because of the seriousness of the condition, anencephalic infants cannot hope to survive more than a few hours or, at most, days after birth.

---

[14] It is an additional problem with the parental interests argument in favour of FAA that there will be many cases in which the burdensomeness on some parents of raising non-disabled children exceeds the burdens on other parents of raising disabled ones, depending only on the individual circumstances. If the general abortion opponent is willing to make an exception for FAA on account of the weight of the burden on parents, he will need to make an exception in all cases where the burden of continuing pregnancy and raising a child is equally weighty, whether or not this has anything to do with defects or disability.

One question for advocates of personhood from conception is what morality dictates in the event of an anencephaly diagnosis during a pregnancy. Conventional moral thinking undoubtedly takes such a scenario to be one of the most readily justified abortions. The human being cannot survive for long outside the womb in any event, so refraining from abortion is not in the interests of sustaining life for any length of time, whereas procuring abortion at the earliest stage possible *is* clearly in the interests of the pregnant woman (and possibly others). On the assumption that abortion amounts to homicide, however, it is not clear that the terminal diagnosis of the fetus/future infant is sufficient to justify abortion. The direct killing of another person is not permitted on the ground that the person has little time left to live and that ending his life even sooner will spare someone else additional emotional distress (consider: a parent whose child is terminally ill cannot request that the child's death be sped up to spare himself the emotional turmoil of watching her suffer). Aware of this problem, Kaczor opts to bite the bullet on the question of fatal fetal abnormalities and argues that even in such conditions, abortion is morally unjustifiable.[15]

While the position taken by Kaczor is consistent, it will seem wildly unreasonable to all but the most hard line abortion opponents. It appears, then, that when it comes to FAA, it is abortion opponents, rather than defenders, who are on the back foot. For general defenders of the morality of abortion, FAA is morally permissible for the same reason that abortion generally is. The fetus has a very low moral status and lacks a strong right to life. Consequently, the burdens associated with unwanted pregnancy, whatever the explanations, are always enough to justify abortion, or to justify it up to a fairly late stage. Even so, defenders of reproductive choice might nevertheless regard FAA prohibitions as particularly draconian in light of the extremity of the burdens they impose on the potential parents.

Yet a particular challenge might face defenders of FAA who wish to maintain that SSA is, by contrast, *im*permissible. That challenge arises when the burdens on parents of bearing a child of a particular sex are, owing to the context, roughly comparable in magnitude to the burdens of caring for a disabled child. We might imagine that in a pregnant woman's individual circumstances, the consequences of giving birth to a girl (financially, relationally, and so on) are more or less equal in measure to the burdens threatening a *different* pregnant woman if she gives birth to a child with Down's Syndrome. If the fetus has a low enough moral status that the parental burdens of raising a disabled child (or, alternatively, giving that child up for adoption) are sufficient to make abortion permissible, why is SSA not also permissible where the burdens of raising a child of a particular sex are comparable? By the same token, some of the arguments that are often deployed *against* permitting SSA can seem to count equally against FAA. I want now to look further at the possible ways defenders of abortion rights could make a conservative exception for SSA, and whether this can be consistent with a permissive stance on disability selective abortions.

[15] Kaczor (n 7) 193.

10.4 Making an Exception for Sex Selection

First, let us recall Kaczor's challenge to anyone who wishes to defend abortion rights generally but make a prohibitive exception in respect of SSA. From the point of view of someone who thinks that abortion is on the whole morally permissible, he says, 'there is some difficulty in explaining why fetal killing for gender preference should be wrong'.[16] Is he right about this? As we saw, Kaczor's argument is that it is difficult to articulate the wrongness of SSA in a way that does not commit one to the protection of fetal rights across the board. We could put this point another way. If it is bad for a fetus to be aborted because of its sex, the fetus must therefore be the sort of being which has a good worth caring considerably about, in which case, it surely follows that we should not terminate the life of the fetus for *other* reasons as well. The fetus does not, after all, know why it is being aborted, and hence cannot be harmed any the more by sex selective than by non-selective abortion.

I think that the logic of this claim is sound. But this only indicates that a serious argument for the specific legal prohibition of SSA will not have anything to do with the moral status of the fetus. A defender of abortion rights can defend the exceptionality of SSA in more than one way. She might claim that SSA is uniquely morally wrong. But she may instead claim only that there are special reasons to prohibit it in law. I wish to focus not on the claims of the person who believes that a woman choosing SSA behaves immorally whereas other women choosing abortion do not, but on the claims of someone who believes that SSA, but not other forms of abortion, ought to be legally prohibited.

For defenders of abortion, the most obvious way to explain the harmfulness of selective abortions is not by reference to the rights of the individual fetus selected against, but by reference to potential harm caused to *persons* possessing the undesired characteristic, particularly when that characteristic defines a disadvantaged class of persons. When considering the legality of sex selection, one cannot rule out of the equation the potential that, if permitted, the practice would be predominantly used to select against female children. Where this is true, or likely to be true, the concern is not that sex selection harms female fetuses, but that it harms *women*.

This concern has been borne out in much of the feminist commentary about sex selection. In short, the worry is that, in different ways, an unbridled practice of terminating female fetuses is likely to contribute to prevailing conditions of sex inequality, conditions which are, in turn, responsible for making female offspring undesirable in the first place. It has been suggested that a wide practice of terminating female fetuses could contribute to sexism and sex inequality in a number of ways. One way is by powerfully symbolizing or expressing the diminished value of women and girls—what is known as the 'expressivist' objection against selective abortion. Indeed, it is hard to think of a more powerful expression of the hatred of women than terminating pregnancies so as to prevent new women from coming

---

[16] ibid 212.

into existence. Through its communicated meaning, the concern is that widespread SSA, especially where that activity is state-sponsored, may help to validate the cultural devaluation of women, resulting in a kind of feedback loop where sex selection helps contribute to the conditions for its own demand. Another way in which it is suggested that sex selection can harm women as a class is by significantly reducing their numbers, and hence, their political might. Political strength depends, to some extent, on numbers. If sex selection skews the sex ratio enough, the sheer number of women could be depleted far enough to erode their overall power, so the argument goes.

Considerations such as these have nothing whatsoever to do with the moral status of the fetus, and they certainly do not presume that the fetus has strong moral rights. If they reflect credible concerns, therefore, they may form the basis upon which someone can object to a legal practice of SSA whilst supporting abortion rights more generally, thus answering Kaczor's challenge. Although such a prohibition would involve some sacrifice in reproductive choice, there is nothing inconsistent in holding that reproductive choice must sometimes be subordinated to other considerations, especially when those considerations reflect much of the value of maintaining reproductive choice to begin with.

Kaczor argues that it is a weakness of objections to SSA which claim that it perpetuates discrimination against women and girls that they only provide a rationale for banning the selective termination of females, not males.[17] Isn't sex selection just as distasteful when male fetuses are terminated because of their sex? Kaczor is right that for someone who argues against SSA on the ground that it contributes to the social disadvantage of all women, it will naturally follow that the selective abortion of males does not produce the same concerns in a patriarchal climate. This is not a weakness of the argument, however. Much of what is found disturbing about the selective termination of females is that it screens out a characteristic which defines an existing, disadvantaged class of persons, and is therefore loaded with meaning in light of the surrounding cultural context. This same meaning clearly does not attach to the selective termination of a male fetus because, say, a pregnant woman feels ill equipped, for one reason or another, to raise a male child. Anyone who makes a case against selective abortion not on the basis of fetal rights but on the ground of collateral harms to disadvantaged groups will rightly be sensitive to these points of distinction. In short, it is not a weakness of an argument against allowing SSA that it depends on the social context if the crux of the argument is that SSA is *only* problematic *given* the social context.

Kaczor does, however, question the empirical claim that SSA exacerbates the inequality of women, arguing that 'no developed account is given for the questionable assumption that SSA perpetuates discriminatory views which negatively affect women and girls in society.'[18] The absence of quantifiable evidence strikes me as a bad reason to disbelieve an assumption that seems to be so intuitively correct, especially when it is not even clear what might count as satisfactory

---

[17] ibid 214.   [18] ibid.

evidence.[19] Still, it is obvious that the extent to which sex selection does or would contribute to the subordination of women depends on a number of factors which vary from context to context. These factors probably include the predicted uptake of sex selection under a permissive policy, whether that uptake is likely to lean heavily towards the deselection of females, and the depth of existing sex inequality and subjugation of women in the context concerned.

As some commentators have noted, these issues are extremely culturally and jurisdiction specific.[20] It is quite unthinkable that a permissive policy of sex selection in Britain would result in as frequent termination of females as it would in India or China. Insofar, then, as concerns about the expression of misogyny and damage to women's inequality need to be balanced against a general commitment to reproductive choice, these contextual features will be highly pertinent. Again, I do not believe this to be a weakness of any argument about the acceptability of sex selection. The claim is not the suspect one that the rights of any individual fetus depends upon the cultural context in which it finds itself. Rather, the starting point is that the fetus has no strong right to life, but that there may exist, nevertheless, strong reasons of public policy and sexual justice to prohibit certain kinds of abortions. If this is the argument, then the aptness of those concerns within any given context will always be relevant. To object that the moral status of the fetus cannot depend on cultural context does not refute a claim that anyone denouncing sex selection on feminist grounds need make, since it does not follow from those arguments that sex selection *ever* violates the rights of the fetus, but only that there may well be reasons, including of a moral kind, to prevent people from practising it.

But Feminist commentators have not been univocal in their responses to the sex selection issue.[21] While there is unity in thinking that it is hugely significant if fetuses terminated because of their sex are considerably likely to be female, far more ambivalence surrounds the question of whether more harm is done to women's interests by prohibiting sex selection or by allowing it. Some of those who equate sex selection with 'femicide' and the future disempowerment of women have advocated an outright ban of the practice as the only tolerable solution. Others, whilst acknowledging the moral dubiousness of sex selection, have argued that abrogating

---

[19] Kaczor refers to the suggestion, by some, that the scarcity of girls as a result of widespread SSA can in fact increase the value of women (ibid 214). But we should regard such a claim with extreme suspicion. As Helen Holmes has written: 'women are oppressed in certain ways when they outnumber men, in other ways when they are in the minority; I see no evidence that skewed human sex ratios correct themselves. In India, for example, the deficit of women does not lead to improvement in the status and value of women and to a desire to have more daughters: quite the contrary' (Helen Holmes, 'Review of 'Gendercide' by Mary Anne Warren' (1987) 1 Bioethics 100, 106–107).

[20] See Sawitri Saharso, 'SSA: Gender, Culture and Dutch Public Policy' (2005) 5 Ethnicities 248 and Sawitri Saharso, 'Feminist Ethics, Autonomy and the Politics of Multiculturalism' (2003) 4 Feminist Theory 199.

[21] For a selection of views, see: Mary Anne Warren, *Gendercide: The Implications of Sex Selection* (Rowman and Allanheld 1985); April Cherry, 'A Feminist Understanding of Sex Selective Abortion: Solely a Matter of Choice?' (1995) 10 Wisconsin Women's Law Journal 161; Clare Chambers, 'Autonomy and Equality in Cultural Perspective: A Response to Sawitri Saharso' (2004) 5 Feminist Theory 329; Jalna Hanmer and Pat Allen, 'Reproductive Engineering: The Final Solution' (1982) 2 Gender Issues 53; Diemut Bubeck, 'Sex Selection: The Feminist Response' in J Burley and J Harris (eds), *A Companion to Genethics* (Blackwell 2002), and Kalantry (n 10).

any of women's reproductive freedoms 'is to nibble away at our hard-won reproductive control' and risks too much in the way of constraining women's autonomy.[22] Some contributions focus their attention on the harm that choosing sex selection causes to existing women and girls, either by reducing their numbers (and, hence, their power relative to men), expressing misogyny (Tabitha Powledge writes that 'to prefer males is, unavoidably, to denigrate females'[23]), or by helping to perpetuate the patriarchal values which make male babies more desirable.

From one perspective, the feminist problem of SSA is, at bottom, a conflict between individual interests in procreative control and a class interest in overcoming disadvantage. Prohibiting SSA so as to protect the interests of women as a class will undoubtedly result in severe hardship for individual women who will suffer as a result of not being able to obtain one (consider the examples from earlier). Without alleviating their difficult circumstances, withholding the abortion option from such women will mean allowing their welfare to be seriously compromised. On the other hand, depending on the context, allowing a rampant practice of SSA might only help sustain sex disadvantage and the conditions in which women find themselves so unfortunately positioned.

This problem is especially pointed where the suffering which threatens the woman (physical or mental) is of a magnitude that clearly meets the law's general abortion permissions. Where this is so, prohibiting abortion only because that threat of harm is related to fetal sex would have the effect of imposing burdens on individual women, which they would not otherwise be required to endure, in the interests of greater sex equality for all. It is understandable if, in the face of this tension, advocates of abortion rights find themselves equivocating over SSA. However, there is nothing about this split-mindedness which commits anyone to the view that fetuses possess strong moral rights.

10.5 Fetal Abnormality and Consistency

We have already seen how the expressivist argument has been deployed against the practice of SSA. But if the expressivist objection is persuasive, it seems to apply with equal force to selective abortion on the ground of future disability. As the philosopher Jeremy Williams comments, the expressivist objection is 'widely known as the signature argument of the disability rights critique of selective abortion'.[24] He writes:

In the hands of disability theorists, the objection avers that the availability and widespread use of selective abortion for fetal impairment reflects and reinforces a number of hurtful and pernicious stereotypes about disabled people – for instance that they have no right to

---

[22] Tabitha Powledge, 'Toward a Moral Policy for Sex Choice' in Neil Bennett (ed), *Sex Selection of Children* (Academic Press 1983).
[23] ibid.
[24] Jeremy Williams, 'Sex-Selective Abortion: A Matter of Choice' (2012) 31 Law and Philosophy 125, 144.

exist; that their lives are uniformly so riddled with misery as to be not worth living; that they bring only unhappiness and no rewards to those around them; and so on. The broadcasting of these ideas is seen both as harmful and disrespectful to disabled people in itself, and as ratifying existing societal prejudices against the disabled, thereby increasing their vulnerability to abuse.[25]

Against the expressivist objection as applied to FAA, some have attacked the notion that an individual choice by a woman not to bear a disabled child carries with it the pernicious suggestion that disabled people's lives are inferior. In essence, such counter-arguments contend that a personal decision by a woman to spare herself the burden of raising a disabled child does not communicate any belief about the lesser value of disabled peoples' lives. Likewise, it might be argued that willingness of the state to provide special permissions for FAA does not signal the view that the lives of disabled people are of unequal value, but aims only to protect the interests individual pregnant women may have in obtaining abortion.[26]

I do not find these sorts of responses to the expressivist objection wholly satisfactory.[27] It goes without saying that pregnant women seeking out FAA are motivated by considerations of personal wellbeing and are unlikely to harbour the belief that disabled lives lack equal value. But the expressive significance of an act can depend upon more than the motivations and beliefs of the person carrying it out. Although the decision by a woman to abort a defective fetus does not necessarily convey the belief that disabled persons' lives are unequal to others or not worth living, it does express the considered belief that, for her, the burdens of raising a child with the relevant condition will not be worth the gains. The fact that the decision is a personal one about her own approximation of the benefits and burdens does not preclude it from making any more general statement about the rewardingness of raising disabled children.

The second main argument against FAA is the consequentialist concern that discrimination against disabled people can be aggravated by the practice. One worry is that the routine termination of defective fetuses will diminish the quality of life of disabled persons by depleting their numbers and, as a consequence, reduce the incentive for social accommodation. With fewer disabled people in the world, the motivation to adapt our environment so as to counter the disadvantage experienced by disabled persons who *do* exist may be weaker. Some have termed this the 'reduced resources argument'.[28] For example, when the number of wheelchair-users is high, there is a greater incentive for the state, and others, to invest in the infrastructure that allows wheelchair access, like ramps or disabled bathrooms, but less incentive when there are fewer wheelchair-users requiring such facilities. The reduced resources argument seems to be strengthened when conjoined with a social model of disability, which views much of the disadvantage attending disability as a product of social discrimination rather than biological difference. If the disadvantages of

---

[25] ibid.   [26] ibid 126.

[27] Williams's account is, however, notable for giving those arguments a fairly persuasive (ibid 144–50).

[28] See, Christopher Gyngell and Thomas Douglas, 'Selecting Against Disability: The Liberal Eugenic Challenge and the Argument from Cognitive Diversity' [2016] Journal of Applied Philosophy 2.

being disabled are predominantly a function of social discrimination, then removing pressure to address that discrimination by reducing the numbers of disabled people will make a significant contribution to them.

As with the expressivist objection, the reduced resources argument has come in for some criticism by those who think it exaggerates the impact of reducing the numbers of new disabled people on the social inequality of existing ones. Some authors have even suggested that in some scenarios, reduced numbers of existing disabled people will augment the resources available to each.[29] Williams's own conclusion is that even if the fears captured by the expressivist and reduced resources concerns are credible, it imposes too heavy a burden on individual pregnant women if their reproductive rights are abrogated so as to avoid them.[30] This calculation may be ultimately correct. However, whatever one makes of the standard objections to FAA, the interesting challenge remains for the person who invokes such arguments in support of a ban on SSA but does not extend the same reasoning to abortion for fetal abnormality.

As Williams notes, the expressivist objection seems to apply in much the same way to both forms of selective termination. If the reason for prohibiting SSA is its propensity to further entrench sexism and worsen the situation of women, we will want to know why FAA is not ruled out for the same reason: that it threatens to exacerbate discrimination against disabled people, partly by communicating the view that disabled peoples' lives are not of equal value. Alternatively, if the concern about further entrenching discrimination is not weighty enough to justify prohibiting FAA, then perhaps it is not weighty enough to warrant the prohibition of SSA, where the burdens on the prospective parents are comparable. As was seen, some have attempted to counter the expressivist objection in the case of FAA by claiming that the personal decision not to become a parent to a disabled child does not express any general belief about the lesser value of disabled lives. But if this counterargument is valid, it should be able to shield SSA from the same objection. Recall the example situations of Women A, B, and C. Here, at least, one could certainly make the case that in choosing SSA the women are not expressing the belief that girls are inferior to boys, but only acting to preserve their own wellbeing in difficult circumstances. If the abortion request and the discriminatory statement can be separated out in the one case, why not in the other? Furthermore, what Williams terms the 'strength in numbers objection' to SSA—the worry that reducing the ratio of women to men will diminish women's political power—seems to be far more powerful when applied to the case of FAA. Since there are far fewer disabled persons to begin with than there are women, it is reasonable to think that a

---

[29] ibid 6.
[30] With regard to the expressivist objection, for example, Williams considers the possibility that even if women who choose to terminate their defective fetuses do not act on the belief that disabled people's lives are inferior, 'the combined effect of what they do will still be to promulgate such [objectionable] ideas throughout society'. His suggested answer to this is to say that the costs to women of prohibiting selective abortion of defective fetuses are simply too high to be justified by the need to avoid reinforcing general prejudices against disabled people. In short, it is unfair to ask women to suffer for such a cause (Williams (n 24) 147).

significant reduction in their numbers through selective abortion will have a disproportionately negative impact on their social equality, if we accept the relationship
between their numbers and their degree of marginalization.

The key question is therefore why the standard objections to permitting SSA
do not apply with the same force to permitting FAA. Or, on the other side of the
same coin, why are the answers to those objections not equally valid answers in the
case of SSA? Most importantly, this includes the answer that, whatever its negative
effects, withdrawing the option of selective termination unfairly burdens individual
women who will suffer as a result, and who are not personally responsible for existing prejudices. Unless the two cases can be distinguished in some way, consistency
requires that we adopt the same attitude towards both kinds of selection. This of
course runs directly counter to popular moral thinking, which sees SSA and FAA as
occupying opposite ends of the spectrum of moral defensibility.

One way of answering this consistency problem would be to concede there are
no principled differences between SSA and FAA, and to suggest that in each case
the correct conclusion will simply be a function of how the relevant concerns balance against women's interests in reproductive freedom, taking into account the
specific surrounding context. Where the culture is such that sexism and sex inequality are extremely thoroughgoing, the potential additive effects of SSA may be worse
than in more equal societies. On the other hand, the burdens for individual women
of not being able to obtain SSA are also likely to be more severe. Likewise, the situation of disabled persons in a given jurisdiction and the depth of existing discrimination and disadvantage may properly influence how one balances the negative
effects of FAA against the imposition of mandated pregnancy on women. Perhaps
it simply cannot be said, in the abstract, whether there is a strong case for prohibition in each instance. But if the devil is indeed in the detail, then it is thinkable that
one could come to different conclusions on each case without being implicated in
inconsistency. It does not seem correct however, that SSA is inherently more problematic than FAA—the standardly accepted position.

Is it possible to distinguish the cases of sex-selective and fetal abnormality abortion in a more general way? One possible argument might be that raising a child
with a serious disability is far more burdensome than raising a child of an undesired
sex. This, however, clearly does not hold true across all cases. Depending entirely
on the particular case, the burdens of giving birth to a female child may be far more
severe than, say, raising a child with Down's Syndrome (consider again the example
cases of women A, B, and C).

Another possible difference is that while the burdens of caring for a disabled
child are objective or absolute, the burdens for women associated with producing
a child of the 'wrong' sex are entirely a product of the social conditions with which
they are enmeshed. If this is correct, then perhaps we would be justified to prohibit sex selection in an effort to counteract the social attitudes responsible for the
burdensomeness of producing the 'wrong' sexed child, whereas prohibiting FAA
will not go any way towards alleviating the burdens of raising disabled children.
How convincing one finds this point of contrast will depend largely on one's conception of disability. If disability is predominantly a social construction, then the

inequality of disabled people will mirror the inequality of women in being socially created, as will be the burdens connected with fetal abnormality pregnancies.

In this respect, then, the comparison of SSA with FAA will turn on whether one accepts or rejects the social model of disability, and to what extent one thinks the burdens of raising disabled children are socially determined and, in theory, eliminable. The debate about the nature of disability is, of course, complex, and I have no intention here of offering a theory of how disability yields disadvantage. However, it is at least clear that the disadvantage entailed by disability is socially imposed to a significant degree, even if it is also, in part, biologically determined, and that positive social attitudes towards disability can help alleviate that disadvantage. The comparison between the burdens of giving birth to a girl in a sexist society, or sub-culture, and those of giving birth to a disabled child therefore goes quite far. And if it is legitimate to restrict sex selection choice as part of the effort to combat the devaluation of women, then it is presumably legitimate to prohibit FAA if it would help counter disability discrimination, if and where the burdens on individual women are roughly comparable.[31]

Next, it does not seem open to us to distinguish the two cases by saying that it is bad for a disabled child to be born but that this is not true of a healthy female child. This would be to invoke the fetal interests argument in respect of disability selective abortions but to argue that it is not applicable to sex selective ones. There are multiple problems with this move. Firstly, it can undoubtedly be far worse to be a girl or a woman in a particular context than to be a disabled person in a different one. These comparative determinations will always depend on many variables: how bad is the disability? How sexist the culture? How discriminatory towards the disabled? And so on. Moreover, even if it were generally worse to suffer from a certain disease or disability than to be a female in an oppressively sexist culture, the fetal interests argument still suffers from the fact that barely any disabled states can be said to amount to a life not worth living. As we saw, this is a condition for the application of the fetal interests argument in favour of selective abortion.

But the fetal interests argument suffers from further drawbacks in the way of the 'non-identity problem'.[32] Non-identity problems arise in ethics where it is claimed that a certain act or practice is wrong because it harms a person, but where it is difficult to identify an individual subject of harm. If fetuses are not yet persons, as we

---

[31] This caveat about comparable burdens is in recognition of the fact that all things may not be otherwise equal. For example, one particular woman may face a far greater threat to her future well-being by the prospect of giving birth to a female child than another woman does by the prospect of raising a disabled child. The prohibition of selective abortion as a means of combating prejudice might only be legitimate when the burdens it imposes on individual women are not unreasonably severe. Consequently, the suggestion here is not that it would be legitimate to prohibit all FAA in the interests of social equality if the same considerations can ever justify SAA, but only that the cases ought to be treated similarly where the interests served by prohibition are equally strong, and the burdens on the individual pregnant women are of comparable weight.

[32] The 'non-identity problem' was originally formulated by the philosopher Derek Parfit as a challenge to a certain way of moral thinking which ties the wrongfulness of actions to their propensity to cause harm to identifiable individuals. See Derek Parfit, *Reasons and Persons* (Oxford University Press 1984) part 4 generally.

are presuming they are not, and not capable of being harmed, then they cannot be harmed by being allowed to live and become persons with difficult lives. Equally, it does not seem correct to say that the later disabled child or adult is the person who is harmed by being brought into existence, since the only alternative for *them* would be not to have existed at all. Even if their life is so terribly poor as to be not worth living (a very rare case), it will not be true that *they* were harmed by not being aborted. To be made worse off by anything, one must already exist in some prior state that can be compared with the latter one. Of course, if the fetal interests argument is deficient for this reason, then it cannot be used to defend either FAA or SSA.

Because of the non-identity problem, the only way to claim that it is worse to bring new disabled persons into the world than to bring new women into the world, even when those women will suffer considerably under male oppression, is to argue that creating new disabled people contributes to an impersonally worse state of affairs. In other words, one must say that although it does not harm the individual brought into existence, it is of some negative moral value when new disabled people are brought into the world, and better when they are not. Suffice to say, I cannot imagine how one could convincingly make such an argument, and by reference to what values and goods the existence of people with disabilities is a bad thing (and of course, much can be said to the contrary).

10.5.1 Choice and coercion

A final way someone might seek to distinguish SSA from FFA is by appeal to the issue of choice. As some feminist discussants have pointed out, SSA in circumstances where the consequences of bearing a girl are hugely detrimental is surely a constrained example of reproductive choice. Especially in conditions where female life is undervalued, we might worry that a decision to terminate a female fetus is not an exercise of free choice by a pregnant woman, but only a response to irresistible social pressure. For this reason, some feminists have suggested that prohibiting SSA could be necessary to protect women from abortions that are not truly consensual. Catharine MacKinnon, for example, writes:

> ... in a context of mass abortions of female fetuses, the pressures on women to destroy potential female offspring are tremendous and oppressive unless restrictions exist. While, under conditions of sex inequality, monitoring women's reasons for deciding to abort is worrying, the decision is not a free one, even absent governmental intervention, where a male life is valued and a female life is not.[33]

MacKinnon is surely right to suspect that, in most cases, the decision by a pregnant woman to abort a female fetus is likely to be the result of immense external pressure, whether from other individuals or from the patriarchal conditions in which she finds herself. Because of this, such choices do not strike MacKinnon as genuinely free. The argument might be made, then, that SSA ought to be generally prohibited

---

[33] Catharine MacKinnon, 'Reflections on Sex Equality under Law' (1991) 100 Yale Law Journal 1317 (n 54).

so as to protect those who would otherwise make a non-autonomous decision to abort because of fetal sex.

But can FAA be regarded as, on the whole, any more consensual than SSA? In a context of disability discrimination, it may be thought that the decision to terminate for fetal abnormality is just as responsive to social pressure. In Britain, the routine gestational screening for Down's Syndrome is indicative of social expectations that a positive diagnosis should at least provoke a serious consideration about termination. Jeremy Williams points out that in Western countries, social expectations now weigh heavily in favour of terminating where fetal disability is detected. If cultural pressure of this kind precludes genuine consent in the case of SSA, he asks why the same would not be true of selective termination on the ground of disability.[34] It certainly seems as though MacKinnon's worry about the freedom of the decision to abort a female fetus in patriarchal conditions carries over to the disability context. In a social world where the lives of disabled people are not valued equally, are decisions to abort defective fetuses not also un-free?

Yet many abortions, perhaps even most, are chosen in the face of undesirable pressures. Abortions we would consider to be freely chosen can be undertaken in response to non-ideal circumstances outside of the pregnant woman's control: her relationship status, her financial resources, her career prospects, to name but a few. Abortions chosen in response to these kinds of pressures are not ordinarily considered non-consensual. Are the pressures often in play in SSA and FAA of a wholly different order? Is, for example, the woman who opts for an abortion simply because she cannot afford to have a child making any less constrained a choice than the woman who aborts because she cannot afford to have a child *that is female*, with everything that entails in her particular situation? Indeed, almost all of the choices we make are taken in response to non-ideal conditions, and are not usually less autonomous for that. The challenge here is to explain why selective terminations of either kind are distinguishable from other kinds of abortion in terms of consent.

It may be argued that where the pressure to abort is applied by particular members of a pregnant woman's social world and is direct and overwhelming enough, it crosses the threshold from mere pressure to *coercion*. That would certainly be true of the extreme case where a woman faces domestic violence, or the threat of being ostracized, if she gives birth to a girl. As Williams notes, threats of harm which come in the way of rights violations by others, like violence, tend to be regarded as destructive of autonomous decision-making in ways that the prospect of other kinds of harm—like financial ruin—are not.[35] Personal threats of force typically obviate consent in a way that circumstantial pressure doesn't.

However, distinguishing SSA from both FAA and what we might call 'financial dire straits' abortions on this basis requires us to believe that SSA is uniquely likely to occur in a context of outright coercion. It is not clear to me that we can make this assumption with any assuredness. Abortion decisions may be coerced in all kinds of situations and for all manner of reasons, with concealment of the sexual intercourse

<hr>

[34] Williams (n 24) 139.   [35] ibid 141.

which resulted in the pregnancy being, presumably, very high up on that list. Many coerced abortions will therefore have nothing to do with fetal sex. A policy of selectively prohibiting only SSA in the defence of reproductive autonomy requires us to believe that where fetal sex is at issue, degrees of force are particularly likely to be deployed which surpass the circumstantial pressures (including personal pressure) that can motivate all kinds of abortions. Unless there is sound reason for believing this, the exceptional prohibition of SSA for the protection of choice appears to be, as Williams concludes, ad hoc.[36]

10.6 Conclusion

Ultimately, prohibiting SSA or FAA as part of an effort to combat sex or disability inequality may impose unfair burdens on individual women, as Williams contends. Such prohibitions would in effect require some women to submit themselves to significant harm in order to help rectify social attitudes for which they are not responsible. Moreover, it is clear that those harms will often be of a magnitude which would ordinarily justify abortion in generally permissive regulatory regimes, were they not linked to particular fetal characteristics—that is, they will pose non-negligible risks to the woman's wellbeing. For this reason, even someone who is persuaded by concerns such as the expressivist objection might well reach the conclusion that prohibiting selective abortion is not an appropriate means with which to counter prejudice against disadvantaged classes of people. Those concerned about sex equality in particular might also reach the conclusion, as some have, that any incursion into women's reproductive rights is not likely to enhance women's freedom more than it will curtail it. Those adopting this view will be particularly alarmed by indications that sex selection abortion prohibitions are intended by their supporters to pave the way to more general abortion prohibitions—indeed, the precise direction of Kaczor's own argument.

But the end determinations about both cases will be invariably context-sensitive. That is, they will necessarily depend on all of the relevant approximations about the domain in question: the likely uptake of selective abortion, the strength of the existing class disadvantage, the correlation between the two, the burdensomeness of the prohibition on women, and whether general reproductive rights are robust enough to withstand some incursions. These are just the main considerations.

Importantly, though, it is entirely possible in principle for defenders of legal abortion to support prohibitive policies on either SSA or FAA on the ground of wider societal harms without ensnaring themselves in incoherence about the moral status of the fetus. Whether those harms really do obtain, or whether their avoidance is worth the restriction of women's reproductive freedoms, is a discussion that will no doubt be on-going. Furthermore, any such discussion must be attuned to the potential that arguments both in favour of and against prohibition

---

[36] ibid.

might apply to SSA and FAA alike. Justifying their differential treatment is not as straightforward as it might seem. In particular, both opponents and supporters of abortion rights may not, with consistency, be able to direct special moral opprobrium at SSA without making the same statements about FAA. All the same, though, philosophical opponents of abortion are simply in error to claim that there is anything theoretically inconsistent about defending abortion rights generally whilst arguing that there are good reasons to support exceptional restrictions on selective abortion.

11

Matters of Conscience

11.1 The Case of the Catholic Midwives

Mary Doogan and Concepta Wood were two experienced midwives employed as 'labour ward co-ordinators' at the Southern General Hospital in Glasgow in 2010. Both women were also practising Roman Catholics firmly holding the view that all life is sacred and that the termination of pregnancy is therefore seriously immoral. They also believed that any involvement in the process of termination would make them accomplices to what was, in their view, a grave moral crime. As 'labour ward co-ordinators', Doogan's and Wood's job description encompassed the management and leadership of the labour ward, which included responsibilities of delegating patient care to individual nurses and providing overarching supervision and support. Eager to ensure that they would not ever find themselves having to participate in abortion treatment on the ward, both midwives registered their conscientious objection to abortion at the beginning of their employment.

Foreseeing that the passage of the 1967 Abortion Act would make a morally controversial procedure commonplace in medical settings, the British Parliament enacting the legislation inserted a conscientious objection clause under section 4, which provided that no person shall fall under any legal duty, contractual or otherwise, to 'participate in any treatment' authorized by the Act to which he harbours a conscientious objection.[1] Pursuant to section 4(2), there is an exception to the protection for conscience where an abortion is 'necessary to save the life or to prevent grave permanent injury to the physical or mental health of a pregnant woman'. The clear purpose of the section 4 exemption is to allow healthcare professionals who morally object to abortion practice to nevertheless serve in contexts in which abortion treatment may be given, without compromising their moral convictions. The Glasgow case concerned the precise scope of that exemption which, quite evidently, rested on the interpretation of the term 'participate in any treatment'.

After some restructuring of services at the hospital, Doogan and Wood became concerned that more terminations were likely to be performed on the labour ward on which they worked. Their roles as labour ward co-ordinators meant that although they were unlikely to be called upon to provide one to one treatment for abortion patients, their host of general managerial responsibilities over the ward were such

---

[1] Abortion Act 1967, s 4(1).

Arguments about Abortion: Personhood, Morality, and Law. First Edition. Kate Greasley. © K. Greasley 2017. Published 2017 by Oxford University Press.

that could potentially entail delegating, supervising, and supporting staff giving front-line abortion treatment. Among other things, it was possible they would be required, in the ordinary course of their duties, to book in terminations and allocate beds for that purpose; to oversee handover of abortion patients to fresh staff at the beginning of a new shift, and to provide guidance and support to the midwives involved in abortion procedures.

Believing that the performance of even these managerial tasks conflicted with their convictions about abortion, Doogan and Wood sought assurance from the health authority that they would be exempted from such supervisory duties in relation to abortion treatment. When their employer refused that assurance, they instigated judicial review proceedings, where the issue became the scope of section 4 of the Abortion Act and whether 'supervising, delegating and supporting' staff giving abortion treatment fell within the definition of 'participate in any treatment' under that section. The midwives argued that the term was to be given a wide reading, which included all of the supportive tasks associated with their roles as labour ward co-ordinators, where those tasks pertained to abortion treatment. The health authority counter-argued that section 4 ought to be more narrowly construed, and that the supervisory and supportive tasks the midwives were required to perform did not amount to 'participation in treatment' for abortion.

The case eventually went before the Scottish Court of Appeal. The key legal question being what kinds of actions amounted to participation in abortion treatment for the purposes of the conscience-based exemption. Did they include only the kinds of activities which directly bring about the termination of pregnancy, such as the administration of pills, or the performance of a surgical abortion? Or did they also extend to the satellite tasks of supervision, delegation, and support, of booking in abortions and allocating beds, and being on standby for more junior staff who needed to seek advice in the process of carrying out terminations? The Scottish Court of Appeal sided with the midwives.[2] Favouring the wider interpretation of 'participate in treatment', it held that the right of conscientious objection in section 4 extends to the 'whole process of treatment' for the purpose of effecting a termination. That whole process encompassed everything that formed part of the 'team effort' involved in bringing about an abortion, including the supervision, delegation, and staff support for which Doogan and Wood were responsible.[3]

The Health Authority appealed to the British Supreme Court, which gave a different answer. The scope of section 4 of the 1967 Act had been considered once before by the Supreme Court (then the House of Lords) in *R v Salford Health Authority Ex p Janaway*.[4] In that case, the question concerned whether a doctor's secretary who objected to typing a referral letter for an abortion would, by doing so, be participating in abortion treatment under section 4. The Court in *Janaway* decided that the conscientious objection exemption in section 4 applied only to the process of treatment for termination carried out in hospital or clinic, and to

---

[2] *Doogan and Wood v Greater Glasgow Health Board* [2013] CSIH 36.   [3] ibid [12].
[4] *Janaway v Salford Area Health Authority* [1989] AC 537.

treatment in which the conscientious objector is required to actually partake. The *Doogan* case effectively asked the Court to refine its interpretation of the scope of section 4 even further. Once *in* the hospital setting, which specific kinds of acts qualified as participating in abortion treatment? Did section 4 apply to *any* act connected with abortion treatment or the conditions required to administer it, or only certain kinds of acts?

In the case of *Doogan and Wood*, the Supreme Court again opted for the narrower interpretation of section 4 placed before it.[5] Delivering the unanimous judgment, Lady Hale determined that to 'participate' in abortion treatment meant 'taking part in a hands on capacity'.[6] On this reading, the section 4 exemption might apply to particular supervisory tasks that required a ward manager to become personally involved in giving abortion care, for instance covering break relief for a midwife caring for an abortion patient by providing the care herself, or assisting in a medical intervention which is part of the course of treatment (like the delivery of the fetus with forceps). However, the general managerial duties of 'supervision, delegation and support' that did *not* involve direct assistance in abortion treatment were outwith the scope of section 4. These managerial tasks the Court regarded as closer to the roles of hospital caterers and cleaners insofar as they facilitated the actual carrying out of abortion treatment.[7] As Lady Hale reasoned, employees whose only job was to provide hospital catering and cleaning services were also 'participating' in abortion treatment insofar as they helped to facilitate the conditions in which abortions are carried out. However, this peripheral kind of involvement clearly would not amount to 'participation' for the purposes of section 4. In the Court's view, many of the tasks from which the midwives claimed exemption were analogous to this. Consequently, it was held that the midwives could not claim the right of conscientious objection in respect of most of the disputed tasks. Since only 'hands on' involvement in abortion treatment would suffice to invoke section 4, the midwives could not rely on the conscientious objection provision to excuse themselves from those duties.

11.2 The Problem of Conscience

Both the *Doogan* case and the *Janaway* case before it illustrate a long-standing problem in abortion ethics and regulation. When a state allows for broadly permissive abortion laws, what provisions ought to be made for medical practitioners who conscientiously object to participating in abortion treatment? Most people believe that some exemptions for conscience ought to be provided for. There is a general interest in not compelling individuals to do things which will sear their conscience. Moreover, it might be thought that the particular nature of the wrong of abortion, as perceived by the conscientious objector, creates a particularly powerful reason to

---

[5] *Greater Glasgow Health Board v Doogan and Another* [2014] UKSC 68.
[6] ibid [38].   [7] ibid.

excuse her from participation in it. It would be extremely onerous indeed to compel an individual to assist in an act which, by her lights, entails the unjustified killing of a rights-holding human being.

But ought there to be any limitations on the right to conscientious objection, and where ought those boundaries to be drawn? We might all agree that there is a strong case for allowing objectors to avoid performing the abortion procedures themselves. But what about less direct forms of participation? Should the doctor's secretary who wishes to avoid typing a letter connected with an abortion be able to avail herself of a conscience exemption? Should the midwives in *Doogan* have been able to excuse themselves from any involvement whatsoever in abortion treatment, including booking terminations and allocating beds? We might well ask whether an objecting nurse sent to fetch abortifacient medicines should be exempt from *that* task. What of an objecting hospital caterer who does not wish to service abortion patients? It is obvious that concern for keeping a clean conscience might provoke objections to evermore far removed contributions to abortion treatment.

Even those who are strongly supportive of abortion rights might nevertheless feel some measure of sympathy for the midwives in *Doogan*, in light of the predicament in which they found themselves. It is certainly understandable that someone who considers abortion akin to murder would feel conscientiously bound to avoid many forms of complicity in it which do not amount to direct participation. It may be cold comfort to such an objector to remind her that she did not perform the terminating act herself if she carried out tasks which were a necessary part of the process. Is it adequate protection of such a person's conscience if she is compelled to allocate beds for abortion treatment, or delegate staff to perform them, or provide those staff with advice?

A similar point might be made in relation to the controversial duty to refer. The section 4 exemption in the Abortion Act 1967 does not impose a duty on objecting doctors who invoke conscience protections to refer patients seeking abortion to alternative, non-objecting doctors. However, National Health Service contracts require anyone exercising their right to refusal under that section to make 'prompt referral to another provider of primary medical services who does not have such conscientious objections'.[8] According to the British Medical Association and General Medical Council guidelines, objectors should even, in some instances, arrange the appointment for the patient with a non-objecting doctor.[9] While there is plenty of support for the duty of referral, a conscientious objector could reasonably claim that even this act amounts to a level of cooperation in abortion that is more than her conscience can comfortably bear. Imagine, for instance, that a doctor who morally objects to a common practice of terminating unwanted infants were told that she need not help carry out the terminations herself, but must display a sign directing

---

[8] See National Health Service (General Medical Services Contracts) Regulations 2004 (S.I. 2004/291), Sched 2(3)(e) and clause 9.3.1(e) of the NHS England Standard Medical Services Contract (cited in: Sara Fovargue and Mary Neal, ' "In Good Conscience": Conscience-based Exemptions and Proper Medical Treatment' (2015) 23 Medical Law Review 1, 5).

[9] See Fovargue and Neal (n 8) 5.

parents seeking the termination service to a willing agent. If we are to believe opponents of abortion that their objection is rooted in the equation of abortion with infanticide, then this is surely what the duty to refer amounts to on their outlook.

Considering all of this, the Supreme Court's decision to exclude the midwives' supervisory tasks from the coverage of section 4 may appear out of line with a serious commitment to protecting conscience. If protecting the moral integrity of objectors was the interest at issue, surely the midwives' wish to be exempt from indirect participation was the central consideration for interpreting the conscience clause. This, at any rate, had been the view of the Scottish Court of Appeal when reaching the contrary decision that the tasks of 'supervision, delegation and support' *did* in fact amount to participation in abortion treatment under section 4.[10] Lady Dorrian (delivering the judgment) placed great emphasis on the grounding rationale for the exemption, which, as she pointed out, was there to protect those morally opposed to abortion from having to perform actions which sully their conscience. This rationale, it was thought, clearly endorsed a wide interpretation of section 4. As Lady Dorrian contended in her judgment:

The right is given because it is recognised that the process of abortion is felt by many people to be morally repugnant . . . it is a matter on which many people have strong moral and religious convictions, and the right of conscientious objection is given out of respect for those convictions and not for any other reason. It is in keeping with the reason for the exemption that the wide interpretation which we favour should be given to it. It is consistent with the reasoning which allowed such an objection in the first place that it should extend to any involvement in the process of treatment, the object of which is to terminate a pregnancy.[11]

There is certainly something appealing about the Scottish Court's approach. If the very point of section 4 is to spare healthcare workers the moral anxiety of being a part of what was, as they saw it, a morally heinous activity, then surely it was for the workers themselves, for whose benefit the clause was inserted, to specify what level of involvement put them ill at ease and, indeed, what in their eyes counted as participation. Put differently, if someone *feels* that writing a letter of referral or delegating staff for abortion treatment compromises her moral integrity, well, that is exactly what conscience protections are there to prevent.

But it is easy to see how far this reasoning could be taken. If conscientious objectors are at liberty to determine for themselves what sorts of activities invoke the exemption, it seems there will be no limits whatsoever on what kinds of activities or tasks could count as 'participation' in abortion under the 1967 Act. Following the Scottish Court's principle of interpretation, the ordinary tasks of the hospital cleaners and caterers, and even the delivery van drivers, could constitute such tasks if an objector only attests that they compromise her good conscience. This leads us to ask whether *any* limits on the right to conscientious objection ought to be imposed.

Any discussion about the right of conscientious objection to abortion and its limits must begin with the assumption that legal abortion is a morally justified

---

[10] *Doogan and Wood* (n 2).   [11] ibid [38].

practice. Writing about rights of conscientious objection in general, Joseph Raz
suggests that the main problem with justifying conscience exemptions is that it
involves showing that a person 'is entitled not to do what would otherwise be
his moral duty to do simply because he believes that it is wrong for him to do
so'.[12] Using the standard example of a pacifist's objection to military service, Raz
explains that '[the] only way to base such a right on moral principles is to concede
that because somebody *wrongly* believes that military service is prohibited for him
he should be allowed to opt out'.[13] Likewise, with abortion, we might say that the
problem of conscience must assume that a permissive legal stance is correct. If the
law is simply wrong to hold abortion to be permissible in many circumstances,
the correct response to this would not be to provide for conscience exemptions,
but to change the law. The question of conscientious objection therefore only
becomes live when we accept, even if only for the sake of argument, that the
duties from which objectors wish to be exempt are in fact morally justified. As
Raz writes:

[T]he argument must proceed on the assumption that the law is morally valid. The conscientious objector, it will be assumed, proposes to act wrongly. Should he have the right to do
the wrong thing because he sincerely holds mistaken or wrong moral views?[14]

Raz goes on to explain that the right not to have one's conscience coerced can only
ever be a prima facie right—one which 'can be overridden to protect other values
and ideals'.[15] This, he says, 'is inevitable, given that it is a right to do what is morally wrong which is given to people who will use it for that very purpose. To give it
absolute importance is to prefer the morally wrong to the morally right whenever
the agent has misconceived moral ideas, however wicked'.[16] This alone may alert us
to the possible necessity of placing some limits on rights of conscientious objection
to abortion practice if and when the exercise of that right threatens the values and
ideals to which the law is committed.

  As we see with Raz's main example, the issue of conscientious objection is most
often discussed in relation to military conscription and the pacifist's right to opt
out. Yet conscientious objection to participation in abortion differs from the case of
military conscription in some key ways. For one, abortion provision is different in
that, insofar as it is a duty, it is not a duty which falls on anyone in particular to provide unless and until they place themselves in a certain position. Most opponents
of abortion will never need to deploy the right to conscientious objection so as to
avoid involvement in abortion treatment, since they will not be so positioned in the
first place that they are otherwise duty-bound to participate in it. No one is plucked
at random and required by law to help deliver abortions. It is only once someone
has positioned herself so that participation is required of her as part of her duties of
employment that the right to conscientiously object is of any relevance. And being
so positioned is largely a matter of choice—the choice to be a medical practitioner,
or an obstetrician–gynaecologist, or a labour ward co-ordinator.

---

[12] Joseph Raz, *The Authority of Law* (Oxford University Press 1979) 277.   [13] ibid.
[14] ibid 278.   [15] ibid 281.   [16] ibid.

These features of the abortion context yield salient differences from the case of military conscription. Ordinarily, avoiding any duty to participate in abortion treatment is extremely easy. The greatest protection for conscience here lies in the fact that *there is no law requiring anyone to perform abortions.* Military conscription is different. Here, pacifist objectors require protection from a law which directly compels them to serve in the military, the imposition of the legal duty being wholly outwith their control. It is clear that these differences affect exactly how the conscience right is deployed in each case and against whom or what. With military conscription, the right to conscientiously object is asserted against the state, which commands compliance. In contrast, section 4 of the Abortion Act is intended not to protect an objector from the consequences of disobeying the state, but from the consequences of refusing to partake in duties of employment associated with abortion. In effect, it shields the objector from the ordinary implications of refusing to perform tasks that arise in her chosen line of work, consequences which may range from legal action for breach of contractual duty, to disciplinary action, to dismissal. Section 4 protects objectors by stepping in to bar employers from penalizing them for refusing to participate in abortion treatment, and is thus only operative *once* an objector so has placed herself that abortion treatment could be part of her job.

Conscientious refusal to participate in abortion treatment is not, therefore, wholly analogous with a pacifist's objection to military service. Nor is the nature of the conscience protection the same. The main question I wish to address in what follows here is how conscience exemptions for abortion practice ought to be framed within the context of permissive abortion regulation and what sorts of factors ought to inform the boundaries of conscience protection. I suggest that there must be some limits on the right to conscientious objection to abortion, and that those limits ought to be determined by a few key considerations pertinent to conscience exemptions in general. One is the imperative that conscientious refusals do not undermine the purpose of abortion regulation and the values and ideals furthered by it. Another is the degree to which the contested activity implicates the objector in giving abortion treatment. A third and final pair of considerations are the cost to individual objectors of shouldering the burden of their objections themselves, and, symmetrically, the cost to others of shouldering the burdens of (presumed) morally erroneous conscientious objections. Relevant to this final question will be the avoidability, for the objector, of the disputed activity, and what avoiding it entails in the way of burdens.

11.3 The Purpose of the Law

One important constraint on the prima facie right to conscientious objection is that the exercise of that right must not frustrate the purpose of the law. All things being equal, it is of course better to fulfil the (presumably) just aims of a legal policy without having to coerce anyone to act against conscience. However, things stand differently if and when allowing for a right to object is not compatible with the aims of the law. Thus pacifism can be tolerated if there are enough conscripts, but not otherwise.

As Raz explains, the prima facie right to conscientious objection is at its strongest in relation to paternalistic laws, imposed for the benefit of the would-be objector. It is particularly difficult to justify coercing someone's conscience for her own good. The right is markedly less robust with regard to laws and policies which aim to promote the public interest. In this context, Raz claims, the right to object will be more defensible when fulfilling the purpose of those policies does not depend on any one individual. As he says, laws that are there to protect the public interest 'normally allow for a certain flexibility because of the insignificance of each individual's contribution'.[17] However:

> ... here as elsewhere one is concerned with balancing the right to autonomy as against other interests. Thus if too many people will, in a particular society and at a particular period, claim the right to object they may defeat the interest served by the law and this may be indefensible.[18]

It is an upshot of this that the right to conscientiously object to military service may well depend on how many others wish to rely on the right in order to excuse themselves. If it is engaged so widely as to defeat the interest served by the law—in this case, fighting a just war—the right must be restricted. The same will be true of other public interest laws where compliance by any individual is insignificant to carrying out the purpose of the law. Raz gives taxation and pollution laws as examples where individual contributions are clearly insignificant. That consideration goes in favour of a right to conscientiously refuse to comply, where a matter of conscience is plausibly implicated. However, since the purposes served by taxation and pollution laws clearly cannot be sustained in the face of widespread conscientious objection, a right to object to such laws cannot be afforded if the predicted uptake is great.

In the case of abortion, then, one pertinent question is what interests are meant to be served by a state's abortion policy, and in what circumstances conscientious exemptions could obstruct those interests. In its decision in *Doogan*, the Supreme Court underscored the fact that the main purpose of the 1967 Abortion Act was to provide for safe and effective abortion treatment, with the section 4 right only included as a 'quid pro quo' of that provision.[19] If the wider purpose of the Abortion Act is read this way, it follows from the above that the section 4 right is subject to the limit that it cannot be exercised in such a way that jeopardizes the very availability of safe abortion within the provisions of the statute. The question then becomes what sort of use or interpretation of the section 4 right to conscientious objection would constitute the frustration of that purpose.

It will not normally be the case that an individual practitioner's refusal to participate in abortion treatment precludes a woman's access to safe, legal abortion. This owes primarily to the fact that there will, in ordinary circumstances, be someone

---

[17] ibid 285.   [18] ibid 286.
[19] *Greater Glasgow Health Board v Doogan and Another* (n 5) per Lady Hale [27].

who can perform the task in their stead—to perform a surgical abortion, or administer a pill, or type a referral letter. Still, circumstances will arise in which the exercise of conscientious objection is at odds with the law's commitment to safe, legal abortion provision, the purpose of the 1967 Act. One obvious circumstance is where a conscientious objector refuses to perform an abortion in an emergency scenario in which no one else is available to perform it. In light of this, it is clear that the section 4(2) qualification for emergency abortions is an essential limit on the right to conscientious objection.

There may be other circumstances, however, in which an objector is so positioned that to exercise the right to conscientiously object would effectively be to obstruct safe abortion provision. One such case might be where a healthcare professional obtains employment at a clinic established to practice abortion exclusively or predominantly, only to then claim her right to conscientiously object to performing almost all tasks associated with her employment. Affording the right to someone thus situated is plainly incompatible with the law's aim of ensuring abortion's availability, for, if safe abortion is to be accessible, then at the very least those who are employed for the sole purpose of carrying it out must be willing to do so.

What we might call the 'effectiveness provisio' limit on the right of conscientious objection might also come into play in relation to the duty to refer, in the right circumstances. Usually, refusal to refer a patient to another doctor for consultation on abortion will not obstruct abortion provision, since the patient will be able to quickly and easily obtain a consultation with a non-objecting doctor. However, there will be circumstances in which this is not the case, for a number of possible reasons. For instance, where the patient lacks the wherewithal to obtain an alternative appointment, or misunderstands the refusing doctor's objection as an authoritative medical decision against the abortion, the exercise of the conscience right will have obstructed abortion provision. The same will be true if there *are* no other non-objecting doctors accessible to the patient. These considerations place limits on the right of doctors to object both to referral and, even, on their right to object to authorizing a legal abortion themselves. Everything here will depend on alternative opportunities for procuring an abortion and the effect of the doctor's refusal. If time is of the essence (say, because the pregnant woman is approaching the legal limit for abortion), then the stalling effect of a doctor's decision to refer rather than authorize the abortion herself, or to refuse to refer, may again function to obstruct the purpose of the law's abortion provisions.

Finally, and most evidently, as is true of pacifist refusal to perform military service, the 'effectiveness provisio' limitation restricts medical practitioners' right to claim conscientious exemption from participating in abortion treatment where there are not enough willing providers to fulfil the law's purpose of making abortion legal and accessible in a number of circumstances. The absence of sufficient willing providers may owe to the widespread invocation of conscientious exemptions, or may be due to a simple dearth of qualified personnel. Either way, the implications for the conscience right are the same. If the right of conscientious objection is subject to an effectiveness proviso, then it can be legitimately restricted wherever, in all of the circumstances, its effect is to preclude abortion access.

11.4 Cogs in the Machine

A second core consideration when attending to the limits of the right to conscientious objection is the degree to which objectors are, by virtue of performing particular tasks, implicated in the conduct which they deem deeply immoral. If the interest in granting conscience rights is that of protecting the moral integrity of objectors, it will clearly matter just *how* morally compromised objectors are likely to feel as a result of different levels of involvement in abortion. Causal proximity to the immoral activity, directness of involvement, the presence of intervening acts, and whether or not one's agency is an essential condition for the immoral enterprise are all factors which can be thought to go to the depth of a person's reasonable self-perceived complicity in what he regards as a morally objectionable activity.

In the British case, this issue bears out in the sorts of activities thought to amount to 'participation' in abortion treatment. What degree of 'participation' ought to invoke the conscience protections of section 4? As we saw, the view of the Scottish Court in *Doogan* was that it was for the objector herself to draw the boundaries of that protection. In other words, what amounts to morally compromising 'participation' was itself a question of conscience. The implication of this answer, we saw, is that there are no limits whatsoever on the kinds of conduct from which objectors can excuse themselves with legal protection. The sandwich delivery person on a hospital ward has as much right to refuse, without repercussions, to service those involved in abortion treatment as a doctor has to refuse to carry out a surgical abortion. Yet it strikes me as wholly inappropriate to regard these two examples as equally serious breaches of conscience from which objectors are in need of equal protection. And considering the fact that the right to conscientious objection must be limited to those refusals which can be tolerated whilst still meeting the legal aim of safe abortion provision, it is reasonable to think that in delineating those limits, the law should be sensitive to the degree of moral complicity which goes hand in hand with different sorts of acts.

The most obvious feature relevant to the severity of a breach of conscience is the directness of involvement in the perceived immoral outcome. The more remote that outcome is from the contentious conduct, the less severe the breach of conscience will be. However, the directness of the causal relationship between the conduct and the outcome is not the only thing relevant to the gravity of a breach of conscience. A notable limitation of the Scottish Court's approach in *Doogan* was its propensity to mask some distinctions between levels of facilitating abortion which are likely to be pertinent to breach of conscience. Lady Hale was of course right that Doogan and Wood's supervisory tasks could be likened to hospital cleaning and catering in the respect that they all facilitated abortion in the widest sense—they might all claim to be cogs in the machine. However, the midwives were very differently situated with regard to the level of responsibility and authority they exercised over the abortion procedures on their ward and the infrastructure required to carry them out. While the supervising midwives may have been no more directly involved in 'hands on' abortion treatment than were the caterers, they were, when on duty, at the helm of the abortive procedures and the ward on which they occurred. Much unlike the caterers, their lack of direct involvement in those procedures did not owe to the fact that they were too insignificant to the process, but to the fact that they were at too *high* a level of responsibility. But morality does not cut any breaks for this. Being distanced from morally prohibited conduct because one is too much in charge of the mechanisms effectuating it is not the same as being distanced because one is too inconsequential. A person is not morally off the hook for refusing to get her hands dirty if she is the one overseeing the entire operation. It is reasonable, therefore, if Doogan and Wood had believed themselves to be in a fundamentally different moral position from that of the hospital caretakers, and thus in need of greater protection for conscience. These important differences were also rendered negligible on the Scottish Court's reasoning which seemed to bring potentially *any* refusal within the scope of section 4.

Lady Hale's comparison of the midwives' supervisory tasks with the jobs of hospital cleaners and caterers might also be considered inapt insofar as they were thought to exemplify the same degree of actual participation in abortion treatment. It is undoubtedly true, as Lady Hale remarked, that the cleaners and caterers would *also* facilitate abortion by contributing to the general upkeep of a hospital in which abortions are performed. Yet the duties of the supervising midwives directly contributed to the effectuation of each individual abortion in a way that hospital caretaking patently does not. Booking appointments, allocating beds and staff, and supervising handovers are essential components of every individual abortion treatment, as well as being causally quite proximate to those treatments. Lady Hale might just as well have pointed out that the drivers of the delivery vehicles supplying the hospital equipment *also* facilitate the abortions that happen there, in a more general way. But hospital delivery drivers who object to abortion are not thereby in the same boat as an objector whose job is to book termination procedures and oversee the staff performing them.

11.5 The Burdens of Conscience

A third and final core consideration when framing a limited right to conscientious objection is the onerousness of requiring objectors to assume the burdens of their own objection, or, in the alternative, of requiring other people to assume them. It is important to hold in mind yet again that right of conscientious objection is not the only thing standing in the way of incurring a duty to assist in abortion—indeed, it is not the main thing. Naturally, the most ideal way for an objector to avoid participation in abortion, direct or indirect, is simply to avoid any situation in which she could be foreseeably called upon to participate. This is never impossible to do—no one need be a health practitioner of any sort—but will at times come at a cost for the objector, the magnitude of which varies depending on their role. As we saw, the function of conscience provisions in law is to protect objectors from the ordinary, possibly detrimental consequences of refusing to perform tasks as part of abortion treatment. A core question is therefore how far the law should seek to ameliorate the consequences of a health practitioner's refusal, which is, at bottom, a question about who should bear the burden of the objection. Refusing an exemption places the burden of avoidance squarely on the objector. Providing an exemption, on the other hand, requires others—the employer, or the health authority—to bear the cost of accommodating the objector by finding alternative providers whilst keeping the objector in her healthcare role.

How much burden can an objector be expected to shoulder in order to avoid being so positioned that she is called upon to participate in abortion treatment? The avoidability of the objectionable activity for the conscientious objector will have much to do with this determination. On the whole, it is acceptable for us to require objectors to shoulder the burden of their own convictions, especially given the assumption that those convictions are morally erroneous. Raz writes:

> [T]he circumstances which lead to the conflict between law and one's perceived moral duty are normally subject to one's control and if one desires to remain faithful to one's moral principles one could, even at cost to oneself, prevent them from arising. Hence, especially given the prima facie nature of the claim that the law should not coerce one's conscience, society is entitled to require the individual to shoulder the burden of his convictions rather than require society itself, which regards them as wrong convictions, to do so.[20]

As Raz claims, it is normally acceptable to expect the conscientious objector to bear the cost to others of his adherence to principles, and therefore little reason for the state to make exemption for liability in damages, or other consequences of refusal. In some situations, however, the burden of avoidance for the objector might be particularly onerous. And where that burden can be eased without undue cost to others, the prima facie right to protection of conscience may legitimately prevail. The avoidability of the disputed activity for the objector and the ease of accommodating his objection will therefore be the two main considerations in the balancing of burdens. With regard to the first consideration, it demands quite a lot in the way of personal sacrifice for the law to tell an objector that the only way she may securely avoid the duty to participate in abortion is by not practising medicine of any kind; slightly less to tell her she cannot be an obstetrician–gynaecologist, and less again to tell her that she simply cannot not work in abortion clinics. In the case of Doogan and Wood, it might be argued that the options for avoiding all forms of participation in abortion were multiple and, hence, that the burden of avoidance was not so great. They might, after all, have only sought employment on wards that did not provide abortion treatment at all. Alternatively, they may have just declined to take up particular positions of responsibility that rendered all disassociation from abortion treatment difficult. Had Doogan and Wood been nurses or midwives on the ward and not ward co-ordinators, keeping them entirely out of abortion care would have been an easier matter for the health authority. It may appear from this that requiring Doogan and Wood to shoulder the burden of their conscientious objection to all forms of participation in abortion would not have limited their options

---

too drastically, even within the healthcare system. Consequently, it might be suggested that the burden on them of avoiding all forms of participation in abortion by simply avoiding employment as labour ward co-ordinators on a ward facilitating some abortions was reasonable.

However, the merging of abortion care with maternal and other gynaecological services is a complicating factor here, as it possibly is elsewhere. Doogan and Wood had taken up positions of responsibility on a maternity ward where abortion treatment represented a very minimal yet increasing proportion of the work. In these circumstances, requiring them to shoulder the burden of their objections to all forms of participation in abortion would potentially exclude them from any managerial position in their field of expertise, which was maternity care and not abortion.

The unique factual matrix of *Doogan* is precisely what makes it a difficult test case for the scope of the section 4 right. It may well be, in the end, that the meaning of 'participation' in abortion cannot be widened so much as to exempt those whose job entails the supervision of abortion treatments, among other things, from absolutely all involvement in facilitating abortion without imposing undue burdens upon the healthcare system and on those wishing to access legal abortion. If this is indeed the case, though, it must still be remembered that the section 4 right is not needed to prevent coerced participation in abortion, but only to provide protection for individuals who wish to refuse participation in treatment whilst maintaining the role of a healthcare professional who is standardly expected to cooperate.

11.6 Conscientious Provision

Almost all of the academic discussion about conscience protections in abortion law concerns the right to conscientiously refuse participation in abortion treatment. But could abortion *provision* not also be regarded as a matter of conscience? In recent years, some scholars have argued that it ought to be. Such scholars have suggested that the respect for moral integrity which justifies exemptions for conscientious 'refusers' of abortion treatment should equally extend to those medical professionals who feel motivated by conscience to *provide* abortion care, and who feel that the refusal to provide treatment to patients requesting terminations would entail a breach of *their* conscience. In the years before abortion was broadly legalized in the United States and Britain, many of the physicians who took personal risks to deliver illegal abortion care to desperate women might well be described as acting out of 'conscience'.[21] Developing this line of thought, some academics have argued that we ought to acknowledge the symmetry of conscientious refusal to provide abortion treatment and conscientious commitment to providing that treatment. In a recent article, for example, Bernard Dickens takes up the long-contested

---

[21] See generally Carole Joffe, *Doctors of Conscience: The Struggle to Provide Abortion Before and After Roe v Wade* (Beacon Press 1995).

matter of conscience rights in the realm of abortion, his stated aim being to 'release "conscience" from capture by those who object to participation in induced abortion'.[22] Dickens advocates a symmetry between conscientious objection to abortion provision and conscientious *commitment* to that provision, arguing that those who are driven by conscience to provide abortion service should enjoy exemption from state-imposed or hospital-specific prohibitions on abortion in much the same way that those morally opposed to abortion are often exempted from duties of provision on conscience grounds. In short, if one medical professional can exempt herself from legal abortion treatment on grounds of conscience, why cannot another medical professional, on the same grounds, insist on providing abortion against a hospital policy or outside the limits of the law?

I have some reservations about this symmetry argument. First of all, it seems to me to matter greatly for the conscientious provision argument *what* the source of the relevant prohibitions are. Where what is in question is a conscience exemption to a state prohibition on abortion, I think it clear that the symmetry argument does not go through. The justification for conscientious objection exceptions to legal duties is the extension of tolerance and compassion to individuals who, as a result of their (presumably misguided) moral convictions will suffer if made to perform them, *where the exemptions can be made without undermining the purpose of the law.* (Hence, as mentioned earlier, pacifists in wartime can be tolerated only while there are still sufficient numbers of conscripts.) These conditions are not met where the law in question is not a positive legal duty but a prohibition, since any exception on grounds of conscience will undermine the very aims with for which the ban was imposed. Such would undoubtedly be true of a 'conscientious commitment' exception to prohibitive abortion laws. The two therefore do not follow the same logic. Likewise, the pacifist's right of conscientious abstention implies no symmetrical right to conscientiously wage an illegal war or form a militia against the laws of the state.

A very different kind of case is where performing an abortion would be legal but the healthcare institution in which a medical professional works will not perform it as a matter of policy. Suppose that the individual physician feels conscientiously committed to carrying out the termination, which she regards as clearly being in the interests of the patient, and therefore part of her moral duty as a healthcare provider. Could the 'willing provider' in the refusing institution plausibly claim a right to defy the hospital's policy as a right of conscience? This kind of case is of greatest relevance in the United States, where a large proportion of healthcare is delivered by, funded by, or affiliated with the Catholic Church, which maintains policies against delivering various treatments, abortion among them, even when they are permitted by law.

Elizabeth Sepper has considered this kind of situation at length, arguing that there is a good case for symmetrical conscientious provision rights for a willing provider working in a refusing institution, to mirror the legal conscience rights that

---

[22] Bernard Dickens, 'The Right to Conscience' in Rebecca Cook, Bernard Dickens, and Joanna Erdman (eds), *Abortion in Transnational Perspective* (Pennsylvania University Press 2014) 210.

objectors may claim when working in institutions willing to provide abortion treatment.[23] As Sepper explains, there are numerous 'conscience clauses' designed to protect doctors who do not want to participate in treatments offered at their place of employment. As she says, those conscience clauses have been extended to entire hospitals and healthcare systems. However, Sepper notes that those conscience protections are asymmetrical, since they offer no similar protection to doctors or nurses who feel compelled by conscience to deliver a controversial treatment to a patient in need. She writes:

[E]xisting legislation generates significant asymmetries in the resolution of conflicts between medical providers and the hospitals, clinics, and nursing homes where they practice—which scholarship has not yet challenged. Whereas a doctor who refuses care for reasons of conscience cannot be disciplined and must be accommodated by her workplace, a doctor in an institution that restricts care . . . can be fired for following his conscience and providing medical care in violation of institutional policy. In one workplace, institutional conscience yields; in the other, it overrides the individual conscience.[24]

Sepper argues that there is no sound basis for this asymmetry. 'Taking conscience seriously', she claims, requires us to negotiate equally between competing claims of health providers and the facilities in which they work—whether they refuse or are willing to provide controversial care.'[25] All doctors and nurses have equal claims of conscience, whether they conscientiously refuse to perform or conscientiously insist on performing abortions.

As Sepper outlines, lawmakers have also recognized institutional conscience claims on the part of refusing healthcare institutions.[26] Entire hospitals and healthcare systems can avail themselves of these conscience exemptions and refuse to deliver contested treatments. As she explains, in some jurisdictions 'broad conscience clauses allow any corporation or entity associated with healthcare— including insurance companies—to decline to participate in, refer for, or give information about any healthcare service for reasons of conscience.'[27] All employees of those institutions, whatever their religious or secular moral beliefs, must then abide by those restrictions. In Sepper's view, this introduces yet another asymmetry, because it is only in respect of *refusing* institutions that the law has recognized the concept of 'institutional conscience'.

This yields asymmetrical results when it comes to conflicts between individual healthcare providers and the institutions in which they are employed. When a conflict arises between the convictions of a refusing individual and a willing institution (a hospital willing to provide abortion care or other contested treatments), the individual's right to conscience wins out. The institution is not taken to possess a comparable conscience-based interest in providing the treatment which can override the individual's refusal. However, when an individual *willing* provider comes into conflict with a *refusing* institution (an employer which maintains a policy against delivering abortion), it is the refusing institution's 'conscience' that wins

---

[23] Elizabeth Sepper, 'Taking Conscience Seriously' (2012) 98 Virginia Law Review 1501.
[24] ibid 1506.   [25] ibid 1505.   [26] ibid 1513.   [27] ibid.

out. Whether institution or individual, it is always the refuser whose claim is pre-eminent. Sepper illustrates the situation with the following diagram[28]:

	Refusing Institution	Willing Institution
Refusing Individual Provider	*No conflict*	*Individual wins*
Willing Provider	*Institution wins*	*No conflict*

Sepper believes that the concept of 'institutional conscience' is in truth a 'bad fit' for refusing institutions, believing that the best arguments in favour of institutional conscience rights better reflect the simple value of moral association.[29] Moreover, as she notes, some institutions which assert a religious objection to certain healthcare aren't actually affiliated with any religion, and the imposition of religious doctrine in healthcare systems, far from being a reflection of the convictions of its members, is often rather owed to changes in corporate ownership or affiliation—for example, acquisitions by Catholic healthcare systems.[30] Her main point, however, is simply that on any conception of individual or institutional conscience, there is no justifi-cation for always privileging refusers over willing providers in conflicts.

Sepper acknowledges that recognizing the 'equality of human conscience' cannot justify exemptions from law for any act of conscience.[31] As she says, the value of con-science might well be outweighed by other considerations, such as public welfare, and a 'well-ordered society' might well demand that people follow the objected-to law 'or face repercussions'.[32] However, she maintains that whenever a contentious issue, such as participation in abortion, is subject to conscientious exemptions that are allowed to 'trump' legal or employment demands, 'fairness requires extending exemptions equally'—meaning, I take it, to all conscience claims about the same matter.

One might wonder whether Sepper does not make the unwarranted assumption here that issues of conscience can *always* go both ways on a contentious issue. This is clearly not so. A vegetarian's decision to abstain from eating meat products is a core example of a practice of conscience, but conscience is not thereby implicated in anyone's omnivorism. However, let us take Sepper's main point to be that abor-tion provision at least *can* be a matter of conscience, and that since this is the case, conscience protection should be symmetrical whether the conscience claimant is a willing provider or refuser.

I do not contest the claim that abortion provision can be an issue of conscience for willing providers, which I think evidently true. The more pressing question for Sepper's argument is whether there exist any salient asymmetries between consci-entious provision of abortion and conscientious refusal to participate in abortion treatment which might be used to explain or justify the asymmetrical treatment of the conscience claims. One obvious suggestion, noted by Sepper, is that there is a morally salient difference between doing and allowing harm that goes to an

---

[28] ibid 1515.   [29] ibid 1526.   [30] ibid 1523.   [31] ibid 1531.   [32] ibid.

individual's depth of moral implication in a bad outcome. A person who is required to participate in an abortion against her conscience has agency in bringing about an outcome which she deems morally repugnant. A 'willing provider' on the other hand, who is barred from performing what she regards as a morally necessary abortion, has only failed to prevent the bad outcome: the refusal of the abortion. Could this difference justify greater protection for conscientious refusers than for willing providers?

Sepper addresses this objection that there is a moral distinction between being compelled to perform an action and being compelled not to perform it.[33] She dismisses the claim that it counteracts her symmetry argument, partly for the reason that the distinction between acts and omissions is 'insufficient to explain moral responsibility in the medical field'. Certain medical omissions, for example, the unilateral decision by a doctor to fail to perform CPR on a patient, render the agent morally and legally responsible notwithstanding the fact that they are not acts. This is of course true, but at most it establishes that omissions are not, by nature, outside the realm of moral responsibility. It does not counteract what we might call the 'asymmetry claim' that, all things being equal, it is worse to compel someone to *cause* harm against their conscience than to allow it. It is no doubt right, as Sepper says, that moral integrity can be damaged by failing to perform an action one believes one is clearly morally required to perform. Still, being compelled to be the agent of harm is, in the eyes of many, more damaging to moral integrity than being compelled to refrain from helping. A person who is compelled to carry out genocidal atrocities is more seriously harmed than someone who is prevented from doing something to stop them.

The genocide example is a good test case for the difference between doing and allowing harm in the compromise of conscience because the harm the individual wishes to avoid participating in or prevent from taking place is the same across the two cases. But this is not true of abortion. The conscientious *objector* who desires exemption from participation in abortion is seeking to avoid being complicit in what she regards as homicide or the immoral destruction of valuable human life. The harm which the conscientious *provider* seeks to avoid allowing by omission is different, being the harms of unwanted pregnancy. These harms can, but very rarely do, entail the death of a human being. This, then, may be another important point of asymmetry between the two cases. For the conscientious objector, being compelled to act is a more morally grave affair than being compelled to abstain is for the conscientious provider.

Thirdly and finally, an asymmetry may also arise with respect to the effect of the conscientious exemption on a hospital or healthcare institution's interest in maintaining its particular policy on abortion. As I said Sepper believes this interest is best characterized as an interest in moral association: the freedom for healthcare practitioners with similar moral goals to unite under the same mission statement. I am sure Sepper is right to suspect that in many cases, the value of

---

[33] ibid 1536.

moral association in a policy of refusal is in fact illusory, in large part because the policy does not reflect the convictions of many, if any, of the associates. However, insofar as operating a policy of refusal is considered to be a legitimate means for an institution to maintain a particular moral identity, it seems clear that accommodating the consciences of willing providers will significantly compromise that policy, and hence that interest, for refusing institutions. A refusing institution cannot maintain a moral identity that is dependent upon refusing abortion treatment whilst, at the same time, allowing for exceptions to protect the conscience of willing providers. But the same does not hold when a willing institution accommodates the conscience of refusing doctors. A providing institution can clearly accommodate *some* refusers without compromising its policy aim of facilitating legal abortion, so long as the number of refusers it must accommodate does not make the implementation of abortion treatment untenable. This is another potentially significant asymmetry, since it will only take one willing provider to undermine the moral aims of the refusing institution, but many more to undermine the aims of a willing one.

Even if we grant that institutional conscience can cut both ways, then, the argument could be made that a refusing institution's claim is stronger against an individual willing provider's conscience claim than a willing institution's is against an individual refuser. Sepper may well be right to believe that conscience is, in the end, a bad fit for institutions. But the considerations here nevertheless go to show that the symmetry argument may be more problematic than first appears. Even where the 'refuser' is an institution, however, the right to conscientiously object to legal abortion provision will still be subject to the limits I outlined in the sections above. In particular, this might limit an institution's right to refuse abortion treatment in any scenario where the effect of the refusal is to preclude a woman's access to safe, legal abortion altogether.

Bibliography

Ashworth A, 'The Scope of Criminal Liability for Omissions' (1989) 105 Law Quarterly Review 424

Beckwith FJ, 'Defending Abortion Philosophically: A Review of David Boonin's "A Defense of Abortion"' (2006) 31 Journal of Medicine and Philosophy 177

Beckwith FJ, *Defending Life: The Legal and Moral Case Against Abortion Choice* (Cambridge University Press 2007)

Bermúdez JL, 'The Moral Significance of Birth' (1996) 106 Ethics 378

Boonin D, *A Defense of Abortion* (Cambridge University Press 2003)

Brazier M, 'Embryos' "Rights": Abortion and Research' in Freeman M (ed), *Medicine, Ethics and the Law* (Stevens 1988) 9–22

British Pregnancy Advisory Service, 'Abortion: A Briefing Document on Why Access to Late Abortions Needs to be Defended' (2004) http://wwwprochoiceforum.org.uk/ocrabort-law9.php (last accessed 5 December 2016)

Brody BA, *Abortion and the Sanctity of Human Life: A Philosophical View* (MIT Press 1975)

Bubeck D, 'Sex Selection: The Feminist Response' in Burley J and Harris J (eds), *A Companion to Genethics* (Blackwell 2002) 216–28

Burin A, 'Beyond Pragmatism: Defending the Bright-Line of Birth' (2014) 22 Medical Law Review 494

Callahan S, 'Abortion and the Sexual Agenda: A Case for Prolife Feminism' (1986) 123 Commonweal 232

Carlson B, *Human Embryology and Developmental Embryology* (CV Mosby 2004)

Carter I, 'Respect and the Basis of Equality' (2011) 121 Ethics 538

Chambers C, 'Autonomy and Equality in Cultural Perspective: A Response to Sawitri Saharso' (2004) Feminist Theory 329

Churchland P, *Matter and Consciousness* (Revised edn, MIT Press 1988) 30–33

Cherry A, 'A Feminist Understanding of Sex Selective Abortion: Solely a Matter of Choice?' (1995) 10 Wisconsin Women's Law Journal 161

Crary A, *Inside Ethics: On the Demands of Moral Thought* (Harvard University Press 2016)

Derbyshire S, 'Can Fetuses Feel Pain?' (2006) 332 British Medical Journal 909

Devine P and others, *Abortion: Three Perspectives* (Oxford University Press 2009)

Diamond C, 'Eating Meat and Eating People' (1978) 53 Philosophy 465

Dickens B, 'The Right to Conscience' in Cook R, Dickens B, and Erdman J (eds), *Abortion in Transnational Perspective* (Pennsylvania University Press 2014)

Donceel J, 'Immediate Animation and Delayed Hominization' (1970) 31 Theological Studies 76

Dupré J, 'Natural Kinds and Biological Taxa' (1981) 90 Philosophical Review 66

Dworkin R, *Life's Dominion: An Argument about Abortion and Euthanasia* (Harper Collins 1993)

Eckerman CO and others, 'Premature Newborns as Social Partners Before Term Age' (1994) 17 Infant Behaviour and Development 55

Endicott T, 'The Impossibility of the Rule of Law' (1999) 19 Oxford Journal of Legal Studies 1

Engelhardt HT, Jr, 'The Ontology of Abortion' (1974) [University of Chicago Press] 84 Ethics 217

English J, 'Abortion and the Concept of a Person' (1975) 5 Canadian Journal of Philosophy 233

Feinberg J, *Freedom and Fulfillment: Philosophical Essays* (Princeton University Press 1994)

Feinberg J, 'The Moral and Legal Responsibility of the Bad Samaritan' in Feinberg J (ed), *Freedom and Fulfilment: Philosophical Essays* (Princeton University Press 1994)

Feinberg J and Dwyer S (eds), *The Problem of Abortion* (3rd edn, Wadsworth Publishing Company 1997)

Finnis J, 'The Rights and Wrongs of Abortion: A Reply to Judith Thomson' (1973) [Wiley] 2 Philosophy and Public Affairs 117

Fletcher G, 'Proportionality and the Psychotic Aggressor: A Vignette in the Compartive Criminal Law Theory' (1973) 8 Israel Law Review 376

Foot P, 'The Problem of Abortion and the Doctrine of Double Effect' (1967) 5 Oxford Review 5

Fovargue S and Neal M, ' "In Good Conscience": Conscience-based Exemptions and Proper Medical Treatment' (2015) 23 Medical Law Review 1

George RP and Tollefsen C, *Embryo: A Defense of Human Life* (Doubleday 2008)

'Gendercide: The Worldwide War on Baby Girls' *The Economist* (4 March 2010)

Giubilini A and Minerva F, 'After-Birth Abortion. Why Should the Baby Live?' (2013) 39 Journal of Medical Ethics 261

Greasley K, 'Medical Abortion and the "Golden Rule" of Statutory Interpretation' (2011) 19 Medical Law Review 314

Greasley K, 'Is Sex-Selective Abortion Against the Law?' (2016) 36 Oxford Journal of Legal Studies 535–64

Green R, *The Human Embryo Research Debates: Bioethics in the Vortex of Controversy* (Oxford University Press 2001)

Gyngell C and Douglas T, 'Selecting Against Disability: The Liberal Eugenic Challenge and the Argument from Cognitive Diversity' [2016] 33 Journal of Applied Philosophy

Hanmer J and Allen P, 'Reproductive Engineering: The Final Solution' (1982) 2 Gender Issues 53

Hassoun N and Kriegel U, 'Consciousness and the Moral Permissibility of Infanticide' (2008) 25 Journal of Applied Philosophy 45

Herring J, 'The Loneliness of Status: The Moral and Legal Significance of Birth' in Ebtehaj F and others (eds), *Birth Rites and Rights* (Hart Publishing 2011)

Hillman NH, Kallapur SG, and Jobe AH, 'Physiology of Transition from Intrauterine to Extrauterine Life' (2012) 39 Clinics in Perinatology 769

Holly Watt H, Newell C, and Khimji Z, 'Available on demand—an abortion if it's a boy you wanted', *Daily Telegraph*, 23 February 2012, 4–5 http://www.telegraph.co.uk/news/health/news/9099925/Abortioninvestigation-Available-ondemand-an-abortion-if-its-a-boy-you-wanted.html (last accessed 15 October 2016)

Holmes H, 'Review of 'Gendercide' by Mary Anne Warren' (1987) 1 Bioethics 100

House of Commons Science and Technology Committee, 'Scientific Developments Relating to the Abortion Act 1967' http://www.official-documents.gov.uk/document/cm72/7278/7278pdf (last accessed 22 January 2014)

Joffe CE, *Doctors of Conscience: The Struggle to Provide Abortion Before and After Roe v. Wade* (Beacon Press 1995)

Kaczor C, *The Ethics of Abortion* (2nd edn, Routledge 2015)

Kaczor CR, *The Ethics of Abortion: Women's Rights, Human Life, and the Question of Justice* (Routledge 2011)

Kagan S, 'What's Wrong with Speciesism?' (2016) 33 Journal of Applied Philosophy 1

Kalantry S, 'Sex Selection in the United States and India: A Contextualist Feminist Approach' [2013] UCLA Journal of International Law and Foreign Affairs 61

Kamm F, 'Abortion and the Value of Life: A Discussion of Life's Dominion' (1995) 95 Columbia Law Review 160–221

Kittay E, 'The Personal is Philosophical is Political: A Philosopher and Mother of a Cognitively Disabled Person Sends Notes from the Battlefield' (2009) 40 Metaphilosophy 606

Lee P, *Abortion and Unborn Human Life* (2nd edn, Catholic University of America Press 2010) 236–48

Lee P, 'The Basis of Being a Subject of Rights' in Keown J and George RP (eds), *Reason, Morality and Law: The Philosophy of John Finnis* (Oxford University Press 2013)

Levin M, 'Review of "Life in the Balance" by Robert Wennberg' (1986) 3 Constitutional Commentary 500–13

Liao SM, 'The Embryo Rescue Case' (2006) 27 Theoretical Medicine and Bioethics 141

Little MO, 'Abortion, Intimacy and the Duty to Gestate' (1999) 2 Ethical Theory and Moral Practice 295

Little MO, 'Abortion and the Margins of Personhood' (2008) 39 Rutgers Law Journal 331

Littleton L and Engebretson J, *Maternity Nursing Care* (Thomson 2005)

Londras Fd, 'Constitutionalizing Fetal Rights: A Salutary Tale from Ireland' (2015) 22 Michigan Journal of Gender and the Law 243

MacKinnon CA, *Feminism Unmodified: Discourses on Life and Law* (Harvard University Press 1987)

MacKinnon CA, 'Reflections on Sex Equality under Law' (1991) 100 Yale Law Journal 1281

Manninen BA, 'Rethinking *Roe v Wade*: Defending the Abortion Right in the Face of Contemporary Opposition' (2010) 10 American Journal of Bioethics 33

Manninen BA, *Pro-Life, Pro-Choice: Shared Values in the Abortion Debate* (Vanderbilt University Press 2014)

Marquis D, 'Why Abortion Is Immoral' (1989) 86 Journal of Philosophy 183

McMahan J, *The Ethics of Killing: Problems at the Margins of Life* (Oxford University Press 2002)

McMahan J, 'Our Fellow Creatures' (2005) 9 The Journal of Ethics 353

McMahan J, 'Infanticide' (2007) 19 Utilitas 131

McMahan J, 'Infanticide and Moral Consistency' (2013) 39 Journal of Medical Ethics 273

Meltzoff AN and Moore MK, 'Imitation of Facial and Manual Gestures by Human Neonates' (1977) 198 Science 75

Meltzoff AN and Moore MK, 'Newborn Infants Imitate Adult Facial Gestures' (1983) 54 Child Development 702

Moore KL and Persaud TVN, *Before We Were Born: Essentials of Embryology and Birth Defects* (5th edn, WB Saunders 1998)

Moore KL and Persaud TVN, *The Developing Human* (7th edn, WB Saunders 2003)

Morowitz HJ and Trefil JS, *The Facts of Life: Science and the Abortion Controversy* (Oxford University Press 1992)

Mulhall S, *The Wounded Animal: J M Coetzee & the Difficulty of Reality in Literature and Philosophy* (Princeton University Press 2009)

Mulhall S, 'Fearful Thoughts' London Review of Books 24 (2002) 16–18.

O'Donnell CP and others, 'Crying and Breathing by Extremely Preterm Infants Immediately After Birth' (2010) 157 The Journal of Pediatrics 846

Olson ET, 'Was I Ever a Fetus?' (1997) 57 Philosophy and Phenomenological Research 95

Olson ET, *The Human Animal: Personal Identity Without Psychology* (Oxford University Press 1999)

Olson ET, ' "Personal Identity", Entry in the Stanford Encyclopaedia of Philosophy' http://plato.stanford.edu/entries/identity-personal/ (last accessed 15 October 2016)

Ord T, 'The Sourge: Moral Implications of Natural Embryo Loss' (2008) 8 American Journal of Bioethics 12

Parfit D, *Reasons and Persons* (Oxford University Press 1984)

Powledge T, 'Toward a Moral Policy for Sex Choice' in Bennett N (ed), *Sex Selection of Children* (Academic Press 1983)

Quinn W, 'Abortion: Identity and Loss' (1984) 13 Philosophy and Public Affairs 24

Rawls J, *A Theory of Justice* (Original edn, Belknap Press 2005)

Raz J, *The Authority of Law* (Oxford University Press 1979)

Raz J, 'Being in the World' (2010) 23 Ratio 433

Raz J, 'Agency and Luck' in Heuer U and Lang G (eds), *Luck, Value, and Commitment: Themes From the Ethics of Bernard Williams* (Oxford University Press 2012) http://papers.ssrn.com/sol3/papers.cfm?abstract_id=1487552 (last accessed 15 October 2016)

Raz J, 'Being in the World: Aspects of Moral Luck' http://clp.usc.edu/assets/docs/who/faculty/workshops/Raz.pdf (last accessed 9 May 2014)

Saharso S, 'Feminist Ethics, Autonomy and the Politics of Multiculturalism' (2003) 4 Feminist Theory 199

Saharso S, 'SSA: Gender, Culture and Dutch Public Policy' (2005) 5 Ethnicities 248

Sandel M, *The Case Against Perfection: Ethics in the Age of Genetic Engineering* (Harvard University Press 2007)

Sanger C, 'Seeing and Believing: Mandatory Ultrasound and the Path to a Protected Choice' (2008) 56 UCLA Law Review 351

Sepper E, 'Taking Conscience Seriously' (2012) 98 Virginia Law Review 1501

Sheldon S, *Beyond Control: Medical Power, Women and Abortion Law* (Pluto Press 1997)

Sheldon S and Wilkinson S, 'Termination of Pregnancy for Reason of Foetal Disability: Are There Grounds for a Special Exception in the Law?' (2001) 9 Medical Law Review 85

Sherwin S, 'Abortion Through a Feminist Ethics Lens' (1991) 30 Dialogue: Canadian Philosophical Review/Revue canadienne de philosophie 327

Singer P, 'Famine, Affluence, and Morality' (1972) 1 Philosophy and Public Affairs 229

Sumner LW, *Abortion and Moral Theory* (Princeton University Press 1981)

Sumner LW, 'A Third Way' in Feinberg J and Dwyer S (eds), *The Problem of Abortion* (3rd edn, Wadsworth Publishing 1997)

Thomson JJ, 'A Defense of Abortion' [1971] 1 Philosophy and Public Affairs 47

Thomson JJ, 'Rights and Deaths' (1973) [Wiley] 2 Philosophy and Public Affairs 146

Tooley M, 'Abortion and Infanticide' (1972) 2 Philosophy and Public Affairs 37

Undurraga V, 'Proportionality in the Constitutional Review of Abortion Law' in Cook R, Dickens B and Erdmas J (eds), *Abortion Law in Transnational Perspective: Cases and Controversies* (University of Pennsylvania Press 2014)

Velleman JD, 'Family History' (2005) 34 Philosophical Papers 357

Waldron J, *God, Locke, and Equality: Christian Foundations of John Locke's Political Thought* (Cambridge University Press 2002)

Warnock M, *An Intelligent Person's Guide to Ethics* (Overlook 2004)

Warren MA, 'On the Moral and Legal Status of Abortion' (1973) 57 The Monist 43–61

Warren MA, *Gendercide: The Implications of Sex Selection* (Rowman and Allanheld 1985)

Warren MA, 'The Moral Significance of Birth' (1989) 4 Hypatia 46

Wertheimer R, 'Understanding the Abortion Argument' (1971) 1 Philosophy and Public Affairs 67–95

Williams J, 'Sex-Selective Abortion: A Matter of Choice' (2012) 31 Law and Philosophy 125–59

Index